The Meanings of Macho

Men and Masculinity

Michael Kimmel, Editor

The Meanings of Macho

Being a Man in Mexico City

Matthew C. Gutmann

UNIVERSITY OF CALIFORNIA PRESS
Berkeley · Los Angeles · London

University of California Press
Berkeley and Los Angeles, California

University of California Press, Ltd.
London, England

© 1996 by
The Regents of the University of California

Library of Congress Cataloging-in-Publication Data

Gutmann, Matthew C., 1953–
    The meanings of macho : being a man in Mexico City / Matthew C.
Gutmann.
        p.   cm.—(Men and masculinity ; 3)
    Includes bibliographical references and index.
    ISBN 0-520-20234-1 (alk. paper).—ISBN 0-520-20236-8 (pbk. :
alk. paper)
    1. Men—Mexico—Mexico City—Psychology.   2. Masculinity
(Psychology)—Mexico—Mexico City.   3. Machismo—Mexico—Mexico
City.   I. Title.   II. Series: Men and masculinity (Berkeley,
Calif.) ; 3.
    HQ1090.7.M6G87   1996
    305.31′0972′53—dc20   95-49535
                                                               CIP

Printed in the United States of America

6   5   4   3

To My Mother
Ann Rosenthal Oliver

In Mexico you begin again every day.

Rodolfo Usigli

Contents

Acknowledgments

It is a pleasure to formally thank some of those who have generously shared their time and wisdom with me in recent years. It is often said that academia and writing in particular are solitary affairs, but as I finish this project I am forced to the conclusion that my role has been less as a writer and more as a compiler of others' insights and suggestions. In guiding my doctoral studies at Berkeley, in widely ranging discussions and correspondence about anthropology, gender, Mexico, and critical theory, with much patience and *cariño*, many people have been helpful in making my return to academia after fifteen years often thrilling and always challenging.

First, my great appreciation to Stanley Brandes for the continuing gift of intellectual redemption and letting me go my own way; and to Nancy Scheper-Hughes for her insights and critiques and for showing a way to make anthropology count. Also in the Berkeley Department of Anthropology, I wish to thank Gerry Berreman, Lawrence Cohen, Meg Conkey, Alan Dundes, George Foster, Nelson Graburn, Gene Hammel, Katie Milton, Laura Nader, Aihwa Ong, Jack Potter, and Paul Rabinow, all of whom taught me more than they may realize or perhaps intended. Elsewhere at Berkeley, my special appreciation to Margarita Melville for her commentary, to Alex Saragoza for his counsel, and to Gwen Kirkpatrick for her encouragement.

In the United States I have been fortunate to know and learn from Thor Anderson, Paco Ferrándiz, Linda Green, Javier Inda, Michael Kearney, Michael Kimmel, Louise Lamphere, Roger Lancaster, Sara

Miller, Roland Moore, Leslie Salzinger, and Lynn Stephen. Additional thanks to many who gave me valued suggestions and assistance along the way: Helga Baitenmann, Tom Bogenschild, Carole Browner, Manny Campbell, Oscar Contreras, Alejandro de Avila, Miguel Díaz-Barriga, Susan Eckstein, Priscilla Enriquez, M. Patricia Fernández Kelly, Renée Friedman, Anita Garey, Paul Gelles, Donna Guy, Sarah Ham, Robert Kemper, Donna Keren, Manuel Lizarralde, Kathleen Logan, Claudio Lomnitz-Adler, Alejandro Lugo, Tanya Luhrmann, María Massolo, Lonnie and Judy McKenzie, Pat McNamara, Kevin Middlebrook, Charlie Moran, David Myhre, John Nelson, Ruben Oliven, Jim Quesada, Linda-Anne Rebhun, Renato Rosaldo, Roger Rouse, Robert Rubinstein, Carol Smith, Carol Stack, Steve Stern, Jim Taggart, Lucien Taylor, Nick Townsend, Don Tuzin, Stefano Varese, Barbara von Schlegell, and Aníbal Yáñez.

My deepest obligation is to those in and around Colonia Santo Domingo, especially Angela Jiménez and Gabriel Saavedra, as well as Miguel Armenta, Mónica Atúñez, Alejandro "Don Doc" Ceballos, César, Dani, Fili Fernández, Glafira, Héctor Jiménez, Valfre Jiménez, Juan López, Noé López, Norma López, Alfredo Pérez, Lupita Pérez, Bernardino Ramos, the River Plate *futbol* team, Marcos Ruvalcaba, Susana, Padre Victor Verdín, and to Francisco Villegas of the Santo Domingo DDF, Herlinda Romero and María Guadalupe Robles of the Secundaria #49, and Maximiliano Sánchez, *colonia* president 1992–93.

In other parts of Mexico, my great thanks to Elia Aguilar, Roger Bartra, Daniel Cazés, Teresita de Barbieri, Elin Emilsson, Néstor García Canclini, Mary Goldsmith, Soledad González, Benno de Keijzer, Pedro Lewin, Francis Lima, Larissa Lomnitz, Nelson Minello, Carlos Monsiváis, Eduardo Nivón, Martha Núñez, Orlandina de Oliveira, Patricia Safa, and Irma Saucedo. My gratitude as well to Tania Carrasco, Pablo Casaubón, Jorge Castañeda, René Coulomb, Margarita Dalton, Ricardo Falomir, Alejandro Figueroa, Luis Gómez, Carolina Grajales, Susana Lerner, Eduardo Liendro, Alejandra Massolo, Marinella Miano, Raul Nieto, Flori Riquer, Mariángela Rodríguez, Robert Shadow, Claudio Stern, Elena Urrutia, and María Waleska.

As models of intellectual commentary, Michael Herzfeld, Louise Lamphere, and Ben Orlove provided wonderfully detailed and lengthy suggestions on an earlier draft of this study. They will not fault me, I know, when I have borrowed some of their comments to clarify points in the book. As my final collaborators on this project, at the University of California Press, I especially want to thank Naomi Schneider, whose vision and enthusiasm were crucial in making this study a book almost before it was a doctoral thesis, as well as Scott Norton for providing a steady hand, Carl Walesa for carefully editing my sometimes twisted prose, and Matt Knutzen for drawing the maps.

Fieldwork and writing were made possible in large part because of the following institutional support for this study: Fulbright-Hays Doctoral Dissertation Research Abroad Grant, Wenner-Gren Foundation Predissertation Grant, National Science Foundation Doctoral Dissertation Improvement Grant, National Institute of Mental Health National Research Service Award, Institute for Intercultural Studies Grant, UC MEXUS Dissertation Research Grant, and at the University of California, Berkeley, the Center for Latin American Studies for small travel grants and the Department of Anthropology for several small Ronald L. Olson and Robert H. Lowie grants. Final revisions on the book were made during a postdoctoral Visiting Research Fellowship at the Center for U.S.-Mexican Studies in La Jolla, California.

During 1992–93, I was affiliated with institutions in Mexico City, which greatly facilitated bibliographic research and brought me into many stimulating discussions throughout the year: at El Colegio de México, the Centro de Estudios Sociológicos (CES) and the Programa Interdisciplinario de Estudios de la Mujer (PIEM); and at the Universidad Autónoma Metropolitana–Iztapalapa, the Departamento de Antropología. At various points while conducting fieldwork in Mexico I had the opportunity to share my research in talks at several institutions there, thus allowing me to receive the comments and criticisms of my Mexican colleagues while still in the field: El Colegio de México, CES and PIEM; UAM-Iztapalapa, Departamento de Antropología; UAM-Xochimilco, Doctorado de Ciencias Sociales; Escuela Nacional de Antropología e Historia; UNAM, Facultad de Ciencias Políticas y Sociales; Centro de Estudios de la Mujer y la Familia (DIF Oaxaca); Instituto Oaxaqueño de las Culturas; and Universidad de las Américas (Cholula, Puebla), Departamento de Antropología. I benefited as well from suggestions after talks on this research and related topics in the following forums: International Congress of Anthropological and Ethnological Sciences, Mexico City (1993); American Anthropological Association meetings (1993, 1994, and 1995); Latin American Studies Association congresses (1994 and 1995); the Biblioteca Benjamin Franklin in Mexico City; the Mexican television program *María Victoria Llamas*; Temple University; University of California, Berkeley; University of California, Davis; and University of California, San Diego.

In my extended family, education is a permanent vocation and a shared responsibility. Besides my thanks for their moral support, I am indebted, fortunately not literally, to the following for financial assistance, great and large, toward my schooling over the years: Ann Oliver, Andrew Oliver, Carl and Audrey Gutmann, James and Jeanette Gutmann, Morris and Helen Rosenthal, and Nan Rosenthal. For his steady faith, my particular gratitude to my grandfather James Gutmann.

I also want to thank my wife, Michelle McKenzie, who shares unequivocally my delight in anthropology's mysteries if not in its mystifications, for originally urging me to study gender issues, for life on Huehuetzin and beyond, and for contributing to so many of the ideas in this study. To my daughter Liliana, who spent her first year of life in Colonia Santo Domingo, Mexico City, for teaching me a thing or two about nuance; I still have a lot to learn, but this is a much better book because of her. And to my daughter Maya, who twirled her way into life just in time for late-night proofreading.

I dedicate this inquiry to my mother, Ann Rosenthal Oliver. Would that Lamarck could be proved correct just this once, yet, alas, I have inherited too little of my mother's wit and charm. I have nonetheless tried to measure up to her standards of moral accountability and living one's life as if it meant a damn. Four decades seem hardly enough time to learn from your example and love, but with this volume, from me to you, Ma, a promise belatedly fulfilled.

My best friends in Colonia Santo Domingo have forewarned me that they are going to mess me up—to put it more gently in print than they have expressed it to me in person—if I get too much wrong about their lives and loves, their convictions, dreams, and secrets. I am not sure they will not allow me an escape, but I offer them *The Meanings of Macho* as part of the tangled process of interpreting, explaining, and changing our world. More than ever, these seem especially pressing tasks today.

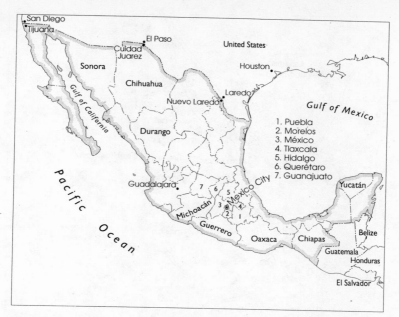

Map 1. Mexico

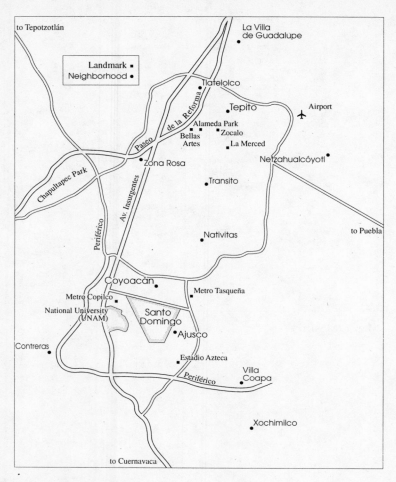

Map 2. Mexico City

Gender Conventions

"Look, he's drooling now! He must have killed a lot of
people. And you invited him in."
"He's probably just poor. Go to sleep."

Juan Rulfo, Pedro Páramo

Hearing me tap lightly on the corrugated metal with the edge of an old
five-hundred-peso coin—this was a month or so before the New Pesos
would be issued at the beginning of 1993—Marcos slid the door gate
open and invited me to enter. It was Saturday, and at 1 P.M. the giant
jackhammers had stopped pounding through the volcanic rock to make
a trench in which to lay the sewer pipes. A pleasant respite for all of us.
As if to celebrate, Gabriel had asked me that morning to stop by Marcos's in the afternoon if I found time after my interviews. Someone had
bought a bottle of Bacardi Añejo, and besides, they wanted to know
more about me and why an anthropologist was living down the block
on Huehuetzin Street in Colonia Santo Domingo.

But when I got inside the gate Gabi and Toño were yelling at each
other, and it looked like it had been going on for a while. Toño was
cursing Gabriel, with sideways laughs at Marcos, and now me, as if to
say, "Can you believe such nonsense?" Gabriel was telling Toño that
he was full of crap. Beyond this it was not immediately clear what they
were fighting about so earnestly. Nor could I tell how serious the argument was.

Yet I do remember privately hoping that my newfound friends, these
working class Mexican men, might be arguing about their past sexual
conquests, or their ongoing capacity for alcohol consumption, or perhaps someone's erstwhile prowess on the *futbol* field, or maybe about
a fantasized future sexual conquest. After all, I had recently arrived in
Mexico City to study Mexican men as fathers and sons, adulterers and

I

celibates, alcoholics and teetotalers. I hoped to enter the affective neth-
erworld of adult males that, I knew, was all but hidden to my female
colleagues, who were still often the only scholars who cared to research
gender issues. The anthropological journey would undoubtedly prove
mysterious and fascinating, for male identity is a topic able to provoke
at once the sacred and lurid, and I was excited when I heard Gabriel
and Toño shouting something about fathers and children.

Leaning on the fender of an ancient VW and waving his empty glass
toward Toño, Gabriel loudly dismissed his friend's suggestion that intricate and already assembled toys were the best presents for youngsters
at Christmas. "Because you see, Toño," Gabi argued, leaning forward
to emphasize his increasingly slurred words, "helping children to become creative is more important than spending a lot of money waste-
fully." Toño countered that only a cheapskate would consider a ham-
mer and a few nails adequate as a Christmas gift, as Gabriel had been
maintaining. Creativity, indeed! Children needed to see a father spend
some money on them to understand how much he cared. "*Pérame*
[Hold on there]," Gabriel the father responded to Toño, who was still
soltero (single). "There is more to being a good father than spending
money."

A thinly veiled flexing of masculine prestige in which disposable income was the operative symbol of competitive power? Perhaps fancy
Christmas presents represented an extension of that infamous desire of
Mexican men to procreate, in this case to have many children who in
turn have many expensive presents. Yet, mindful of Freudian cigars,
I wondered if an argument between men about children's Christmas
presents could ever be mainly an argument about children's Christmas presents. And if it was, what might this tell us about men and male
identities?

At the very least, I eventually came to conclude, many of the images
anthropologists have been creating about Mexican working class men
are erroneous and harmful. For instance, whereas the "typical Mexican
man" was often portrayed as a hard-drinking, philandering macho, that
image largely ignored the activities of fatherhood in the lives of millions
of Mexican men. A new analysis of masculinity and modernity in Mexico was clearly needed.

Nonetheless, an inquiry into working class men as fathers and
friends, husbands and lovers, could hardly avoid confronting conse-
crated stereotypes, especially the cherished varieties bandied about concerning Mexican working class men. Throughout this study, therefore,

examples of what men say and do among themselves, and occasionally with women, are raised as illustrative of several central issues, from images of what *ser hombre* (to be a man) means to different men and women at different times, to moves toward a degendering of certain aspects of daily life among sections of the urban poor today in Mexico. Yet if such episodes provide microcosms of larger sociocultural phenomena, they do so partially in Lila Abu-Lughod's (1993) sense that the stories are meant to "undo the titles." That is, in the course of subverting facile expectations of Mexican male gender identities, the episodes seek to undo our ability to speak of a unitary Mexican man, or Mexican urban man, or even a Mexican urban working class man, in any reasonable manner.

A concluding chapter in this study is devoted to examining the etymologies of the terms *macho* and *machismo*. Conventional methodology, of course, would place all historical sections of this study toward the beginning, but to have defined *macho* and *machismo* in contemporary or historical terms at the outset would have been premature. For instance, what it means to be a macho—whether the macho is considered brutish, gallant, or cowardly—changes over time for various sectors of Mexican society, and we must not ignore the often elusive and mutually exclusive ways in which these catchwords are employed today. Machismo is best understood after and not before other ethnographic details have been developed. I therefore reserve most discussion of the word *machismo* until late in this study in order to provide a fitting coda—and a reflective punch line—to the anthropological descriptions in the preceding chapters.

Like some Weberian ideal type run amok, scholarly and popular images of Mexican men as often as not serve other theoretical and political agendas. Yet despite the many sayings, commonplaces, accepted judgments, and assumptions about Mexican men and machismo, precious little scholarly attention has been paid to the subject. The result of this situation, briefly put, is that by capriciously glossing over significant differences among men based on class, generation, region, and ethnicity among other factors, such generalizations have come to invent and then perpetuate sterile ideal types and stereotypes.

Nonetheless, the objects of scorn and pity who populate these categories, Mexican working class men as well as women, have learned to manipulate the cultural rituals and social laws of machismo. Just as much recent social history has brought to light the previously overlooked customs, agency, and consciousness of popular classes, so too

analysis of modern gender relations in Mexico City should provide a
potent antidote to the notion that especially virulent strains of sexism
are to be found only in Mexico. Further, and of more long-term scholarly and political significance, through investigation of the vagaries of
gender identities amid the realities of gender oppression, we may come
to better understand the persistence of gender variations and instability
amid enduring patterns of inequality.

In early January, stalled in traffic on a *combi* minibus, I spotted Don
Timoteo sitting with his wife in the grassy median of a major boulevard
where for twenty-two years customers have sought him out to repair
their wicker furniture. I got off to talk with Don Timo, who is originally
from the aptly named Valle de Bravo, and his wife, Catalina, also in
her early seventies, and someone who neighbors say is one of the most
submissive and self-sacrificing women you could ever hope to meet. A
notorious drinker and wife beater in his earlier days, Don Timo at least
no longer abuses liquor. We talked about my research on families and
parenting, and about recent changes in domestic divisions of labor in
Mexico.

"What about your children?" I asked. "What did you do with them
when they were young but not yet old enough for school?"

Don Timoteo pointed to a spot in the grass where, he said, his children had grown up. Catalina nodded, rocking a little on the wicker
chair, as if recalling the scene. Don Timo told me he brought the two
girls and the boy with him to work each day, whether his wife joined
him or not, and they played while he waited for business.

A few minutes later I asked each, "What do you find has changed
between men and women in your lifetime?" Catalina surprised me with
a quick response: "*¡Pues, la liberación de la mujer!* [Well, women's liberation!]" She did not care to expand on this opinion except to add that
it had been women who had changed the most since her youth, implying
that the men were lagging behind. Still startled by her phrase, I turned
to her husband.

"Don Timo?"

His response came quickly as well. "*¡Hay mucho maricón que deja
de ser hombre!* [There's a lot of queers who've stopped being men!]"
Then he stared at me, as if to say, "There's really nothing more to say
about the matter."

In the months that followed, I came to view Timoteo and Catalina
not so much as representative of Mexican men and women in general,
but rather as typical of the enigmas inherent and common in most gen-

der identities that are constructed and transformed each day on the ancient lava fields that make up much of southern Mexico City. Throughout my research on masculinity in Colonia Santo Domingo, my approach has been to study men and women who are typical *because* they are enigmatic. Men like Don Timo, who play an active part in raising their children and at the same time regularly voice their hatred and fear of men who have sex with other men, are not marginal or unusual except in studies in the social sciences. The complex riddles of real lives are the stuff of good ethnography, and they require of the reader as well as the writer an openness to alternative approaches, in this case with respect to gendered images, practices, and beliefs in Mexico City.

CROSSING THE BORDER

As we entered Mexico through the Laredo–Nuevo Laredo checkpoint in our new used car, my wife, Michelle, and I were unprepared for the reception that our other rider would receive. At our first stop, a roadside stand where we paused to purchase sodas in the desert heat, our seven-week-old daughter, Liliana, was taken from us. Not permanently, but just long enough for her to be passed around among the women and one old man who lived and worked at the stand. They delighted in Liliana's baldness and plump cheeks, inspected her for infection, and checked to see that she was well clothed. It was ninety-five degrees that August day, but all over Mexico for several months to come, no matter the temperature, the refrain "¡Tápala! ¡Tápala! [Cover her! Cover her!]" would be as constant as were the strangers who, at the same moment they were asking us if they could hold Liliana, were grabbing her away without waiting for a reply.

Strangers, usually women but sometimes men, would approach us on the street to look at Liliana and offer the advice that she should be better wrapped. A man in a gas station questioned me closely one afternoon about the security of the straps on her car seat. Reassured, he nonetheless directed me, "Drive carefully with her." As much as this study is dedicated to debunking stale generalizations about common national culture traits, children and parenting do seem more central to more people in Mexico than has ever been my experience in the United States. What might constitute busybody behavior in other locations is in Mexico quite often customary cultural parenting practice.

If anthropology, including that devoted to understanding Mexico, has often trafficked in simplistic versions of geographically bounded cultural practices, it has in addition sometimes lacked an ability to treat seriously specificity and confusion—for instance, with regard to male gender identities in Mexico in the late twentieth century. Fortunately, in response to this situation, some researchers have recently begun to reappraise hallowed truths (see Brandes 1988 and de Barbieri 1990),[1] and to reject a superficial categorization of Mexican men and machismo. Gender characteristics long presumed quintessential and immutable have belatedly come under closer scrutiny. Even if generalizations about Mexican men and women had in the past been somewhat appropriate—and there is little to recommend such a conclusion—they should be discarded now.

Nor are we are dealing simply with the pressing need for social science to catch up to history in its theoretical formulations. In fact, today in Mexico, what it means to be a man or a woman may be less evident than ever before. Among the young in Mexico City the model of aggressive masculinity is no longer the pistol-packing *charro* cowboy of yore looking for a tranquil rancho where he can hang his sombrero. He has been replaced by the submachine-gun-spraying Rambo launching assaults on the Vietnams or Afghanistans of the moment. No one would suggest that Rambo is a product of Mexico, yet there as in his land of origin, is he not known as the ultimate macho? Local symbols become globalized and then relocalized and reglobalized.

Neither is this book a straightforward study that traces the compass and course of modernity as it lurches fitfully ahead in Mexico, as if following painfully but faithfully in the tracks of the United States. Hanging outside a second-floor window in Colonia Santo Domingo, a banner reads, "Kinder Quetzalcóatl. Antes Mickey Mouse"; the school formerly called the Mickey Mouse Kindergarten is now named for a Toltec and Aztec deity, Quetzalcóatl, the Plumed Serpent. The geopolitics of Mexico's two-thousand-mile border and historically unique relationship with the United States weigh heavily on all aspects of Mexican society. But there are also particularities to Mexican modernity that, while often related to the country's unequal economic and cultural connections to the United States—a $100 billion debt, for instance—are not reducible to these ties.

Mexico has a long and unique history, and its approach to modernity has been equally complicated. Rampageous urbanization, epitomized by the massive and widespread land invasions of metropolitan peripheries; the massacre by the national army of hundreds of leftist students in a working class housing project at Tlatelolco in 1968, just before Mexico hosted the Olympics; devastating banking and financial crises like those of 1982 and 1995; an earthquake in 1985, which pancaked the imaginary development of democracy into the boggy foundations of Mexico City; state-run antipoverty programs, like the one called Solidaridad (Solidarity), which is broadly ridiculed instead of welcomed by the poor, the presumed beneficiaries of such government largesse; fractious political dueling at the national level that on occasion leads to speculation about electoral upsets, as in the presidential elections of 1988, and political assassinations, as in 1994; an armed uprising in Chiapas in 1994 that gained popular support throughout the country because "Chiapas is Mexico"—these are but a few of the signposts of modernity in Mexico City that have arisen in recent times.

Yet people in Mexico City's Colonia Santo Domingo and other poor neighborhoods of Mexico are also fascinated by international events and topics as varied as U.S. military activities in Iraq and police brutality in Los Angeles because they see these events as part of their world and their future. For example, the subject of Rodney King, the Black man whose 1991 beating by Los Angeles police was shown to the world on videotape, confronted me with great regularity in Mexico in the year or two following the incident. It came up one afternoon at the house of a relative of a friend in the town of Tepotzotlán, on the northern reaches of the Mexico City area, where in the course of an afternoon I was subjected to a two-hour interrogation on King and many other issues by half a dozen men and women. My smiling hosts explained that it was only fair that the anthropologist be so interviewed every once in a while, though as a guest of honor I was given one of the two or three collapsible chairs to sit on. The others stood or sat on the ground outside the two-room concrete dwelling, which had been "under construction" for some years and boasted no other furniture save a fold-up cot and a black-and-white television set. Cooking was done on the makeshift *comal* (grill) outside.

The owner of the property, Armando, initiated the inquisition. "Listen, Mateo, you are welcome, you are very welcome in my poor home. But, listen, Mateo, I must know one thing. Mateo, why is the U.S. bombing Iraq? What the hell can you tell me about this?" He had attended school for less than one year, some fifty years earlier, but Armando enjoyed watching the TV news. As I incautiously tried to explain what I knew of U.S. strategic planning for the Middle East, others interrupted, "And what's with this Rodney King beating?" We discussed

racism and recent police campaigns against African American youth in
the United States. "So how much do you bribe the cops in the U.S.?" I
responded that while bribing police was far less necessary in the United
States than in Mexico, clipping a twenty-dollar bill to your driver's license used to be a common practice in working class areas of Chicago
when I lived there. "Why won't Blacks work as hard as Mexicans
there?" The nasty feelings of some Mexicans for African Americans,
with whom few have ever had contact, is largely a product of Southern
California's economy and provides another indication of the ambigu-
ities of national borders.

"What Mexican food do you like best?" Politics and cuisine were
beginning to mix. "Did you know that Taco Bell is opening up here?"
Which led to a discussion of why the Mexican upper middle class, the
main group that frequents such establishments, might wish to eat U.S.-
style Mexican food. "How did you learn Spanish?" "What do you hope
to accomplish with this anthropology?" "Why did you choose to live
in Santo Domingo?" "What kinds of jobs have you had in the U.S. and
how much did you get paid?" "What are the gangs like in Houston?"
There followed questions about the Mexican film comedian Tin Tan,
Mexico City's pollution, finding a job in Oakland for someone's niece,
and how many children Michelle and I were going to have.

The consequences of modernity require an analysis of changing
structures and events by lay practitioners and professionals alike. Why
certain changes occur and what happens to the men and women who
are the actors and critics of modernity as they themselves change is the
subject of this study. But though emerging cultural practice—what used
to be called culture change—is a focus here, Arrom's (1985:231) description of early-nineteenth-century Mexico City remains relevant:
"Although Mexicans believed that wives should be subordinated to
husbands, they disagreed on what that meant in practice." Nonetheless,
fewer Mexicans, especially Mexican women, share such beliefs today,
and a broad comparison between life in the Mexican capital then and
now would probably indicate an even greater disparity between the ideals of familial authority and responsibility and their practical realities.
The diverse ways in which power is manifested and wielded at the
household level do not, however, prevent us from recognizing recurrent
elements in the wider sociological context.

In the financial and governmental elites in Mexico, men routinely
control economic and political power. At all wage-scale levels, women
get paid a fraction of what men receive. Rape and domestic violence are

widespread and, some argue, increasingly characteristic of the subordination of women to men. The rising rate of single abandoned mothers is but one indication of the double standards that are broadly utilized to exculpate men by absolving them from parental and marital responsibilities.

To adequately allow for both structure and agency, therefore, the study of men and male gender identities in Mexico City requires a constant refocusing of one's vision. This is necessary, first, in order to apprehend the Durkheimian invisible hand of social facts—how we are all in a very real sense products of our societies—and second, in order to accent the existential issue of cultural accountability. For, as suggested by Nancy Scheper-Hughes (1992:22–23), "the ethical is always prior to culture because the ethical presupposes all sense and meaning and therefore makes culture possible." What constitutes good and bad gender identities and relations for women and men in Santo Domingo is not knowable through abstract discourse on culture, any more than changes in culture can be explained without examining previous changes in ethical standards of belief and behavior.

FALLING FROM CONVENTIONAL GRACE

After spending nearly a year living and working in the *colonia popular* of Santo Domingo, Mexico City, I sat with a friend going over some questions that I had asked him six months earlier. I do not know if he remembered his initial answers, but the second time around his personal history had changed in significant ways. No doubt this change reflected a mutual trust that had developed between us in the interim, but I think that the ethnographic process had also allowed him, as it had me, to increasingly bring certain events in his life to light, to put into words many of the actions and feelings that had remained hidden from his consciousness.

Precisely because ever more men and women throughout Mexican society are today reflexively considering their multiple gender identities, the process of documenting these identities grows more complex. One reason to avoid thin and sweeping conclusions about gender relations in Mexico, and in Latin America as a whole, is that we still know too little about them. But the main reason to avoid such overly ambitious generalizations is that there exists no stable set of determining and essential gender qualities that can adequately capture the situation for the region as a whole; relentlessly emergent gender variations see to that.

Whenever I was in doubt, for persuasive evidence I had only to walk through my section of Colonia Santo Domingo, beginning with the agnostic printer who bragged to me about his vasectomy a week after I met him, who worked in front of the house with a single mother and five young children, who lived a block over from the woman who resided openly with her children and a series of male lovers, who was next door to the woman who could not leave home without her husband's permission, who was across the street from the cobbler who ridiculed state- and church-sponsored marriages in the same breath as he rebuked unfaithful husbands, whose shop was below the home of a notorious and belligerent wife beater and his alcoholic sons, one of whom was the boyfriend of a young mother of two small children who lived in a home in which all the males were waited upon by all the females of the household, all of whom were surrounded in the *colonia* by young women who would be the first people in their families to graduate from high school.

These are but a few of the numerous men and women whose lives may at first glance appear too mundane to merit attention but in whose everyday activities, if we look closely, we might just glimpse the creative efforts of people coping with the gender relations they have inherited from past generations while simultaneously striving to fashion new approaches as best they can.

ONE

Real Mexican Machos Are Born to Die

Imagination can't create anything new, can it?

Tony Kushner, Angels in America, Part One: Millennium Approaches

DIFFERENCES AND SIMILARITIES

In this book I examine what it means to be a man, *ser hombre,* for men and women who live in the *colonia popular* of Santo Domingo, Mexico City. The ethnographic focus of this study is on understanding gender identity in relation to the changes in cultural beliefs and practices that have occurred in urban Mexico over the course of several decades of local and global upheaval. By looking at how gender identity is forged and transformed in a working class community formed by land invasion in the Mexican capital in 1971, I explore cultural categories in various incarnations, some relatively fixed, others shifting. That is, I look at how cultural difference and similarity are constituted by diverse social actors who in turn limit and expand the meanings of gender identity.

While the cultural and political issues raised in this ethnography are necessarily sweeping, the events, sentiments, and activities described here have occurred, as often as not, on a far smaller scale as part of the daily lives of the residents of one neighborhood in the Mexican capital. As a prelude to the discussion in the chapters that follow, it may be helpful to first clarify certain questions related to gender and cultural identity in Mexico and to explain the underlying theoretical and methodological framework of this study.

If we understand gender to refer to the ways in which differences and similarities related to physical sexuality are understood, contested, organized, and practiced by societies, then we should expect to find a diversity of gendered meanings, institutions, and relations within and between different social groupings. At the same time, more than is commonly acknowledged, what it means *physically* to be a man or a woman must not be taken for granted but must be explained. As will be seen in chapter 5, an understanding of the body and sexuality requires an examination of cultural and historical factors and not simply an inspection of genitalia. Regardless of the importance of gender and sexuality in many aspects of human existence today and historically, the gendered character of social life is never transparent.[1]

In my own case, I did not so much set out to find gender as a topic of study as gender found me. Serendipity initially drew me into thinking about Mexican men as fathers. In the spring of 1989, while walking through downtown Mexico City, I took a photograph of a man in a musical-instruments store who was holding a baby as he talked to a customer; the reactions of friends to this photo provided my first impulse to study Mexican men as fathers. (We will return to the photograph in chapter 3.) Later, as I reviewed the social science literature on Mexican men and masculinity, the topic of my research became clear: widely accepted generalizations about male gender identities in Mexico often seemed egregious stereotypes about machismo, the supposed culture trait of Mexican men that is at once so famous and yet so thoroughly unknown. Even when I read of individuals and groups who for some reason did not fit a pattern of machismo—which, however it is defined in the social sciences, generally carries pejorative connotations—those cases were routinely judged to be unusual. Nor did such views come from academia alone. In casual conversations in working class areas of Mexico City over a period of years, I was often told, "Well, you know what Mexican men are like, but my husband [or brother or son or father] is different." It appeared that there were a multitude of exceptions to the rule of machos.[2]

Is this study, then, designed to deconstruct a unitary meaning of Mexican masculinity into multiple Mexican masculinities? In part it must have such limited and negative aims. However, my overall purpose is greater than this. The book is indeed concerned with meanings and understandings, but it is also a study of expectations, judgments, and actions. Most of all, this book is an examination of the dialectic between engendered meanings and social power.

Seen in this light, another goal of this study—beyond the deconstruction of hollow clichés of Mexican masculinity—is to contribute to the theoretical and empirical reconstruction of gender categories in their constantly transforming and transgressing expressions. While not directing himself to gender studies in particular, Néstor García Canclini (1989:25) infers such reconstructive intellectual work when he observes, "The totality may be forgotten when one is interested only in differences between men [people], not when one is also concerned with inequality." Certainly questions of inequality, identity, and power are of interest and importance not only to social scientists and their kin, but also to the ordinary people who constitute the subjects of most ethnographies.[3]

While certain notions of innate and essential male sexuality are being deconstructed every day in the *colonias populares* and the halls of academia in Mexico City, other sexual meanings, identities, and power relations are emerging in novel configurations. A central conclusion of my research in Colonia Santo Domingo, Mexico City, points to the creativity and capacity for change with regard to gender on the part of numerous actors and critics of modernity, an epoch, Giddens (1990) points out, that is characterized by the progressive socialization of the natural world. These circumstances make it all the more incumbent upon anthropologists and other scholars to imagine and invent new ways of describing, interpreting, and explaining cultural emergence and variation.

This process requires cognizance of both general and particular cultural mores and practices associated with gender relations. For example, if a man walking down the street alone at midnight in Santo Domingo hears footsteps rapidly approaching him from behind, the possibility of assault and robbery will usually cross his mind. A woman in the same circumstance will generally worry about assault, robbery, . . . and rape. Men from the *colonia* are rarely concerned about being raped, except when they are in circumstances such as prison or the army.[4] For all practical purposes, men and women in Santo Domingo share many concerns and experiences, while at the same time there are distinct gendered differences in their daily lives.

Yet even to formulate the issue as one of similarity and difference can fatally skew any attempt to penetrate beyond superficial gender identities in Santo Domingo. If you ask people in the *colonia* about the differences between men and women, for example, they will invariably respond with pat answers of the opinion-poll variety and, not surprisingly, highlight differences between men and women. That is, simply by couching the issue in these terms you can usually get predictable answers of some sort, but this does not mean that these people necessarily see gender differences as interesting or worth talking about, much less as paramount.

There is not a Mexican or Latin or Spanish-speaking cultural system of generally agreed-upon gender meanings and experience. Not only is there tremendous intracultural diversity with regard to gender in *colonias populares* in Mexico City, but there is wildly uneven knowledge and power in the field of gender relations there.[5] Gender identities in Colonia Santo Domingo, as elsewhere, are products and manifestations of cultures in motion; they do not emanate from some primordial essence whose resilience bears testament to perpetual forms of inequality.

CONTRADICTORY CONSCIOUSNESS

One of the key theoretical concepts employed throughout this study is that of contradictory consciousness. In an attempt to explain the often conflicting influences of practical activity and self-understanding on individuals, and to get beyond mere acknowledgment of confusion, Antonio Gramsci developed the formulation of *contradictory consciousness*. While Gramsci's references to the term were quite brief, what he did write can provide us with a starting point from which to develop a fuller understanding of how male identities develop and transform in societies like Mexico's today. Specifically with reference to "the active man-in-the-mass," Gramsci explains:

> One might almost say that he has two theoretical consciousnesses (or one contradictory consciousness): one which is implicit in his activity and which in reality unites him with all his fellow-workers in the practical transformation of the real world; and one, superficially explicit or verbal, which he has inherited from the past and uncritically absorbed. (1929–35:333)

As employed in this book, *contradictory consciousness* is a descriptive phrase used to orient our examination of popular understandings, identities, and practices *in relation to* dominant understandings, identities, and practices. For instance, with regard to the practices of Mexican men as fathers, many are aware of a social science image of poor urban Mexican men typified by the Macho Progenitor. Yet whereas the beliefs and practices of many ordinary men do not accord neatly with this monochromatic image, ordinary men and women are themselves often acutely aware of and influenced in one way or another by the dominant, often "traditional" stereotypes about men.

That is, these same working class men and women share both a consciousness inherited from the past—and from the experts—that is largely and uncritically accepted, and another, implicit consciousness that unites individuals with others in the practical transformation of the world.[6] (To speak of traditions and inheritance should not be misconstrued to mean that the world was changeless until the contemporary era. Tradition and past customs provide questions and characterizations that confront every generation anew.) While there are historic, systemic, and bodily facets of machismo, figuring out exactly how the pieces fit together is another matter. With respect to some of the attributes frequently cited as manifesting machismo on the part of men— wife beating, alcoholism, infidelity, gambling, the abandonment of children, and bullying behavior in general—many men, and more than a few women, in Santo Domingo exhibit certain of these qualities and not others. Some alcoholic men are known as good providers for their families; children in Santo Domingo are said to receive more whippings from their mothers than their fathers; most public violence in the area has as much to do with unemployment and youth as it does with gender itself; adultery and drunkenness among women are becoming increasingly common; some husbands who abstain from drinking nevertheless brutally batter their wives, sons, and other men; and gambling is not a common activity.

Distinguishing inherited from transformative consciousness has been one of the urgent tasks of feminist anthropologists over the past twenty-five years, a part of their efforts to reveal the relevance of gender where often it has been overlooked or marginalized. Through ethnography and theoretical debate, anthropological gender studies have documented male biases in research results, detailed the salience and the changing nature of gender (variously defined) in social formations throughout history, and challenged notions of universal male authority.[7] Taken as a whole, gender studies in the last two decades make up the most important new body of work in the discipline of anthropology overall.

Of particular interest for the present study is the fact that, following initial overgeneralizations in most feminist anthropology regarding the extent to which commonalties could be found in the status of women historically and globally, more recently emphasis has been increasingly placed on studying the particularities of gendered differences in diverse cultural processes and milieus. In like fashion, and flowing from the attention given here to the notion of contradictory consciousness, this book aims to contribute to the newer, emergent effort in critical feminist theory by emphasizing the variety, as opposed to the homogeneity, of masculinities among working class Mexicans.[8]

As to the study of men *as men,* following in the wake of the second wave of feminist theory some male anthropologists began in the 1980s to examine men as engendered and engendering cultural beings in various parts of the world.[9] Customary anthropological practice had long entailed male ethnographers interviewing male informants, so there was nothing inherently remarkable about men talking to men about themselves. What was novel, rather, involved not the study of men but the study of men-as-men. Today gender studies have to include research on both men and women as engendered subjects, which is why examining masculinity in contemporary Mexico is thus both a methodological question and a cultural issue.

Although much more research and analysis is needed, important strides have nonetheless been made in gender studies in Latin America—for instance, studies on women and work, women and households and families, women and ethnicity and class, and women in social movements.[10] But why is there virtually no scholarly material on men-as-men in Latin America? In the case of Mexico, we need to correct the fanciful and static portrayals with which even some of the best ethnographies of the region too often characterize men, if now less often women.

Overlapping with some of these examinations of gender, particularly as they relate to questions of inequality and difference, new theoretical work in anthropology has been produced in the past two decades that examines relations between power and agency on one hand and between hegemony and consciousness on the other, effectively building on classic earlier attention in the discipline to oppositional ritual and political organization.[11] The emergence of this new work coincides with excited debate in the field concerning textual critiques of anthropology, and especially ethnography, which have been raised to counter idyllic notions of objectivity.[12] The best anthropology today successfully navigates these invigorating though sometimes chilling currents.

HOMBRES DE VERDAD—REAL MEN

"Identity is not as transparent or unproblematic as we think," writes Stuart Hall. He continues:

> Perhaps instead of thinking of identity as an already accomplished fact . . .
> we should think, instead, of identity as a "production," which is never com-
> plete, always in process, and always constituted within, not outside, repre-
> sentation. (1990:222)

The concept of identity has a long scholarly history, and has been discussed in the modern era in the West by philosophers such as Locke,
Hume, and Schelling. By the mid–nineteenth century, at least, the term
had gained some currency in broader intellectual circles.[13] Identity lies
at the very heart of Marx's famous first chapter of *Capital* (1867).[14]
Here I adopt an explanation similar to that of Marx, seeing identity as
an interminable process residing in the *abstraction* of equivalency. Because identity does not stand still or fall outside what it itself represents,
this indeterminate understanding of identity allows for the nuanced appreciation of the elusiveness of gender identities that are constantly
shifting in terms of both history and place.

My definition of male identities focuses on what men say and do *to
be men,* and not simply on what men say and do. Male identities do
not, for instance, reflect elemental or eternal cultural differences between men and women. If courage is an attribute that is valued in men
by both men and women, is courage therefore masculine? What if courage is also valued in women by both women and men (or only women)?
Are courageous wives to be considered only as extensions of their husbands? This would be a serious mistake.

Or what are we to make of the historical development in which many
men who used to drink together in specific places at specific times in
Mexico City are now more frequently being joined by women and are
in fact drinking their Coronas, Vickys, and Don Pedros together with
these women at these times and places? The specifically (essentially)
male aspects of these activities and relevant attitudes will consequently
have changed too. As we will see in chapter 7, this development does
not necessarily mean that such drinking patterns are more degendered,
less heavily associated with gender identities, though this may be the
case. But it does often lead to changes in the gendered character and
quality of drinking at such moments and in such locations, and may
entail confusion on the part of the male and female drinkers regarding
gender identities.

Somehow, with regard to gender identity, we must account for both
change and persistence in what it means to be women and men,
avoiding the twin errors of, on the one hand, assuming that acquiring

gender is the same as acquiring a social identity that is already fixed and, on the other, assuming that there exist no prior social categories and that gender is constructed anew with every social encounter (see Barrett 1988:268).

Erik Erikson (1963, 1968) brought the philosophical term *identity* into modern social science discourse, especially in the field of psychology. Parts of his analysis of identity remain valuable, especially his insistence that one identity may be understood only relative to another, that identity must be seen as a process and not something permanent, and that the relation between identity and history is fundamental. But whereas for Erikson identity was ultimately epigenetic in nature, identity here is treated as thoroughly cultural and variable. Further, for Erikson, identity was relatively fixed following a period of "identity confusion" in adolescence, whereas I argue that identity can and does continue to change throughout one's personal and historical life.[15]

In this investigation of the meanings of masculinity in Colonia Santo Domingo, I historicize gender identities, whether for children of six or grandparents of seventy-six, and show that identity and identity change (and, yes, identity *confusion*) play important roles throughout peoples' lives.

As a direct refutation of both the older melting-pot theories and the newer banalities about the necessarily homogenizing impact of modernity, identity politics are gaining in importance not only in the United States, but also in many other parts of the world including Mexico. Racial, ethnic, political, sexual, and national identities are powerfully asserted in Colonia Santo Domingo, Mexico City, and not merely imposed from without. And the very acts of assertion testify to the comparative, processual, and historical nature of cultural identities. When men and women in the *colonia* raise their own concerns about being confused about gender identities, they are giving voice to the psychological components of cultural changes otherwise reflected in developments as varied as the gay and lesbian rights movements, the church's teachings on abortion, and the gender identities beamed south via U.S. television sitcoms.

Although the assertion of identity can be used to exclude and control oppressed peoples, it can also be used by these peoples to counter such domination as well. Much depends on whether the assertion of identity is initiated from above or below, which points to the need for a critical consciousness that simultaneously asserts and challenges identities, as women and men rediscover what Gramsci (1929–35:333) calls "the sense of being 'different' and 'apart' . . . an instinctive feeling of independence."

MANLY DOMINATION

The need for such a critical consciousness raises the issue of hegemony and ideology, terms employed to different ends by different people today.[16] As used here, *hegemony* speaks to the dominant ideas and practices that are so pervasive as to constitute common sense for members of society, and through which elites gain the popular consent necessary for their continued rule. *Ideology*, on the other hand, describes the outlook and conscious beliefs of particular social groups as distinguished from other social groups. As Jean and John Comaroff write,

> Hegemony is beyond direct argument; ideology is more likely to be perceived as a matter of inimical opinion and interest and hence is more open to contestation. Hegemony, at its most effective, is mute; ideology invites argument. (1992:29)

While Mannheim (1936) along with many other sociological theorists correctly locates the origins of ideology in society, thus linking knowledge decisively with social formations, his notion of "relationism" (as opposed to relativism) still does not incorporate as fully as necessary the power struggles—and attempts to defeat others' ideologies—inherent in people's use of ideologies. Yet these struggles are of cardinal importance, as is the need to discriminate between the ideologies of more and less powerful social groups.[17]

A central component of the argument that follows is that at various levels of society, power is contested by dominating and dominated groups and not just by individuals, as Foucault often contends in his arguments against the reification of societies and classes (for instance, 1980a, 1983). This occurs at the society-wide level between elites and popular classes, as well as within elite and popular classes. And it is found in the cultural spaces inside households between women and men, men and other men, women and other women, the young and the old, and so on. This is why I am not proposing that emergent cultural practices are the products only of the poor, for instance, since culture and class do not so neatly coincide. Contrary to mechanical materialism, there is no isomorphic correspondence between class and culture, just as there is none between material reality and ideas. But there is a definite relation between dominant and emergent cultural practices, and there are definite components to them that must be linked with particular social formations such as classes and genders. For instance, in Mexico City, certain ideas and practices concerning men's roles in parenting are more associated with certain classes than with others.

Power differentials emanate from social groups to significant degrees and are not found just in Foucault's capillary forms of existence (1980a). In an atomized manner, "[p]ower moves in mysterious ways in Foucault's writings, and history, as the actively made achievement of human subjects, scarcely exists" (Giddens 1992:24). Recognizing the role of complicity in perpetuating subjugation does not mean forfeiting the ability to distinguish greater and lesser powers. Individuals and groups do not wield power in the same ways, much less with the same consequences. As the Comaroffs (1991:17) point out, ignoring such a truth has left too many scholars dismissing power: "Now everywhere, it is nowhere in particular."

Critical theory has benefited from the renewed attention to constraints on historical agency, just as it has from discussions of historical contingency versus evolutionary inevitability. Further, there is something akin to the later Marx's commodities in Foucault's institutions, in that both can and do seem to assume lives of their own and can turn on their creators. These are similar forms of power. Yet with Marx we also find another form of power, agency—a concept providing us with a way to understand how power in the form of social groups contributes to creating things that do not yet exist. In terms of historical transformations, it is true that with Marx, and even more so with many subsequent Marxists, progress is at times portrayed simply as the quixotic sense of improvement. But generally with Marx, progress is shown as merely the manifestation of impermanence. With Foucault, we are too often left everywhere all at once, and thus too often never anywhere.

In some feminist theory, the relationship between power, ideology, and masculinity is depicted as one of uniformity. This is why, as Yanagisako and Collier (1987:26–27) point out, models of homogeneity among men falsely and inexorably lead to "the notion that there is a unitary 'man's point of view,' " whereupon confusion often results when the dominant ideology is equated with the point of view of men. For this reason, in the case of Santo Domingo I am interested in men's points of view seen in processual flux and not as some one thing permanently molded into a particular configuration, and in men's points of view over a specific time period and not, for instance, "since the Spanish Conquest."

My argument is not that such circumstances are immune to analysis on any but an individual basis. Rather, the notion of a unitary maleness, whether conceived of as national or universal in character, is wrong and harmful. Odd as it may seem, it was Durkheim (1895 [1964]:6) who thought that "sociological phenomena cannot be defined by their universality." The multiple expressions of male gender identities in Mexico City contradict all such stereotypical notions of a uniform Spanish-speaking masculinity that crosses class, ethnicity, region, and age.

For both material and ideological reasons, *los hombres* (men) and *los machos* are indeed valid anthropological categories in Mexico today. Often, though not always, these terms are popularly conceived in contradistinction to *las mujeres* (women) and *las mujeres abnegadas* (self-sacrificing women). In line with Behar's (1993:272) call to "go beyond first world representations of third world women as passive, subservient, and lacking in creativity," we should recognize that there is always both acquiescence and dissension with regard to these concepts, and that no category is popularly regarded—or should be seen—as homogenous. Nor is the following discussion based on a structuralist binary opposition, in this case that of man/woman or *macho/abnegada*. "Manliness" and "womanliness" (to say nothing of "femininity") are not original, natural, or embalmed states of being; they are gender categories whose precise meanings constantly shift, transform into each other, and ultimately make themselves into whole new entities.

What is the relation between what people believe—about their identities, for example—and what they do? How does what people do affect what they believe? Some critiques of the notion of false consciousness, for example, have reached the not-so-challenging conclusion that if oppressed people are quiet, this reveals not mystified thinking but rather a superior and resigned grasp of their utter powerlessness to do anything but survive and resist. A corollary to this view is that it is high time for intellectuals to recognize the truth of this reality as well.[18] But the issue would seem to be not merely whether intellectuals accept some preordained fate of the oppressed but why intellectuals may do this (see Gutmann 1993b). An important issue for critical theory is to get beyond mere acknowledgment of illusion in order to understand the powerful ideological hold that illusions may have. Experts and ordinary people alike can be deluded, misinformed, and prejudiced.

These are old intellectual questions, variously formulated as the matrix of structure and agency on one hand, and tensions between determinism, voluntarism, and free will on the other. As applied to Santo

Domingo, key questions arise as to whether and how gender relations there faithfully reflect (or mimic) larger social norms; the causes of divergences that do occur, both when compared with broader populations and within the *colonia*; and the importance or insignificance of popular consciousness in fomenting and/or registering such counter-hegemonic practices and pockets of difference.

CULTURAL CREATIVITY

If one of the characteristics of modernity is a pluralism of contradictory convictions, as Habermas (1985) contends, then the impact of this situation on people who live in Colonia Santo Domingo is revolutionizing and not even superficially predictable. In the tension of contradictory convictions and contradictory consciousness in the *colonia* lies the impulse for cultural creativity, this book's other key theoretical concept (the first being contradictory consciousness).

Surely one factor determining the course of events in Santo Domingo is the conscious and unconscious agency of the men and women there, and what Raymond Williams (1977) calls the "elements of emergence" and "emergent cultural practice." For our purposes this insight is valuable in identifying emerging gender meanings and practices that challenge dominant social ideas and structures, particularly those pertaining to machismo. While we must be cautious in our attempt to analyze changes in gender identities, we must also guard against what is frequently the even more debilitating contemporary notion that nothing ever does change, especially when it comes to life between women and men.

How much room is there for ideas and actions, whether consciously motivated or not, that do not come from the elites and do not automatically benefit them, and how can these phenomena be shown? Bourdieu's analysis of symbolic capital remains a key point of reference here in accounting for the hegemony, dominance, and constraint of the elites over societies. But it is insufficient in explaining change and, in particular, agency from below. This is why Bourdieu is mistakenly led to conclude:

> Those who believe in the existence of a "popular culture," a paradoxical notion which imposes, willy-nilly, the dominant definition of culture, must expect to find—if they were to go and look—only the scattered fragments of an old erudite culture (such as folk medicine), selected and reinterpreted in

terms of the fundamental principles of the class habitus and integrated into the unitary world view it engenders, and not the counter-culture they call for, a culture truly raised in opposition to the dominant culture and consciously claimed as a symbol of status or a declaration of separate existence. (1984:395)

Minimizing the creative capacity of popular classes is tempting, especially in moments of relative quiescence that are only periodically broken by public protest. Yet while acknowledging the persuasively "realistic" invocation by Bourdieu of elite domination, we must not become overawed by the common-sense approach that would relegate nonelites to robotic existence and deny Gramsci's sense of emancipatory agency or Williams' remarks concerning emergent cultural practices.[19] Theories of distinctions may tell us important things about many social differences and how these are created and developed by dominant groups, but they do not necessarily provide an indication as to whether and how change may take place.[20] The rub, of course, lies in distinguishing how far symbolic capital *does* extend, and how deeply some of the historical determinism accurately reflects the lives of the poor. Nor can we forget that the role of accident in history must be added to these factors, for in terms of both individuals and groups, happenstance plays a part in determining how change occurs.

In Santo Domingo, the very indeterminacy and ambiguity of social life provides an opportunity for both men and women to negotiate male identities. This is a particular illustration of the point made by Rosaldo (1993:112) that, with regard to the combustible mix of diversity, creativity, and change, "sources of indeterminacy . . . constitute a social space within which creativity can flourish."[21] Still, though cultural creativity may thus spring from myriad and amorphous sources, rarely are matters so ambiguous as to entirely obviate differences in coercive and consensual power.

Although gender identities and practices are not fixed, automatic, or predestined in Colonia Santo Domingo any more than they are in the broader Mexican society, in ordinary and anomalous ways most men who today live in the *colonia* continue to benefit as a group from aspects of the subordination of women. The fact that some men in Santo Domingo regularly eat before women and eat better than women is not necessarily a matter of mere convenience. Similarly, though decision making about matters as diverse as buying kitchen appliances and choosing birth-control methods is shared in many households, when one person dominates the choices, this person is usually a man.

Yet gender identities and practices are changing in Mexico City, and these changes are in many respects characteristic of gender relations there in the mid-1990s. By simply acknowledging these transformations we may begin to account for the changing perceptions and actions of many men and women, including those men (described in chapter 8) who, after they beat their wives, insist, "The macho culture made me do it."

Masculinity in Mexico, as elsewhere, is definitely more subtle, diverse, and malleable than is generally assumed. This evaluation is linked in turn to one of the central conclusions of this study: where changes in male identities and actions have occurred in Mexico City, women have often played an initiating role. Social groups that hold power, no matter how circumscribed, rarely give it up without a fight, much less out of a collective sense of fairness. In Santo Domingo, whether or not women are physically present with men at work and at leisure, the initiating role of women in challenging received gender wisdoms and customs is profound.

The fact that the ground is shifting under the feet of many men in Mexico is due as well to large-scale socioeconomic transformations generally involving women at first, or at least initially attracting their attention: greater numbers of women working outside the home for money; parity of girls and boys through junior high school; a sharp fall in the number of children women have been having in the past twenty years; the feminist movement; and further changes (see chapters 4 and 6). The process I am describing does not mean that women's initiative has produced an automatic (and predictable) reaction among men. But, seen dialectically and not as a dualism, women's initiative—often in the form of arguing, cajoling, and issuing ultimatums—should be understood as part of a process by which women and men creatively transform themselves and their gendered worlds in consequential new ways. The outcome of these confrontations and resolutions provides ample evidence of cultural creativity and how social life is constantly engendered and degendered in the *colonia*.

ANTHROPOLOGY'S AFFINITY TO THE MEXICAN MACHO

Many finely wrought ethnographic explorations of Mexico and Latin America have documented just such creativity as it has emerged from within conflicting power struggles and desires for emancipation, whether at the level of families, communities, regions, or whole states. At the same time, as Sapir long ago recognized, "[c]reation is a bending of form to one's will, not a manufacture of form *ex nihilo*" (1924 [1949]:321). Though for Sapir this was too often reduced to a matter of national cultures providing platforms from which creativity could spring, in Mexico creative tensions have often appeared as contradictions between the pre-Hispanic and modern, the mestizo and Indian, the local community and the national or global. Child-rearing and family studies conducted in Mexico in the 1960s were not immune from the quest for unique national traits, but at their best they provided sophisticated analyses of how local communities fit into a historical context.[22]

Along these lines, and because of his crispness, scope, and vigor in presentation, Oscar Lewis (1951, 1959, 1961) has been a central anthropological ancestor for me in my study of masculinity in Mexico. Though he contradicts himself on occasion—for example, regarding paternal child-rearing patterns in rural Tepoztlán (see chapter 3)—his descriptions are still a constant point of reference for all contemporary students of the changes and continuities of life between and among women and men in Mexico. His theoretical formulations are also still delightfully provoking, if unfortunately too often insufficiently developed with regard to several topics, including the concept of machismo.

In trying to understand Mexican men, however, numerous other scholars have utilized details from Lewis's ethnographic studies to promote sensationalist generalities that go far beyond anything Lewis himself wrote. For instance, in David Gilmore's (1990) widely read survey of the "Ubiquitous" if not "Universal" male in the world, machismo is discussed as an extreme form of manly images and codes. Modern urban Mexican men are useful to Gilmore mainly as exaggerated archetypes; with other Latin men they constitute the negative pole on a continuum—from machismo to androgyny—of male cultural identities around the world. Mexican machos are thus employed as a foil against which other men less concerned with virility are compared. Gilmore cites Lewis to make his ethnographic points about Mexican men.

> In urban Latin America, for example, as described by Oscar Lewis (1961:38), a man must prove his manhood every day by standing up to challenges and insults, even though he goes to his death "smiling." As well as being tough and brave, ready to defend his family's honor at the drop of a hat, the urban Mexican . . . must also perform adequately in sex and father many children. (1990:16)[23]

To be sure, such a characterization of "the urban Mexican [male]" does find echoes in popular culture—for instance, in a line from the Mexican hit song of 1948 "Traigo mi .45" (I'm carrying my .45): "*¿Quién dijo miedo, muchachos, si para morir nacimos?* [Who's talking scared, boys, if we were born to die?]"[24] But even if Lewis's ethnographic descriptions, compiled in the 1950s, were just as valid decades later, in *The Children of Sánchez* Lewis did not usually generalize in this fashion about the lives of the father, Jesús Sánchez, or of Jesús's offspring. His anthropology was often artfully composed and some of his theories were naïve, but Lewis generally tried to keep "mere" romance and fancy out of his ethnographic descriptions.[25]

To cite another example of social science depictions of Mexican men, Lola Romanucci-Ross's 1973 ethnography set in rural Mexico carries an epigraph, attributed to a village proverb, that reads, "*El macho vive mientras que el cobarde quiere* [The macho lives as long as the coward wills it]." To call this a proverb implies ancient wisdoms. As we will see, however, not only is this notion of the death-defying macho of fairly recent vintage, but indeed the use of the word *macho* in this manner is quite modern.

In a frequently quoted paper on machismo, Stevens (1973:94) calls the popular acceptance of a stereotyped Latin American macho "ubiquitous in every social class," a summation that has led some scholars whose geographical interests lie outside the region to utilize the concept of machismo in their own studies.[26]

connotation In a sense, then, the words *macho* and *machismo* have become a form of calumny, shorthand terms in social science and journalistic writing for labeling a host of negative male characteristics in cultures around the world. A researcher at the Center for Gender Studies in Moscow told a reporter in 1994, "Before the view of Russian men [was] . . . as creatures without willpower who drink too much. Now they have the ability to make money, they want everything in this life. They have that macho feeling" (cited in Stanley 1994:7).[27]

This last case is illuminating: men who drink too much are not called macho, yet those who have money more easily acquire "that macho feeling." In earlier examples cited, male sexual conquest and procreation are central themes, as are bragging and the defiance of death. Machismo is said by some to be most prevalent among certain social classes, and by others to be found among all strata. One way or another, the assumption is that we all know what machismo means and what machos do and that the task of social scientists is principally to find cultures in which machos flourish as much as they supposedly do in Mexico. Who calls whom a macho and why and when is, as we will see in chapter 9, a key question whose answers do not come easily.

An equation of machismo with Mexican culture as a whole has occurred well beyond the confines of mere social science; it has also been common in the stories Mexicans tell about themselves, both in daily discussions among Mexicans and in the grand proclamations of the scholarly elite. Stereotypes about machismo are critical ingredients in the symbolic capital used by ordinary Mexicans. Even if verbally denigrated by many, machismo is widely regarded in Mexico as constituting part of the national patrimony in much the same way as the country's oil deposits are considered a source of national if not necessarily individual self-identity. In this manner machismo has become part of the more general political economy of cultural values in Mexico.

Before anthropologists even began discussing the issue of machismo, of course, the foremost men of letters in twentieth-century Mexico, writers like Samuel Ramos, Octavio Paz, and Juan Rulfo, were making this situation known and drawing psychologized connections between Spanish conquests of Indians and male conquests of women.[28] Herzfeld (1987:146) points out in his discussion of "disemia"—the contest between official discourse and everyday usage—that usage is often "serendipitously subversive of accepted meanings."[29] Thus the partial coincidence, or overlap, in the utilization by both Paz and my friends in Santo Domingo of the same key terms should not lead us into simplistic thinking that there is only one meaning of macho in Mexico.

Dissatisfied with habitually adopted representations of masculinity in Mexico, as well as with widely accepted models of male-female relations in Latin America more generally, I have in this study sought to complicate matters. When analyzing changing male identities in *colonias populares* of Mexico City, for example, categories that posit static differences in the male and female populations—the drunks, the loving mothers, the wife beaters, the machos, the sober family men, the submissive women—hinder one's efforts more than they assist them. Gender identities, roles, and relations do not remain frozen in place, either for individuals or for groups. There is continuous contest and confusion over what constitutes male identity; it means different things to different people at different times. And sometimes different things to the same person at the same time.[30]

Plasicity

LILIANA

Not to look, not to touch, not to record, can be the
hostile act, the act of indifference and of turning
away.

> *Nancy Scheper-Hughes,*
> Death without Weeping

There are limits to anthropological inquiry, and otherness is not merely
an illusion. Nonetheless, anthropologists may sometimes impose obsta-
cles in their research when the subjects of their studies see more commonalties, including those between the researcher and themselves, than
simple native-outsider images would account for. How we interpret
otherness often says more about our own culturally driven opinions
regarding incommensurability than it does about cultural others.[31]

But what is the fieldworker to do when the father of thick description, Clifford Geertz, warns that "[w]e cannot live other people's lives,
and it is a piece of bad faith to try," because really and truly ethnography is "all a matter of scratching surfaces" (Geertz 1986:373)? When
Geertz exhorts us to abandon this kind of effort, we ethnographers take
notice. Elsewhere Geertz is more blunt: "The responsibility for ethnography, or the credit, can be placed at no other door than that of the
romancers who have dreamt it up" (1988:140). This assertion is connected to "the un-get-roundable fact that all ethnographical descriptions are homemade, that they are the describer's descriptions, not those
of the described" (1988:144–45).

Geertz is correct in pointing out that no pretense of "just quoting the
natives" can absolve anthropologists of their own responsibility for
their publications and teaching. Yet ethnography is not necessarily so
solitary an enterprise as Geertz implies: good ethnography inevitably
contains the influences of diverse sources, including other anthropologists and the descriptions of the described about *themselves* that arise
in the course of what might be called ethnographic friendships and col-
laboration.

Further, the argument that anthropologists bring too much cultural
baggage with them to truly penetrate the consciousness of others is
based on a set of unstated and unfounded premises. After all, how can
the ethnographer be sure that all she knows is mere surface phenomena?
The advice offered by Geertz ironically implies prior (and superior)
knowledge of precisely what is said to be unknowable. "How [do] you

know you know?" is the anthropological question Geertz reinvents (1988:135); "How do you know you do not know?" is the one he neglects. Finally, and worst of all, Geertz's counsel implies that "native" informants cannot see and communicate anything significant about themselves and their lives to others, including ethnographers.

This whole approach can treat the subjects of research as thoroughly exotic objects, and hostile ones at that. But the ethnographic process need not consist in such mutually unintelligible relations. Ethnographic research inevitably involves contradiction, yet this need not be antagonistic contradiction. Indeed, self-awareness on both sides of the research divide can reveal not only what we do not know about the other, but also how much there is to know. Ideology, as part of culture, is likewise not automatically a hindrance to the process.[32] What Geertz may view as a liability—having hybrid points of view and practices—can in fact be a source of advantage in gaining knowledge of others that goes beyond the superficial.

My own cultural and personal hybridity played a determining role in the questions I asked in my ethnographic fieldwork and how I asked them. First of all, I was a new father and my daughter Liliana was my unwitting field assistant. Many of the thrills, tensions, and traumas of being a parent during the first year of a child's life have become for me impossible to distinguish clearly from life as an ethnographer. My wife, Michelle, and I truly became parents in Mexico City. The fact that I was studying men as fathers had everything and nothing to do with being a new father myself. Michelle and I are certainly different parents because of these particular experiences.

For instance, we are undoubtedly more likely than we would have been without our year in Mexico to hold infants for hours on end rather than let them play on the floor or ground. Our standards for warm clothing have changed dramatically: today, back in the United States, we instinctively shudder in horror when we feel that a child is not adequately covered. And we are truly dismayed by the hostility we see on the part of so many adults and establishments in the United States toward noisy, even screaming children. This last reflects not so much "Mexican culture" as the cultural politics of class, because in the poorer strata of Mexico *and* the United States children abound at social gatherings, whether parties for family and friends or neighborhood political meetings. The routine separation of children from adults in a variety of social settings is the more exclusive prerogative of the wealthy in both societies.

Shortly after we began renting an apartment in the *colonia*, our neighbors in Santo Domingo began asking why we were being so mean to Liliana. They, women and men alike, were concerned about what they saw as one particular act of cruelty on our part. Or, rather, about the perceived cruelty of a particular instance of inactivity on our part: why had we not pierced Liliana's ears? Were we embarrassed to have a girl? Didn't we know that daughters were as wonderful as sons? The responses we considered making—easy, decontextualized analyses of what difference has to do with inequality, and whether treating boys and girls differently necessarily reveals inequality—seemed pathetically abstract and lifeless. We pierced Lili's ears.

To draw again from the well of my personal history, in addition to my willful confusion regarding my position as Liliana's father and as a visiting North American anthropologist, I similarly could not and did not wish to sharply delineate the ethical standards that had led to my studying one aspect of culture change in the slums of Mexico City in the early 1990s from those that had led to my activities during the 1970s and 1980s in political and community organizing in Chicago, Houston, and other cities in the United States. Like many ethnographers before me, in learning how to be a good parent and anthropologist, and in trying to understand the world better in order to change it, I have had to depend on the kindness of many strangers.

INFORMANTS' FAME, INFORMERS' INFAMY

Like all ethnographies, this one is based especially on those people who were most receptive to and curious about themselves, the issues, and the anthropologist. Some of the people I tried to meet, interview, and learn from in Santo Domingo, however, remained hidden to me. And though for my formal interviews I originally intended to use more random methods of selection, I was quickly dissuaded from this approach. It seemed that I had arrived on the heels of some rather unpleasant confrontations between certain residents of the *colonia* and a group of U.S. Protestant evangelists who had given gringos in the area an even worse reputation for arrogance than they already had. My technique for meeting many people and interviewing some therefore became reliant in the initial instances on the introductions of people I already knew, which were often prefaced by the statement "He's OK, he's not one of the evangelists." Within a few months such formal introductions became far less necessary.

It is deadly for the researcher in an anthropological exploration to try to act like an ethnographic sponge—the infamous fly on the wall—soaking up life around her. It is merely the silly flip side of those who try to "go native," against whom Geertz's admonition was directed. My style in interviews was therefore usually more conversational than interrogatory. My opinions, and not just my questions, were raised throughout. With one or two exceptions—for instance, I rarely used the word *machismo* until others raised it with me, because I was studying the use of the term—I felt free to speak my mind, as I believe my friends generally did with me. Teasing, arguing, flattering, guilt-tripping, and boasting were essential to my daily interactions with friends and neighbors.

Some reactions to my research were playful. One day after he knew me better, Lolo, a teenager, responded to my request to interview him by saying, "Whenever you want. Who are you anyway, the police?" Others were unexpectedly calculating. After an article I had written appeared midway through my fieldwork in the Sunday literary-magazine supplement to the newspaper *La jornada* (see Gutmann 1993a), my status as a published neighbor became an issue for some friends and contacts; I represented potential fame or infamy for many. A mechanic friend, Gabriel, had told me before the essay appeared that if he did not like what I said he was going to "*partirte la madre*," which loosely translates as "fuck you up." [33] Afterward both Gabi and others seemed to view my research somewhat differently, as if they were thinking that anything they told me now might one day end up in print. This meant that attempts were made to keep things from my attention. But it also led to people telling me about experiences and ideas that I was expected to write about for them. Anthropology provides many instances of the ethnographer as ghost writer and informer.

Originally I intended to make up names for all my informants, and in the course of fieldwork I would sometimes ask my friends if they had any special requests. Partly in response to my article as well as to my appearance on a national television talk show, *María Victoria Llamas*, over and over friends asked me to use their real names in whatever I wrote. And I usually have done so. In those cases where I was asked to change names, I have always changed them. To respect the wishes of those who wanted to remain anonymous, I have also sometimes combined life-history details and comments in order to form composite informants. I have kept the citations from informal discussions and more formal interviews as accurate as possible, cutting only some repetitious verbal mannerisms within and between paragraphs, though usually not within phrases. Unless otherwise specified, all dates in the ethnography refer to the period from August 1992 to August 1993, and unless otherwise noted, all translations into English are mine. In addition, all photographs in this book were taken by the author, with the exception of the one on page 191.

.   .   .

In the pages that follow, I describe and analyze how different aspects of men's lives—for example, fatherhood, sexuality, alcohol, and violence—have recently combined as part of the process of transforming gender identities in Mexico City in the late twentieth century. In a variety of surprising as well as more predictable ways the men and women of Colonia Santo Domingo, as part of the broader society and because of certain specific conditions pertaining in this largely self-built community, show that the *macho mexicano* stereotypes are today inappropriate and misleading. These stereotypes are in fact inaccurate and will help us but little if we sincerely hope to understand large sections of men in this area—how they see themselves, and how the women with whom they share their lives see them, their history, and their future.

TWO

The Invasion of
Santo Domingo

Today, whoever says they know Mexico City is lying; at
best, we intuit it.

Carlos Monsiváis, in La jornada

¡HAY TIERRA!

During the night of 3–4 September 1971, a call went up in the southern
outskirts of Mexico City: "*¡Hay tierra!* [There's land!]" Within a
twenty-four-hour period, four to five thousand families, some twenty
thousand people in all, "parachuted" into the sparsely inhabited area
today known as Colonia Santo Domingo. It stands as the largest single
land invasion in the history of Latin America.

Mexico's president, Luis Echeverría Alvarez, proved the uninten-
tional instigator of the invasion when, on 1 September 1971, he declared his intent to respect the rights of all Mexicans to decent housing,
called attention to the need to legalize de facto tenancy on public lands,
and emphasized the obligation of the federal government to support
those living in the worst conditions.

In the early 1970s, the squatter settlements and slums of Mexico
City were part of what Castells (1983:175) calls the "fastest and most
dramatic process of urbanization in human history." The short- and
long-term success of self-built areas such as Colonia Santo Domingo
during and since that time has been predicated on extensive labor by
members of the communities themselves, tolerance on the part of state
authorities for the technically illegal land occupations, and investment
by capitalist speculators, often through local front men.[1] In fact, self-
help housing in Mexico City in the early 1970s was not so much tolerated by the government as it was recognized and fostered as the only
viable option left at a time of crisis. And self-construction offered an

extraordinary way to reduce the cost of the reproduction of labor power.

Colonia Santo Domingo lies in the heart of the area known as the Pedregales, which since the eruption of the volcano Xitle around 200–100 B.C. has been covered with twenty to thirty feet of igneous rock.[2] Because of this solid foundation, the Mexico City earthquake of 1985, which crumpled many central neighborhoods of the capital, did virtually no damage in the Pedregales a few miles to the south. Before the invasion of 1971, the area was a wasteland of volcanic rocks, caves, shrubs, snakes, and scorpions. Writing in the 1840s, Fanny Calderón described the area:

> The robbers who, in hopes of plunder, flocked down at the time of the [gambling] fête, like sopilotes [turkey buzzards] seeking carrion, hide themselves among the barren rocks of the *Pedregal*, and render all cross-roads insecure, except with a very strong escort. (1843:391)

Of the invasion and the metamorphosis of Santo Domingo nearly 130 years later, Alejandra Massolo writes that from one night to the next morning thousands of families

> transformed the immutable and silent volcanic ground of Santo Domingo into a place of feverish movement, murmured signals and orders, the hammering of spiked posts as boundary markers, the noise of sheets in the wind and cardboard roofing fastened down in first shelters. The pedregales were becoming a city. (1992b:148)[3]

After staking out their plots and building makeshift dwellings, the newcomers made the securing of a steady supply of water their top priority. Women carried pails and buckets over long distances, water trucks occasionally entered the area, and eventually neighbors gathered the labor power and funds to bring in water lines and communal spigots. Candles and kerosene were used early on for illumination and cooking. Later, electricity was stolen from lines running into neighborhoods surrounding Santo Domingo. From the beginning of the occupation in 1971 until 1992, sewage was usually funneled down *grietas*, cracks in the volcanic rock; to be habitable, each land plot had to have at least one large *grieta* or the residents would have to maintain an expensive septic toilet. Schools and streets were built by residents of the *colonia*, with minimal government financial or technical assistance in the first several years. Today there are six elementary schools and three junior high schools in Santo Domingo.

Massolo (1992b) estimates that the construction of each street

Since thousands of squatter families "parachuted" into the area in 1971, Colonia Santo Domingo has been largely a self-built community. Residents were able, however, to force the city to pay for laying sewer mains in 1992.

extending three kilometers through Santo Domingo required an average of eight hundred *faenas colectivas,* collective work days performed by residents. Each *faena* required approximately 120 people, and thus each street required a total of ninety-six thousand work hours, as well as eighty boxes of dynamite to break through the rock and one hundred truckloads of dirt to later form the surface of the street. The government saved over 280 million pesos just on the potable water lines, which the residents themselves built for the community. In November 1977, in recognition of these communal efforts, Santo Domingo received a prize of 2 million pesos from city officials.

Today Colonia Santo Domingo consists of about eleven thousand lots within 263 city blocks covering some 654 acres (261 hectares), bordered by the National University (UNAM) on the west and by upper and upper middle class neighborhoods on the north, and on the east and south by other squatter communities like Colonia Ajusco as well as middle class housing projects. A few neighborhoods that dot the area around Santo Domingo call themselves pueblos and trace their roots to pre-Hispanic times, like Copilco on the northwest and Los Reyes on the northeast.

Despite Santo Domingo's having lost much of its raucous reputation since the invasion of 1971, strangers to the neighborhood, including those from other working class areas in the city, still sometimes comment that they think of it as *un lugar feo* (an ugly place) where *los hombres malos* (the bad men) live. A taxi driver, shaking his head sympathetically when I gave him my address one evening, asked, "*¿Le tocó vivir allá?* [You're (stuck) living there?]" But residents insist that Santo Domingo has calmed down considerably in recent years. Today there are roofed markets for fruits and vegetables and small-appliance repairs, *tortillerías,* separate butcher shops for beef, chicken, and pork, *panaderías* for pastries and rolls, unisex hair salons, lumber-supply and junk yards, auto-parts and plumbing retailers, pharmacies, and stationery stores equipped with photocopiers as well as telephones, the use of which in 1993 cost people a peso (then about thirty-five cents) a call.

Santo Domingo today is gray. A dull, concrete tone dominates things and social life in the *colonia,* from the masonry walls that shield homes from the foot traffic if not the noise of its streets to the dingy sky above, from the packs of roving dogs underfoot to the rocks boys and girls throw at rats caught in the open. When asked about how the neighborhood has changed in recent years, people will often point to the piles of gray cinder blocks in the street, which are taken as a sign by neighbors that a congregation or household has saved enough funds to add another room to a church or home. Trees in the neighborhood hardly break up the pallid color scheme; their leaves and trunks preserve a sooty, gray coating—even, it seems, in the rainy season. And besides, trees are so scarce in Santo Domingo that the boys who fly their kites from the rooftops and in less congested streets worry only about keeping the bright *papalotes* out of the telephone and electric wires.

As in other new and old *colonias populares* in Mexico City in the 1990s, an improbable combination of elemental horrors and an invigorating sense of community pervades much of daily life for the residents of Colonia Santo Domingo. Today there is water—except in the dry months of *la temporada de secas* and, even more infuriatingly, in the rainy season, when flooding is widespread. At these times water pressure can be so low that not even a drop is to be had between 6 A.M. and midnight, and in the middle of the night women can spend hours washing clothes and men filling buckets for use the following day. More than a few families still share communal outdoor water taps, and though showers are now common, washtubs are still used by many for bathing.

Today there is electricity for almost every home, except when the power goes off in the *colonia* during the torrential *aguaceros*. When this happens, usually at night, it seems even darker than it is, because often you can see from the rooftops of the one- and two-story homes in Santo Domingo that, curiously enough, the nearby middle class neighborhoods are still lit up.

Santo Domingo has been a noisy place since the invasion of 1971. At dawn it is common to hear the click-click-click-click of a car that will not start. But today at least some families in the *colonia* have cars. If the engine refuses to turn over, men, and sometimes women, will curse under their breath, "*¡¿Qué chingaderas . . . ?!* [What the fuck?!]" While they decide what to do, some will buy a *tamal* from the vendor who comes by walking his bicycle cart, announcing through a microphone his fresh, hot treats: tamales with red or green sauce, and *dulces también* (sweet ones, too). But people try to spend less time in the street on winter mornings, when, emerging from their homes, they inevitably walk into a *tovanera* (dust storm) whipping through the *colonia*. As Chicagoans do when it is especially chilly, many curse the weather as they walk with their backs to the wind, covering eyes and mouths with hands and scarves. But in Santo Domingo, unlike Chicago, assuming

this position has less to do with the cold and more to do with not want-
ing to directly suck in the dried fecal matter being swept by the wind
from the open sewers and piles of dog excrement in Mexico City.

Feeling a little overwhelmed one day by water, wind, howling dogs,
and a screaming child, I complained to our neighbor Angela that it was
taking all my time and energy just to get through each day. She replied,
without condescension, "*Así es* [That's how it is]."

THE HISTORICAL EXPERIENCE OF SANTO DOMINGO

Twenty years after the invasion, Santo Domingo is today largely a con-
solidated bedroom community with a population estimated to exceed
150,000.[4] The *colonia* is typical of self-built communities throughout
Mexico City, which share certain amenities and indignities that make
up life in popular urban neighborhoods. And because this *colonia* was
more stabilized than even newer settlements, by the early 1990s the
social safety nets were more in place to catch the poorest families from
falling through the cracks. Thus in Santo Domingo, unlike other areas
of the capital with more significant levels of malnutrition, some families
can receive food rations in the mornings and afternoons at the local DIF
(Desarrollo Integral de la Familia, the government-run family-services
agency) and milk for their young children early in the morning at the
government-run *lechería* next door.

Today other services are available, if intermittent. Refuse collection
is often a problem, because, as Lima (1992:26) notes, garbage-truck
drivers prefer to go to other *colonias* where more objects in people's
trash can be resold and recycled. One never knows whether the garbage
truck will come today or in a week, so at the sound of the garbage
bell one must be ready to leap into the street dragging whatever has
accumulated since the last trash pickup. Still, however irregular, there
is service. And although food prices in the 1980s consistently climbed
faster than real income, at the open-air markets twice a week at least
some of the grains, vegetables, and fruits are within the financial reach
of most families. In some ways, Santo Domingo is typical of many other
colonias populares in Mexico City.

In the 1970s and 1980s, migration from the impoverished countryside exacerbated an already serious housing shortage in cities all over
Mexico. Many of the current residents of Colonia Santo Domingo were
born in the nearby states of México, Hidalgo, Morelos, Puebla, Guanajuato, Michoacán, Tlaxcala, Querétaro, and Guerrero. Upon arrival,

they moved into older parts of Mexico City. Later they moved to the Pedregales, during or after the land invasions. Large numbers of people born and raised in Mexico City also took advantage of the opportunities to own a plot and a home of their own in Santo Domingo. Prevalent among the early invaders of the Pedregales were young couples who had been living with parents and in-laws in the immediate area. For instance, in the northwest section of the *colonia* where I lived with my family, most of the older residents were born in other parts of the capital. Even people born in *la provincia* (the provinces) had frequently spent decades living and working in Mexico City before arriving in Santo Domingo.

Since the beginning there were, among those who migrated directly to the Pedregales from outside the capital, many who identified themselves as and were considered by others to be ethnic minorities. A section of Santo Domingo that abuts the Universidad metro stop, for instance, is known for its concentration of people from Oaxaca. At the same time, on Huehuetzin Street where I lived, in another part of the *colonia,* among the Day of the Dead altars in homes I visited were several that older women had framed with marigolds, as is the custom among the Zapotecs in Oaxaca. In other words, people who are originally from various indigenous communities of Mexico are scattered throughout Santo Domingo.

Returning from the metro one day, I walked several blocks with a man who pointed to a house and informed me that in it lived a family of Mazahua. "You know," he added, "the guys are a bunch of lazy bums who make their women go out and work while they stay home and get drunk. No wonder they are so insecure." In his depiction of this Otomí-speaking family from the state of Guanajuato, my companion sought to distinguish himself and other mestizos of "mixed ancestry," as the euphemism goes, from the supposedly uncultured Indians who were of course from the rural *campo*.[5] Not so coincidentally, the most common image of the Mexican macho is a mestizo, whether urban or rural, and thus my companion was defending the honor of Mazahua *Marías* (women)—who often work as domestic servants in the homes of well-to-do mestizos in other *colonias*—from the abuses of their men.[6]

In the everyday lives of most of my friends in Santo Domingo, the issue of ethnicity commonly arises in three ways: in terms of clothing, language, and skin color. With the exception of rebozo shawls, most men and women in the *colonia* who consider themselves mestizos would not want to be seen in public wearing anything that might be associated with indigenous dress. (Though certainly during public holidays neighborhood groups of *danzantes* perform in "traditional Aztec costumes.") As for language, many of the monolingual speakers I know in the *colonia* refer disparagingly to neighbors who speak a *dialecto,* by which they invariably mean not a dialect of Spanish different from their own but rather an indigenous language. As is common in other parts of the world, minority languages in Santo Domingo are broadly stigmatized. Finally, with regard to skin color, in many families darker-skinned brothers and sisters are often the targets of ridicule in which they are portrayed as Indian hayseeds in mestizo disguise.

Masculinity is involved in the *colonia*'s diverse ethnic identities, not only in the insulting portrayals of Mazahua men and their exploited *Marías,* but in a reverse fashion whereby traits and customs associated with indigenous peoples are valued and those associated with the colonialist *mestizaje,* such as machismo, are scorned. Certain aspects of the relationship between ethnicity, national identity, and male identity became clearer to me through my friendship with Gabriel. A Spanish speaker, Gabriel nonetheless sees the true Mexican nation as the product of an ancient, indigenous spirituality and not as a modern mestizo hybrid. (As such, Gabi's views are akin to Bonfil Batalla's [1987] notion of "Deep Mexico.") Gabriel's identification with indigenism, he says, also makes him less susceptible to the appeal of other oppressive ideologies like machismo. Ideas like Gabriel's are not predominant in Santo Domingo, but they are part of the subterranean currents of the ethnically heterogeneous populations of this and other *colonias populares* in the Mexican capital.

THE BERLIN WALL

People generally have moved to Santo Domingo for housing, not for jobs. Most paid employment is to be found only outside the *colonia.* Some men and a few women travel to distant factories in the Vallejo industrial belt on the northern side of Mexico City, or to other, closer-by parts of the city. Yet Santo Domingo is far from many work sites and shopping areas not because it lies on the outskirts of the city but because Mexico City is a gigantic metropolitan area; in fact, its location near a metro line means this *colonia* is much more convenient than hundreds of others on the ever-expanding outer fringes of the populated zone.

The *colonia*'s location near the National University and well-to-do sections of southern Mexico City such as San Angel and Coyoacán has attracted some middle class families to Santo Domingo, and large complexes of upscale condominiums were under construction at the edges of the *colonia* in 1993. But until these are completed the community will remain overwhelmingly composed of working class households living from week to week on the pooled incomes of one to three minimum salaries—around twenty-four to seventy-two U.S. dollars a week in the early 1990s. Though most parents in Santo Domingo dream of greater financial security in the form of middle class membership for their children, at the same time being part of the *clases populares* for many carries with it an inherent if nebulous dignity, because, among other things, it means that you are not an exploiter of others.

Many men and women who live in Santo Domingo are engaged in the service sector, quite a few as janitors at the nearby National University or as drivers of minibus *combis,* taxis, or trucks. Still others sell food and wares on the streets, in markets, or from their doorways. Directly and indirectly they are participants in what David Harvey (1989:189) describes as "a sea-change in the surface appearance of [international] capitalism since 1973." Harvey's analysis of what he calls "flexible accumulation" is especially pertinent to the working people of Santo Domingo, because flexible accumulation "rests on flexibility with respect to labour processes, labour markets, products, and patterns of consumption" (p. 147). For women and men in Mexico City and globally, flexible accumulation has given rise to a remarkable "surge in service employment since the early 1970s" (p. 156). In many respects the study of changing male identities in Santo Domingo is part of what Harvey refers to as "the ways in which norms, habits, and political and cultural attitudes have shifted" since the transition to flexible accumulation (pp. 170–71).

Though cultural changes in Colonia Santo Domingo never occur as a necessary consequence of economic changes, neither do they take place in isolation from socioeconomic contexts. What is more, though some analysts might seek to carefully distinguish between the culturally symbolic and the materially economic, in practice such dichotomies often conceal more than they reveal.

The working class composition of Santo Domingo and the specific history of self-reliance in the *colonia* are both revealed in the waning but still flickering sentiment that neighbors share some collective responsibility toward one another. For example, in Santo Domingo certain "private" and "domestic" issues such as wife beating and household budgets have in many instances become more "public" concerns, brought from the relative obscurity of households to the greater scrutiny of friends and neighbors. Unlike those who dwell in middle and upper class neighborhoods of Mexico City, residents of Santo Domingo know something about their neighbors and experience some sense of local community, often revolving around children and activities on the street in front of their homes.

The distinguishing public spaces in the *colonia* are its streets. During the day women and men hurry through them on errands and small children play along their edges dodging the occasional car. In the early evening, neighbors pause at doorways to exchange greetings and gossip. From then until midnight, the streets belong to the youth, who gather in the shadows of abandoned cars to listen to loud music, argue, and make furtive love. If they stay out later, they are careful not to stray too far from doorways, preferring the prying gazes of family to the intimidation of gangs.

Some festive occasions, especially the pre-Christmas *posadas*, bring together block residents in joint celebrations. Others are more family oriented, like the Día de Muertos, the Day of the Dead, which revolves around altars built inside homes, usually by older women. If a large fiesta is required, however—in honor of a *quinceañera* (a girl celebrating her fifteenth birthday) or after a wedding, for example—the party inevitably becomes semipublic. Rented loudspeakers in banks six feet high are set up inside doorways or in the street, and for blocks around, the music and fireworks rattle windows until 2 or 3 in the morning. Then, when most of the revelers are heading for bed, the street drunks begin their sacred revelries; they wander until dawn, serenading the moon and anyone foolish enough to try to hush them, sharing the streets with the stray dogs.

The homeowners who sponsor these giant celebrations, and who often go into debt for years afterward, are generally middle-aged or older. Very few young people in the *clases populares* will ever again have enough money to buy a house and a lot in Santo Domingo. Their parents and grandparents took advantage of a unique opportunity in the 1970s, an accident of history, to build themselves a future with concrete blocks and laminated asbestos roofs. The fact that it is overwhelmingly older people in the *colonia* who own homes and lots has severe implications for the future social mobility, stratification, and immiseration of the younger generations growing up there today. Depending on the fate of regional, national, and international economies, many households

A residential side street in Colonia Santo Domingo.

are likely to experience great hardship and bitter conflict in the future because of still-unresolved problems like property inheritance, made all the more pressing by the already dangerously overcrowded conditions in the city.

In 1993 there were still some rickety shacks in the *colonia,* but in the main the structures were more solid. Even small homes went on the market for one or two hundred thousand pesos (then, thirty-five to seventy thousand dollars). Crowding, however, was an ongoing and in some cases growing problem. Whereas about half the households in the *colonia* consisted of one family, in the remaining homes two, three, or more families squeezed together, sharing stoves, refrigerators, toilets, family squabbles, and child care.

From the beginning, the struggle to create Santo Domingo required many radical measures and sacrifices on the part of the creators, and numerous community leaders and residents have long histories of opposition to city and federal authorities. Still, it would be wrong to overestimate the extent to which most people in the area see their interests as inimical to those of other sectors of the populace. Most people in the *colonia* have long struggled to assimilate into whatever they see as mainstream capital-city life. For them the fight has been to become more a part of the society rather than oppose it in fundamental ways.

This is quite a fortunate development for the upper middle class resi-

dents of Colonia Romero de Terreros, bordering Santo Domingo to the
north, who after the invasion in 1971 erected a ten-foot wall making
passage between the two communities impossible. Today the wall remains as a guardian of class privilege, a barrier protecting the rich from
the poor. Residents of Santo Domingo call it El Muro de Berlín—the
Berlin Wall.

THE PREDICAMENT OF STABILITY

With so many men working outside the *colonia* during the day, from
its inception much of the daytime responsibility for constructing and
defending Santo Domingo fell largely upon women. They were the ones
in charge of communications during the early days when private and
police-connected goons roamed through the community trying to extort
or evict less than vigilant squatters. With wooden poles, clods of dirt,
rocks, and shovels the women had to physically guard their new proper-
ties and those of neighbors. Such exploits on the part of many women
became emblematic of the invasion, not simply because of the courage
and determination they evinced, but because women throughout the
area were coming to be widely regarded as key decision makers and
leaders.

Such was not the case in all parts of Mexico City, and in this respect
the events of the past twenty years in Santo Domingo are not typical
of all *colonias populares*. Still, elsewhere in the Federal District and
throughout Mexico and Latin America, similar popular struggles took
place in the 1970s and 1980s, one of whose outstanding characteristics
was the prominent role of women. Although in the *movimientos urbanos populares* (MUPs; popular urban movements) and *nuevos movimientos sociales* (NMSs; new social movements) in the region men have
generally been leaders and women have filled the ranks as militant activists, this has perhaps been true to a lesser extent in the Pedregales.
There, women have been more consistently among the leaders as well
as the foot soldiers, though in that area other problems eventually beset
the once-vibrant popular organizations.

The historical and ongoing association of women with community
leadership and organization in Colonia Santo Domingo has had important implications for how gender identities and relations have developed there in the past two decades. Citing the role of women in the
NMSs and other social changes—for example, growing numbers of

women working for money, sharply falling birth rates, rising educational levels, and increasing national and international migration—several recent studies have focused on recent changes in gender and class identities among women in Mexico and Latin America.[7] In the chapters that follow I examine concurrent changes in gender identities among men—not in isolation, but precisely in relation to those prevalent among some women in the region. I have taken this approach for two reasons: first, it is rarely useful to isolate gender identities as if men and women led quarantined lives; second, and even more importantly, women in Colonia Santo Domingo have often played a catalytic role in the changes in male attitudes and behaviors that have taken place over the past twenty years.

When asked to compare the early days of Santo Domingo with the present, many of the *colonia*'s founders say they preferred it back at the beginning. Hauling buckets of water was a horrible way to spend the day, women will often point out, but at the same time there was a spirit of mutual dependency and belonging at the time that is lacking nowadays. Women as well as men attribute the disappearance of this goodwill partly to the fact that because their living conditions are not so desperate, they have less practical need to rely on each other. Many long-term residents of the *colonia*, women and men, also point to the role of the ruling Partido Revolucionario Institucional (PRI; Institutional Revolutionary Party) in the demise of group solidarity in Santo Domingo. In a textbook example of a more widespread phenomenon, in the Pedregales, too, the "state has sought to use the land issue as a means of extending its influence over the poor and to maintain their quiescence" (Ward 1990:155). Through co-optation, coercion, and, if these do not work, repression, the city and federal governments, with batteries of land-office bureaucrats, lawyers, police, and politicians, have striven to incorporate ever more independent community political activities and organizations into their spheres of influence. The intricate and timeworn strategies employed by the PRI and its functionaries in Santo Domingo do not directly concern us here, but they are important as a background noise that has sometimes served to drown out the voices of change.[8]

In Santo Domingo, as Safa (1992:51) notes, an antiauthority attitude on the part of community activists has nonetheless long been evident. This sentiment helped women to justify their armed attacks on police thugs in the early days of the *colonia*, and today it reinforces for many the need to stand up to men who try to bully their wives and women neighbors on the grounds of male prerogative. With or without the presence of popular urban movements, all areas of Mexico City have undergone major dislocations and shifts over the past twenty years. Residency in Santo Domingo during this time has conferred certain historical experiences on the people there, but never so in isolation. Whereas my friend Miguel, who grew up in Santo Domingo, told me that he was ten before he went to downtown Mexico City for the first time in 1973, by the early 1990s travel within the capital was part of most people's regular experiences: for work throughout the city; for recreation in the Xochimilco gardens to the southeast; for "regularizing" property deeds in government buildings downtown; for household purchases in Tepito, on the near north side; and for visits to family and friends in the surrounding countryside. The Copilco metro stop on the Universidad-Indios Verdes line is a short walk or *combi* ride away, and from there one can join several million other riders each day for fast and clean, if often severely cramped, service throughout the city. In 1993 the price of a ticket was forty centavos (then about thirteen cents).

COMMUNITY

Globalisation can thus be defined as the intensification
of worldwide social relations which link distant
localities in such a way that local happenings are
shaped by events occurring many miles away and vice
versa.

Anthony Giddens, The Consequences
of Modernity

La Capital is today home to nearly one out of five people in Mexico overall. The population of the metropolitan area has grown from 344,000 in 1900 to just over 1 million in 1930, 5 million in 1960, 9 million in 1970, 14 million in 1980, and nearly 20 million in 1990. Projections raise the possibility that the area could grow to over 30 million in the early years of the twenty-first century (see DDF 1988:126, 147). Though it is the manufacturing, financial, political, and information hub of the country, the capital is also the site of millions of long-term unemployed and underemployed, as well as an enormous "informal sector" disproportionately made up of women, children, and the elderly.

Lying in the first ring of expansion from the old urban core of Mexico City, self-built communities such as Santo Domingo have constantly been subjected to the vicissitudes of the capitalist accumulation process through real-estate agents, spiraling costs for construction materials, the utility industry, and the Mexican state itself (see Ward 1990:192). For these and other reasons, Cuauhtémoc Cárdenas, an opposition candidate in the 1988 presidential elections, swept many of the settler communities in and around Mexico City. In terms of post–World War II patterns of migration and urbanization in Mexico, Santo Domingo represents a relatively young *colonia,* especially with respect to densely populated areas in the center of Mexico City, which have been inhabited since pre-Hispanic times.[9] On the other hand, this neighborhood is hardly new when compared with the sprawling settlements where hundreds of thousands lack basic amenities like running water and sewage systems, areas like Chalco to the east of the Federal District and Ecatepec to the northeast of it.

Despite the continuing migration to Mexico City, there is a special love-hate relationship many citizens of Mexico maintain with their capital. Although people continue to migrate to Mexico City from other impoverished parts of the country (some estimate that as many as one thousand newcomers arrive in the capital daily), in *la provincia* there is bitterness, jealousy, and resentment expressed toward the natives of Mexico City, the *chilangos.*

The political economy of shrinking growth rates for Mexico as a whole has meant that the country's growing population has had to get by on fewer financial resources. Annual rates of growth during the period 1940–80 averaged over 6 percent; the growth rate for 1980–88 averaged −1.9 percent (see Barkin 1990:123). With fewer resources available, competition heated up in all sectors of society. This competition is linked to growing class polarization, which has resulted in fabulous wealth for the top 1 or 2 percent and stagnation or falling standards of living for the lowest 60 or 70 percent. Real minimum salaries have fluctuated considerably in the past fifty years, but by the early 1990s they stood at roughly the same levels as they had in 1960. Workers' real earnings in 1990 were less than half what they were before the 1982 crisis (see Barkin 1990:144).

The 1982 financial collapse had cataclysmic consequences for the working class in Mexico, and since then, as Selby and his colleagues conclude, "[t]he crisis for poor people has been permanent" (1990:175). This is in stark contrast to the situation during most of this century, and especially during World War II and shortly afterward, when even the poor in Mexico justifiably felt confident in their chances for future economic improvement. Since the early 1980s, widespread cynicism and profound mistrust of the government and industry in Mexico have replaced the erstwhile optimism. Many of the poor in Colonia Santo Domingo, for instance, think that the recent North American Free Trade Agreement (NAFTA—ironically, TLC [Tratado de Libre Comercio] in Spanish) portends even more dismal economic times ahead for them. Many believe that the wealthy classes within Mexico, the United States, and Canada are becoming "denationalized" and in the process are trying to manipulate the treaty in order to fatten their own coffers. This analysis of NAFTA by Mexico's *olvidados,* the forgotten ones in the title of Buñuel's famous movie—who were, after all, those most immediately and practically affected by international finance charges in the wake of major banking and monetary crises in 1982 and 1995—is not only justifiable but brutally accurate.[10]

The present study concerns a small section of the population of a neighborhood community in Mexico City, but in order to make a fruitful analysis of the findings there we must have a clear idea of broader community contexts. For the people of Colonia Santo Domingo, one's individual and group identities depend upon contexts and communities in the broadest sense. Gender identities, for instance, may be different in significant ways in particular communities. Colonia Santo Domingo exists as a limited community in some respects, while in many other and more absolute ways it represents a community of international significance.[11] Hence we find in Santo Domingo something that Appadurai (1991:199) notes is true more broadly: "the possibility of divergent interpretations of what 'locality' implies." There is a constant interplay between the local and the global, between homogeneity and heterogeneity, and the complex back-and-forth of dominant and popular cultures in working class areas of Mexico City restricts and transforms gender relations there. This process is also marked in part by conflicting global, national, and local identities, and includes contested notions about what *ser hombre* means today at these different levels of community.

Yet if my descriptions of Santo Domingo and the people who live there appear to the reader as in any sense exotic, or, still worse, quaint,

I will have neglected to heed the words with which Eric Wolf opens his famous study of world history:

> [T]he world of humankind constitutes a manifold, a totality of interconnected processes, and inquiries that disassemble this totality into bits and then fail to reassemble it falsify reality. (1982:3)

I hope that in looking at the lives of the people living in the *colonias populares* of Mexico City as the millennium approaches, readers of this study will recognize more than a little of themselves and their own experiences.

THREE

Imaginary Fathers, Genuine Fathers

[M]arriage cannot be defined as the licensing of sexual intercourse, but rather as the licensing of parenthood.

Bronislaw Malinowski, "Parenthood, the Basis of Social Structure"

FATHER TIME

"When you were younger, did you spend much time with your fathers?" I asked a group of young men I was talking with in the street one afternoon.

"No, I spent more time with my mother," said Jaime.

"With both," said Esteban.

"Always with my mother," said Felipe.

"No, I was always with both of them," said Pancho. "From when I was little my father took me around a lot. He used to take me along wherever he wanted to go. I always went with him."

What do men *do* as fathers in Santo Domingo, and what relation does being a father have to being a man for them? When I arrived in Mexico City in the summer of 1992, I was especially interested in learning about men as fathers: how, why, if, and when they spent time with their children. In addition to the fact that I was myself the new father of a infant girl, I had a suspicion that in Mexico fathering might be more important to male identities than is acknowledged in many of the sociological and psychological theories that, based largely on studies of the U.S. white middle class, posit a general absence of fathers in developmentally significant parenting activities (for example, Chodorow 1978 and Ruddick 1989). By talking and being with fathers and mothers, as well as with their sons and daughters, I learned to better distinguish between cultural customs that have been uncritically adopted from the past and new ways of challenging these manners and habits that men and women in Santo Domingo are creating every day.

   Minimally, I wanted to find out how images of fatherhood and fathering activities might be related to notions of masculinity among working class men and women in Mexico City. My status as Liliana's father certainly helped me in my research. Throughout our year in Santo Domingo friends and acquaintances would regularly check with me about her: Was she sitting up yet? What was she eating? Who watched her when she was sick? Did we need any clothing for her? When would she ever get hair? Nicknames our friends and neighbors attached to Liliana were part of their commentary on both little children in general and, more particularly, our presence in Santo Domingo. Walking along streets in the *colonia,* friends would shout out for the *gordita güerita* (chubby little light-skinned girl). Mothers would smile when they asked if she was still such a *cabroncita* (bossy little thing). Older children liked to touch her chubby cheeks and stroke her bald head, giggling at the *peloncita* (little baldy).[1]

   After our arrival in late summer 1992, it quickly became apparent to me that fathers in Santo Domingo were a diverse group, and that there was no uniform sociological standard of fathering in the *colonia.* So, guided by Margaret Mead's method of "negative instance" and the "anthropological veto," I began looking less for consistent patterns of fathering and more for differences and "exceptions."[2] For instance, the prodding of new friends and neighbors in Santo Domingo soon compelled me to understand what they saw as culturally significant differences between fathers in the rural *campo* and those in the city, between rich and poor fathers, and between fathers of different generations.

   In the pages that follow, starting with what might appear to be the uncomplicated and relatively unimportant question of holding children, and continuing with a more detailed survey of parents' responsibilities toward their children of different ages, we will explore the fatherly meanings and practices of some men in Santo Domingo, and some of what region, class, and age have to do with changing male identities in contemporary Mexico. Using fathering as a window through which to understand a number of broader issues, we will also have cause to reexamine certain past ethnographic discussions of fathers in Mexico.

THE BANK OFFICIAL'S REMARK

While living and working in Santo Domingo, I sometimes had occasion to attend academic and social functions outside the *colonia*. In mid-August 1992, I left for the day to attend a conference on contemporary Mexican society. Before speaking about the economic crisis of 1982, neoliberalism, and the Free Trade Agreement, a Mexican government banking official introduced himself to those in attendance as *un esclavo* (a slave) to his wife and to the women who worked for him. It was the kind of joking comment about gender-role reversals that one sometimes hears in Mexico, a society that often seems painfully aware of its outside notoriety as the land of unbridled machismo.

Later that evening I attended a cocktail party with my wife, Michelle, and our then nearly two-month-old baby in the fashionable *colonia* of San Jerónimo. I was carrying Liliana in a *canguro* (literally, "kangaroo"; a Snugli-type carrier for infants) when the same bank official grinned at me and offered, "We Mexican men don't carry babies!" Nonplussed, I honestly responded that where I lived in Mexico City men did carry babies and young children, and that indeed this was quite common.

The bank official's remark raised a number of points, not the least of which concerns differences in fathering attitudes and behavior in upper and lower class settings. That is, with fathering, as with all other aspects of male identities and practices in Mexico, there is not one Mexican pattern of masculinity against which all men compare themselves or should be compared. The diversity of fathering practices in Mexico is in fact central to the ambiguous character of masculinity there.

Back at the cocktail party, the pedagogic point could also not be missed that here was a Mexican explaining "Mexican culture" to a North American anthropologist who was living in Mexico to learn such things. There was also an implied allusion to culture change, as if he had been thinking, "We Mexican men *still* don't do that." In any cultural context key background assumptions influence actors' words and conduct; in this case assumptions concerned fathering in Mexico mingled with a perceived U.S. model of male parenting.

In the course of fieldwork on male identities in Mexico, I found that nearly everyone had a ready opinion on and explanation for various gender-related attitudes and behavior. Colleagues and acquaintances of the bank official, for example, insisted that other factors were critical to understanding his declaration about Mexican men not carrying babies. Regional differences within Mexico were involved, I was told. The official originally came from Durango, a state with a cowboy-country reputation, where, they said, the men were just a little wilder and more *bravo* than elsewhere in the Republic. No doubt, my informants offered, men in Durango had little physical contact with children.

Then there was the government functionary's political history, a university professor later told me. He had enjoyed a brief though illustrious career in the late 1960s as a Maoist radical; perhaps the severe political shift to capitalist banking had similarly led him to later reaffirm the status quo in gendered divisions of labor in parenting. That, at least, was what the professor believed. Yet whether these interpretations reflect generally agreed upon history and labels or simple capital-city chauvinism toward *la provincia* becomes a less mystical question when we consider that how people characterize themselves and others in part constitutes who and what they are. Authoritative and popular interpretations and analyses of cultural identities in turn become part of what makes up social life.

It is also quite possible that the bank official's comment was meant as a joke. Humor is to be taken seriously, for what is funny to some is not necessarily so to others, and we can learn as much from jokes, taunts, nicknames, ridicule, puns, and witticisms as from any other genre of human discourse. In Santo Domingo, I often used the example of my excursion into high-class cocktail-party life to clarify through comparison the experience and opinions of women and men in the *colonia* about carrying babies. Whether or not the official's remark was intended as a joke, however, the reviews he received from Santo Domingo residents were uniformly negative. Often people responded with criticisms of the parenting engaged in by *los ricos* (the rich), making comments like, "What do they know? They all have maids to carry their kids around." Sometimes I was offered a specific example to refute the generalization that Mexican men don't carry babies. One young woman told me, "That's silly. Haven't you seen the vegetable man at the *sobre ruedas* [open-air market] on Saturdays who keeps his baby in a cardboard box under his table?"

The bank official's remark raised a number of questions about fathering in Mexico in general (such as whether significant differences existed with regard to fathering in the working class and among the elite), fathering in various regions of Mexico, and fathering in distinct historical epochs.

THE PHOTOGRAPH OF JOSÉ ENRÍQUEZ

In April 1989, while walking through downtown Mexico City, I passed a musical-instruments shop and something inside caught my attention. I took a photograph of a man holding a baby. When I later showed the photo to anthropologists and other friends in the United States, many had a curious reaction. "That can't be," one said in surprise. "We know they're all machos in Mexico." The implication was that although machos may sire many children, they do not attend to them later because that is women's work and machos by definition shun those kinds of duties. The photograph, or more precisely the responses of various people to it, provoked my initial interest in the subject of what we know and do not know about Mexican men and male identity.

I always carried this photo with me in Mexico, and in the course of the 1992–93 field season I recorded several dozen responses to the photo from people living in Santo Domingo as well as from anthropologists and residents of other areas of Mexico City and other parts of the country.[3] This approach allowed me a way to more easily explain the nature of my research project, and, even more importantly, it got me into many discussions about fathering that might not otherwise have transpired.

Among the comments I recorded were those of Carlos, a long-haul truck driver and the father of three girls in their early teens, who asked, "Is his woman sick? His face looks like he's suffering." An anthropologist with a rich knowledge of Mexico and the complexities of ethnicity in the country told me that the man in the picture was probably *indígena* (Indian) because one would seldom find this behavior among mestizo men.[4]

Sitting around drinking with me one afternoon, three male friends in their mid-thirties to early forties passed the photo among themselves, and each in turn announced that he found the situation "*muy normal.*" The six-year-old daughter of one of the men came by, and I asked her if her father had taken care of her like this when she was a baby. She said he had, and that he had done so with her little brother and sister, too. An older man, in his fifties, told me, "*Muy bien* [Very good]," when he glanced at the shot and said that he had always carried his five children, though, he added, a neighbor still gave him a hard time for having done it. He linked his neighbor's thinking to the fact that the neighbor was an alcoholic.

Norma, a neighbor of ours and the mother of a five-year-old son,

I gathered dozens of comments about this photo of José Enríquez cradling an infant in a musical instruments store. Mexico City Centro.

told me she thought the man "*se ve muy tierno* [looks very tender]" with the baby. A community organizer and feminist who works in Santo Domingo but does not live there told me the man looked *alejado* (bewildered) and that the situation seemed forced. Eugenia, the mother of four who runs the corner store on Huehuetzin Street where we lived in Santo Domingo, insisted that "in the city men do these things [carry and care for children]" but not in the village in the state of Hidalgo where she is originally from. Fernando, a parking attendant at a Gigante supermarket near the *colonia*, who identifies himself as a *campesino* farmer from the state of Puebla, said emphatically "*I* carry *my* daughter," implicitly acknowledging that he knows men who do not carry theirs.[5] "Sure," someone else informed me, "this guy is carrying the baby because the boss lady made him. Look at that head. That's not his baby."

An anthropologist friend told me that the photograph was *irreal* (unreal) and that her husband had never carried their children. I asked what social class he came from. "Educated, upper class, liberal. We always had at least two servants living with us when the children were young." Herlinda, a junior high school teacher who lives and works in Santo Domingo, called the scene depicted in the photo "the most natural thing in the world: the way Mexican men are at being fathers." Curiously to me, on two occasions when I showed the photo to separate groups of older men in Colonia Santo Domingo, the first comment was a question: "So you like mandolins, do you?" In both cases I had to point out the man holding the infant and ask what they thought of this. "*Normal*" was the most common response. María Elena, who was several months pregnant when I showed her the photograph, called it "realistic, what they have to do" and then asked, "Haven't you seen men here who do the same thing in their shops?"

It is worthwhile to note that responses to the photograph were not just different but fell into two completely opposed categories: the photo depicted either the most natural, common situation in the world, hardly worth commenting on, or an anomaly, an aberration that it would be irresponsible of me to interpret as representative of any significant number of men in Mexico. Also noteworthy is the fact that "*normal*" was by far the most common description of the situation by residents of Santo Domingo, whereas anthropologists and other professionals felt it to be a very rare sight indeed.[6] Not satisfied with merely examining their own personal experiences, many people revealed in their responses a desire to summarize what fathering entails for men generally in Mexico, and thus the widespread and profoundly contradictory consciousness regarding masculinity in the capital city and beyond.

On 18 January 1993, almost four years after taking the photograph, I went looking for the musical-instruments shop and the mustached man behind the counter. I could not remember the address, but after wandering the streets of downtown Mexico City for a couple of hours I passed by a doorway and spotted mandolins hanging against a wall. On showing the photograph to a young woman behind the counter, she shouted excitedly, "José, come quickly, it's you! A man's got a picture of you!" José emerged. He had shaved his mustache, but he had on a similar blue shirt. Finally the truth would be known. Was he from an indigenous group? Was he comfortable or ill at ease that day as he held the infant? Was it the child of his employer or his own? Was this a common occurrence or a once-in-a-lifetime responsibility? In short, why was he taking care of that baby that day?

José Enríquez patiently explained to me that he really had no idea why he was with the baby that day. It was the child of a woman who lived upstairs in the building; he smiled as he mentioned with pride that the boy was now in kindergarten. The mother often left her son with José when she had to run out for an errand. What was so strange about that? He was right there, not going anywhere, and he was happy to oblige. It happened all the time, he told me. How could he remember that particular day? he asked rhetorically; he was always watching kids for others. José also spoke of having grown up in Mexico City, of his family and his own children. After showing me a picture of them, I left him a couple of copies of the one I had taken of him and the child.

The responses to the photograph of José Enríquez reveal something about the viewers' own life experiences with fathering as well as myriad preconceptions about the fathering experiences of others. They also illustrate, I think, that conscious recognition of cultural patterns may lag behind actual changes in practice. Many if not most of the interpretations must be judged as correct—not in the sense that there are as many different "realities" as there are interpreters, but rather because there is a broad spectrum of fathering practices—despite the ever-present temptation to consider one's own experiences as normal and those of others as odd. In short, the varied commentaries on the photograph of José Enríquez illustrate a true diversity of expectations about fathering based on truly divergent fathering experiences in Mexico City.

PARENTAL HOLDING

The first concept of childhood [in Europe]—
characterized by "coddling"—had made its
appearance in the family circle, in the company of
little children.

Philippe Ariès, Centuries of Childhood

To gauge the extent to which actual fathering practices in Santo Domingo might diverge from broader stereotypes about Mexican men and
how much the photo of José Enríquez might represent an extraordinary
situation, and partially as a result of the bank official's observation that
Mexican men do not carry children, I decided to conduct an informal,
random survey of "parental holding."[7] I wanted to know who, in a
couple of one man and one woman, holds children when the family is
out in public. For purposes of the survey I chose the open-air markets
and streets of Colonia Santo Domingo, on Saturdays and early on weekday evenings, when men and women are commonly found together outdoors.

Of sixty couples I spotted in which one child was being held, in forty-
three cases the man held the child, in seven cases the woman held the
child, and in ten cases both held the child between them. Of twenty-six
couples with two or more children being held, in three cases only the
men and in one case only the woman held both children, whereas in
twenty-two cases both held the children separately. These results are
summarized in Table 1.

In Colonia Santo Domingo, when a man and a woman are out in
public and one of the adults is holding a child, that adult is probably, if
there is a choice available, the man. Indeed, in some sense this task is
culturally induced, if not mandated, for younger men. Initially I assumed that men's carrying children was mainly related to musculature.
But numerous examples in my survey were of couples leaving the open-
air market, when not uncommonly the man would still be carrying the
smallest child (and if there was another child, that one might then be
walking) and the woman would be weighted down with several heavy
bags of produce, meats, and other goods.

Men do not shoulder the main burden of carrying children overall;
brawn does not dictate cultural behavior. But the straightforward results of the survey in Colonia Santo Domingo stand in contrast to other
studies, and widespread perceptions, indicating that many men in Mex-

TABLE 1

PARENTAL HOLDING BY COUPLES IN COLONIA
SANTO DOMINGO

Holder	One Child Held	Two or More Children Held
Male	43	3
Female	7	1
Both	10	22

SOURCE: Observations by author, 11 September to 23 October 1992.

ico do not wish to be seen in public doing such traditionally female tasks.[8] According to my friend Fili, who is a grandmother, generational differences are pronounced when it comes to men's participation in parenting. She told me that her husband, who spent a lot of time at home once he had been laid off from his job as a curtain man a few months before I met him, used to get ridiculed by his brother when their children were young because her husband would hold them, change their diapers, and in general help in raising them. Her brother-in-law's attitude was typical of his generation, Fili reported with a satisfied and toothless grin, but now the tables had turned a lot and "the father who doesn't do things like carry babies is more likely to be the one being ridiculed." So we see once again the development of new attitudes and practices that often directly contradict older ones.

There is a widespread sense among women and men in Colonia Santo Domingo that significant, though by no means uniform, changes have occurred from one generation to the next regarding men's active participation in parenting. There were always a few men who spent a lot of time with their young children, some people will say, but today they are far less exceptional. Paternal holding is simply one piece of the larger, more complex puzzle of male parenting practices and symbolic reasoning. But it is a fine illustration that the (seemingly) irrelevant can still illuminate.[9]

RURAL SAVAGERY AND *CHILANGISMO*

There are many assumed conventions and "known" customs regarding Mexican men in general and how they think about and conduct themselves as fathers, all of which makes it difficult to tease out actual cultural habits and beliefs about *la hombría* (manliness). In Colonia Santo

A young father carrying a baby in a *canguro*. Mexico City Centro.

Domingo, people often remark about how different life is for men and women in the city in comparison to almost anywhere in the rural *campo*. When I interviewed Tomás, a metalworker, in his workshop one day, he told me that thirty to forty years ago there had been far more machismo in Mexican society.

"Of course there's still a lot in the pueblos. They are really different there," he said, not needing to make explicit the distinction *different there than we are in the city*.

I chuckled at his derisive portrayal of rural life. Taken aback because he was not sure why I had laughed, Tomás insisted, "I'm serious!"

He went on to describe what he thought was a typical situation in the countryside: a man riding a horse along a path, his wife walking alongside him struggling to keep up. "You see it all the time out there," he told me.

Eugenia said of her native state of Hidalgo, "In the villages men are real *salvajes* [savages]. They don't lift a finger to help with the kids or anything else around the house." Valfre, a day laborer who was awaiting the birth of his first child when I interviewed him, is from the Zapotec village of San Pablo Yaganiza in the mountain sierra of Oaxaca. After looking at the photograph of José Enríquez holding the infant in the guitar store, Valfre offered that at most "two or three percent of the men" in his village would carry babies.

It is striking that few men mention the issue of ethnicity when they discuss masculinity, especially given the common preoccupation with questions of racial ancestry in Mexico. It may well be that because the dominant discourse in the country regarding masculinity has centered on questions of nationalism and *mestizaje*—and thus indigenous peoples have often been excluded from this conversation—even those from indigenous backgrounds seldom think about male identities in terms of race and ethnicity.

Despite speaking Zapotec and regardless of the fact that he would be seen by many people in Mexico City as probably coming from an indigenous community—because he has dark skin and wears the clothes of a day laborer—in our discussions of men and male identities Valfre seldom made reference to the issue of ethnicity. Generally he made comparisons of what it meant to be a man in rural and urban areas or explained what he thought were the differences in the ways of rich and poor men. When I asked Valfre why he made such a sharp distinction between Mexico City and rural Oaxaca, with no references to ethnicity, he told me a joke that for him captured the essence of relations between women and men and fathers and children where he grew up:

"A guy is trying to marry off his son. He tells the father of a potential bride that his boy is a responsible and tireless worker. Why, his son doesn't ever drink or smoke, and he's very respectful toward women. The young woman's father shakes his head and says no, he's sorry, but he's not interested in marrying his daughter to such a man. The only son-in-law he will even consider is one who's a real man: a guy who drinks, smokes, and isn't afraid to go after his wife with a machete."[10]

One day as I was talking with two young women working behind the counter in a *papelería* (five-and-ten) on Las Rosas Avenue in Santo Domingo, our discussion led to the topic of marriage and what they might look for in a husband. While they were telling me about their relations with their parents and the differences between how their fathers treated them and their brothers, one of them bounced Liliana gently on the countertop. The other emphasized that, whatever other qualities he might or might not have, her husband could not come from the *campo*. Men from the countryside are *necios*, ignorant and stupid, she said, and they expect their women to be more obedient, submissive, and *abnegadas* (self-sacrificing). "How do you know?" I asked her. She had cousins in the town where her father was born, and they visited often. She insisted that boys born and raised in the city are different

than those in the *campo* because the former have probably been raised
to share housework and decision making with girls.

Justo tells a story of *campesino* relatives from Hidalgo coming to
work for a month on a project in the canals of Xochimilco in Mexico
City, during which time they stayed with Justo and his family. One
Sunday, before sitting down to dinner, Justo handed his nephew of
twenty a plastic bag and some coins and told him to go buy fresh tortillas. The young man responded, "*¡Eso es para las viejas!* [That's wom-
en's work!]" Embarrassed at the prospect of him, a man, being seen
carrying a bag, he didn't want to go.

People in Santo Domingo commonly distinguish between how men
treat women in urban and rural areas of the country. Their comments
reveal, among other things, Mexico City chauvinism. As in the United
States, where New York City residents, simply because they are from
New York, can be both insulted by and insulting to inhabitants of other
parts of the country, so too in Mexico *los chilangos,* residents of the
capital, share in a game of mutual recriminations with the rest of the
Republic.[11] Thus, despite frequent complaints about the capital itself,
the constant references by many to how much worse everything is outside Mexico City is in part a reflection of *chilangismo,* Mexico City–
ism.[12]

"The *campo*" refers to an area in Mexico that is too varied to war-
rant generalizations such as those mouthed by residents of Santo Domingo. Not since the folk-urban continuum model of Robert Redfield
have anthropologists of Mexico seriously utilized such a dichotomous
description of city and country, and I am not proposing that we return
to this paradigm now.[13] Any attempt to equate, say, the parenting attitudes and behavior of an eighty-year-old Maya-speaking grandfather
from Quintana Roo with those of a rural proletarian in the agribusiness
tomato fields of Sonora who is the young father of a newborn, just
because both come from the countryside, should demonstrate the futility of any such strict urban-rural classification. In addition, ethnographers have found a wide disparity in gender relations, even within the
same geographic region and ethnic group—in Oaxaca, for example, between the Zapotecs in the Isthmus of Tehuantepec (see Chiñas 1973;
Miano 1993; and Campbell and Green 1994) and those of the Sierra
(see Stephen 1991).

But the perception of my friends in Santo Domingo that there are
significant regional differences in male identities and fathering points to

some of the historical transformations in which they themselves have participated in recent decades. Understanding what is similar and what is different about being a father (or a mother) today in Santo Domingo is a critical element in the negotiation of contemporary gender relations in late-twentieth-century Mexico.

One factor involved in the disparaging remarks about the *campo* from residents of Santo Domingo who come from rural areas is that these people are often remembering less-than-contented childhoods. This means both that unhappiness in childhood may act as a filter on their memories and, more significantly, that despite periodic return visits to see family in the *campo,* they are most familiar with their natal villages of fifteen or twenty years ago or even before that. In a similar manner, people born and raised in Mexico City frequently refer to how difficult and different life was between men and women in their childhood neighborhoods. Much of this is undoubtedly well remembered; some, however, is probably embellished.[14]

For many in Colonia Santo Domingo, the *campo* has come to symbolize many of society's ills and their own sufferings, so their comments about the rural hinterland often reveal more about their own values than about the state of affairs outside Mexico City. Some friends in Santo Domingo who considered themselves more politically savvy (or cynical) also pointed out to me that as long as the urban poor are content with comparing themselves favorably with the poor in the countryside, social divisions between rich and poor throughout the country tend to be obscured. Nevertheless, despite the fact that Mexico's countryside is itself quite varied, there are sharp differences as to how gender relations are experienced by residents of Santo Domingo as opposed to people living in other parts of the country.[15]

Finally, partial but revealing research has been done on the differential impact on men and women of migration to the cities of Mexico from different rural regions within the country, including its impact on parent-child relationships (see Arizpe 1975, 1982, 1985). One implication of these national migration studies is that stable, uniform, and timeless gender relations simply do not exist in the Mexican countryside any more than they do in the cities.[16] This is especially true in the 1990s in Mexico, an expression of the regionally fluid nature of fathering in Mexico and the need for analyses of parenting that go beyond acultural (U.S.) models. Above all, debates in Santo Domingo over rural savagery and *chilangismo,* and whether rural or urban men make better fathers, speak to the liminal quality of contemporary gender identities and relations in Mexico.

NATURALIZED FATHERS AND MOTHERS

Margaret Mead (1949:188) wrote that the distinctiveness of human societies lay "in the nurturing behaviour of the male, who among human beings everywhere helps provide food for women and children." If not nearly measuring up to Mead's idyllic classification, in Colonia Santo Domingo, as in other parts of Mexico today and historically, active male participation in parenting does not necessarily mean an improvement (or worsening) in the position of women vis-à-vis their husbands and men in general.

Women in Colonia Santo Domingo usually spend more time with children than men do. In the minds of most women and men there, children, especially young children, "belong" with their mother or other women. When I arrived at the corner store one morning carrying Liliana, César Sr., an elderly neighbor, asked me, "Doesn't she miss her mother?" Eugenia, who was working in the store at the time, nodded in agreement with the question. I tried to explain that although her mother spent a lot of time with Liliana, so did I, and that to my mind proximity was a principal determining factor in an infant's attachment to others.[17] To them this was beside the point: there was a natural and physically overwhelming bond involved in mother-child mutual dependency that took precedence over all others, a qualitative relation that no amount of time spent with me could unseat. In Mexico, toddlers are said to suffer from *mamitis* (mommy-itis), whereas *papitis* is to date an unknown affliction (see Gutmann 1996).

Certain prevailing notions of maternal instincts are accepted as natural, as much by women as by men in the *colonia,* and therefore beyond reproach. These are some of the products and reflections both of standard Catholic doctrine promoting female domesticity and, for those who read popular magazines like the Spanish-language edition of *Readers Digest,* of the latest scientific theories of biologically driven mother-child bonding.[18] In this particular case, older men and women and younger women are most likely to expound theories of natural mother-infant bonding; younger men, and I refer here especially to young fathers, are more likely to mention that they and their wives simply found it most convenient for the women to care for their infants because the women were nursing, because the husbands could make more money working than the wives, and so on.

After we had been in Santo Domingo for several months, and after our neighbor Angela, in her late fifties, had begun caring for our daughter Liliana in the afternoon, relations between our families became very close. Angela was now the *abuelita* (grandmother), and as Lili's parents, Michelle and I became Angela's ex officio adoptive children. This meant greater emotional warmth and mutual reliance between our two families, and it opened the way to playful teasing—often, as it happened, at my expense.

Liliana was occasionally quite colicky. I am sometimes gruff, with a quick temper. To christen our newfound family ties, and as if to test them at the same time, Angela invented the expression *¡Se pone matea!* to describe Liliana when she was upset about something or other. Simply put, it means, "She's acting Mattish!" Everyone seemed to enjoy the neologism, which denoted being spirited, with a low flash point, and the expression continued to be used throughout the year by members of Angela's family (and by my wife, I am sorry to say). Although employed largely in jest, for Angela the phrase also carried the sense that traits such as temper and poise are directly inherited from one's "natural" parents. In Santo Domingo, men and women often speak of children behaving in this manner because they "have the same blood" as their mothers or fathers.

A sense that genetics controls at least the physical appearance of children is widespread. Norma likes to joke that Miguel married her because she is tall and strong, and in this way Miguel, who once played professional *futbol* but was eventually cut from the sport because of his small stature, could hope for larger sons who might have greater athletic success. I was implicated in a discussion about genetics and adultery, according to a third party who related the following exchange to me: a woman was holding Liliana one evening when another woman asked her if Liliana was her child. "No, she's Mateo's," came the response. The second woman, pointing to Liliana's blue eyes, then commented, "That's true. You couldn't have one like this. Not with *your* husband." The first replied with a smile, "No, but I know how to get them to come out like this." [19]

At the same time, I was not as light skinned as Michelle, so in the eyes of many in Santo Domingo my symbolic-genetic capital as progenitor was less than hers. As I arrived at her aunt's house one chilly, overcast February morning, five-year-old Sara examined me carefully. She

My daughter Liliana proved to be an invaluable, if unwitting, field assistant. Here she is held by her Uncle Noé.

finally indicated what was puzzling her: "*Nació la mamá güera, la bebé también. ¿Por qué no naciste así?* [The mother was born light-skinned, and the baby too. Why weren't you born like that?]" Her implication was that my parents were to blame. But then she quickly tried to turn it into a joke, adding as an explanation "*¿Porque traes mugre?* [Because you don't wash?]" Sexual and racial characteristics often clash with one another, as in this case in which my seed, carrying the promise of darker children, would not fully enjoy the advantage I generally obtained from being a gringo male.

While the belief in such biological constraints is widespread, parents do try to influence their children's acquisition of particular personality traits in other ways. This can be seen in how some children are named for their parents. Girls may be named for either mother (for instance, Lidia's oldest daughter is also named Lidia) or father (Gabriel's daughter is named Gabriela). But to my knowledge, boys are named for only their fathers, never for their mothers. The point of this naming strategy, it appears, is that girls may take after their mothers or their fathers, whereas boys are more often culturally encouraged to emulate their fathers alone.

Though there are generational differences with respect to fathering, with younger men usually more active and involved in parenting than were their fathers and grandfathers, even some men in their seventies today who describe themselves as "more macho than Jorge Negrete" (the old *charro*-cowboy film star) talk about having had a lot of responsibility for raising their children—boys in particular. These men frequently relate that they took their boys with them when they went out on errands or to visit friends during their free time, especially on weekends. This is often the case with fathers today as well, beginning when their children, more often boys than girls, are three to five years old.[20]

Fathers of the older generation also say that when their children were young, the men were responsible more than the mothers for teaching their boys technical skills and a trade—things that would later be necessary in fulfilling their adult masculine responsibilities as economic providers. Angela and Juan's son Noé, now a security consultant in his early thirties, was sent to live with Angela's brother Héctor in Santo Domingo when Noé was still in his mid-teens. Noé told me that he and his parents had been living in another barrio at the time, and that he had been spending his days hanging out in the streets, drinking, smoking, and stealing sheets of chewing gum at a factory where the guard had a bum leg and could never catch him and his friends. Santo Domingo was considered, by comparison, a less sinister environment. Perhaps just as important, his uncle Héctor had already started a machine shop in Santo Domingo and could offer Noé a job and teach him how to operate the lathes and drills. Héctor has long played the same role, that of surrogate father, with other young men having drinking or other problems, offering them jobs and instructing them in a trade.

ANTHROPOLOGICAL FATHERS AND SONS

Discerning historical differences in the meanings of fatherhood and the practices of fathers in Mexico often requires a careful reexamination of ethnohistorical materials, particularly the contradictory conclusions of Oscar Lewis, whose writings are still often referenced by anthropologists in Mexico and the United States. The ethnographic record compiled by Lewis and others is too fragmentary to draw any firm conclusions, but it may well be that in many societies where rural economies predominate, such as Mexico until the last few decades, ties between fathers and sons are often reinforced systematically through the training and later joint work done by men in agricultural production. To note that capitalist production relations have torn these bonds asunder, as they have so many others, does not mean that family life was in any sense bucolic in earlier epochs, but merely that gender roles and relations do change, and that they do so—though *never* automatically—in relation to changing economic systems of production and organization.

The following statement on men's roles as husbands and fathers is taken from Lewis's (1951) classic ethnography of rural Mexico, *Life in a Mexican Village.*

> In contrast to the wife's central role within the home, the husband's actual participation in family and household affairs is minimal. . . . The division of labor is clear-cut, and the husband, except in emergencies, never does anything in connection with the house or children. (1951:321)

This characterization of family relations in the village of Tepoztlán, Morelos, in the 1940s, could stand for prevailing contemporary views (or assumptions) on Mexican male parenting. It is the perspective many may have had in mind when they commented to me that my photograph of José Enríquez was unusual or unreal. However, as we will see presently, Lewis's theoretical summary contrasts sharply with some of his own ethnographic detail concerning the role of men in parenting practices and sentiments. The Mexican-men-have-nothing-to-do-with-the-children perspective corresponds in part to an antiquated image many in and outside Mexico have of gender relations there, a picture largely based on real and/or imagined, past and/or present social relations in the Mexican countryside.

Anthropologists from the United States and Mexico bear some responsibility for this confusing state of affairs, since they have long been recognized as among the foremost interpreters and chroniclers of cultural ideas and behavior with regard to parenting. Of great significance, Lewis contradicts himself on the subject of the relation between fathers and children, perhaps because he saw parenting as an intrinsically domestic activity. A few pages after the summary statement regarding men's avoidance of household affairs and child rearing, Lewis offers ethnographic descriptions that stand in marked contrast to what he (and others) had long summarized about Mexican men's roles in parenting,

> The father assumes an important role in the life of his son when the boy is old enough to go to the fields. Most boys enjoy working in the fields with their father and look forward with great anticipation to being permitted to join him. Fathers, too, are proud to take their young sons to the fields for the first time, and frequently show great patience in teaching them. (1951:338)

This description accords with most other ethnographies of rural Mexico, though, again, not with many of the characterizations of fathering in the social science literature.[21]

Some of the modern, and urban, twists to these patterns may also provide a source for new parenting problems. Justo, who was born in a rancho in the state of Hidalgo, noted to me one day that in the *campo* young children can go with either their mother or father, whereas in the city to a far greater extent they have to stay at home, which usually means remaining with their mothers and other women. According to Freudian theory, this greatly complicates a developmental hurdle already considered problematic enough: the need for boys to break their primary bonds with their mothers in order to develop into psychically mature men. If young boys today spend even less time with their fathers than in earlier eras, then in line with this theory mothers become even more involved in their sons' male identity development, and the break with the mother becomes even more difficult and traumatic.[22]

BOYS AND GIRLS

In earlier studies of families and parents in rural Mexico, anthropologists have emphasized how economic pressures have often influenced couples to have more children (for example, Arizpe 1982). The presence of more children has meant more family members can work at home and in the fields, and more can be sent to work in the cities. The presence of more children has also served as greater insurance against the uncertainties of old age in a society with meager or nonexistent social-security benefits.

But families throughout Mexico, including Mexico City, are today having fewer children than did previous generations. In chapter 6 we will examine some of the meanings and goals of *not* having so many children. Here it is worthwhile to briefly consider some of the reasons men and women in Colonia Santo Domingo *do* want to have children. Understanding these reasons is complicated by the fact that for most of my friends in the *colonia,* having children after marriage is a matter of course; few people I know in Santo Domingo have a conscious strategy about having children or, conversely, have decided never to have children. Far more frequent are shotgun marriages prompted by an unwed woman's pregnancy—in other words, marriages brought about to sanctify parenthood. When Angela told me her eldest daughter got married at sixteen, I asked her how old she'd been when she married Juan.

"Seventeen. And my daughter was born when I was eighteen."

"And why are you criticizing your daughter?"

"All right, precisely because of my experience. I never thought my daughter was going to marry. I had so many hopes, so many goals for her. And then she got pregnant and got married."

"You weren't pregnant when you got married?"

"I was too. Finally, the truth!"

Though some men want children in order to demonstrate their procreative abilities and prove their virility, for many more men, and for many women, children provide a way to prove one's worth in other, more important ways. In the manner of vicarious projections, parents in Santo Domingo often talk about the dreams and goals they have for their children, ranging from lucrative incomes to happy and stable marriages. How children turn out is also taken by many as a test of their parents' most significant accomplishments in life.[23]

There is another reason many adults in Santo Domingo want children. At once a most uncomplicated reason and for some readers in the United States—where children are broadly regarded as nuisances much of the time—perhaps the most difficult and naïve explanation to fathom is this: many poor women and men in Mexico City become parents for the fun of it. Finding pleasure in the company of children is considered by people of all generations in Mexico, even childless adults, to be one of the most natural and wonderful things in the world.

In Santo Domingo, some men speak with great pleasure about having jobs that allow them to spend time with their children while they are working, such as those furniture repairmen or cobblers who have little workshops in their houses, or others like car mechanics who work in the street in front of their homes. When the tanker truck arrived at 8 A.M. each Saturday morning to deliver natural gas to the *tortillería* across the street, two boys between six and eight years old often accompanied the men pumping the gas, and sometimes helped them with the hoses. During the summer, when the mailman came putt-putting down the street on his little motorcycle, his young son ran along the opposite side of the street, stuffing letters through mail slots. Other men, of course, talk about staying at work later than they need to because they would rather not go home. More than one man told me that the hardest part of every day was right after work, when he had to decide whether to go home, which meant "returning to my screaming children and wife," or kill time until the rest of the family might have fallen asleep.

Even for men who seem to take little interest, and less pleasure, in their children, most feel some cultural pressures to provide periodic guidance for their sons and daughters. Luciano is a welder who no longer lives in Santo Domingo but whose first family lived near us and who still often works there during the day. While recounting his life one day, Luciano talked to me about the four boys and five girls (including one who had died) in this family: "It makes sense that a boy becomes responsible as a result of the father, of education. And with a girl it's the same, because of education by her mother. Not because of nature, but because it is the obligation of the father to guide his son."

As part of his paternal duties Luciano feels that he has to impart a skill to his sons and then leave them to fend for themselves: "The boys are the ones I am helping. Oscar already knows the *chamba* [job] more or less, so he's going to teach the others. I already told him that I'm going, I'm going to look for work somewhere else so as not to be here. I'm beginning to make myself independent of them so they can teach themselves to be responsible about their house, because if I'm around they don't do anything. They are waiting for me to arrive, or for me to do it all."

This sentiment was echoed by another man who insisted that I not use his name in my book: "If you're a *canijo* [son of a bitch] in your life, your children are going to turn out worse than you. Take women, for instance. If your woman or you is a *canijo*, then the girls are going to turn out *canijas* and the boys *canijos*. If you're *tranquilo* [even-tempered] and the woman is a *canija*, like in my case, well then, most of the girls are *canijas* and the boys are *tranquilos*, because they don't smoke, don't drink—nothing besides *futbol*."

What happens if there are no boys? I spoke with Leti, the mother of

This construction worker often brought his son to the job site on Saturdays. Colonia Santo Domingo.

three girls between ten and fourteen years old. She speculates that the main reason her husband has never taken much responsibility for the children is that they have no sons. She laments that had there been three boys instead, he would have had to live up to (*cumplir*) his obligations as a father, and life would have been very different for her. This situation is felt by neighbors to be rather typical of old-fashioned relations between mothers and fathers, and in this sense more exceptional in a community that has undergone innumerable changes in recent years. Whether she is right is impossible to determine, but she is sure of her perception that with boys her husband would have been at least culturally pressured if not obligated to take on certain accepted male parenting duties.

Leti's husband, Carlos, the long-haul truck driver, chooses to emphasize his participation in raising the girls rather than his absence. As with other couples interviewed, Carlos talked of a division of labor he and Leti worked out when the children were young. Leti had them by day, and he got up with the infants at night (he had a different job at the time that permitted him to remain in the Federal District). The first time I met Carlos he told me of his knowledge of world geography. "Test me!" he challenged. I asked him, "What is the capital of Germany?" and he answered, "Bonn and Berlin before; not yet decided today." Over a lunch of rabbit *adobo* that he, with Leti's help, had prepared, Carlos said that when his daughters were very little and he was getting up all the time in the night, he had pinned a map of the world to the ceiling. He would lie on his back, sometimes for hours, rocking a daughter back to sleep and studying the world. "That and being a truck driver is how I know so much about geography," he told me.

Also indicative of how some parents distinguish between their sons and daughters and others do not is the fact that there is great variation in inheritance patterns today in Santo Domingo. Angela and her husband, Juan, will leave all their property to their three girls and one boy, all grown and all married, only the youngest of whom, Norma, still lives in the *colonia*. The children will have to decide how to divide it among themselves. Similarly, Marcos and Delia will leave their lot and home to their two girls. However, though he no longer lives there, Luciano as legal owner of the land and house his first family lives in, has decided that only his four sons will get the property, because, he reasons, his four daughters can find men and move out.[24]

A division of labor, fathers-sons and mothers-daughters, still prevails in some younger families in Colonia Santo Domingo, but many men with small children today like to claim as a point of pride that they treat their boys and girls the same. If they spend more time with the boys outside the home, they sometimes explain, it is because it simply "works out that way," because it is "more convenient" for both the father and mother, or because the boys want to spend time with them more than

the girls do. To this must be added the fact that mothers—probably
more so than fathers—are often reticent to have their girls go out with
the men. Diego told me that he used to take his girls with him when he
went out drinking with his friends, but that he now regrets having done
so because such situations are improper for girls—because girls (and
women) should not have to hear and witness the vulgarities that are
common when men are drinking together. Diego's wife agrees, and so
overall it remains the case that from very early on boys are sent off with
their fathers by their mothers in a way that girls less often are.

MALE AND FEMALE PARENTING OBLIGATIONS

In addition to those regional and historical differences already described
as to how men have approached the tasks of fathering in Mexico,
within Santo Domingo there is also significant diversity based on generation and individual proclivities. These last two factors were especially
apparent in forty-two semiformal interviews I conducted with fathers
and mothers of various ages in Colonia Santo Domingo. In addition to
questions about marriage, work, and what it means to be men and
women, I asked what it was people regarded as the principal parenting
obligations of men, and whether those of women were different.

There were six questions centering on how (and if) parenting responsibilities are divided between fathers and mothers with infants, young
children, and adolescents: Who takes care of the children's daily needs
(washing, feeding, play)? Who is affectionate with them? Who helps
them with their homework? Who helps them in doing their household
chores? Who scolds and who rewards them? Who gives them moral
instruction? [25]

Overwhelmingly, the people I interviewed stated that there were pronounced differences in parenting obligations: to oversimplify, men
should first and foremost provide for a family economically and women
before all else should care for the home (meaning children, husband,
and house, often in this order of importance). There was variety in the
responses, with many men and women calling attention to the important role of men as fathers, for instance, but the consensus was unmistakable in terms of the ideals enunciated by both women and men.
For men: "to work," "bring in money," "earn money," "support the
family economically," "fulfill marital duties economically." For
women: "take care of the children," "see to one's husband," "care for
the children and husband," "keep the house clean."

Though I was more interested in who *actually* did what and less concerned with what was supposed to happen in the opinion of the person I was interviewing,[26] and whereas the main purpose of the survey was to prompt freewheeling discussion about parenting and gender relations, specific questions were asked and concrete answers sought and recorded.[27] The survey was designed in part on assumptions I had developed while living in Mexico previously, and in part on questions about which I knew too little to even hazard a guess. For instance, the query about who was affectionate with the children was suggested by an image of cooing mothers and distant fathers. I meant it to be in direct contrast to the question about discipline, where I thought men would come to the fore. As to moral training, I expected women to stand out as the parents mainly responsible for religious instruction and the like.

The commentaries elicited through the survey were unambiguous about the fact that mothers were responsible for washing and feeding infants. Tasks involving older children and teenagers were often answered more vaguely. It is also revealing that in the course of the interviews, women were far less able to absent themselves from caring for very young children, preparing dinner, and so on in order to answer my questions than were men. When men are "available" they may and often do care for children, but women are more present and are expected to be, and women generally have less flexibility than men with regard to child care overall.

But why men care for babies less is not a simple matter. The belief that women are naturally more adept at caring for the very young is an ideological manifestation of the value systems of most women and men in Santo Domingo. Yet it is also not the case that men are seen as necessarily less tender or caring. A system of constraints is perceived by many such that infant care is routinely equated with maternal care. Societal norms into which people discover themselves born and reared—that is, an "inherited consciousness"—interact with individual decision making and practical consciousness, leading people to acquiesce to or challenge the status quo in the lives of their infants, and in their own lives as caretakers. It is an ideological concern intimately connected to a practical one.

For example, in a baby's first year, breast feeding is more common in Santo Domingo than formula feeding.[28] This requires the mother's rather constant presence with her baby and establishes a fairly rigid division of labor early on, setting a precedent for the first years of the child's life. Yet, as Laqueur (1990) reminds us, destiny is anatomy: in those cases in which babies are given formula from the outset, men's participation in infant care shows no appreciable increase. The body—in this case, men's inability to lactate—influences but does not in any sense dictate culture, yet the body is routinely used to justify and explain cultural fortunes.

Even if one were so inclined, to dispute systemic norms regarding maternal infant care would be a challenge for even the most dedicated iconoclasts. Work pressures make infant care on many jobs impossible, especially for men. From the perspective of individual couples, the imperatives to conform are prodigious. Through local branches of the family-services agency Desarrollo Integral de la Familia (DIF), the state provides day-care facilities beginning with forty-day-olds for a small number of children and in so doing may inadvertently promote "desertion" of families by fathers.[29] Space is extremely limited, and *madres solteras* (single mothers) who have jobs are given top priority. According to the cook at one DIF day-care center in the *colonia,* many families lie when they apply for spaces: a woman will sign up for her children as an abandoned mother; a week or two later, lo and behold, the father will "return" and begin to drop off and/or pick up the children.

To my surprise, although most people I interviewed felt that both mothers and fathers are affectionate with children of all ages, a sizable number said that fathers are more or much more tender with their children. The fact that many mothers spend more time with children than do the fathers may lead some men to indulge their children when they are with them. Yet affection does not invariably follow from relative absence. Older men often emphasized to me the need for men to remain aloof in order to maintain their authority over wives and children.

As I was talking one day with a man from outside Santo Domingo, our discussion turned to fatherly affections. Joaquín, in his early thirties, told me that he had never felt maternal or paternal tenderness from his own mother and father, and that he was thus especially determined that his daughter of ten should never want for this kind of affection. Even though he was suffering from AIDS at the time of our conversation, he said, he could never be as removed and *seco* (dry) as his own parents had been with him. In living with AIDS, Joaquín is very much a product of the 1980s. But his portrait of that decade is colored with very personal hues:

"Funny things happened in 1982. My brother died. He was the youngest, and he was adored by my father and mother. They wanted me to suddenly take his place emotionally for them. He died in August. My daughter was born in September. My wife left me in December of that year with an infant girl. She told me, 'You know what, I'm going.' 'What do you mean you're going? Where are you going?' 'I'm going. Where? I'm going from your life forever.' 'But why?' 'Because I've come to realize that I'm not mature enough to take responsibility for a daughter.' She was nineteen years old. So that's why I have a lot of ideas about marriage, about having a family. Then, later, in 1986, I got the disease when I had my first homosexual relation."

It appears that the temperaments and conduct of younger men have undergone a process of "naturalization," so that the greater affection of these men toward children is said to stem from something characteristically male within this realm. Few argue that men are by nature more patient or understanding than women in all situations. Rather, it is sometimes noted that with their own children fathers are often more doting than mothers. "Men can't help themselves when they get around *esquincles* [kids]," I was informed on more than one occasion.

Mothers enforce the rules far more than fathers, even when it comes to beatings. Men in Santo Domingo talk of beating their children, just as they were slapped, spanked, and whipped with belts as youngsters. But the most violent punishments inflicted on children today are often at the hands of mothers, a situation many also take as "normal."[30]

A less gendered division of labor pertains to helping children with their homework and household chores. Often the key factor is which parent or other adult is home with the children more, though in the case of schoolwork, which adult has received more formal education is also important. Neither task is necessarily or generally considered especially male or female, which may be why responses to these two survey questions less frequently included defensive justifications and tangential anecdotes. Whereas people often seemed to be thinking about how their responses to questions about affection and discipline might reflect on them, with regard to schoolwork and housework people seemed to have fewer precepts about which answer was "right" or "wrong," which more modern or traditional, which more typical of the rich or the poor, which more reflective of how things are done in Mexico as opposed to the United States.

As I expected, even when both parents were concerned about emphasizing to their children the importance of ethical conduct, the mother was most often the parent involved in gathering the children to attend church and religious celebrations and, when they were young, to pray.

The communication and organization of religious morality by women corresponds to the preponderance of women at church services throughout Santo Domingo, and it is a reflection of the great importance of churches, church sites, and priests in the lives of many women. Men in Santo Domingo are less likely than women to seek out the counsel of a priest when morally or emotionally troubled—a neighbor disclosed to me one afternoon, "I'm Catholic, but I don't normally go to church"—and this explains in part why church doctrine is less central for men when they teach their children about morality.

Still, with regard to parental guidance on subjects as diverse as children's sexual dalliance and school attendance, I have not seen mothers play a greater role than the fathers in Santo Domingo. Beliefs and practices differ enormously from family to family (and within many families), but I find no basis for either those generalizations that posit an exclusive, or ultimate, male authority on ethical matters or those that paint women as the standard-bearers of (conservative) public morals in an age of increasing "male depravity."

If we are to appraise the extent of generational differences in parents' care of their children, an additional matter must be considered: the impact of changes in the composition and size of households, and how changes in parenting responsibilities have been stimulated in part by the fact that in urban Mexico it is no longer as common to find extended families living together, and attendant older women in particular, as it was until recently.[31] Undoubtedly many men are assuming certain responsibilities left by grandmothers and other senior women who are no longer as commonly resident in many homes. And parents still routinely drop off young children with grandparents—for instance, when the children are sick and both parents work. But such arrangements are not always practical, especially if the grandparents live in distant parts of the city.

Nor is it always easy to enlist the support of older men in parenting. Augustín, who lives in Colonia Santo Domingo, frequently complained about having more daily contact with his grandchildren than he ever had with his own children. Sometimes he would take a walk just to get away from their noise. Then, after smoking a cigarette, he would calm down and return. It was all well and fine that his sons did not seem to mind children, but he was a different kind of man. And he was not going to change now.

Although transformations in family and kinship structures and the shrinking grandmother option have had a hand in the greater participation of younger men in parenting duties, the changing practices of fathers are not mainly due to such kinship factors. Where such emergent cultural practices have appeared, they have developed, consciously or not, in spite of formidable barriers in the form of dominant cultural ideologies that extol the virtues of fathers as breadwinners and mothers as caregivers.

Responses to the survey on parenting indicate the perils of oversimplifying fathering practices in urban Mexico, especially of making generalizations that posit bland homogeneity among lower class men in the form of erratic participation in day-to-day care and little interest in anything more than procreation. In addition, though male identity, especially with regard to Mexican men, is often thought of as equivalent to irresponsibility and violence, for most of the men and women interviewed, at least, being a dependable and engaged father is as central to *ser hombre,* being a man, as any other component, including sexual potency.[32]

BEING A FATHER NEVER ENDS

"My father almost never visits me. He visits my brother more, almost daily. He's over at Emiliano's house really late sometimes," Arturo told me as we sat in his car talking one afternoon. "Often I feel bad, you know, because how can someone have five children in Mexico City and only pay attention to one?"

Studies in anthropology regarding the relations between parents and their children have usually focused on child rearing during the first few years of the child's life.[33] This focus is related to infant and toddler dependency upon adults, which in turn is associated with biological and evolutionary neoteny and "retardation" among primates with respect to most other mammals, and humans as compared with most other primates.[34] Relatively slow maturation and long lives require and allow intensive parenting of very young offspring. In turn, according to many psychological models, the first few years of life are by far the most important in terms of one's long-term and overall psychic development. Thus by studying child rearing, researchers have sought to catch in microcosm the key cultural elements of societies as they are being imparted to impressionable youngsters.

But parenting as understood by women and men in Santo Domingo continues through children's adolescence and well beyond. Though the forms of parenting change during the life course of both parent and

child, being a mother or a father is a responsibility until parent or child
dies. For this reason I speak primarily of "parenting" and not "child
rearing" in this study. Arturo, who is forty-seven, said his father, who
is seventy-one, justifies paying more attention to Arturo's younger
brother by telling Arturo, "I can't visit you because you're doing fine. I
already helped you for a long time." Arturo told me he had to admit
that this is true.

"So is being a father [*ser padre*] forever?" I asked Arturo.

"Yes, I guess it is, until you're gone, right? But my father has always
come by. When my father finds out that I'm sick, he comes to see how
I am, what I need, if I have my medicines. So he tries to see us. But now
he goes to see my brother because he says that my brother needs him
more than I do, you see?"

I told Arturo that it seemed to me his father was simply trying to
help the child who he thought needed it most. Arturo responded, "On
the one hand, it's OK. But what happens is that this help isn't what it
should be. My brother hasn't taken advantage of this help but instead
he has just continued to flounder in his problems."

Children grow up, marry, and often move out of the neighborhood.
Most return to see their families on weekends and especially holidays.
Such visiting is sometimes attributed by scholars to "the importance of
family in Mexican society." But as much feminist scholarship has
pointed out, it is a mistake to treat families as homogenous and undif-
ferentiated structural units.[35] Often grown children in Santo Domingo,
for example, will talk of returning to see one particular parent, or of
moving nearer to be closer to one parent. And if parents are separated
or divorced, it is common for children to talk about and seek out one
more than the other. When one parent dies, if the other was estranged
from particular children, past difficulties are not necessarily forgotten
and relations patched up.

Gabriel was thirty-eight at the time he and I drove up into the mountains ringing Mexico City to the south. Of his background, Gabi says
he's "almost *chilango*," because he was brought to Mexico City shortly
after being born in a little village in the state of Guanajuato, and because he has few ties with relatives still living in Guanajuato. "My way
of thinking is very different from my cousins, really different," he tells
me. "I get along with strangers better than with my own family."

Gabriel and I sat and talked at the foot of the now-extinct volcano
Xitle, which long before had spread the lava that now covers Colonia
Santo Domingo. It was Sunday morning, and Gabi wasn't fixing cars or

Gabriel at the foot of Xitle volcano, talking about his dreams and secrets.

minibuses in the street where he has worked for years Monday through Saturday. After commenting that he started "using his memory" when he was about two and a half after his little sister died at only a few months of age, Gabriel began discussing his parents:

"They didn't mature. My father always carried the traumas of his childhood with him. He'd been an orphan left by his mother; he grew up with an aunt and uncle. Just before he passed away I realized that he'd begun to mature. That made me sad because I saw him differently and I felt bad because everything he managed to give us as adults I would have liked to have had as a boy. I have very bad memories of him . . . because he broke my toys."

We had been talking about many emotional subjects having to do with his childhood, marriage, and intermittent drinking problems, but now for the first time that morning Gabriel began to cry. He wiped his eyes, glancing at me to see whether I noticed the tears, but not necessarily because he was embarrassed. I think Gabriel wanted me to know how badly he was hurting just then.

"It was worse than getting beaten, because I had worked hard to get enough money to buy those toys. Since I was ten years old, I was always collecting garbage, washing dishes, selling *paletas* [popsicles]."

I wanted to know how Gabriel thought he was different from his father in his marriage and with his children.

"My father was very irresponsible," he said. "I'm irresponsible—but with myself, not with my family."

"What does that mean?"

"My soda pops [which were causing Gabriel serious kidney problems], my drinking binges—all that is my irresponsibility."

"Oh, that makes sense," I sarcastically commented. "So if you died, what would happen to your family?"

"I've thought about just that. My head still isn't big enough to understand everything I've got to understand."

Gabriel insisted that he was different than his father with regard to family responsibilities, that his father often deserted his mother and Gabriel would never do that. He noted that he always provided for their economic well-being, though he admitted that his drunken sprees were remarkably similar to the ones with which his father had tormented his childhood.

Teaching one's children to learn from the mistakes their parents have already made, and sometimes avoided, is an important element in fathering for many men in Santo Domingo. Marcos says he likes to chat with his teenage girls about lessons he has learned. As children he and his brothers and sister were often left alone. Their mother was a servant in the home of a Spanish family, and their father worked as a driver or mechanic's assistant much of the time. As the supervisor of other janitors at the National University today, Marcos also has to spend a lot of time away from home, but, he says, he tries to be there for his two daughters when they need him.

"I've told them what I've been, what I am, what I've done. I've showed them what a prostitute is, what a—"

"Why?" I interrupted.

"So they'll know more or less . . . this . . . so they'll see the difference between a normal woman and a prostitute."

"Why is it important for them to know this?"

"So they never get into a situation like that. A while ago we went to Tepito.[36] Every time we go to Tepito I take them [his two daughters] so they can see the prostitutes, how they're dressed, how they present themselves, how they stand, how they approach men, what they can gain from this situation, economically or physically, right? Because there are women who are sick. You can get a venereal disease and that makes it really hard for you. So I try to teach them all the good and the bad in this life, not keep them sheltered and all that. Because if you cover their eyes . . . then they do go out on the street and say, 'OK, I don't get what this is. What's going on?' I try to tell them how life is so they don't go out with their eyes closed. Because in fact I have given them an education, a training. They have to decide where they're going and what they're going to do."

FATHERING AND SOCIAL CLASS

Changing economic conditions in Mexico, especially since the crisis of 1982, have fostered additional changes among broad sectors of the male population with regard to fathering. Differences in what men from various social strata think and do about being fathers provide further evidence that generalizations about universal, modern, or even national (Mexican) cultural patterns of child rearing cannot be made without taking into account the effects of class divisions and inequalities on parenting beliefs and practices. As we will see, however, such socioeconomic "environmental" factors do not necessarily impact families in predictable ways. But they do once again suggest the importance of taking into account questions of class, generation, ethnicity, and region when analyzing the contradictory cultural politics of masculinity in Mexico.

Among intellectuals in the middle classes, tougher times financially have sometimes meant learning to do without the live-in *muchacha* (maid-cook-nanny), who was ubiquitous only a short time ago. Thus men in these strata find themselves caring for their young children far more than ever in the past, and the expression *"Estoy de Kramer* [I'm *Kramer*-ing]" has come into modest vogue. The expression, which comes from the Hollywood movie *Kramer vs. Kramer,* means "I've got the kids," and it reflects a cultural image of the modern U.S. family prevalent in Mexico. I have noticed its use exclusively among male intellectuals, normally preceded by an invitation, for instance over the phone, from another male colleague to take part in some leisure activity. The response *"Estoy de Kramer"* means not only that the invited party is busy, but that he is busy taking care of his children. Implicit in the statement is the sense that the speaker finds this task somewhat onerous; nonetheless, it reflects the fact that men in the less-well-off middle classes are participating in fathering to a greater extent than they might have only a few years ago.

In this light it is interesting to recall the statement the banking official made to me, that Mexican men do not carry babies, with its implication that they have as little to do with the female duties of infant care as possible. In addition to the explanations already offered for the official's remark (that it was a joke, that the speaker came from Durango, and so forth), there is another that must now be considered: that the banking official was expressing contempt for those without the financial resources he enjoyed. In a complex tangle of class and gender issues, he may have been indicating his idea of what money, after all, is for—to pay others to do life's disagreeable chores for you. Whereas even men in the middle strata have in the recent past been forced to confront issues related to their role in parenting, and thus a confusing welter of emerging and often contradictory male identities, wealthier men have for the most part had the financial latitude to maintain their immunity to such changes in gender relations.

Superficially, at least, the critical differential ingredient here is the *muchacha,* and being able to afford such hired help and thereby relinquish at least a good share of daily child care.[37] In Hospital Ángeles, an elite medical center where the signs are always in Spanish and English and patients with cellular telephones are as plentiful as wheelchairs, it is not unusual to see a well-heeled couple walk briskly into a waiting room followed closely by a uniformed *muchacha* carrying the couple's young child.

A man I know has worked for many years as a butler on an exclusive family estate at the edge of the city. He enjoys telling neighbors in Santo Domingo of the extravagant lifestyle that fabulous riches will buy, including how on whimsy the lady of the manor might commission the family jet to the Pacific Coast hundreds of miles to the west to pick up fresh prawns for dinner. When the meal is served, however, the children are nowhere to be found. Or rather, not to be found by their parents, for they are not allowed to eat with these adults. The children eat with the servants in the kitchen until deemed old enough to behave themselves in decent company.

Larissa Lomnitz and Marisol Pérez-Lizaur conducted an ethnographic study of an elite Mexican family for seven years. They write that generally within elite families,

> [the father's] participation in raising children is indirect; he may occasionally play with his small children or, when they grow up, gradually introduce his sons to certain aspects of a man's world. Child rearing is the direct and formal responsibility of the mother. (1987:210)

For at least many fathers in Colonia Santo Domingo, this is hardly the situation. Simply to note the greater responsibilities that women in both elite and popular classes have in parenting misses the enormous differences in the content of fathering in each context. Fathers in the *colonia* to a far greater extent are integral in all stages of their children's lives. Beyond a merely quantitative, time-allocation difference in fathers' attention to their children, most of these men define their own and others' masculinity in part in terms of their active role in parenting.

I am not maintaining that being born into the *clases populares* makes one a better or a more attentive parent in some abstract sense. But belonging to the lower social classes may, among other things, result in more active parenting, especially in Mexican society, where those from better-off strata can still afford to hire others to care for their children. That is, we should recognize a relationship between fathering and social class in Mexico City that, in turn, involves many men (and women) in the practical transformation of their social lives and therefore, too, their consciousnesses. And I do wish to affirm the ongoing importance of class as a pivotal, if complex, category.[38] As Stuart Hall (1988:45) writes, while not sufficiently determinate in explaining the movement of ideas and practices, "class interest, class position, and material factors are useful, even necessary, starting points in the analysis of any

ideological formation." Class makes a difference in parenting practices
and should consequently be brought into any such description and analysis.

When I attended a symposium on "La Pareja" (couples) at the Centro Cultural in the quaint upper middle class community of Coyoacán,
I brought Liliana in her *canguro*. She was the only child present. Who
but an outsider of one kind or another would bring such potential dis-
rupters to social events when they could be left with the *muchacha* at
home and everyone would be much happier? Yet such an absence of
children would be inconceivable in Santo Domingo. At community
meetings there, like the biweekly *junta de jefes de manzana* (block captains' meeting) and the *reuniones de animadores* (organizers meetings)
of the Christian Base Communities, children are always present, being
shepherded by mothers and fathers, brothers and sisters, fidgeting between their father's legs or absorbed in drawing on the blackboard near
an older cousin.

As Lourdes Arizpe makes clear in the conclusion to her study of belief systems in the city of Zamora, Michoacán,

> All the foregoing allows us to conclude that there do not exist two distinct
> subsystems of beliefs between men and women which simply overdetermine
> all class differences. (1989:253; emphasis removed from original)[39]

It is not a sign of intellectual diffidence to note that the very concept
and relevance of social class must now be explained and defended in
some scholarly quarters, where today, as Michèle Barrett (1992:216)
notes, "social class is definitely *non grata* as a topic." Mechanical materialism, often in the form of economist connections that make beliefs
spring automatically from class membership, is no doubt partially to
blame for this state of affairs at present. Yet the situation does not justify the exile of class analysis from contemporary scholarly work. Examples drawn from Mexico historically and today indicate that ideas
and activities regarding fathering have consistently, if elaborately, developed in relation to class formations.

FATHERING AND GENDER EQUALITY

Child rearing and child care are considered by some feminist scholars in
the United States as habitually and often exclusively feminine domains.
Whereas their arguments are, ironically, based on the premise that such

practices are universally cultural and need not be permanent features of human relations, they write as if these parenting patterns varied little cross-culturally. Sara Ruddick (1989:17), for example, writes, "To be a 'mother' is to take upon oneself the responsibility of child care, making its work a regular and substantial part of one's working life." Nancy Chodorow (1978:3) begins her famous study *The Reproduction of Mothering* with the simple declaration "Women mother." She then adds, "Though fathers and other men spend varying amounts of time with infants and children, the father is rarely a child's primary parent."

As they pertain to Colonia Santo Domingo, I agree with much of Ruddick's commentary and Chodorow's analysis, especially the implication that parental divisions of labor are eminently cultural and not biologically determined, and hence more amenable to prompted change. I think insufficient attention is paid by these authors, however, to cultural variation—and to the fact that we still have precious little knowledge about parenting practices historically and globally.[40] The child-rearing and parenting practices of the white middle class in the United States are hardly representative of every other cultural context.

The point about men not being nearly as active as women with infants was also characteristic of the situation in Colonia Santo Domingo in the early 1990s, for instance, yet it is a mistake to reduce all parenting, motherhood, and fatherhood to those activities occurring during the first years of life. Mothers and fathers are parents for life, with greater and lesser degrees of influence and obligations depending upon a host of factors. In addition, though parents may exert great influence, the socialization of children, including their guidance as to whether and how to be parents someday, takes place not just in the family but through school, television, and other sources.

If Chodorow were correct in arguing that the cultural origins of masculinity must be understood as an oppositional stance to boys' overexposure to their mothers, we would expect to find less acute concern with male identity in the working class in Mexico City, where many fathers play an active part in their children's upbringing, than in the upper social echelons, where fathers are indeed generally absent from the family. Such, however, is the opposite of official discourse regarding Mexican men and machismo, where working class men are said to valorize brute virility and ignore their offspring. Nor do sweeping cross-cultural analyses of capitalist modernity help us much in understanding fathering and fatherhood in Santo Domingo.[41] In "the isolated nuclear family of contemporary capitalist society," Chodorow writes,

[m]asculine development takes place in a family in which women mother and fathers are relatively uninvolved in child care and family life, and in a society characterized by sexual inequality and an ideology of masculine superiority. (1978:181)

To note that not all capitalist societies are the same does not deny the importance of capitalism. It is simply to call attention to the particular cultural forms that capitalism itself has assumed (see Smith 1984 and Watts 1992).

Both Chodorow and Ruddick discuss women's primary responsibility for infants and children as integral to the subordination of women, and they argue that the extent of shared parenting between men and women is the key test of the degree of gender equality in all societies. I think parenting is a measure of gender equality, but perhaps not so accurate a gauge as has been argued. In Colonia Santo Domingo, as in other parts of Mexico today and in the rural and urban past, we find forms of parenting so distinct as to make us question such conclusions, which are based almost exclusively on particular U.S. settings.

With regard to the issue of women's equality, in Santo Domingo active male participation in parenting does not necessarily mean that the situation of women is better (or worse) there than elsewhere in the world. We should revise our beliefs that all men in Mexico today and historically have little to do with children. Instead, more active and less active parenting by men seems to correspond more to other factors such as class, historical period, region, and generation. For numerous, though not all, men and women in Colonia Santo Domingo, Mexico City, in the 1990s, active, consistent, and long-term parenting is a central ingredient in what it means to be a man, and in what men do.

FOUR

Motherly Presumptions and Presumptuous Mothers

It's true what they say: a docile horse becomes worthless, and a good man becomes an asshole.

Jesusa Palancares (quoted in Hasta no verte Jesús mío, *by Elena Poniatowska)*

CHANGING MEN

How much men are or are not changing is a subject of frequent and lively debate among women in Colonia Santo Domingo. So is the role that women play in changing men. As many women residents of the *colonia* reason, if sons are going to be better men than their fathers, then mothers have some work to do. As for the men in the *colonia*—though this varies from one individual to another, and from one point in an individual's life to another—most define their masculinity in relation to the women in their lives, whether they be the mothers or lovers, community activists or teachers, nurturers or breadwinners. That is, as often as not for these men, manliness is seen as whatever women are not.

In Colonia Santo Domingo, older women and men of the *tercera edad* (literally, "third age," meaning senior citizens) seem to have an easier time than other residents in responding to questions about what difference it might make to grow up in an area where women are community organizers and leaders, as opposed to one in which even if women work outside the home they do not play a substantial or integral role in the public political life of the neighborhood. For those who have grown up in Santo Domingo, or in other parts of Mexico City where *movimientos urbanos populares* (MUPs; popular urban movements) have taken place in the past fifteen years, it is difficult to even imagine a situation in which women are not community activists.[1]

When I asked her what made Santo Domingo different than some

[handwritten: Community words are met by male + female Participation]

other *colonias* in Mexico City, the director of a day-care center told me,
"In Santo Domingo women by nature tend to be leaders. I'm talking to
you about Santo Domingo because I have lived with them for longer.
[The woman in Santo Domingo] is characteristically a leader in her
community, in her family. Why is this? I think it's because of the needs
of the *colonia*. In Santo Domingo you often hear, 'Let's get together on
such-and-such a date at such-and-such a time to petition the *delegación*
[city district authorities] to put in a sewage system.' And a whole bunch
of women take off. We've seen it. And they all take off for the *delegación,* and they get what they want because they're born leaders. Even
now they're born leaders. Still today."

The director wanted me to understand both the history of women's
activism and leadership in Santo Domingo, and the fact that, in her
opinion, this new tradition continues: "They bring the grandfathers and
the fathers. None of this business of 'Men say . . . ' When it comes time
to explain this or that, we women can do it too. It's when everything
we carry inside comes out. Born leadership. This is reflected in their
families one hundred percent. Because thanks to this group of women
which insisted on them putting in the sewage system, now it's been
done. And who enjoys it? Everyone in the family. Who saw it happen?
The children. And the children say, 'My mama is going all over and
she's a leader of lots of stuff and she made them do it.' "

"Do the children really talk like that in your day-care center?" I
asked.

"Yes," the director told me. "Yes, the children have a [role] model
in their own house."

Yet not all barrios are created equal.

The difficulty many younger residents of Santo Domingo have in
imagining a situation in which women are not politically involved in
the community was brought home to me by the tough time I was having
one day in explaining my research to Herlinda Romero, who for fourteen years had lived in Santo Domingo and taught there at the José
Vasconcelos Secundaria Técnica, the technical junior high school.

"Could you tell me about the impact on men of women's involvement in these political activities?" I asked.

"I don't understand what you're getting at," Herlinda replied. She
explained to me that because men work outside the *colonia,* "in our
community of Santo Domingo I'd say that it's been a question of
women running things [*es la mujer la que manda*]." It was a relatively

straightforward issue, Herlinda tried to explain to me, and she was not sure why it was even worth discussing.

I was clearer with my questions when we began talking about the *colonia* where Herlinda had grown up. She drew on her experiences as a youth in Colonia Moctezuma, near the airport, to make comparisons with life in Santo Domingo: "There [in Colonia Moctezuma] women are busy with their homes. Some of them work [outside the home], but they have to be back before their husband returns. Because if they're not, who knows! For example, there education was different for boys than for girls. And the boy could go out in the street, though the girl could not. If she did go out, the poor thing, she'd get it. I still have family there, and that's what it's like for my nieces."

"So it is different here in Santo Domingo?" I questioned.

"Of course! Here there's not a situation like, 'You, as a girl, you're going to . . . clear the table.' They're treated equally. It's a matter of letting them do what they want to do. Yes, there are differences [in the treatment of boys and girls], like in one family [on the street] where I live there's a difference. Twenty years ago women went to *primaria* [elementary school], and that was that, and the boys went off to *secundaria* while the girls stayed home and swept, made the beds, washed, ran errands, and so on. But as soon as a girl is as much a part of education, well, that's when it's, 'You know what, *mijito* [my son], you go run this little errand and you, *hija* [daughter], you're going to study.' That's where it all comes from."

Other people, young and old, report continuing and sharp distinctions between sons and daughters in their families in Santo Domingo, but the point is that this particular neighborhood has experienced changes that, although not unique, are also not uniform throughout Mexico City. One of the chief reasons Colonia Santo Domingo is a good location to study cultural creativity—and more specifically how and the degree to which gender relations and identities are changing in Mexico today—is that during the past two decades women there, as independent social actors, have played such a powerful, initiating role in creating and sustaining the community.[2]

DIFFERENT AND DIFFERING WOMEN

In this constant, complex interaction among spaces of
conflict and alliance, there are moments of greater
change or transformation.

Florencia Mallon, Peasant and Nation

In most recent studies of popular urban movements in Mexico City and
other parts of Mexico and Latin America, the central role of women
has been emphasized.[3] Most studies dealing with these issues in Mexico
and elsewhere in the world today argue convincingly that women's participation in political struggles as militants and sometimes as leaders
represents a radical break with certain popularly conceived traditional
female roles and that at the same time women often utilize their positions as mothers to enter into "public" politics (see Kaplan 1982; Sacks
1988; and Martin 1990). This analysis is both correct and timely,
though the modern notion that Mexican women remained submissive
during the centuries of colonial rule, as well as the era following independence in the early nineteenth century, has recently been sharply critiqued by historians of the region (Taylor 1979; Arrom 1985).[4]

Women in Santo Domingo in the past two decades have been speaking truth to power, especially to government authorities, but also to
their men. In particular, these women have flouted stereotypes of the
submissive, self-sacrificing, and long-suffering woman—*la mujer sumisa y abnegada.* Bearing no more necessary relation to all women in
Mexico than do generalizations of machismo to every man there, notions of *marianismo* (the cult of the so-called long-suffering Latin American woman [see Stevens 1973]) have recently been critiqued by scholars (Ehlers 1991), as have presumptions of universal traits among all
Spanish-speaking women (Stephen 1991). Yet how men in recent years
have reacted to women's recent involvement in social struggles in Latin
America has remained largely unstudied in the ethnographic literature.

Even to the casual observer, though, it should be clear that in Santo
Domingo and elsewhere in Mexico, transformations among women
have had a profound impact on men in direct and indirect ways. Recent
changes in gender identities among men may indeed often be traced to
the conscious or unconscious initiative of women and to the tensions
that at first affect women more than men in the *colonia.* That is, in these
particular historical circumstances, and intentionally or not, women
have often played the role of catalysts for change among the population

more broadly, and not just with regard to gender inequality. And part of the process in which women challenge men to change their thinking and practice involves the contradictions between consciousness that has been uncritically inherited and that which arises in the course of practically transforming the world.

In various venues, from block captains' meetings in the *colonias populares* to the pages of mass-circulation periodicals, the feminist movement in Mexico has effectively challenged the notion that women's sole creative function is to reproduce the labor force (see Franco 1988:513). The Mexican feminist magazine *fem*, for example, achieved widespread distribution in dozens of *colonias populares* like Santo Domingo throughout the Federal District when it was a supplement to the newspaper *Uno más uno* in the late 1970s and early 1980s. Teresita de Barbieri (personal communication), an editor of the magazine at the time, says that in many *colonias* thousands of copies were sold and that according to research done at the time, each copy was in turn read by many women—and no doubt by a few men. This is no longer the case, and I know of no feminist publications that were broadly read in Santo Domingo in the mid-1990s. Nonetheless, feminist and generally leftist ideas about gender relations undoubtedly continue to reach an audience in Santo Domingo through many, often circuitous routes.

Some people read the daily "opposition" newspaper, *La jornada,* including its monthly *Doble jornada* feminist supplement.[5] Many more watch the long-running television program *Aquí nos tocó vivir* (This is where we're [stuck] living) every Saturday at 9 P.M., when reporter Cristina Pacheco shows how particular families, often female headed, are, amazingly enough, managing to survive in Mexico today. Also popular in 1992–93 was the prime-time television talk show *María Victoria Llamas,* which frequently discussed issues relating to gender and sexuality while a national audience phoned in its opinions during the broadcast. On the radio, women's centers in Mexico City regularly run spots offering assistance to women suffering spousal abuse.

Women public-health workers have been leading workshops in the Pedregales since at least the early 1980s, offering classes on childbirth training and sexuality. For much of our year there, my wife, Michelle, worked as a health educator in our neighborhood with Salud Integral Para la Mujer (SIPAM; Women's Whole Health) on campaigns favoring legalized abortion, promoting condom use and "safe sex" among teenagers, and providing access to tests for sexually transmitted diseases.

Perhaps from a casual acquaintance with the efforts of organizations

"In memory of the suffering and the deaths of women who have had to abort. No more silence!" This altar was built by women public-health activists to commemorate women who had died from illegal abortions, a reflection of the influence of grassroots feminism in the area. DIF family-services agency, Colonia Ajusco, 1993.

such as SIPAM, the grandmother Catalina responded as she did when I asked her what had changed between men and women in her seventy-plus years. "Well, women's liberation!" she answered. Such is the pervasive, if diffuse, influence of feminism and its vocabulary in many barrios in Mexico City.

Certainly the amorphous but no less real presence of tens of thousands of women and men who identify themselves as part of the "sixties generation" of rebellion against the Mexican state and bourgeois authority also exerts an intangible yet no less consequential influence on everyone who lives in Santo Domingo and Mexico City. Consequently, because its creative aims are for emancipation and not simply resistance and withdrawal from modern society, since 1968 the feminist movement in Mexico has to a greater or lesser degree been on the offensive, in Habermas's sense of this term.[6] Similarly, when the Zapatista Army of Chiapas burst into city halls and international headlines in January 1994, its bulletins reflected equally emancipatory aims, as well as a stated desire to confront issues of gender inequality in immediate ways.

By the late 1980s in Mexico, Bennett (1992:255) concludes, "[t]he collective memory of the urban poor now included organizing as an expected feature of city life." The presence of women in these broad mobilizing efforts as well as in autonomous women's organizations also had become a commonplace in areas of the capital like Colonia Santo Domingo.[7] Carlos Monsiváis estimates that women in the early 1990s constituted between 40 and 50 percent of the leadership in *colonias populares,* unions, and the "informal economy" in Mexico (interview by author, 20 February 1993). In Santo Domingo, women make up about half of those attending and participating in the biweekly Block Captains' Meetings. On 24 October 1992, for instance, twenty-six women and twenty-two men attended. On 7 November 1992 there were thirty-seven women and thirty-six men. After the meeting of 7 November, I wrote in my field notes:

> There seemed to be few distinctions made (consciously or explicitly) between men and women, either in terms of who raised what, who supported what, or how people referred to each other and each other's ideas. In the discussion on a possible abduction attempt of three children it was clear that neither are kids simple "women's affairs," nor did the men assume more of a role as "heads of households and ultimate decision-makers." Men refer to women who have spoken before them in the same manner in which they refer to men: seconding suggestions a woman has made, and recounting struggles the woman has previously initiated in the community, as a way of reminding others of her past contributions.

Some of the women at the meetings are *jefas de manzana* (women block captains), and many of these *jefas,* today in their fifties and sixties, were among the "invaders" of Santo Domingo in the early 1970s.[8] Nonetheless, the top three elected positions in the *colonia* were held by men in 1992–93.

Women have also been making inroads as leaders in other venues in Mexico City. The *cacica* (neighborhood boss) Guillermina Rico, to cite one notorious example, was reputed to have some seven thousand people who carried out her bidding in the old central barrios of the capital. Whereas the new wave of women leaders in popular struggles is one manifestation of the breakdown of some "traditional" female roles, notes Monsiváis, the *cacicas* and female business executives represent an extreme and opposite product of the same social processes.

MEN LEFT BEHIND

"Every established order tends to produce . . . the naturalization of its own arbitrariness," writes Bourdieu, who then follows this analysis with the following example:

[I]n the case of domestic conflicts to which marriages often give rise, social categories disadvantaged by the symbolic order, such as women and the young, cannot but recognize the legitimacy of the dominant classification in the very fact that their only chance of neutralizing those of its effects most contrary to their own interests lies in submitting to them in order to make use of them. (1977:164–65)

Bourdieu's is a rather sweeping prescription for those dominated by male privilege. Such are the vagaries of being passive receivers of history.

In Santo Domingo such muted, covert subversion of the established order is indeed actively carried out by women and the young all the time. But simultaneously there is overt and organized rebellion against male privilege that has occurred since the invasion of the Pedregales in 1971, and the interplay between the open and hidden forms of creative contest indicate the fallacy of reducing the activities of the oppressed to their recognizing and submitting to the powers that be.

I first met Bernardino Ramos in mid-October 1992, when he was twenty-nine years old. Berna was born and raised in Colonia Ajusco. Having grown up in the years following the invasion of the Pedregales, he has memories that include events like the time his mother heard that there was a new electric line going up and sent Berna to tap into it; ever since, his family has had electricity. But only after the invasion, he says, "did we figure out that the women had definitely played a fundamental role. I didn't notice it at the time, but it was clear afterwards."

Bernardino's father was originally from Guanajuato, and when he wasn't selling candies in the street he sometimes returned to this state, which lies to the north of Mexico City. His mother, who speaks Otomí and was born in a village in Puebla, to the east of the capital, used to sell clothes door-to-door. Bernardino himself has held down a variety of jobs, but he says that since 1982, except for a year and a half when he was drunk most of the time, he has been a community and political activist. He was elected president of Colonia Ajusco in the late 1980s.

When we first talked, I asked Berna about changes among men and between men and women as a result of the participation of women as leaders and organizers in the area—for example, how male power and prerogative might have been challenged in the Pedregales. His first response was a common one among political militants: "Very few men have consciousness about women's oppression."

When I asked what he meant, Bernardino expressed the view that such consciousness can come only from participation in organizations such as the one he was involved with, the Unión de Colonias Populares (UCP), which explicitly grapple with issues of oppressive ideologies and practices. Numbers were down in the UCP, Berna informed me, and therefore, by definition, most men remained ignorant about unequal gender relations in the area. The implication was that without an organization to lead them in raising their consciousness, men had little opportunity to be affected significantly by women's leadership and involvement in popular struggles in the Pedregales. Bernardino was articulating a central tenet of the Leninist theory of vanguards, adapted to the needs and abilities of the UCP: without an enlightened group to spell things out for them, people do not and cannot significantly alter their understanding and practice.[9]

Bernardino is no doctrinaire, and he may have worried that his first comments about consciousness of women's oppression sounded a little wooden. In an interview two months after our initial discussion, we returned to the theme of men and women in the *clases populares* and how twenty tumultuous years in the Pedregales had left them. "Check it out, because there are two phenomena," Berna said. "We find families in which the best is for the son, while the daughter has to wash, clean things up, and serve the son. It's a situation which is still widespread in Mexican society: the man has to be waited on, has to have his wash done, has to be served, because he is the one who works and brings home money. This makes men act like machos.[10] But where the popular movement, the urban movement, exists, it has also raised a new consciousness about sharing responsibilities. Because a man also has to get into the struggle. What happens is that many men are urban leaders and they must get into the struggle. So they face a lot of economic limitations. And they have to share [with women] the economic responsibilities as much as the domestic ones."

This topic has broader theoretical implications, because although distinctions between popular and governmental politics have grown in Mexico and much of Latin America since 1968, the opposite has been occurring in terms of what is considered public and private in society (see Foweraker 1990). As people in the *clases populares* have come to rely less on promises of future assistance from government social services—through "poverty alleviation" programs like Solidaridad, for example—they have had to rely increasingly on their own efforts and organization.

A middle-aged woman explained to me one chilly afternoon in December, "That's why I say that the government has not helped us much,

A block meeting of neighbors was called to discuss street paving. Colonia Santo Domingo, 1994

because they don't recognize the work we've done here. We have limited means. For example, I have worked in houses, cleaning and ironing,
in Coyoacán, in rich areas, in Jardines de Coyoacán, in Villa Coapa.
There they buy houses with everything in place. They don't end up having to build the roads as we do. They get sewage lines and everything."

In Santo Domingo widespread forms of mutual assistance have fostered a sense of shared histories, as members of the community, at least
for a time, have become more united through a series of common rites
of passage—for instance, through *faenas,* collective work days, which
usually occur on weekends and for which neighbors gather to donate
their labor for tasks such as laying concrete for roads, building street
altars, and constructing community centers. In these ways, in the 1970s
and 1980s, Santo Domingo and other communities organized and re-
made themselves anew every week. And in the midst of such chaos and
shared experience, gender identities simply could not stay the same.
This last point, says Bernardino, has been a real source of conflict in
families and popular organizations:

"What's more, the groups—which are feminist or not feminist—the
groups of women who are organizing themselves in the *colonia* begin
to see that, 'Oh, *chihuahuas,* my old man won't let me go to the meeting.' They begin to talk about it with other *compañeras,* and to criticize
men because they [the men] are getting in the way of the advance of the

organization, reducing the capabilities of the group. They even tell the men, 'Look, *compañero*, either get involved in the committees or let your *compañera* do it. Because there is no other way. We need community participation.' This has meant that little by little relations in the family are beginning to change. In organized groups, it's changed a lot."

CHRISTIAN BASE COMMUNITIES

In the invasions of the early 1970s in the area that today includes Santo Domingo and Ajusco, the ensuing establishment of the shantytowns, and the later stabilization of daily life in the Pedregales, nuns, priests, and lay workers of the Iglesia de la Resurrección were among the most earnest and consistent advocates of the self-organization and self-management of the population. The Iglesia de la Resurrección promotes the iconoclastic views of liberation theology, which throughout Latin America for the past twenty-five years has attempted to make the ancient gospel of the Catholic Church relevant to the existential needs of its parishioners. The Iglesia is one of five churches in the greater Mexico City area associated with *comunidades eclesiales de base* (CEBs; Christian Base Communities). Base Communities represent a grassroots movement in the past thirty years organized by clergy and lay people within the Catholic Church in Latin America who are committed to improving their communities through direct efforts to secure justice in their societies.[11] In Colonia Ajusco, the Iglesia de la Resurrección is a center for many neighborhood and occasionally citywide political activities. For example, the Iglesia served as the venue for a talk, to a standing-room-only audience, by Rigoberta Menchu in late January 1993, shortly after she had won the Nobel Peace Prize.

In winter 1993, the head priest of the Iglesia, Padre Víctor Verdín, told me that there were some sixty-five Comunidades de Base, each made up of at least five (and often many more) people, affiliated with the Iglesia de la Resurrección. Though there had been many more in the past, numbers were again growing. Of great significance is that at least 70 percent of the members of the Comunidades are women. Thus, as in most other religious communities in Mexico, most of the participants are women. In Santo Domingo, women are also closely associated with liberation theology, which has had a long and significant history of opposition to official discourse and elite domination.

As *animadores* (activist-organizers) in the Base Communities, these women are known for their dedication to serving the poor, and for their skills at public speaking. The CEBs insist that women as well as men be trained in public speaking so that they can carry out their responsibilities more effectively. Because of the example and preaching of the CEB representatives, advocates of liberation theology have paid special attention to changing gender relations in the Pedregales. The results have been mixed, but Padre Víctor and the *animadores* have persisted in trying to find new ways to resolve older problems in families in the area. One day I asked Padre Víctor about single mothers and the economic pressures and cultural conventions that impel and allow men to abandon their families.[12]

"I don't know what to tell you. Yes, you find cases of single mothers, and still it is often the case that if a girl gets pregnant they make sure the two get married in the church right away. But if they are very young we try to dissuade them, because marriage in this case is not appropriate."

"What do you say? That they should not get married?"

"That they should not get married at that time. What we propose is that they live together if they wish, without being married, and that in this sharing—because clearly there is a responsibility toward the third party in this arrangement!—they test themselves to see if they are going to be a family and if they want to be a family, not assuming anything permanent that later they would have to break, but before this to mature a little to see if they really are a couple. It seems better to us this way than marrying in the church, or in a civil ceremony, and then a few months later deciding to divorce, which is the same thing."

Through the efforts of the Base Communities to encourage novel approaches to pressing issues such as pregnancy among unwed mothers, women in the Pedregales are once more linked in the popular imagination to radical and progressive political efforts aimed at changing society from the ground up.

THE REPRODUCTION OF FATHERING

They've killed my son, but now all of you are my sons.

> Celia Castillo de Chávez (quoted in Massacre in
> Mexico, by Elena Poniatowska)

Our neighbor Angela, the grandmother who began caring for Liliana in the afternoons shortly after we arrived in Santo Domingo, often empha-

Resting outside her kitchen, Angela offers her perspective on Mexican machos and the women who tolerate them.

sized to me that the only time I would find changes in male attitudes and behavior was when I encountered women (mothers) who were no longer willing to tolerate machismo. She and I often talked and sometimes argued about why men and women think and act in the ways they do, and in particular about the relative influence social factors outside immediate family relations have on gender identity. I sometimes tried to accuse her of blaming victims for their suffering and the like, but Angela always insisted that women, by refusing to indulge macho men, can do something about changing the situation.[13]

Raised by her grandmother in Mexico City, Angela went to school through *primaria*, the sixth grade. She married Juan in 1956, and, she says, though like all couples they have had their problems, they are still together. She is the mother of four grown children, and is a grandmother many times over. Because her back has been in bad shape for years and it is hard for her to visit others as much as she would like, Angela's sisters, nieces, nephews, and other family members stop by to see her regularly. So do numerous friends and neighbors from Santo Domingo, including an old friend who always stops by to tell Angela a new dirty joke, an aspiring young rock guitarist whose long hair embarrasses his mother, and a feisty junior priest from a small church in the *colonia* who comes by periodically for a good lunch. People who have rented a spare room in her home at one time or another also drop in for confessions and gossip, and to ask Angela for advice about their lovers, jobs, and assorted aches and pains.

Though all her daughters were encouraged to do so, Angela herself has never worked outside the home. And though she resents what she sees partly as a domesticity enforced on her by others, at the same time she insists that women be held accountable for their situation. This view is linked to her belief that women's mothering duties are their most important tasks. Angela's view that parenting is a mainly female responsibility thus reflects unmistakable cultural conservatism based in part on Angela's reasonable assessment of how power is distributed within her family, most particularly a mother's authority over her children. To Angela's way of thinking, changing this configuration— through, for instance, greater joint parenting when children are young—might threaten the loss of one of the mainstays of women's cultural power. This would be especially true if such a change had not been part of larger sociocultural transformations in gender relations. Angela's predicament is thus that attempts to maintain the status quo regarding mothering can paradoxically entail a stubborn sense of agency on the part of some women. This paradox is related to what Steve Stern (1995) calls the "myth of complicity"—that is, the entanglement of women in their own domination. This "myth," says Stern, is not so much wrong as incomplete. It entails an argument that can be used to exonerate men from their responsibilities.

Regardless of whether both parents work outside the home, little boys in Colonia Santo Domingo learn a lot from their mothers about how to be men and not women, about what boys may do and girls may not and vice versa. There *are* many women in Santo Domingo who have actively participated in the construction of the *colonia* and struggles in the broader social arena in Mexico City, and these women have truly stood many aspects of oppressive gender relations on their head. Yet even these women may trivialize one particular matter that, despite its seeming triteness, some of their husbands and sons privately admit is a continuing source of frustration for them as men.

Among the most common admonitions of women to little boys in Mexico City is "*¡No llores como niña!* [Don't cry like a girl!]" The persistence and seriousness of men's complaints among themselves about not being able to cry is striking. No doubt aware that to some the male-crying issue might even seem silly, some men occasionally ex- press anger that because crying is culturally proscribed behavior for men, they have since childhood been physically unable to cry.

In meetings that I attended of men who had histories of beating their spouses, the subject of crying was an incongruously recurring theme of male subjectivity. (The men voluntarily attended these gatherings, indicating a greater desire for changing gender relations than would perhaps be true of their male brethren in general.) This involved not simply the agony and humiliation of crying in front of others, perhaps especially strangers, which frequently occurred in these meetings. Some men vividly recalled mothers forbidding them to cry at all when they were children. As one participant put it, " 'Machos don't cry!' they tell us. But, yes, we men do cry—alone, silently, hidden. Yes, we do cry."

Some men in Santo Domingo voice the objection that they are ex- pected to change in certain ways in relation to women but not allowed to change in others. Unless sanctioned by women, behavior such as cry- ing by men in public often remains forbidden in the minds of many men. At Ricardo's house in Santo Domingo one afternoon, the sixty- year-old grandfather was recounting how the fates had conspired against him throughout his unhappy life and eventually brought him to his present pitiful and unemployed state. He was very tipsy after nip- ping on a bottle of rum most of the morning. He felt worthless, he said, and he began to sob. His wife, a woman who has stoically tolerated his alcoholism for decades, nonetheless could not abide his bawling, which she saw as an unbridled form of (male) narcissism.[14] "Shut up your crying, old fool. At least don't whine in front of the company." It was reminiscent of a scene from Vicente Leñero's (1970:109) play *Los albañiles* (The laborers):

> ISIDRO [teenager]: Are you crying? Don't tell me you're crying.
> DON JESÚS [old man]: Yes, I'm crying. And now make fun of me for it. Go tell everyone about it. "Don Jesús was bawling like an old woman."

How to cope with the traumas of childhood and old age and the modern dilemmas of "flexible" unemployment and *ser hombre* (being a man) are a few of the challenges facing men in Santo Domingo at a time when they see certain of their male prerogatives eroded, with no compensation in sight. Given the perception among many men that women such as those in Santo Domingo have been stirring up entirely too much trouble, it is no wonder that many feel the need for at least cathartic release—but they are still not allowed to cry.

GENDER MARKING AND THE THANKS MOTHERS DESERVE

As part of a taken-for-granted process through which boys become men, it is common in Santo Domingo for women to joke with little boys about how many *novias* (girlfriends) they are going to have. Girls are seldom if ever asked about numbers of *novios* (boyfriends). In Miguelito's case, at the age of four he was encouraged by his mother and others to proudly announce that he already had several girlfriends. Shortly after becoming acquainted with us, Miguelito, Angela's grandson, generously announced that if my daughter Liliana (then barely three months old) also wanted to be his *novia,* she could easily be added to the list. As our families became more familiar within a few months, a curious thing happened. When Angela began to refer to herself as Liliana's grandmother, to Miguelito's mother, Norma, as Liliana's aunt, and so on, Miguelito was no longer prompted to consider Liliana as his girlfriend. Instead Angela and Norma began calling the children brother and sister. As young Miguelito knew, this made even play-acted romantic attachments between them out of the question.[15]

Women and men do unconsciously pass on habitual ways of looking at social life and participating in cultural events. At the same time, as Giddens emphatically states, "every social actor knows a great deal about the conditions of reproduction of the society of which he or she is a member" (1979:5; emphasis removed from original). So it is that an elaborate performance of emphasis and de-emphasis upon gender distinctions is begun at birth in Santo Domingo. For instance, certain popular expressions about newborns, prompted by an examination of an infant's genitalia, are increasingly, if often jokingly, contested by women in the *colonia*. For boys, the comments have often been: "*¡Qué grande y fuerte!* [How big and strong!]"; "*¡Va a tener un pegue!* [He's going to be quite a catch!]"; "*¡Qué cara inteligente!* [What an intelligent face!]" For girls: "*¡Qué ojos bonitos!* [What pretty eyes!]"; "*¡Qué piernas bonitas!* [What pretty legs!]"; "*¡Carne para los lobos!* [Meat for the wolves!]" Boys and girls from infancy on are commonly referred to as *papacitos* and *mamacitas,* little daddies and little mommies. In daily conversations among women, and far more seldom among men, such expressions increasingly elicit explicit challenges such as "Girls can be intelligent, too!"

Yet marking "differences" between boys and girls is certainly an active practice of mothers and other women throughout Santo Domingo. Whether differences necessarily imply inequalities is, as we have seen, itself a contested issue, as many women seek to call attention to the "positive qualities and capabilities" of girls and women.

Gender marking gathers force among many families in Colonia Santo Domingo beginning when children are four or five years old. During a Mother's Day festival in May at which children in a day-care program danced and performed, there was little difference in costuming or choreography for the youngest entertainers; they all hopped around dressed up as big balls, like rotund pieces of fruit. The participation by four- and five-year-olds was an entirely different matter. Each child wore a costume specially designed and made by her or his mother (or, in Miguelito's case, by his grandmother). Conveying a sexy, come-hither look, the girls were dressed in black miniskirts, fishnet tights, red leotard tops, and berets. The boys strutted about in black pants, white shirts with suspenders, bow ties, and black fedoras cocked back gallantly on their heads. Unlike the younger children, who when they danced all ran and jumped alike to the music, among the older children the boys led the girls, twirled them around, and even dipped them across their knees as best they could. The crowd applauded enthusiastically throughout.[16]

Conflicting interpretations of the gendered aspects of such events represent certain shifts and unresolved contradictions that are broadly characteristic of gender relations throughout Mexico today, where few habits and customs are immune to reinterpretation. Take the case of how new meanings are placed on old dolls.

At the gala celebration of one *quinceañera* (a girl marking her fifteenth birthday) that I attended in November in Oaxaca City, a large
white doll played an important symbolic role in this rite of passage. The
doll was first seen being carried on a silver platter during the church
ceremony. Later, during the party at her family's remote hillside home,
Eugenia marked her transition to womanhood by holding the doll in
her right hand while a bouquet of red roses rested in her left.

I never had a chance to ask the *quinceañera* about the doll, but two
interpretations were offered to me later by friends in Santo Domingo as
to the significance of the doll at the Oaxaca fiesta. One friend held that
the doll announced that the girl was now ready to *have* a baby. Another
felt that the doll symbolized that the girl no longer *was* a baby. In the
first interpretation, girls are raised to be mothers; in the second, they
are raised to be women. It may well be that such vying interpretations
are more fully offered in *colonias* such as this where debates over
"women's work" have achieved public prominence, but in this age of
large-scale transnational migration and satellite television transmis-
sions, I rather think that reinterpretations are the stuff of conversations
throughout Mexico.

The differences voiced in the two explanations about the *quinceañera* doll reveal some of the tensions that have developed in female identities in many parts of Mexico, and how motherhood there is not being
simply and identically reproduced from one generation to the next in
Santo Domingo or elsewhere. And if women who play an integral role
in the construction of masculinities are changing, so too are their men.

MEXICAN MOTHERS AND OTHER VIRGINS

Official representations of women in Mexico often define women
through recourse to national iconography, specifically the Mexican
Mother and the Virgin of Guadalupe. Despite these appeals, in Santo
Domingo I find little evidence for a particular theory, popular among
psychologists, of a timeless "Mexican national character": that relationships between sons and mothers are usually the closest in families
and thus constitute a widespread and relatively stable cultural pattern.[17] Instead, mother-son relations in the *colonia* depend far more on
specific family history and individual personalities than on any overriding cultural imperatives. Sons in Santo Domingo are not more (or less)
doting toward their mothers than toward their fathers in any general
sense. Nor are mothers routinely more (or less) attentive to their sons

than to their daughters, though both mothers and fathers are often more tolerant of their boys than of their girls.

To conclude that mother-son relations are unique in Santo Domingo—perhaps because of women's greater involvement in extra-household political activities, for example—would be a mistake. A more accurate assessment is gained by contrasting once again the official discourse on motherhood with popular uses of this same imagery. In Santo Domingo and elsewhere, mother-son relations (or those between mothers and daughters, for that matter) are often embraced or creatively contested as an integral part of people's dialogue with larger national symbols.

On an abstract, theological plane, if you ask women and men in Colonia Santo Domingo today to name the *santos* to whom they pray and with whom they feel a special affinity, the Virgen de Guadalupe—the Virgin of Guadalupe—and Jesús are the most common responses you will receive.[18] People's relationship with the Virgen—Mexico's national symbol, the mother and queen of the Mexicans, the mother of the Indians—is very personal and in some cases is possibly related to psychological anxieties stemming from human mother-child relations. But the key symbolism of the Mexican Virgen mainly lies elsewhere, as a national(ist) cultural feature. Tracing the history of Mexicans' relationship with the Virgen during the past several hundred years provides insights into gender and maternal relations overall and into the changing connotations of what it means to be a Mexican man in particular.

According to other popular representations, sons' worship of their mothers is a prime element in defining "Latino society" in general. Though they may love their own mothers dearly, Mexican male immigrants in Chicago, where I spent several years as a political organizer, sometimes refer to these women in less than chivalrous ways to distinguish themselves from the Puerto Ricans in that city. On more than one occasion in the Mexican barrio called the Pilsen I was told, "The difference between us and the *borinqueños* [Puerto Ricans] is that you can say '¡Chinga tu madre! [Fuck your mother]' to another Mexican and live to tell about it." This is a gross exaggeration, but it makes the point that the code of defending one's mother's honor—to the death!—may be more important in some "Latin" cultural contexts than in others. It is yet another illustration that we generalize about all Spanish-speaking males at our peril.

The socioeconomic traumas of modernization weigh heavily on mothers who every day scramble to provide sustenance for their children. One afternoon Berta described to me her own parental anguish: "You neglect your children by going to work. I neglected mine a lot in terms of food." Yet Berta's concerns are not reducible to those of just one more guilt-ridden working mother. Not all women entering the paid work force share the same anxieties, for neglect can take many forms, and Berta's children have never wanted for emotional nurturance. She continued:

"When I began working, my husband started cooking beans or whatever there might be. As he worked nights, he saw to it that our little girl got to school. He took her there and gave her whatever was left to eat— soup, beans. Then, as soon as they paid me, I'd bring them home milk and fruit. I'd get home at night and I'd say, 'Look, I've brought you milk and bread for tomorrow.' "

The modern Mexican nation has routinely been presented in politics and the fine arts as male in character. Yet because women are expected to contribute to the national project, they inevitably come into conflict with its engendered values and goals. Women as domestic beings cannot provide for the needs of their families; hence increasingly they must work outside the home alongside their men. Women's challenge to domesticity in Santo Domingo and other *colonias populares* in the Mexican capital is as widespread as it is varied in conviction. And it is a key source and consequence of modern transformations in gender identities.

MOTHERLY CONTRADICTIONS

My friend and neighbor Miguel does not remember a lot about the invasion of Santo Domingo because he was still young when it took place. He and his family were among the few people already living in the area in 1971, and he does recall that in those days he had more freedom to walk wherever he wanted and that he used to be able to see rabbits, squirrels, snakes, and other animals. He also remembers that during the invasion "the women took care of things in the day. The women were the ones in the day and the men at night." I asked Miguel how women took care of things. "Well, with guns, with rifles, with pistols, and some with rocks and others with sticks, whatever they could." Miguel noted frankly that invading women sometimes fought the few women who were already living in the area, and that their pitched battles were a noteworthy feature of the origins of the *colonia*. His is not a portrait of women playing a unified role in the invasion.

And this is partly why questions about "the role of women" in the invasion seem odd and unanswerable to many residents of the *colonia* today. Whom are you talking about? At what time? Over what issues? Women in the neighborhood did not act as a unified group, nor simply as two groups—those who went out in public and those who stayed in their homes. Bernardino, the community organizer from Colonia Ajusco, told me about confrontations he had had when defending lands occupied by invaders who refused to pay bribes to police and to the *caciques* (bosses) in the area:

"I'm telling you, women were the ones who every time some invader got kicked out would beat him and smash his things in the street. They'd beat them with sticks. These women came with Fidel Torres [a *cacique* in the area] and would tell me, 'Hey, you, asshole! What are you doing? Don't you know that I'm the owner of this lot?' I'd tell them that we were improving the housing because they'd abandoned it."

On the one hand it is no coincidence that community activists like Bernardino have long advised women in the Pedregales to get title to their homes and land so they will not be evicted if their husbands should one day leave them. On the other hand, in no one's experience have the political or the physical battles in the area involved men on one side and women on the other. Women and men have fought side by side, and they have faced off against one another.

Few people in the *colonia* employ the expression "the woman of Santo Domingo," not because of any sociological unsophistication, but because the term is woefully deficient in expressing the realities of women's lives, individually and collectively. When I asked Fili, who has been a leftist leader in the Pedregales for nearly two decades, about whether a certain other woman was a role model for youth in the community, she deliberated for a moment and then replied that she thought not. She felt that the daughters of this other woman were very "traditional," and therefore concluded that the other woman's radical history was not seriously affecting the younger generation. When I expressed the belief that such leaders might have influence beyond their immediate families, Fili allowed that this might be true.

Few residents of the *colonia* associate community activism and opposition to state policies with men or manliness particularly, and in this sense male identities in Santo Domingo stand in contrast to those in other contexts, such as the one examined by Herzfeld (1985:23) in Crete, where "one of the true marks of manhood is the ability to hold one's head high in the face of government repression." Detailed ethnographic portraits of specific historical circumstances, such as the present study and the one by Herzfeld, allow us to analyze what constitutes masculinity and its dialectical opposites in different times and places, and to refute generalizations such as those that argue that male violence against women is largely a displacement of the modern state's "original" violence against men.

Though there is much that has not changed in the *colonia*, there is broad consensus that life for many women today in Colonia Santo Domingo is irrevocably different from what it was for their grandmothers and mothers, and that although there is continuity from one generation to the next, there is also a transformation taking place in ways of thinking and doing that is ushering in novel arrangements and imaginings. Where women find themselves in the course of this transformation has consequences for men—particularly in the area of sexuality.

FIVE

Men's Sex

There is something compelling about being both male and
female, about having an entry into both worlds.

Gloria Anzaldúa, Borderlands/La Frontera

SEX EDUCATIONS

Alfredo Pérez's wandering father, like many men of the older generations according to Alfredo, was absent for most of his son's life. Before
his father died, however, Alfredo Pérez found him and, as he recounts,

"I took my wife and children to see him. He asked me to forgive him.
I told him, 'Don't worry about it, Papa. I'm no one to judge you, only
God.' A week later he died. I went to see him one Saturday, and by the
next Saturday they told me he had died. When he died, well, we went
to the burial and to the vigil. A lot of people began looking at me. I saw
my sisters, and they said to me, 'Look, we want to introduce you to
Papa's son.' So a man said to me, 'Glad to meet you, my name is Alfredo
Pérez.' And then another, 'How are you, my name is Alfredo Pérez.' I
met five Alfredos, all with the same last name, all my half brothers—
Alfredo Pérez, Alfredo Pérez, Alfredo Pérez, each one."

Like his many namesake brothers, Alfredo Pérez was born in Mexico
City, and he has lived there all his life, arriving in Santo Domingo a few
years after the initial invasion. He describes himself as a carpenter,
though like most men in the *clases populares* in Mexico, Alfredo counts
carpentry as just one of many skills he has acquired over the years, and
not one for which he has regularly found employment. Alfredo spent
decades doing factory jobs, driving trucks, and occasionally hammering
nails, and today he likes to look back on his working life and how he
has kept trim over all these years. He had wild years with alcohol and

affairs, he tells me, but those days are long past. Now his family is what counts.

"I've been married for thirty-two years, and we've had our ups and downs. I fight with her, we say things to each other. But she respects me, and I her. Even though we fight and we stop talking for a day or two, afterwards we're happy. And that's the way we will go through life, God willing. But the fine thing is to have some children who respect and admire you. I see now how they respect and admire and love me, and it's a *semilla* [seed] that I planted and taught to grow straight and tall." For Alfredo, one's self-identification as a man is closely connected with insemination, financial maintenance, and moral authority, all of which are in turn largely predicated on men's relationships with women.

People in Colonia Santo Domingo speak of men like Alfredo's father as more common in the past. If many Mexican male identities used to be wrapped up in adultery, polygamy, and siring many children, especially male children, today these are less central concerns. These issues are still important to varying degrees to some men, but in the *colonia* many younger men in particular have begun thinking more reflexively about their bodies than their fathers ever did, and today there is a growing sense that sexuality is as much a possibility as it is an ultimatum, that there are multiple sexualities—not just two—and that sexuality can and does change. In short, men in Santo Domingo are participants in what Sedgwick (1990:1) calls "the long crisis of modern sexual definition."

These men today express greater self-consciousness about sexuality, not in the sense that they talk more about sex, but that their manner of talking about sex is different. Two key factors have contributed to these transformations: one, the greater accessibility and widespread use of modern methods of birth control in the past twenty years in Mexico City; and two, in a less obvious but still significant fashion, the open challenge of homosexuality as a major form of sexual life and expression.[1] Both these factors have had direct and indirect ramifications on the construction of contemporary, modern sexualities in Mexican society.

Adult men have rarely died from childbirth in Mexico or anywhere else, of course, but the separation of sex from pregnancy, childbirth, and child rearing has had a profound impact on them as well as on women, and altered more than just fertility rates for men and women.[2] Sexuality increasingly has the ability to culturally transform personal and family life. And more than ever before, sexuality, potentially at least, can similarly be transformed, including sexuality in relation to romantic love.[3] Sexuality in this context is less and less tied to biological imperatives and more associated with desire, which is subjective and transitory. Yet this analysis of desire must always follow from its contextualization, because, as Lancaster (1992:270) insists, "[d]esire is thus always part of the cultural, economic, and ideological world of social relations and social conflicts."[4]

In the wake of studies such as those by Foucault (1980a, 1980b) and others, sex is now less taken for granted in (Western) academia. In a parallel manner, in Santo Domingo and other *colonias populares* in Mexico City, too, sex is less certain, and as Laqueur (1990:13) notes in his historical study of sexuality in Europe, to a growing extent "the comfortable notion is shaken that man is man and woman is woman." In the Pedregales of Mexico City, for instance, people talk not only of distinctions between the sexualities of men and women, but to a greater extent now also of differences among men and among women. Sex has a social history today and not just a biological evolution. One implication of this development that I will explore in this chapter is that, rather than sanctify as cultural shibboleths those particular mores and practices popularly linked to sexuality in Mexico—male lechery leading to adultery and the *casa chica,* for example, or the promiscuous sex of single men—we would do better to reexamine them under a well-ground historical lens.

In my formal interviews with residents of Santo Domingo I asked men and women who was responsible for teaching their children about sexuality. After several interviews I also began asking people with whom they had discussed sex when they were young. Most had never discussed sexuality with either of their parents. All but a few said that they themselves felt a responsibility to teach their own children more about sex, though people differed, not clearly along gender lines, as to who should do it. Some thought both parents should handle the task together; others believed mothers should talk with their daughters and fathers with their sons. Several parents admitted that they preferred to wait until their children came to them with questions based on what they had heard or learned at school or elsewhere rather than initiate discussions on the topic.

In Santo Domingo mothers report that they do commonly talk with their daughters about menstruation. Sometimes in these discussions women explain that with their periods the girls have also reached an age when they can become pregnant, and mothers may impart to their daughters whatever they know about the functioning of the female reproductive system. Few fathers and fewer mothers, it seems, talk with their boys about these issues. Thus if there is great ignorance among all youth regarding sexuality, however uninformed girls may be about sex, it seems probable that boys know even less and have even fewer adults with whom they can discuss their concerns regarding their bodies and reproduction.

Based on interviews in Santo Domingo, on discussions with students at the José Vasconcelos Junior High School in the *colonia,* and on figures compiled in the 1988 (Mexican) *National Survey on Sexuality and the Family among Youth,*[5] most young men speak with male friends or with their fathers about sexuality. Around 40 percent of high school students, according to the *National Survey,* had spoken about the subject with male teachers. As for young women, most receive information about sexuality from their mothers and some from female friends and (for high school students) from female teachers.

At least some discussion about sex and bodies is beginning to occur—in contrast to what took place in earlier generations. This situation contributes to an expanding awareness of the distinctions between sex and procreation and a retreat from the perceived difference between what Adrienne Rich identifies as "fathering" and "mothering" (in the United States):

> To "father" a child suggests above all to beget, to provide the sperm which fertilizes the ovum. To "mother" a child implies a continuing presence, lasting at least nine months, more often for years. (1976:xi–xii)

While parenting and fathering practices vary significantly across space and time, in Mexico historically there has been a greater cultural significance for men than women regarding insemination, and therefore a closer identification for men than for women between the act of generative sex and social status. Recent studies have called attention to women's bearing and caring for children as distinguishing social markers in Mexico and have discussed how some women utilize the culturally esteemed status of motherhood to further their involvement in political activities (see Logan 1984; Nader 1986; and Martin 1990). But all this is a long way from identifying coitus with mothering.

Perhaps it is significant that there is no direct translation into Spanish for the English expressions *fathering* and *mothering.* Simply to render the former as *ser padre* clarifies nothing, since this phrase may be understood as either "to be a father" or "to be a parent." That is, even to state "to be a father" implies in Spanish (in its own linguistically biased manner) "to be a parent," just as being a parent in Spanish is lexically also being a father. This does not mean that Mexicans or other Spanish speakers are in any fundamental sense restricted in what they do by the peculiarities of their native tongue, but it does indicate that in Spanish some cultural concepts are expressed in more linguistically convoluted ways than are other concepts.[6]

PROCREATION

The importance of "blood ties" between parents and children came up unexpectedly in my discussion with the *muchachos* on the street one day. I happened to mention that one of my brothers had died fourteen years earlier. I told the youths that Andrew was not my brother by blood, but that nonetheless my mother continued to grieve for him, her stepson, as she would have for me. I told them that my mother still sometimes cried when she thought about my brother.

"I say if you had died instead," responded Esteban, "she would cry more because you were her son, right?"

"Maybe. I don't know."

"Sure, she loves your brother, but not like she loves you," said Celso.

"You can't compare a child born from your insides [*entrañas*], who you know is yours, who belongs to you," Jaime added.

I tried to take the discussion away from Andrew by saying, "If you have four children maybe you're going to love one more than the others."

"I think so," said Enrique.

"I don't think so," said Jaime.

"I say no, Mateo, because I have two children and I love them both the same," countered Celso.

Enrique, ever the diplomat, tried to resolve the debate. "What happens is that there are different factors. Maybe your mother cries for the boy because he spent a lot of time with her, he won her affection, he knew how to treat her with respect. Maybe the *muchacho* behaved better toward her than you did."

"That's what my mother sometimes says," I confided, and the *muchachos* smiled sympathetically.

Gabriel talked to me a lot about his four children. It was not until I'd known him for several months that I realized that the oldest two are

stepchildren from his wife's previous marriage. Gabi says he loves each
child equally and seeks love from each in return. For Gabi, ignoring the
ties of blood is a point of pride.

In his late thirties, the skeptical Gabriel has worked for years as a
skilled mechanic on the curb of the same side street in Santo Domingo.
By fixing cars and *combis* on the street, Gabriel not only avoids costly
garage rental but is also able to engage passersby in conversation. He is
known among friends as a free spirit, and religion and spirituality are
precisely the issues that animate him most. He is especially interested in
the Aztecs and has a collection of posters and pamphlets about them.
He has taken Nahuatl classes from time to time, and he uses Nahua
names for his two youngest children. For Gabriel, it does not matter
how children come into the world. When they come into his life, a man
must relate to them as a father; this is what adults do, he says. It is of
little consequence from whose loins or seed they come. Gabriel's ideas
may be exceptional in the *colonia,* but they are not unique.

I met Raúl, who describes himself as bisexual, outside Santo Domingo, yet what he told me about men in other areas being afraid of
bisexuals and homosexuals applies equally to some men in the *colonia.*
"This is a *machista* society of total machos. If you're not macho, if you
don't have children with five or six women, you're not macho. But I
don't think it's necessary to have five, or six, or seven women to show
you are a man."

I asked Toño, a single man of twenty-seven, about whether having
children, especially boys, was important to him. "For me," he replied,
"having a lot of kids to prove you're macho is *una chingadera* [equiva-
lent to "a lot of bullshit"]. Those ideas are forty years old." Though
not everyone would agree with Toño's assessment, he touches upon a
sentiment that is more widespread than certain dominant images would
lead us to believe: that Mexican men have to confirm their virility
through fathering many children (in Rich's sense), especially male children.

Nor has the valorization of those who are fruitful and multiply been
an issue solely for men as inseminators. Pronatal policies have been
given boosts not only by Catholic Church doctrine, but also by the heart
of the modern, liberal elite in Mexico. Following the lead of its not-so-
distant neighbor to the north, on 13 April 1922 *Excelsior,* Mexico's
newspaper of record, launched a campaign to celebrate the tenth of
May every year as Mother's Day. Every year from 1922 until 1953, the
newspaper awarded a prize to *la madre más prolífica,* the most prolific

mother. Beginning in 1953, the Mexican widow who had made the most sacrifices to educate her children was honored. Mothers who had given birth to only girls were not allowed to compete. In 1968, the prize was given to the mother who since 1910 "had given more sons to the defense of the Fatherland, either as revolutionaries or as members of the National Army" (Acevedo 1982:60–62).

Efforts such as those by the publisher of *Excelsior* in 1922 may have been in part a response to popular will. Margarita Melville (personal communication) reports that her grandmother was active in a 1922 campaign to celebrate Mother's Day in Mexico City, and thus it is possible that the publisher was also supporting a preexisting demand. And, after all, if there were not a deep affection for mothers in Mexico, *Excelsior* never would have proposed celebrating Mother's Day, and the holiday never would have been accepted as it has been. Yet the more critical question would seem to be, how do ventures that are at least in part orchestrated by elite social classes create, reshape, and channel, and not simply reflect, the desires of so many nonelites? Returning to Gramsci's formulation of contradictory consciousness, the initiation of Mother's Day celebrations in Mexico provides one case of how uncritical consciousness came to be accepted and spread.

The other aspect of contradictory consciousness relates to consciousness that arises from and is reflected in the practical transformation of the real world.[7] If fatherhood in the minds of people in Santo Domingo is less associated with profligate behavior than the stereotypes would indicate, or at least if such behavior is becoming more proscribed, then these changes should be evident in the practical, everyday experiences of men in the *colonia*.

Bruner's distinction between behavior and experience is relevant in this regard. The former, he says,

> implies an outside observer describing someone else's actions, as if one were an audience to an event; it also implies a standardized routine that one simply goes through. An experience is more personal, as it refers to an active self, to a human being who not only engages in but shapes an action. (1986:5)

My concern here, with regard to the pragmatics of motherhood and fatherhood in Santo Domingo, is above all to take the uncritical acceptance of standardized routine, which is implicated in behavior, and contrast it with the active shaping of human life experiences.

The point was brought home to me when I went one day in early spring to the butcher shop on Huehuetzin Street to get some meat for Liliana. Although meat is a little more expensive there than it is in the supermarket, Guillermo and his brother always grind the beef twice when they know it will be fed to an infant. As I was leaving I thanked Guillermo and said something to the effect of "OK, gotta go cook this up with some pasta and—" Before I had time to add "vegetables," Guillermo interrupted me and said, "No, not pasta. That's just going to make her fat. *Sabes, el padre no sólo los engendra sino también tiene que atender a su alimentación* [You know, the father doesn't just procreate, he's also got to make sure they eat right]." Guillermo felt that since I was a new father he had the right and responsibility to give me advice when warranted. By wording his counsel of fatherly love and care in contrast to the familiar image of Man the Procreator, Guillermo was, probably consciously, positioning himself in opposition to a history, or at least a story, of Mexican men.

MALE POTENCY

I would recommend that at least once a week men
have sexual relations, since, for example in boxing, it
stimulates masculine responses which are very
necessary for combat. It's false that abstention is
necessary or positive. If you have sexual contact, even
twice, before the fight, you feel more like a man and
your masculinity surges forth.

> Bernardo Vargas, psychologist for the Pachuca
> futbol team (quoted in Escenas de pudor y
> liviandad, by Carlos Monsiváis)

At least one history of Mexican men has told of them desiring not simply offspring in general but male heirs in particular, and of using their issue as irrefutable confirmation of the potency of their seed. In retrospect I realize that I sometimes baited men for statements that might confirm this "well-known" male cultural standard. I asked César one day, "Come on, tell the truth. Doesn't it bother you that you don't have a son?"

"No, I've never had a preference," he responded, content with his two teenage daughters.

"Because, that's the notion that—"

"Yeah, it's that machismo, that 'If it's not a boy, you leave the house.' No, no. I have always told my woman—she knows, my family knows—that whatever God brings us, great! I never asked for a boy, but there are a lot of folks who do prefer boys."

"Still?"

"Yes, still. I have a brother-in-law, and he just had a son. He told his woman that if it hadn't been a boy, she shouldn't have bothered to find him. I think that this kind of person is sick in the head, because we are already living in a modern age, and we should realize that it's not what one wants. Because if you want a boy, it's so easy to say, 'I want you to have a boy,' but then the whole world would be full of boys! It's like they say, 'Go to the corner, at an intersection, and when the moon is full, do this, and do that, so you'll get a boy.' That's a lie. Nature is so pretty that she provides us with everything we need. If she wants a boy, then a boy; if not, a girl."

I was determined, however, to find men who esteemed their male children more than their female, and were not too "modern" to say so. Elena told me that her husband, Carlos, had always wanted a boy, as did she, but that they had three girls. Yet when I talked to Carlos he said he was happier with girls, because they were easier to control. Then Diego Trujillo and his wife, both active in the Christian Base Communities, told me about their children: first a girl, the oldest, then another two girls, and then a boy. "Finally!" I exclaimed. Diego looked at me with a puzzled expression and politely responded, "No, we don't feel that way." Perhaps in my zeal to uncover the renowned preference for sons among Mexican men, I had left informants wondering instead, "Is this how they think in the United States?" [8]

In my own defense, I think that Diego probably understood just what I was getting at: an insulting image of Mexican men and their alleged need for male offspring. Therefore, I took his comments as more than a simple affirmation of his feelings and those of his wife about their personal situation. He was also attempting to refute inaccurate, idealized, and often racist beliefs held in the United States about Mexican men, at least the "traditional" ones.

Men and women speak easily of men who want to keep their wives pregnant all the time. But, curiously, among the people I know in Colonia Santo Domingo, no man wants to identify himself as such, nor does any woman want to label her husband in this way. (This is yet another instance of people approving stereotyped characterizations of others while insisting that those generalizations do not apply to themselves.) Referring to men other than her husband or brothers, Lupita the nurse summarized:

"The husbands who are Mexican machos say, 'I want to have children all the time.' And they want to have the woman pregnant while they are on the *otro lado* [other side—that is, the United States] doing whatever. And when women who have a lot of children, when they have a cesarean birth, they are asked if they want a tubal ligation. The woman who has a Mexican husband says, 'No, because my husband will get angry. Don't sterilize me until God lets me do it.' People get upset as well if you put in IUDs."

The impact of feminist ideas and practices is decidedly mixed in Colonia Santo Domingo, as was revealed in a seemingly exceptional story that Daniel told me about birth control and abortion. During his wife's second pregnancy, Dani told me, she wanted to get an abortion. Daniel was adamant that every life is sacred and that this one had already begun, despite the fact that he is an avowed agnostic and someone who openly ridicules the Catholic Church. On hearing Daniel's story, it was easy for me to conclude, "Here's a guy who's forcing his wife to bear his progeny." Before I had a chance to broach this idea with him, however, Daniel added slyly, "So you know what I did then? I went out and got myself cut"—that is, he got a vasectomy, something that puts him in a rather exclusive category among my friends in Santo Domingo. This was Dani's way of making short- and long-term deals with his wife. Dani's feelings and actions also illustrate that contradictory male identities—in this case, those relating to male sexualities—are to be found not only when comparing groups of men in the population as a whole, but within individual men as well.

According to statistics compiled in a survey titled "Report on the Survey Regarding Knowledge, Attitudes, and Practices in the Use of Birth Control Methods by the Working Class Male Population of Mexico City," which was commissioned in 1990 by the health department of the Mexican government, slightly less than 2 percent of the male participants who were at least thirty-five years old had had vasectomies, whereas the figure for younger men was so low as to be negligible. Men were the active users of birth control only about one-quarter of the time, even when withdrawal and rhythm methods were employed. Among couples using some form of contraception, tubal ligations had been performed on over half the female partners of the men over thirty-five interviewed in the survey, whereas the IUD was the most common method for women having sexual relations with the men under thirty-five. Condoms, according to the report, were used by 5 to 6 percent of the men.[9] These figures agree with my understanding, based on field-work in Santo Domingo, that birth control is popularly seen as mainly a female responsibility.

The experiences of one woman neighbor illustrate government-sanctioned pressures on women (and men) to keep contraception a woman's concern. My friend went to get condoms at the ISSSTE, a state health service, where she was told by a male government doctor that prophylactics were only for promiscuous women. Besides, the doctor added, condoms are painful for men, so she should give her husband a break and get an IUD. Despite other changes in attitudes and practice concerning sexuality, the doctor's policies match a common one among men in Mexico City concerning who takes responsibility for birth control.

The Mexican government's continued refusal to legalize abortion is another form of controlling women's reproductive options (see Lamas 1992). In the case of abortions, however, class distinctions result in highly unequal consequences. Whereas women of means can easily arrange for an abortion in Mexico City, those in the *clases populares* must resort to unsafe practices or carry unwanted pregnancies to term.

BODIES

Beginning in the early or mid-1960s, in many junior high schools around Mexico City academic administrators suddenly appeared on school yards toward the end of recess and announced to students that they would not all be returning to their classes as usual. They told the sixth graders that boys were to go upstairs to their next classes but that girls were to go to the auditorium. Once inside the auditorium, the girls watched a short sixteen-millimeter movie about menstruation, produced by the U.S. manufacturing company Kimberly-Clark. The film ended with a sales pitch: "When this happens to you, use Kotex."

An entire generation of middle and upper middle class women who attended public school was taught the basics of menstruation in this manner (see Riquer 1989). Thus, in its efforts to sell sanitary napkins to young women just experiencing menarche, Kimberly-Clark was at the same time an unusual actor in sociocultural change concerning knowledge of and attitudes toward this aspect of sexuality. Whether Kimberly-Clark suggested that boys be excluded from the auditoriums, whether this was decided individually by school administrations, or whether the subject of boys learning about menstruation even occurred to those organizing the programs is not known. What is evident is that, in this official view, menstruation has nothing to do with boys. To this day, most men in Colonia Santo Domingo are unlikely to learn much at all about menstruation before they marry, and even then it is sometimes a subject shunned by both women and men.[10]

Some men take special care to not touch their wives or girlfriends when they know that the women are having their periods. For various reasons, men may try to avoid eating food prepared by menstruating women. A young woman who was our neighbor in Santo Domingo was rumored to have given her boyfriend tea that she had brewed with a soiled sanitary napkin. According to some, a man will automatically fall under the spell of the woman whose menstrual blood he has ingested. Héctor had another reason for not enjoying food prepared by menstruating women: he informed me one day that women do not cook as well five days a month, because during those days they lose their sense of smell.

By no means do all men fear contact with menstrual blood or menstruating women. Shortly after meeting him, and after a few too many drinks at a relative's party we were both attending, I mentioned to Enrique that I was having trouble sleeping at night. He leaned over and offered me some well-considered advice: "¡Echate el palo de una vez! [You gotta stick your pole!]" he whispered in my ear, adding, "Even if she's having her period." Enrique's knowing grin conveyed the moral of the message: after all, we are men, and we need to take care of our bodies—or, even better, have someone else do it for us.

Casual comments about male sexual organs are more common among younger than older men. At the same time, although such commentary was a recurring theme among most men in the colonia, sometimes it seemed to arise more out of a sense of obligation to "talk as men are supposed to" than from any great interest in the subject. One man told me in earnest that sex held little attraction for him, yet this same man liked to joke that what men really want is "una vida larga y dos bolsas de oro [a long life and two bags of gold]"—in other words, a long penis and two priceless testicles. All in all, it would be a mistake to infer from this that all men in Colonia Santo Domingo equate their manhood with their genitalia. Rather, I think, it would be more accurate to say that for many men they are a favorite reference point.

The use of the words *huevos* (literally, "eggs"; slang for *testicles*) and *verga* (slang for *penis*) in everyday vulgarities reveals a symbolic ambivalence toward the male body on the part of men, who are more prone than women to use these expressions. *Tener muchos huevos* (to have a lot of eggs [balls]) means about what it does in English, "to be gutsy," thus linking courage with physical masculinity in a rather direct fashion. At the same time, the insult *¡Huevón!* is hurled at someone precisely to express the meaning of "Lazy good-for-nothing." Both are symbolically related to the male testicles but have very different connotations.

The use of *verga* is even more complicated. Consider the following expressions: (1) *vale verga* (is worth a dick); (2) *no vale verga* (isn't worth a dick); (3) *me vale verga* (is worth a dick to me); and (4) *es una verga* (is a dick). The first refers to someone (or something) who is no good. The second, semantically the negative of the first, means someone (or something) who is even worse than one who *vale verga*. The third is the rough equivalent of the English "I could give a shit." The fourth, on the other hand, though not as common, is a compliment meaning "He's really something."

In Mexico City, the uses of *verga* are diverse.[11] To be "worth a dick" is bad, yet to be "not worth a dick" is worse. And "to be a dick," unlike the English literal translation, is a good thing. The word *verga* appears in derogatory and complimentary expressions commonly used by men in Santo Domingo, employed more for emphasis and shock value than for any culturally inherent negative or positive property that penises are considered to have.

If men are fickle in referring to their penises, many show greater consistency about physically revealing them in front of other men. There are culturally sanctioned times and places in which men may bare themselves in front of other men. Some men in Santo Domingo seem to delight in urinating together as if it were for them a consummately male activity (and ability, according to some). While accepted procedures vary regarding talking and looking while peeing with other men, for many there is something egalitarian about the act that promotes friendship and male affection.

There is a lot of touching that occurs between men in public in Colonia Santo Domingo. The most obvious form of contact is when two men shake hands on encountering one another. Shaking hands in Mexico City is very common among and between men and women when they have not seen each other recently. Of significance, the form of

handshake between men often differs from that between women or between men and women. In the *clases populares,* among men in their
teens through their forties (men of the 1960s generation and later), the
"power shake" is very, very common.[12] As in many contexts in the
United States, it is used as a sign of mutual respect and equality; such
handshakes would rarely take place between an employer and an em-
ployee, even if both were men of the same age. Most of my friends in
Santo Domingo are quite surprised when I tell them that I believe the
origin of the handshake lies in the Black Power movement in the United
States in the 1960s. But most appreciate this history, perhaps because
they are sympathetic with the goal of physically affirming "common
cause" with other oppressed people, which in Mexico City, as in the
United States, is inherent in the handshake. At the same time, women's
relative exclusion from the practice of the power handshake bears witness to popular though unconscious assumptions that men more than
women may casually engage in symbolic political statements.

Other than greetings, physical contact between men usually involves
arms, hands, heads, or shoulders, with one man leaning on another's
shoulders, for instance. Often a younger man, perhaps a teenager, will
rest himself against an older man who in turn is engaged in a conversation with a third man. Or a teenager will walk down the street with his
arm around another boy's shoulders—men, unlike women, do not walk
down the street holding hands—with such contact indicating close
friendship or family ties. Generally only if both men are intoxicated
does each put his arms around the other. Such physical contact among
men in no way necessarily implies romantic or sexual relations between
the men, as it might in other cultural contexts—for instance, in many
contexts within the United States.

SEX BETWEEN MEN

Actually, in an imperceptible fashion, diverse ways of
thinking had come of age in the country.

> Carlos Monsiváis, *"Paisaje de batalla entre
> condones"*

Friends in Santo Domingo occasionally mention *las casas de las locas*
(the houses of the crazy-queens), where gay cross-dressers and transvestites are said to live. But reference is usually made to these houses in the

past, and no one ever seems able say where such a house might be today. During my fieldwork in Santo Domingo, on only one occasion did
I meet someone in the Pedregales who was openly gay: one day as Gabriel and I walked into his *vecindad* (a group of one-room apartments
with a communal water spigot and bath), we were greeted by a man
shouting from the shower on the side of the patio. He looked out at me
from behind the curtain and in an uninspired come-on told me that he
had dropped his soap and asked me to hand it to him. Gabriel cursed,
calling him a *"pinche maricón* [damned queer]." As we entered his
room, Gabriel told me that the real problem with the man was not that
he was homosexual, but that he was an alcoholic and was always making trouble for others.

Despite the fact that political movements for homosexual and lesbian
human rights are less visible in Mexico City today than they were in the
late 1970s and early 1980s, the organized struggles of lesbians and gays
and their supporters in Mexico have had real, if often collateral, importance for men and women in Colonia Santo Domingo.[13]

Some of this influence is evident in self-consciously "neutral" comments about gays. As we watched Gabriel repairing a car one day, I
asked Enrique, in his late sixties, about people he knew in the *colonia*.
When I asked him about homosexuals, he said that although there were
homosexuales and *lesbianas* in Santo Domingo, he did not know any
personally. He then hastened to add, as if anticipating a follow-up question, "And they are treated the same as everyone else." He had contradictory theories on the subject of why some people are homosexual
(and, implicitly, why some are heterosexual): on the one hand, he said,
people are born men and women; on the other, he felt, homosexuality
is a result of parenting problems. In other words, although Enrique, like
most of my male friends in Santo Domingo, would occasionally make
insulting remarks about *maricas* and *maricones,* revealing unremark-
able prejudices about homosexuality, he also tried to demonstrate impartiality through what were for him newer, democratic ideas. An
emerging and transforming cultural ethos regarding sex between men
can be traced largely to the inchoate influence of the gay and lesbian
rights movement among residents of the *colonias populares* of Mexico
City.

Of all the men with whom I conducted life-history interviews, only
one told of having had sex with other men. Joaquín, who in fact is not
from Santo Domingo but rather from a town in Hidalgo, told me about

sitting in cars late at night with men—married and "straight" men—who know he is bisexual. After a few drinks they might begin to stroke Joaquín's leg:

"I ask them, 'What's going on?! I'm tipsy but I'm not loaded. Easy there, what's going on?' And they tell me, 'But don't you like it?' And I tell them, 'This is what I'm about, but I know with whom, when, and where, and I'm not going to do it with just anyone. There's a place for everything. So all right, but now we're just friends.' I ask them to forgive me. But no. No." Joaquín would sometimes counsel the men: "It seems strange to me that you're really *machito* when you're in your right mind, with all the women. But look what happens with alcohol, all these things you've got buried inside, I don't know what. You're heading toward homosexuality." Then he added to me, "I think that if you put a barrel of rum in anyone, anyone, even the most macho, and he gets loaded, a lot of the homosexual in him is going to come out."

When I asked male friends in Santo Domingo about sexual experiences with other men, everyone denied having had any. They all may have been lying, yet this is not likely. Given the frankness with which they revealed other aspects of their sexualities, I think it more probable that, coincidentally or not, most of these men had never had sexual relations with other men.

Gaining even a rough picture of the sexual practices of men is complicated enough, not least of all for lack of common definitions: What *is* a heterosexual act? What *is* homosexuality? There is the possibility that men denied to me, or even to themselves, these episodes of their youth. Carlos Monsiváis says that, at least in the past, sex between males sixteen to twenty-five years old used to be "a habit of youth" in the *colonias populares* of Mexico City (interview by author, 20 February 1993). Still, regardless of the sex practiced or dreamed about by men in Santo Domingo, many have undoubtedly been greatly influenced through what they have seen, heard, and in some cases done outside (or inside) the *colonia*.

Although writing mainly with an eye to U.S. and European contexts, Giddens describes a social history that is also shared by men in Colonia Santo Domingo, Mexico City:

> The "coming out" of homosexuality is a very real process, with major consequences for sexual life in general. . . . On a more personal level, however, the term "gay" also brought with it an increasingly widespread reference to sexuality as a quality or property of the self. (1992:14)

It is hardly coincidental that the Zona Rosa, the part of Mexico City best known as a converging area for homosexuals, is also a major tourist district and the site of Metro Insurgentes, the busiest stop on the city's subway system. Millions of people pass through the Zona Rosa each day on their way to and from work and shopping. In addition, the Zona Rosa is a favorite spot among more adventurous teenagers from Colonia Santo Domingo, a place they go to hang out on Friday and Saturday nights. In sites such as the Zona Rosa, people in Mexico City have great access and exposure to people of different cultural orientations, including people of different sexual preferences. Such cross-cultural, and cross-sexual, intermingling is one feature of life in Mexico City that makes the capital stand out from most other parts of the country.[14]

The Alameda Park is where many young women who work in wealthy homes during the week as *muchachas* go on Sunday, their day off, hoping young men will buy them sodas or *paletas*. The Alameda, next to Bellas Artes, another tourist attraction, is also where young *prostitutos* (male prostitutes) cruise the pathways looking for business. Many of the *prostitutos'* clients are foreigners, and nearly all are men from the middle and upper strata—some of the people who frequent this part of the Centro Histórico of Mexico City.[15] According to Patricio Villalva, who has conducted over three hundred interviews with *prostitutos* working in Mexico City, the great majority of them are adolescent and darker-skinned *indígena* migrants from the countryside who are hired to have sex with other, often lighter-skinned men.[16]

Many of these young men come to Mexico City from the *campo* looking for work. Every Monday morning, for instance, the Central San Lázaro bus terminal is filled with such recent arrivals. Some of the youth are tricked when they are approached by unscrupulous men who ask, "Do you need a place to work? A place to stay? Some food?" "*Carne nueva siempre llama la atención* [New meat always attracts attention]," the *prostitutos* have told Villalva. Whereas young women may arrive on the same buses already wary of such guile, many young men are caught wholly unprepared.

Once initiated into the life of prostitution, young men can earn $50 (U.S.) a day, and some on occasion make over $150 (U.S.). These youth seldom have any other means of earning this much money, so even if they stop selling their bodies for a time, they will often return to the business whenever they need quick cash. In fact, reports Villalva, more than a few of these young men marry women, have children, and con-

tinue working as *prostitutos*. Nor is being married to a woman considered strange, because although they have sex with other men, the *prostitutos* do not consider themselves homosexuals or bisexual. Their clients
do not see the *prostitutos* as homosexual either, though they usually see
themselves as homosexual or "*gay*."

For the *prostitutos* and their gay clients, definitions of homosexuality
are determined primarily by *why* one has sex with other men, and only
secondarily by *how* one has sex. Nearly always the client plays a passive
role in anal intercourse, and the *prostituto* plays the active, penetrating
role. "Just like with a woman," the *prostitutos* say.[17] *Prostitutos* generally insist that other men may come into physical contact with only
their penises: *prostitutos* penetrate and get masturbated (though they
also sometimes have sex with the wives of their clients). In this they are
different from the *chichifos*, homosexual prostitutes who, at least at
times, play a passive role in sex. Another indication that for the *prostitutos* sex with other men is considered equivalent to sex with women
can be seen in the taunts that are common among these youth, such as,
"You're a *puto* if you *don't* do it with a man."[18]

Some poorer areas of the Federal District are known as havens for
prostitutes and *travestis* (transvestites); in Cuidad Netzahualcóyotl
travestis are widely reputed to play an active role in street fiestas. But
in Colonia Santo Domingo, there are no *travestis*, *prostitutos*, or *prosti-
tutas* regularly walking the streets. Still, the challenges of reimagined
sexualities in Santo Domingo are there and in other *colonias populares*,
in large part an indirect product of the gay rights movement and the
open display of alternative sexualities in other parts of the city.

Younger men in Santo Domingo who are particularly prone to using
sexual innuendo are also more inclined to make insulting and/or defensive comments about homosexuality. However, the contemporary homophobic language used by young men in the community reveals cultural creativity in response to the new challenges of multiple sexualities
in Mexico City. While riding together on the way to matches, the young
men on the River Plate *futbol* team, who come from Santo Domingo or
the neighboring pueblo of Los Reyes, usually slap and pinch each other
a lot. Amid all this grabbing and touching, two or three of the fifteen
young men regularly and loudly jeer the others. Often, employing a
kind of generic slur, they accuse one or another of their teammates of
being a *maricón*, a queer. Instead of merely responding in kind, the
accused often retorts with the more sophisticated insult "Yeah, well
you're a *bisexual*."[19]

Such rejoinders show no more expansive understanding than the frequent opinion voiced by older men in Santo Domingo that there are more *maricas* (faggots) and machos among the rich, as if to imply that (what they see as) sexual deviance—and sexual *access*—is greater within the elites. But comments about *bisexuales* do announce a growing lexicon that in turn points to new understandings on some level that people *have* sexualities, that these sexualities are part of what makes someone who she or he is, and that alternative sexualities are viable, at least for some.

Among youth in Santo Domingo the tensions of contradictory consciousness and practices with respect to sexuality are often evident. In addition to the most vocal members of the River Plate *futbol* team who give voice to homophobia, there are also youth in the *colonias populares* for whom homosexuals and bisexuals are not so much seen as a group apart as they are accepted as one group among many within the culturally accepted boundaries of sexuality. Among some working class youth, sexual experimentation among youth of the same gender is considered positive and a rite of passage.[20] This makes it all the more impossible and erroneous to categorize youth, as individuals or groups, as even heterosexual, homosexual, or bisexual. After all, it is precisely from such labels that these youth are attempting to escape—even as they articulate and manipulate such markers.

Sexualities in Colonia Santo Domingo are thus thoroughly implicated in constructions of gender identities, yet they also operate to a real degree on their own trajectories. That is, sexuality is considered by many in the *colonia* as a discrete category that is never simply subsumed by considerations of masculinity and/or femininity, and indeed plays as much of a role in the constitution of gender categories as gender plays in forming ways of thinking about and acting on transformations of sexuality.

URGES AND *AVENTURAS*

After I had spent several months in Mexico, my research suddenly assumed an explicitly sexual character in a very personal way when my wife and daughter returned to the United States for a couple of weeks. Before leaving, Michelle talked casually one day with Angela and Norma about her planned trip. Angela asked if she was worried about leaving me alone for so long, hinting not so subtly at the opportunity this would present me for *aventuras* (adventures)—in other words, adultery. When Michelle responded that she trusted me and was not concerned, Angela countered, "Well, sure, but do you trust the women?" Michelle had not understood the real threat, Angela counseled: men cannot help themselves when sexual opportunity presents itself.

The day after Michelle and Liliana left, I bumped into Norma and another neighbor, Lupita, at the *sobre ruedas* (open-air market) that is set up on Coyamel Street each Wednesday. After asking if Michelle and Liliana had gotten off all right, Norma turned to me and, forefinger pointing to her eye, said, "*¡Te estamos vigilando!* [We're keeping an eye on you!]". Lupita added, with the same gesture, that she too would mount a vigilant lookout. It was mainly a joke by these two married women who had already become like family. But it was also a warning to the husband of one of their absent friends that no fooling around would be tolerated—or go unreported. Implicit, again, was the message that men will try to get away with whatever they can sexually, unless they believe they might get caught.

What is interesting is not that the actual frequency of cheating is that high (or low, for that matter), but the insights all this provided into what many women and men in Santo Domingo view as an innate core of male sexuality. As Angela told me later when I asked about her comments to Michelle, "*¿A quién le dan pan que llore?* [Who cries (i.e., does something inappropriate) when they're given bread?]" Everyone knows what you do with bread: you eat it. The stereotype of men in Mexico being subject to uncontrollable bodily urges and needs is widely held in Santo Domingo—which just proves that some stereotypes about sexual identities in the region are shared by those living there.[21]

Many men tell of having had affairs with women other than their wives. "*No soy santo*," confides Alfredo, "I'm no saint." The justification for adultery on the part of men is often that men have peculiar "natural desires." Further, men sometimes snickered to me that "*el hombre llega hasta donde la mujer lo diga* [men will get away with whatever women let them]." One of the most common expressions for an extramarital affair is *cana al aire*—literally, "a gray hair to the air," the image being that when you find a gray hair you pull it out quickly and fling it away; you do it, and it is over.

Such "flings" are said to be distinguished by their purely sexual as opposed to romantic content. One woman described to me how when her husband was younger he would often disappear on Friday night and

I asked Norma to repeat a gesture she'd used earlier in the day when she told me, "I'll be keeping an eye on you [while your wife is out of town]."

not return until Sunday night. She would tell their children that he was working, to protect them, she said. Taxi drivers have an especially wide reputation for casual rendezvous with women fares. After waxing most poetic on the qualities of his wife, one *taxista* told me that he and she have an agreement that *aventuritas* are fine so long as they are not discussed between them later. "Twenty-one years is a long time to be married," he told me, suggesting that the underlying rationale was boredom in the marital bedroom. He also insisted that she has the same freedom to find lovers as he. After all, he reasoned to me, otherwise it would not be fair.

Affairs are discussed and joked about casually by many people in Santo Domingo. On boarding a *combi* driven by my friend Rafael, I asked how his infant son was doing. He said the boy of four months was doing great. There was one thing, though, that concerned my friend.

"What's bothering you?" I inquired. It was noisy on the minibus and we had to shout to make ourselves heard.

"Every day the boy looks more like people from the 'other side' [the United States]," he screamed.

"How?"

"He's got bright green eyes. I don't even think he's mine!"

He laughed heartily. The other passengers seemed oblivious to this self-disparaging and semi-lewd commentary. His was not the storybook image of a shamefaced and cuckolded husband.

Marcos told me that his wife, Delia, has been joking for years that Lolo, a neighborhood boy of fourteen, is her second husband. It all started when Delia's sister spread a rumor that Lolo had slept with Delia, Marcos related. "Sometimes I chew Lolo out," he continued, "telling him that I had to go to Tepito to buy my girls shoes when he should be the one doing it."

The documentary record leaves open to question the extent to which such banter is new. For example, the use of the term *cabrón,* which can figuratively refer to a cuckold, is widespread, but by no means necessarily tied to this one meaning or even to a negative quality.[22] Regardless of the history of jokes about infidelity, humorous quips about adultery today take place in a shifting context. Men continue to have affairs; this is nothing new. What has reportedly changed is the number of women who do so, and the fact that some are quite open about having lovers. A particularly promiscuous woman in Santo Domingo has even earned a nickname, La Tasqueña, for her amorous liaisons. La Tasqueña is married to a man who spends ten or eleven months a year in Detroit and returns for only short stays to Santo Domingo to visit her and their two children. Whenever her legal husband is in the United States, she has a series of men (one at a time) living with her, each of whom moves out temporarily when the legal husband returns to the *colonia.* Her nickname derives from an episode that occurred several years ago during one of her legal husband's infrequent visits. She was very late returning to the house one night, and when she finally arrived she complained that she had missed all the *combis* from the Tasqueña metro stop. The problem was that her neighbors had seen her elsewhere and knew this was a ruse to cover up her date that night.

Thus one of the creative responses of some women to men's adultery has been to take lovers of their own. Women's activities as varied as community organizing and paid work have led to far greater opportunities to meet other men and to have affairs with them. To whatever extent sexual "needs" were ever associated with men alone, this seems far less the case today in Santo Domingo.

In refutation of the commonplace that many or most Latin American men have their first sexual escapades with prostitutes, none of the men

I interviewed from Colonia Santo Domingo save one admitted to ever having been to a prostitute. Nor had any men taken their sons to prostitutes "to become men." Once again, it is possible that my friends and informants were simply covering up sexual escapades from their pasts. More probable, I think, is that paying for sexual services is today more common in some areas of Mexico City—for instance, around the Centro Histórico—than it is in others. Then, too, it is possible that for many of my friends, paying for sex implies an unmanly inability to attract women sexually.

Going to prostitutes may be more of a tradition among young men from the middle and upper classes. In the survey on sexuality among high school students cited earlier, 20.5 percent of the well-to-do boys reported that their first sexual relation was with a prostitute (Consejo Nacional de Población 1988:120). Men from upper middle class homes also speak of the convention whereby the father hires a maid with whom his sons can have their first sexual encounters. Making caustic references to "the excesses of the feminist movement," one lawyer sarcastically told me that young men are often raped by these older and more sexually aggressive *muchachas,* adding, "I know this from personal experience." The lawyer's comments regarding feminism and rape bore witness to a defensive posture assumed by many men in his milieu today. Still, for this man and others of his class background and generation, it was taken for granted that males would lose their virginity prior to marrying whereas females should be virgins until their wedding night.

Female virginity continues to be an important issue for many men, but this double standard is far less an issue among younger men and women, especially as knowledge about and use of birth control by teens becomes more widespread. But the matter is contested—among teens, and between teens and their parents. As part of this gendered and generational confrontation over virginity, a particularly bizarre rumor about adolescent sexual behavior in the United States was making its way through the Pedregales in 1993. Some people had heard, and were convinced, that many girls in the United States have their hymens surgically removed so that the first time they have sexual intercourse they will not experience so much pain. This example, among others, was put forth to my wife, Michelle, to demonstrate that women in the United States have much more sexual freedom and know how to better enjoy themselves sexually.

NORTHERN PENETRATIONS

Due especially to factors such as migration and television, cultural boundaries that coincide with geographic divisions are far less prevalent today than at any time in the past. This is true both within Mexico and, of fundamental importance, across the international border with the United States. As Rouse notes,

> the growing institutionalization of migration to the United States . . . means that more of the Mexican population is oriented to developments outside the country and that this orientation is becoming steadily more pronounced. (1991:16)

The numbers of human beings involved in international migration is staggering. A recent study suggests that "14.8 percent of Mexico's labor force is, at one time or another, employed in the United States—legally or otherwise" (California Chamber of Commerce 1993:14). If these figures are correct, the experience of living and working in the United States is common to one out of every seven adult Mexicans. The impact of this transnational migration on cultural standards and manners within Mexico is evident in the realm of sexuality.

Because of migration and the fact that English has a certain cachet among youth throughout Mexico, and no doubt as a partial result of commercial dumping by the U.S. apparel industry, T-shirts with slogans in English are popular and commonly worn in Colonia Santo Domingo. Some merely appear bizarrely out of place, like one with the words "I love Ollie [North]!" over the Stars and Stripes. Others seem grotesque until you realize that surely most people haven't the foggiest idea what they mean. An eleven-year-old girl walking next to her older brother wears a T-shirt reading, "If I weren't giving head, I'd be dead. . . ."

According to recent figures, at least 3 million households in Mexico City have televisions (perhaps 95 percent of all homes), which are watched daily, and 59 percent of all families in Mexico City have video-cassette recorders (García Canclini 1991:164). When we moved into Santo Domingo in mid-1992, in one neighboring household there were four televisions and four VCRs for seven adults and one child. Also of special relevance to the discussion of sexual practices and role models is the fact that every day in Mexico City and throughout the country new and old television programs originating in the United States and dubbed into Spanish are broadcast on major channels. During a random week (24–30 July 1993), the following U.S. television shows were seen: *Murphy Brown, Los años maravillosos* (The Wonder Years), *Beverly Hills 90210, Miami Vice, Los intocables* (The Untouchables), *Bonanza,* and *Alf,* as well as the cartoon shows *Los Simpsons, Las tortugas ninja* ([Teenage Mutant] Ninja Turtles), and *Los verdaderos casafantasmas* (The Real Ghostbusters). That same week, viewers of the major television stations could watch such classic cinematic fare as *Body Double, Absence of Malice, The Bigamist, My Man Godfrey, The Fugitive,* and *The Mummy.*

To call attention to the cultural, economic, and political power of the United States as well as the Catholic Church in Mexico, Arizpe (1993:378) refers to those bodies as the Regional Caciques. Most of my friends in Santo Domingo are acutely aware of how Mexican and other Latin American men and women are portrayed in U.S. television and cinema. Questions related to sexual roles and machismo, illegal immigrants and racism are noted and judged by audiences throughout Mexico. This does not mean, however, that all reactions are the same, as certain analysts of the "culture industry" would have it. Frequently there is debate over the meaning of episodes on the TV, as some more than others are able to transcend oversimplified representations and messages.

Regardless of the extent to which U.S. television and film do or do not accurately reflect aspects of sexual experiences occurring in the United States, they are reference points orienting international viewers' attention to alternate sexual lifestyles and relations. Following the opening in Mexico of the Hollywood movie *Pretty Woman* (released there as *La mujer bonita*), knee-high leather (or simulated leather) boots such as those worn by Julia Roberts in the film enjoyed enormous popularity for several years among young women in the *clases populares* in Mexico City. Whether or not these boots were directly associated with Roberts's occupation in the movie (she plays a prostitute) or with the story's outcome (she goes off with a handsome young billionaire), such highly gendered fashions are increasingly tied to direct U.S. influences.

Young women in Colonia Santo Domingo also began watching the Miami-based Spanish-language talk show *Cristina* as soon as it appeared on Mexico's Channel 2 at the end of 1992. "Look at what fifteen-year-old girls in the United States are talking about! They know it all!" seventeen-year-old Carmen exclaimed to me one day. Interestingly, Mexican intellectuals are likely to label *Cristina* a "U.S. program" or a "Cuban-American program," whereas young working class women, its main viewing audience in Santo Domingo, seldom care about where it comes from and simply refer to it as "my show."

As I was talking about witches one day with Martha, a friend who sells diapers in bulk in the open-air markets, she said to me, "You know what? There aren't as many witches in Mexico as there used to be. And do you know where they're coming from now? Your country." She smiled and related that she had seen a lot of (U.S.) witches on a *Cristina* program. I suggested that maybe they were part of the North American Free Trade Agreement.

WHEN THE MAN'S AN ASS

In Santo Domingo in the 1990s, if, with respect to women, virginity is less an issue and adultery more of one when compared with the situation twenty years earlier, divorce rates remain approximately the same. In Mexico City, 2 percent of women older than twelve reported their civil status as divorced in the 1990 census, whereas in the country overall the figure was 1 percent (INEGI 1992:22). The fact that of the women I know in Santo Domingo far more than one in fifty says she is divorced leads me to believe that many of these women had common-law marriages, and thus splitting up did not officially constitute divorce. Or perhaps some of them are still legally married yet call themselves divorced because they no longer live with their legal spouses. For whatever reasons, many of them have never gotten formally divorced.

Attitudes about divorce are changing, especially on the part of women, and in some instances this in turn has had dramatic effects on their men. In an interview in June 1991, Marco Rascón, president of the citywide Asamblea de Barrios, told me that divorces were on the rise among the influential organization's membership. He attributed the initiative in most cases to women militants who were no longer willing to tolerate husbands who opposed their wives' political efforts. Increasingly, according to Rascón, conflicts of this type were resolved either in divorce or in the husbands' following their wives and becoming Asamblea activists themselves. Nevertheless, the *muchachos* I talked with on the street were intrigued when they learned that my parents divorced when I was quite young, and they asked me a lot of questions about what it was like to grow up in that situation, indicating that divorce for them still carried a somewhat exotic flavor.

Rosa, a deeply religious and devout Catholic, repeated a story to me that her granddaughter had told her: "Oh, Grandma, in school they assigned us to write about the worst thing that has ever happened to us in our lives, and I put that for me the worst was my parents' divorce." But, Rosa confided to me, "I told her, 'Don't be an ass. It's the best thing that has ever happened to you.'" Rosa never thought highly of her former son-in-law, and for her, church stricture or not, there were some times when divorce was the best way out of a bad situation.

Men in Santo Domingo enjoy complaining about being married, some saying that marriage is to be endured (usually for the sake of the children). Numerous others, both newlyweds and those who have been married for many years, snipe at wives and marriage. But these attacks should not always be taken at face value. In many ways complaints of this kind by men in Santo Domingo are similar to *albures*. Ostensibly and superficially about sex, *albures* are more frequently double-entendre jokes and quips that use sex to comment on other topics and issues.

When they make wisecracks about the miseries of marriage, men likewise frequently use familiar codes, albeit often sexist ones, to vent their rage at life's iniquities and to blame especially loved ones for keeping them in their sorry state of affairs. If pressed on the issue, even some of the most ornery insulters of wives will tell you they pray they will die before their spouses, because they would not know how to live alone. Although male dependency upon wives to feed and clothe them doubtless focuses important aspects of women's subordination to men, such unvarnished sentiments on the part of men are not merely venal attempts at control, nor are they expressed without contradiction.

In the same way that men use *albures* and complain about marriage, those who are caught for their *aventuras* commonly raise the excuse that appearances can be deceptive and that extramarital flings do not necessarily mean what they might appear to mean. (And most of my male friends in Santo Domingo who admit to affairs say that they were eventually caught.) Needless to say, most of my male friends have a more difficult time sifting through the layers of meaning when a question of women's delinquencies arises. Juan came into the kitchen of his home one day as Angela and I were talking about adulterous friends and neighbors. Angela looked up and said to Juan, "Now, tell Mateo whether a man would forgive a woman for such an offense. Would you forgive her?"

"Men almost never forgive such women, and when they do it's because they really love them—" Juan started to respond.

"Or 'because he's an ass!' That's Juan's expression," Angela shot back.

"Men like it," Juan continued, "when their wives say to them, 'Look, I bought you this and—' "

"I bought you a sombrero!" Angela interrupted, making reference to covering the "horns" growing on a cuckolded man's head.

LA CASA CHICA

In Oscar Lewis's (1961) affectionate portrait of Mexican working class family life, *The Children of Sánchez,* he discusses many sexual practices in the capital in the 1950s. Overly confident in the resilience of cultural practices, I was sure when I began fieldwork in 1992 that one of these, *la casa chica* (the small house), was still an entrenched social institution. After all, Jesús Sánchez, whose children are the subject of Lewis's book, usually seemed to have a mistress or second wife, depending upon how you defined the relationship, whom he maintained in *la casa chica* (or *segundo frente* [second front]).

A concept and a practice regarding male gender identities in Mexico that social scientists have more often assumed than studied, *la casa chica* is usually thought of as the arrangement whereby a Mexican man keeps a woman other than his wife in a residence separate from his main (*casa grande*) household. It is generally discussed as a modern form of urban polygamy that is common in all social strata in Mexico and is by no means the prerogative of only wealthy men.[23]

Information on *la casa chica* was initially easy to come by. One man in a Christian Base Community in Colonia Ajusco spoke to me disparagingly of a brother of his who maintained *three* different households simultaneously, and did this on a factory worker's wages. A few weeks later, Luciano was welding a pipe in our apartment. Neighbors had already told me Luciano had a *casa chica,* so I was especially looking forward to talking with him. I asked Luciano about his family, and he told me that he and his wife were *separados* (separated). They had not lived together for years, he said. When I asked where he was living then, he replied, "Not far from here." But though he no longer shared a home with his "wife"—a couple of times Luciano fumbled over what to call her—because the house and the land were in his name, getting divorced was out of the question; in a divorce he would risk losing all the property.

On another occasion I mentioned to a friend, Margarita, that I was surprised I had not encountered the famous *casa chica* in Santo Domingo. Margarita paused a moment and then said to me carefully, "*¿Sabes qué? Carmela es la casa chica.* [You know what? Carmela is *la casa chica*.]" Carmela, a woman in her late thirties whom I had previously met in the *colonia,* had lived for twelve years with the man she always referred to as her husband. But, it turned out, this man was legally married to (though separated from) another woman with whom he had four children, the youngest then thirteen. Carmela's "husband" had legally adopted her son from an earlier relationship, and she and this man later had a daughter who was then nine.

After a few months of fieldwork, I was getting quite wary of what *la casa chica* meant to different people, and how everyone referred to the "husbands" and "wives" of those involved in *las casas chicas.* By the time Rafael told me in December that his brother was living in their home with his *casa chica,* I had also grown a little weary of the term.

"Is he married to another woman?" I asked Rafael.

"Yes, he's been married for years," came the reply. "Of course, they haven't been together since he's been with this new woman, but he's still married to the first one."

Then a neighbor happened to mention a remarkable but more "classical" *casa chica* arrangement a couple of blocks from where we lived in Santo Domingo.

"You know the tire-repair place on the corner? Well, a guy used to live over it with two sisters. He lived with them both!"

"In the same house?" I asked suspiciously.

"No."

"But each sister knew about the other one?"

"They knew about it and each tried to outdo the other, trying to get him to realize that she was better. He lived with the two sisters, two days with one, two with the other."

"What were they thinking?"

"Their mother was the really stupid one. She used to say that he was her *doble yerno* [double son-in-law]. If the mother thought this, what could you expect from the daughters?"

Yet how the phrase *la casa chica* is used in daily discourse is often quite removed from such classical patterns. Rafael works in maintenance at the National University (UNAM), which borders Colonia Santo Domingo. He once told me that 60 percent of his fellow employees at the university have *casas chicas.* Astonished, I questioned him further. "Yes, I am talking about women as well as men." It soon became apparent that Rafael was talking about people having extramarital affairs; for him *casa chica* was a catchy analogue.

So too, although Margarita refers to Carmela as "*la casa chica,*" and although by Carmela's own account the man she lives with cheated on her early in their relationship, this man has been faithful to Carmela for seven years and he is her "husband." As for Luciano's arrangement, a few weeks after fixing our pipes, and after we had gotten to know each other better, he told me that for several years he had lived with a woman other than his "first wife." He and the second woman now have two children together. In responding to questions about "your spouse" in the survey I conducted, Luciano always answered with regard to this second woman.

Most of the *casas chicas* that I know of in Mexico City that conform to a pattern of urban polygamy—where a man shuttles between two (or more) households and the "wives" are often ignorant of each other— are maintained by well-paid workers or men from the middle and upper classes. Other than the rather extraordinary arrangement of the man married to two sisters, and the factory worker with three "wives," generally the only workers who can afford this kind of set-up are truckers or migrants to the United States, or men who have high-paying jobs in the electrical, telephone, or petroleum industries.

So what, then, *is* the meaning of *la casa chica,* and what shape does it take in the lives of people in Colonia Santo Domingo? At least in some instances, rather than referring to urban polygamy, *la casa chica* is used to describe second (or later) marriages. In other words, it frequently refers to serial monogamy, and if adultery occasionally occurs, it does so within *this* context. The approach many people take to *la casa chica* is in part a product of Catholic doctrine and antidivorce sanctions. Mexican working class men as well as women have learned to manipulate the cultural rituals and social laws of machismo, not unlike the sixteenth-century rural French, who were, as Natalie Davis (1983:46) writes, a people with "centuries of peasant experience in manipulating popular rituals and the Catholic law on marriage."

This is especially true for the poor, who cannot as easily arrange and afford church annulments of their marriages. Men are culturally expected to financially maintain their (first) "wives" forever, just as these women expect to be supported—not that this situation always obtains. That is, for many men and women *la casa chica* is the best resolution to a situation in which legal divorce is out of the question. It is the way serial monogamy is practiced by many people in a society in which one often must be "married" to one's first spouse for life. The fact that few women and men necessarily intend in this manner to subvert Catholic rules regarding marriage-for-life does not take away from the creative (and subversive) quality of their actions—one of the ways, to paraphrase Ortner (1989–90:79), in which arenas of non-hegemonic practice can become the bases of a significant challenge to hegemony.

In addition to prohibitions against divorce emanating from the Catholic Church, there are other factors that impinge on the situation. After divorce, first wives can more easily prevent fathers from seeing their children. And men such as Luciano can also lose property rights if their de facto divorces become de jure, and if they marry other women and end up living elsewhere.

The traditional *casa chica* arrangement in which one man lives simultaneously with more than one woman and "family" may or may not persist in the upper echelons of Mexican society. But it is not common in Colonia Santo Domingo, at least not in this sense of urban polygamy. At the same time, none of my analysis regarding serial monogamy minimizes the traumatic financial and emotional impact caused by men who do desert their wives and children, regardless of whether these men take up with other women.[24] My argument is instead threefold: first, that the expression *la casa chica* is used in a variety of ways in *colonias populares,* many of which have little to do with adultery as this latter term is defined by men and women involved in these unions; second, that these multiple meanings of *la casa chica* are illustrations of a cultural practice that has emerged in the context of Catholic laws on marriage; and third, that this cultural practice should be seen as part of a manipulative popular response to the church's ban on divorce.

Popular approaches to the *casa chica* in Santo Domingo are thus exemplary of Gramsci's notion of contradictory consciousness, as the unpredictable exigencies of the living enter into lively contest with the oppressive traditions and sycophantic bromides of dead generations. And, therefore, as Herzfeld (1987:84) makes clear in another context, in instances such as the daily references and practices to the *casa chica* we should, rather than merely bearing witness to an "enforced passivity" induced from on high, especially and instead see "the quality of active social invention" in defiance of official discourse and control.

LOS SOLTEROS: MASTURBATION, CELIBACY, AND ASEXUALITY

During the same period in January when my wife and daughter were away and I was temporarily "*un hombre abandonado* [an abandoned man]," as some neighbors joked, I expected to hear comments from men about my temporary single status, opportunities for adultery, and much more. Reality proved not so much disappointing as unexpected.

During this time, I spent a Saturday afternoon, as I often did, having a couple of drinks on the corner with a few friends. Marcos, Gabriel, Marcial, Pablo, and Marcelo were all there drinking *anís,* on the rocks or straight, out of plastic cups. Eventually the discussion wound around to the fact that I was alone for a couple of weeks. There were initially some mild inquiries as to whether I would go out looking for some *jovencitas* (young women), but then the comments took an abrupt turn.

"You do know what we say about single guys, don't you?" asked Marcelo. " '*Los solteros son chaqueteros* [Single guys are meat beaters]' and '*No le aprietes el cuello al ganso* [Don't squeeze the goose's neck].' " Everyone laughed, especially when they made me repeat the phrases back to make sure I had learned them correctly. Then they insisted that I copy them down. "You should put them in your book," Marcos recommended.

Masturbating men may not conjure up as romantic an image as a *mujeriego* (womanizer). But I imagine this representation is infinitely more accurate, if mundane, in describing the sex lives of most single men in Santo Domingo than portraits of rapacious young Mexican men always on the prowl for female conquest.[25] Although I briefly hesitated to do so, I checked with Angela the next day to see if she was familiar with the expressions about masturbation I had heard and to make sure I had copied them correctly. She approved my transcriptions and then mentioned that she and her sisters often lament the bachelor status of a nephew by saying to each other, "*Le jala la cabeza al gallo* [He yanks the cock's head]." So much for my worry about embarrassing this grandmother.

Eventually I discovered that in Colonia Santo Domingo one of the most popular ways to describe a single man is to refer to him as a masturbating man. Roberto, a muffler repairman near where I lived, introduced me to his cousin Mario one day. Noting that his cousin was unmarried, Roberto added, "He's a *maraquero* [another slang expression for a man who masturbates]." No joke was made about the cousin being free to run around with a lot of women because of his single status. On another occasion, when we were discussing parents' roles in teaching their children about sexuality, Roberto told me that he and his wife both consider it important to teach their three boys about masturbation, so that they come to see it as part of a transitional stage and a good way to deal with "*estrés* [stress]." He did caution, however, that masturbation could be overdone and that it was only a stage through which one should pass in adolescence.

The assumption that all men love to have as many orgasms as possible is a view about male sexuality that is widely shared by men and women in Santo Domingo. This premise is basic to understanding the connections between men, masturbation, and womanizing, and to examining many of the sexual justifications and intimations heard in the *colonia*.

Héctor and I were walking through the famous La Merced market one overcast afternoon. We had already visited the Sonora market, where herbs, spices, Buddha statues, and love potions are sold. As we passed by a doorway marked "#4" leading to a series of indoor stalls, Héctor pulled my arm and said he wanted to show me something. He found a stall selling sweets made of squash, nuts, and other delicacies, and bought two pieces of *queso de tuna* (tuna-cactus cheese), a sweet made of the nopal cactus that looks like a light brown hockey puck, only smaller. I bit into one as we went back out on the street and continued walking.

After I had finished about half, Héctor smiled, pointed to the remaining portion, and mischievously informed me that *queso de tuna* has a marvelous side effect. About four the next morning, he told me, I would have an erection so hard that it would wake me up. Héctor must have also been sure that I would then want to wake Michelle and have the best sex of my life, because he added, "In the morning you can tell me if it worked." I asked him the obvious question: why hadn't he bothered to mention this little supposed attribute of *queso de tuna* before I ate it? He just laughed, sure that I was really grateful for having been given a food that would unleash my essential male sexual proclivities.

But the view that *all* men have the same sexuality fails to account for multiple sexualities—homosexual, heterosexual, bisexual—and it overlooks androgyny and *a*sexuality. It also overlooks changes in sexuality experienced throughout individuals' lives, from childhood through adolescence, early adulthood, middle age, and old age. And this outlook skirts around significant variations based on class, generation, and family histories.

After a man I know in Santo Domingo confessed to me, "I'll tell you honestly, sex has just never been as important to me as it seems to be for a lot of other guys," I decided to seek out a professional celibate, a Catholic priest, to talk more about male sexuality and asexuality. So I went back to see Padre Víctor Verdín of the Christian Base Communities, at the Iglesia de la Resurrección. I asked him, "For you, the church is your family in a way. But have you never thought that you might be missing something by not having a regular family? It's a naïve question, but a serious one."

"That's a little question, all right! Look, at the level of ideas, a lot of the time I have known that celibacy is right, in terms of leaving you time for others. You have to have a heart which is open to all, and your family is people and your personal relation is an intellectual one with God. But emotionally, in the heart and feelings, I lingered a long time and still I don't think I've got it, really experiencing with serenity and peace an acceptance that there will be tremendous incoherencies, a giant emptiness. It hasn't been easy. There are theories of Freudian sublimation, and in this sense, yes, you can cope. But one goes through various crises. Sometimes what hurts is parenthood. Sometimes it's the lack of tenderness. Sometimes you miss the sexual relation. Sometimes it's everything all at once."

Padre Víctor is a man nonetheless, by which I do not mean here simply that he is biologically male, but that he is a social male. Because of this fact, sexual tensions with women are not obviated by his office: "With women, you have to exercise certain obvious discretion, most of all so that no one misinterprets a certain closeness, or a certain friendliness. People are very sensitive, including in how you greet them, and you have to be careful to avoid ambiguous signs. In this culture, that's the way it is." [26]

Yet in the culture to which Padre Víctor refers, physical intimacy is "the way it is" for some more than others. And, really, there is only so much one man can do about the fact that men's and women's sexualities are increasingly open to ambiguity and misunderstanding. Sex is changing in important if uncalculated ways partly in response to pressures such as those the good padre and his iconoclastic church bring to bear on pregnant teenagers and their lovers. Throughout this Catholic land, youth continue to reach puberty knowing precious little about their and others' bodies. Yet birth control in some form is the standard procedure, albeit a women's procedure. Divorce restrictions remain in place, though they are routinely and creatively dodged, by some through *la casa chica*. Homophobia is a code of boyish insults, whereas sexual experimentation by young men with young men and by young women with young women is increasingly seen as legitimate. Though men are still acting like men, women too are experiencing urges and *aventuras*. The sexual contradictions of a generation have effectively transformed very little and quite a lot.

SIX

Diapers and Dishes, Words and Deeds

The sayings of the wise men won't wash any more.
Everybody, at last, is getting nosy.

Bertolt Brecht, Galileo

ENGENDERED WORK

By 1992, most of the five-year-old boys in the San Bernabé Nursery School in Colonia Santo Domingo cheerfully participated in the game called *el baño de la muñeca* (the doll bath). Aurora Muñoz, the director of the nursery school, noted that the boys also now swept up, watered the plants, and collected the trash. When she began working at San Bernabé in 1982, however, many of the boys, if asked to help out with these tasks, would protest, "Only *viejas* do that!" (an expression similar to "That's girl's work!").[1] Muñoz attributed the changes to the fact that, as the boys themselves reported, their older brothers and fathers often did these things now, so why shouldn't they?[2]

Describing what is changing in the mundane world of domestic chores in Colonia Santo Domingo, what has remained more constant from one generation to another, and why particular reformations in domestic divisions of labor might be occurring will be the focus of this chapter. The discussion in chapter 3 indicated both that intergenerational changes regarding fathering are occurring and that social scientists have sometimes allowed their preconceptions about male parenting to get the better of their ethnographic details. That is, there has been active participation by men in parenting in specific cultural situations for a long time. In chapters 4 and 5, changes in male attitudes toward women and sexuality were linked to particular political developments and movements in Colonia Santo Domingo and more widely in Mexican society over the past two decades. In this chapter the impact of demographic factors on gender identities and relations will be highlighted, especially as these manifest themselves in intergenerational changes and challenges.

It may seem odd that the focus of this chapter, and in fact of this book, is decidedly on men's domestic practices, activities that are largely unstudied and unreported in the social sciences. (Even the expression *men's domesticity* sounds like an oxymoron.) My point is not that masculinity is unimportant in other contexts like work environments, but that the "breadwinner" role of men, which is so often tied to masculine identities in modern capitalist economies, is not inherently a work-related gender construction. Indeed, even descriptions of manly activities such as "going to work" and "coming from work" imply a domestic frame of reference for this often crucial aspect of masculinity. Just as Benería and Roldán (1987) have shown that women's gender identities are constructed in the workplace as much as in the home in Mexico City, so conversely we must grasp that men's gender identities are developed and transformed in the home and not just in sites considered to be typical male reserves, like factories, cantinas, and political forums.

To better understand the relation between domesticity, economics, and masculinity we should reexamine one of feminist anthropology's hoary debates: the association of public life with men and of private life with women. As an early proponent of this dichotomy came herself to conclude, such typologizing can tend to overlook the numerous situations in which such associations do not apply (see Rosaldo 1974, 1980; see also Strathern 1980). Yet if Rosaldo's original formulation remains awkward, perhaps, as Ortner (1989–90) points out, a public/private distinction should nonetheless not be jettisoned too hastily.

I argue in the pages that follow that if instead of a rudimentary public-is-to-men-as-private-is-to-women model we adopt the more expedient concepts of Habermas regarding public and private spheres, we will be able to gain important insights into the particular cultural processes having to do with housework that were under way in Santo Domingo and other *colonias* populares of Mexico City in the early 1990s. Because although Habermas (1987:318 ff.) sees private as similarly associated with family affairs and public with collective social life, for him both public and private spheres are part of what he terms the "lifeworld," which by definition is subject to manipulated change by men and women. That is, while not making specific reference to gender, Habermas argues that men *and* women can and do engage in transforming both public and private life.

Habermas contrasts the public and private spheres of the lifeworld with "social systems," of which the two most important are the economy and political administration. Social systems in this understanding are likewise the products of social actors, but, significantly, their actual manifestations are not necessarily the intended consequences of any individual actors. Thus the economy, for example, is not associated by Habermas particularly with public life. Indeed, for him the economy is more connected to the private sphere of the modern nuclear family, whereas the public sphere is more connected to the state administration of society.[3]

As Nancy Fraser (1987:45) points out, although Habermas neglects gender as a major component of his theories of public and private spheres, his formulations do allow for an understanding that "gender identity is lived out in all arenas of life." The relevance of this insight for our present purposes is the need to document and analyze how women are linked with the extradomestic/public just as men are associated with the domestic/private. That is, the problem lies not so much with the terms *public* and *private* as with the inappropriate application of these concepts, as though they everywhere coincided with rigidly delineated gender categories.

A postulate of cultural anthropology is that factors such as women's paid employment, falling birthrates, higher educational levels, and so on never mechanically lead to particular cultural formations or changes in cultural practices. Nor do changes in ideas necessarily reflect or result in creative changes in activities—for example, changes on the part of men with respect to their participation in housework. Yet it would also be wrong to argue that demographic changes have no significance whatsoever with regard to cultural identities and relations, especially when many social actors themselves make connections between women's employment and men's domestic chores. At the least, we might recall Durkheim's (1915:30 n.) remark that "social disturbances result in multiplying mental disturbances." Throughout this discussion we will examine whether changes in men's share of housework are more verbal than material and explore several probable connections between demographic shifts and changing gender identities.[4]

HOUSEWORK

Most women in Colonia Santo Domingo who work outside the home continue to do most of the cooking, cleaning, and laundry. Significantly, though, the perceptions of many men (and some women) in Colonia Santo Domingo contradict the notion that all men do little to nothing around the home. Men and women speak in particular of intergenerational changes; younger men, for instance, routinely assert that they do far more housework than their fathers ever did. The extent to which changes from one generation to the next are occurring is not necessarily constant from one locale in Mexico City to the next. Therefore the perceptions of change and the changes themselves in Santo Domingo should not necessarily be taken as representative of transformations that are occurring in households everywhere in the capital.

That said, it is also true that no changes take place in Santo Domingo outside the context of contradictory consciousness regarding the cultural values that each generation has inherited from the past and new ways of approaching practices like housework and domestic divisions of labor. When old and young friends in the *colonia* speak of generational differences with regard to domestic chores, it is seldom without mention of the struggles between women and men that have precipitated these changes.

What counts as housework—and therefore what it means for men to participate or not in such activities—is not easy to determine, but among other things it generally refers to unpaid labor.[5] In self-built communities like Santo Domingo, rooms are often added on one by one over the years, as households save enough money to buy materials and as families grow larger. The overall construction of the home is most often shared by women and men, though the erecting work—laying bricks, pouring cement, hanging doors, building closets—is typically performed by men in their "free time," sometimes with the help of children. House repairs, too, are generally men's responsibilities. Such activities are not, however, usually included in definitions of domestic work, which is generally considered to encompass cooking, washing, cleaning, and child care—in other words, activities that in social science writings are traditionally associated with women.

Let me cite another example. In Santo Domingo some households have a car or access to a car. But none of my friends or acquaintances in the *colonia,* even if they have a car, have one that is in good running condition. Many men perform large and small repairs on their cars

more or less constantly, at least several hours a week in the late afternoons and/or on weekends. Scouring junkyards for parts, walking several blocks to borrow tools from a friend, and helping others lift trans-
missions and engines out of their housings for overhaul are among the
most common forms of "leisure" activity of adult men in the *colonia*.

Because their households have in most cases come to depend on the
vehicles, this is not simply a matter of men's hobbies. On the other
hand, car repairs inspire social gatherings, stories and gossip, and the
training of young men by older men (in technical questions of auto
mechanics, the etiquette of alcohol consumption, and broader issues of
politics and morality), and in this sense they are usually far less isolated
affairs than hanging up the clothes or feeding the baby.

Yet what of the traditionally female duties in the home? On the
whole the picture is quite varied in Santo Domingo, with most men,
including younger men, doing little to nothing in the way of laundry
and food preparation, although many now wash dishes and go shopping, and some iron their own clothes. Similarly, though there is a cor-
relation in the minds of some men and women between wives working
outside the home and men therefore taking on more domestic chores,
the *doble jornada* (double day) persists to one extent or another in most
households. Instead of men now sharing in domestic chores as women
share more in contributing to families' incomes, women report having
to work a *doble jornada*.

I tried to probe the issue of men's participation in housework while
I sat one day on a stool in Marcos's kitchen admiring the masonry work
in his brick walls and the colorful ceramic bowls hanging from pegs
above the sink. He was washing the morning dishes before leaving for
work in the early afternoon. I asked Marcos if he had always done this
chore. He paused for a moment, thinking, and then, turning around to
face me, shrugged and said, "I began doing it regularly four years and
two months ago." Skeptical by nature and more than mildly surprised
by the precision of his response, I inquired as to how he so clearly remembered his initiation into this task. "Quite simple, really," he replied
with a grin—he knew exactly what I was driving at with my questions
about men doing housework—"that's when my *vieja* began working
full-time. Before that she was around the house a lot more."

On another occasion, Gilberto Echeverría, a grandfather of sixty-
eight, offered his own experience. "Things used to be much more simple. For forty years, I earned the family money as an *albañil* [laborer in
construction], and my wife, before she died, she was responsible for

everything in the home. Now," he mused in a meditative tone, "now it's a wonder you can tell who's who. My daughter is also making money, and my son-in-law helps [ayuda] her all the time in the house."[6]

It is not uncommon for husbands and fathers in their twenties and thirties in Colonia Santo Domingo to wash dishes, sweep, change diapers, and go shopping on a regular basis. They will tell you about it if you ask, as will some of their wives, mothers, and sisters, and you will see them in their homes, in front of their houses, and in the neighborhood markets. A good friend boasted to me one day, "Why, sometimes I'm the one buying my daughters their sanitary pads. And, I'll tell you, I've got no problem with this as some guys still do . . . well, so long as they tell me what brand to buy. After all, I'm not going to stand there like a *pendejo* [asshole], just gaping at all the feminine-hygiene products!"

THE GENDER OF TORTILLAS

One day in early December, from our apartment window I spotted Miguel with Miguelito, who was then not quite five, stepping out of his gate onto Huehuetzin Street. After handing his son a cloth, Miguel stayed in the doorway while the boy walked the thirty feet to the *tortillería*, looking back frequently. Miguelito walked to the head of the line, not understanding that he had to wait his turn, threw down the cloth (in which the tortillas were to be wrapped), and ran back to his father. With a nudge, the boy ran back, picked up the tortillas, and returned to a beaming Miguel. Though Miguelito is more closely protected than many boys his age, his experience was nonetheless typical of many girls and boys in Santo Domingo.

Whereas older generations may still associate "picking up the tortillas"—something that is done two or three times daily—exclusively with girls and women, in Santo Domingo it is now not so gendered an activity. For boys as well as girls, being allowed for the first time to buy tortillas by oneself marks a minor rite of passage. One way to measure changes in gender roles and identities is to determine the extent to which activities become less (or more) gendered—less (or more) identified with women or men in particular. Picking up the tortillas is today less and less associated with women; thus a symbolically charged activity has become less gendered.

Several times fathers and mothers told me with pride of challenging what they perceived as being culturally assigned gender roles, from

The *tortillería* near where we lived in Santo Domingo drew lines of women and men, boys and girls, from 8 A.M. to 7 P.M. every day.

changing diapers to mending clothes. For example, Jesús García said that while he was building a sidewalk in front of his home, neighbors complained to him that not only Jesús's son but also two of his daughters were up to their knees in a ditch shoveling dirt. This was not, said the neighbors, something that females of any age should be seen doing. Jesús had enjoyed provoking the scene. Although he is of the same generation as his neighbors, the differing approaches to whether some activity—like ditch digging—is considered appropriate for women are often described by men like Jesús as a conflict between antiquated and newer ways of doing things. And, for Jesús as well as others, it is not an abstract moral issue, but rather a practical matter of what is needed in the family, the *colonia,* or even the nation.

According to many residents of Santo Domingo, more than at any time in the past men participate in chores involved in running a household. The most common exception to this is cooking, which among older and younger men—and not a few women—in various classes in Mexico City is still commonly seen as the consummately female task. Miguel once told me that, although his own father had done little around the house, "before I got married, my mother taught us to do the wash, to iron, to mop, and to do the dishes. The only thing I didn't learn was to cook." Rare is the man who prepares his or others' meals on a regular basis.[7] Many men do cook when their wives or other women are not around, though this generally takes the form of reheating food the women have left for them. And a lot of men like to cook for fiestas and festive events, often preparing a special, signature meat dish (like calf-brain tacos or a spicy goat stew). When asked why they do not cook more, some men explain that their wives will not even let them enter the kitchen area, much less cook. Some of these same wives clarified for me that the real issue was that their husbands are far better at giving excuses than working.

In attempting to distinguish between words and deeds, when it came to housework duties performed by men in Santo Domingo I was continually confronted with not only the more straightforward issue of men not doing as much as they claimed they did, but also the far more perplexing question as to why men (and often women) sought to convince me that men were sharing in chores previously regarded more as women's work. That is, analyzing the words of my friends was important in its own right, and not just as a counterpoint to deeds. This is particularly significant because even men who participate relatively little in domestic affairs in Santo Domingo will often comment on how much *las cosas* (things) are changing in the world of housework. Perhaps especially because they were explaining the situation to a North American, many men would describe the changes in terms of "this is the way things used to be for men in Mexico." Their words made it plain that to live in Mexico City today means to participate, to one extent or another, and willingly or not, in contemporary debates on engendered topics like housework.

Despite indications that changes intergenerationally have occurred regarding domestic chores, Sánchez Gómez (1989:70) is correct when she writes: "Most research [on housework in Mexico] concludes that the participation of men in domestic work is scarce, inconsistent, and sometimes nonexistent." Time-share, work-allocation studies point to definite and continuing inequality in the sharing of household chores (see de Barbieri 1984 and Rosenblueth 1984). Even when considerations such as men's longer hours of paid work are factored in, women in Santo Domingo and throughout the working class in Mexico City generally work (whether for money or not) more than men and have fewer leisure hours. This fact is both cultural and fundamental, an expression and nexus of broader and ongoing gender inequalities.

Beyond indicating the difficulties in determining what constitutes "significant" contributions to the household, at a minimum these studies point to the need for further research on male participation in house-work.[8] A pattern of historical change regarding housework is also prob-able—that is, change as experienced by younger generations, and not simply cyclical change whereby patterns of change are continually re-peated and reproduced from one generation to the next.

When I approached them on a warm spring day in April, the *mu-chachos* were bantering about their sisters. I joined in about my own two sisters, and after a while I asked if I could tape the discussion. They laughed and assented, flattered, I think, because they thought their words so inconsequential. We talked at first about how young women they knew were demanding a lot of things that their mothers never had, that this was going to require them as husbands to treat women consid-erately, and how they envisioned living their lives differently than had their fathers.

Esteban told me, "In that sense, something has changed. Men have become more . . . not exactly *mandilones* [men bossed around by women], but more like . . . now they share the housework, they go shopping, make the beds, prepare the food. In other words, check it out, there have been more divorces."

"Why?" I asked.

Felipe answered this time. "Because women now feel able to take care of themselves, to get ahead even if it's with kids, so now it's . . . a single life. There are more single mothers now."

Esteban continued: "But also for the same reason, because now they [women] are becoming independent. Now they're beginning to work [outside the home], right?"

It seemed to me that the young men were thinking of concrete, per-sonal experiences and probably challenges they had faced, but I re-mained curious about the extent to which they were actually taking part in housework. I asked, "If both husband and wife are working full-time, is housework still more the woman's duty?"

Pancho said, "If both are working, both have the same responsi-bility."

"Really, or are you just saying that?"

"No, no, really," he insisted. "What women want now is for the man to get up first and make breakfast, and also do the housework."

"I don't think it's so ridiculous that a man get up and make break-fast, that a man make the bed," chimed in Rodrigo, who had been silent until then. "Why? Because as we're saying now, everything's changed, everything's evolving. I think that a family can last a long time [to-gether] if it shares its experiences."

"Do you guys cook?" I asked.

"Yes," said Esteban.

"The truth is, no," said Felipe.

"I do . . . now," said Rodrigo.

"I cooked for the whole family . . . once," added Jaime bashfully.

Later our talk turned to what each person considered the easiest and the worst household chores. As we debated the relative agonies of hand-scrubbing dirty collars, greasy pans, and younger siblings' ears, I had the sense that although this was not a common topic of discussion for the young men—indicating that housework was presumably not as inte-gral to their lives as it was for their sisters—they were speaking from real experience. When we discussed sewing, they might have felt awk-ward talking about it with other men instead of women, but they also knew something about bobbins and a hem stitch.

On another occasion, I asked students in an eighth-grade social sci-ence class at the José Vasconcelos Technical Junior High School in Santo Domingo about housework. In a boisterous class "interview" the young men and young women all assured me that today boys do a lot of chores that their grandfathers would never have done. I asked for a show of hands regarding who regularly performed different tasks, and, with the exception of cooking, the young men claimed they did as much as the young women. I then asked for a show of hands from just the young women, the *muchachas,* asking them whether their brothers re-ally shared these chores. Once again, the response was overwhelmingly that they did, with a couple of comments to the effect of "And they'd better, if they know what's good for them."

I was starting to believe them, chastened for wondering whether the students were merely putting on an egalitarian appearance for my bene-fit. And, feeling less skeptical, I began to think that here were signs of some transformations in gender roles in the realm of housework. So I added a final, loaded question for the young women: "So you, the *muchachas,* are not going to marry men who think that housework is just for women?" A hand went up, followed by the simple, firm reply "Of course we will!" A dozen heads nodded in agreement. "But why?" I asked. "Well, sure it would be better if he did housework, but there is a lot more to a good marriage than that," the student advised me.

After concluding several interviews with family members from different generations, and hearing from many of these people about the greater participation of younger men in domestic work in Colonia Santo Domingo, I interviewed Tomás, who was thirty years old and the father of two children. Tomás stated categorically that he did no housework whatsoever. I thought Tomás's responses were more typical of older men than younger and that Tomás was a rather exceptional case among my younger male acquaintances. In the course of our chat he also happened to mention that he felt a special love for his older daughter. Why? Tomás told me that when the girl was young he spent a lot more time with her, and that he did a lot of the cooking, cleaning, and other household chores. I was puzzled, since his housework contributions at the time of the interview were, according to him, nil. Tomás was in turn surprised by my confusion. It was really quite natural, he explained. His wife used to have a paying job. Now she did not because Tomás was making enough to support the whole family. If his wife was home all the time now and he was working all day, why, he asked, should he continue doing housework?

POR NECESIDAD

Social life is essentially *practical*.

> *Karl Marx, "Theses on Feuerbach"*

The most common explanation offered by men and women of varying ages in Santo Domingo as to why some men are now taking greater responsibility for household duties that have previously been the rather exclusive tasks of women is "*por necesidad* [by necessity]"—because they have to. What they usually mean is that in numerous families it has become economically necessary for both husband and wife to have paid work, and that this has sometimes led the husband to do some of the household tasks.

What few men state, but what many women discuss with a certain relish, is that *por necesidad* can refer also to men being coerced by women to take on some of these responsibilities. That is, in terms of changes in cultural attitudes regarding housework, quite regularly it is women who change first and then make—or try to make—their men change. This process is undoubtedly part of a larger development that Lomnitz-Adler (1992:282) calls the "emergent forms of coherence in some of the more stabilized urban underclasses." We can also see here one aspect of regional distinctiveness within Mexico that has so occupied the attentions of historians of the country recently (see Joseph 1988; Lomnitz-Adler 1992; Mallon 1995; and Stern 1995).

The causal chain of events in emergent cultural practices such as those involving male participation in housework is remarkably consistent according to my friends in Santo Domingo: women usually initiate the changes; at first, men normally resist them. The issue is rarely resolved but instead often becomes a source of ongoing tension in the marriage and the household. In addition, and related to their often privileged position compared with women in Mexican society as a whole, men in Santo Domingo sometimes admit to trying to take advantage of the situation by attributing greater natural energy to women and greater innate *flojera* (laziness) to men.

The partial, relatively recent, and multiform changes within the division of labor in some households in the *colonia* are not simply a reflection of economic transformations—for example, more women working outside the home—but also relate to cultural changes in what it means to be a man today in at least some working class neighborhoods of Mexico City. It is a further indication of the actual duties performed and of the cultural values still placed on these household tasks, by women as well as by men, that the expression used by nearly all to describe men's activities in the home is *ayudar a la esposa* (helping the wife).[9] It is not inconsequential that the term *ayudar* is also used very commonly by women to describe how their remunerated employment fits into maintaining the household. Women "help" with the household budget, as men may "help" with the housework.[10] Men generally do not share equally in these responsibilities, in word or deed, and the cultural division of labor between men and women is still regarded as important and therefore enforced by many. Yet women in Mexico are working outside the home for money more than ever before, and this applies even more to women in the capital (see table 2).[11]

Whereas in Mexico City in 1990 around 30 percent of women worked for money, the figure was slightly less than 20 percent for the country overall. Statistics by age group reveal an even starker contrast: over 40 percent of women between forty and forty-four in the capital were economically active in 1990, whereas only 23 percent of women in Mexico as a whole in the same age category reported having remunerated employment at that time (see table 3).[12]

The extent to which women work outside the home is a social question reflected in statistics, public mores, and governmental policies, and

TABLE 2

ECONOMICALLY ACTIVE POPULATION, AS
PERCENTAGE OF RESPECTIVE POPULATION OVER
TWELVE YEARS OLD (1990)

	Mexico City	Mexico
Women	31	20
Men	67	68
Women and men	48	43

SOURCE: Data from Instituto Nacional de Estadística, Geografía e Informática 1990, *Cuadro* 27, p. 316.

TABLE 3

ECONOMICALLY ACTIVE POPULATION BY AGE GROUP, AS
PERCENTAGE OF RESPECTIVE POPULATION (1990)

	Women	Men	Women and Men
Mexico City			
20–24	40	70	54
25–29	45	89	66
30–34	44	94	68
35–39	43	95	68
40–44	41	95	66
Mexico			
20–24	29	77	52
25–29	28	89	57
30–34	27	92	58
35–39	25	92	57
40–44	23	91	56

SOURCE: Data from Instituto Nacional de Estadística, Geografía e Informática 1990, *Cuadro* 27, p. 316.

in citing statistics such as those regarding women's paid employment there is always a danger that they will be misinterpreted as the *cause* of changing cultural patterns. My intent here is, if anything, precisely the opposite: to highlight the cultural changes by showing one of their effects: women's work outside the home.[13]

Whether women work for money is also a personal issue for individuals and individual households. In most situations with which I am familiar in Colonia Santo Domingo, men's steady employment is normally a shared goal of husband and wife, though one that is often unattainable. Periodic and chronic unemployment and underemployment are constants for many men in the *clases populares*. Whether women work for money is far more variable and depends not only on factors such as job availability but additionally on more particular questions concerning the individual desires of wife and husband, the ages of children, the financial resources of the family at any particular moment, and so on. The question of whether women should work and how much is a frequent source of conflict in many households, for both financial and moral reasons.

Miguel and I discussed the fact that he was working while his wife, Norma, studied for two years to become a bookkeeper. Miguel, who began working when he was eight years old by carrying bags for shoppers to their houses or cars, told me about the plans Norma and he had.

"There will come a time when both of us will be working," he said.

"But will you always work more than she?" I inquired.

"Of course."

"Why?"

"Maybe because women have more to do taking care of the children in the house. And men, they can more easily find work. Norma is going to have a harder time than I do working. She's not going to be able to leave at eight or ten at night or stay all night working when it's needed. I sometimes have to do this."

I asked Roberto, who repairs car radiators in Santo Domingo, if his wife had a paying job. He told me she did not, because she suffered from a long-term illness. Then he added, "Besides, women would have to work a lot more just to make the same money men make."[14] Women in the working class seldom earn a higher salary than their husbands, and Roberto's point thus alludes to social discrimination against women and indicates the way in which many households may feel themselves caught in a catch-22: for a wife to work while her husband stays home would require not only mocking cultural conventions, but probably also suffering even greater economic hardship than they already are.

THE CONDITIONS OF WOMEN'S WORK

There is frequent and sometimes acrimonious controversy within households over whether women want to, should, and will be "allowed" to work outside the home. When he turned five, the child of one couple went off to kindergarten in the mornings, and the mother found a full-time job for the first time since before her son was born. The boy's grandmother was to watch him in the afternoons. The mother was elated, she told me, not so much because she was earning money herself—the husband had always given the wife his paycheck to do with as she wished—but because she was free of some of the tedium of day-to-day housework and child care. An older woman was hired to come in once a week to clean and cook some for the family. Unfortunately, however, the boy quickly began to get into trouble in the afternoons, and the husband insisted that his wife stop working at once, before it was too late. Despite tears and pleas from the wife, and promises from the grandmother and the grandfather that they would watch the boy more closely, the husband was unmoved.

Angela told me that her grandmother was a single mother who worked as a servant for a wealthy family who arranged for Angela's father to get a scholarship at a school for rich children. Even with this help, however, Angela's father was not able to succeed in his career like the other youths. But he was able to make the acquaintance of a man who many years later had a powerful post in the state health service and was able to offer six positions to members of her father's family. Angela's father asked her if she wanted a job.

"I already had all my children," Angela recalled. "So my father arrived one afternoon and said to me, 'Bring me all your papers and we'll see what's missing.' "

When Angela's husband, Juan—the *cabrón* (bastard), she called him—arrived, he said to her father, "So, you're going to arrange for work for your daughter?"

"Yes, yes, I am going to arrange it. She wants to work."

When Juan heard this, Angela continued, "he said to his father-in-law, 'Well, the only thing I'm going to tell you is that if anything happens to my children it's your responsibility, because she is going to work because you want to arrange for work for her. So if she doesn't take care of the children as she should, or something happens to them, it's going to be your fault, because you went around putting all these ideas in her head.' So my father said, 'No, forget it. Don't count on me, daughter.' And he ripped up the papers."

"Would you have wanted to work full-time?" I asked.

"No. I have a very maternal character. Extremely so," Angela replied. Even so, she never again had the chance to get even part-time work.

Many women wish to work for money but their men are against the idea. Yet in more than a few situations, men have to persuade their wives to seek paid employment, and the women still resent having to leave their homes each day and express their dreams of someday being able to return to lives as housewives. These women and men live in an era in which service-sector (and "informal"-sector) semi-employment is surging if irregular (see Harvey 1989), requiring all the more flexibility and mobility on the part of wage laborers. Even many of the terms that characterize the economy of flexible accumulation—terms like *informal economy* and *domestic work*—are themselves officially and popularly linked to gender categories, being especially associated with women's paid or unpaid labor. This is reminiscent of Habermas's (1987) point that economics is not to be thought of as connected neatly to male gender identities and the public sphere. Rather, as here, the interchange between economics and the private sphere of women and men must be recognized as an integral part of the relation between systemic and household circuits within society.

The private lives of men and women in the *clases populares* often conceal powerful economic pressures that do lead to severe strains in most households of Mexico City. Then, too, even in the wake of much recent and valuable analysis regarding gender and intergenerational conflicts in families, we should also acknowledge that love, generosity, and mutual agreement are not altogether unknown phenomena in Santo Domingo. That is, shared desires and rationales can play a cohesive role, in some families more than others, at some times more than others, and around some issues more than others.

Part of the issue involves money. As an older woman who had worked as a cleaning woman for rich families told me, "It's nice, because after working awhile, you get used to having your own money. You don't have to go asking for money from your husband all the time: 'Give me money for this, give me money for that, because I don't have any left.' "

The *muchachos* told me that although their fathers had sometimes initially opposed their mothers' desires to seek work in factories or as cleaning women at the National University, things had changed both in terms of who earned money for the household and regarding certain consequences of outside employment.

"What's happening is that women are becoming independent a little more, because men are now giving women more freedom to work. Before, men didn't let them work, only men worked and supported the women. Now women and men work and help each other out. That's why they both have opinions. Only because of that."

Long ago Frederick Engels (1884b:137–38) stated that "the first con-

dition for the liberation of the wife [in the modern individual family] is
to bring the whole female sex back into public industry."[15] This view
has been variously misinterpreted, most often to mean that once women
get out of the home and find paid employment (preferably in factories),
their liberation will quickly and necessarily follow.

As Hartmann (1981) explains, women's wage labor does not necessarily lead to sharing housework duties with men or to women's equality more generally. But recent social science research on these questions
is nothing if not contradictory. Although Young (1993) recently has
shown that women in Ciudad Juárez may gain a measure of "bargaining power" with men through their paid employment, Benería and
Roldán (1987:165), working in Mexico City, "did not find that wom-
en's control over their incomes empowered them significantly in the
bargaining of gender relations within the home." And although Zavella
(1987) argues effectively that Chicanas working in Santa Clara, California, continue to be chiefly responsible for housework, in a study by
Zavella and others (Lamphere et al. 1993) it is reported that in practice
Hispano and white working class men in Albuquerque are assuming a
number of "women's chores."

Even allowing for some mechanistic currents in Engels's thinking,
however, it is hard to accept the interpretation that he saw a simple
cause-and-effect relationship between women's employment and liberation. His comment comes at the end of a passage in which he discusses
the historical mutability of the social form he calls "the family," and
his emphasis is not on the emancipatory splendors of factory work per
se, but rather on the stultifying confines of modern capitalist families.
Engels's point was not that remunerated employment in itself liberates
women, but that liberation will never come about as long as women
remain in cloistered domesticity.[16]

The ongoing relevance of Engels's formulation is seen in the caustic
comments of women who have been active in the community struggles
of the past decade, whether they have held paying jobs or not, concerning women who are still housebound. Sometimes they voice anger at
"*los pinches machos mexicanos* [the goddamned *machos mexicanos*]"
who think women are their slaves. More often they speak disdainfully
of the women who put up with such abuse. Once again, whether or not
their sense of generational changes is accurate, it is noteworthy that
they often couch their critiques in terms of historical change: "Women
who *still* tolerate men like that deserve what they get." Either way,

many women see the home as a prison if it circumscribes one's entire life. In this sense, they view simply getting out—whether for employment or community activism—as potentially, if not inherently, positive.

BOOKS AND BABIES

Enrollment at the elementary school level in Mexico was by 1975 roughly equal for boys and girls. Only in the decade of the 1980s did girls begin attending junior high school in the same numbers as boys (see table 4). For the upper middle and upper classes as well, change becomes especially apparent in the universities in the 1980s. Fifty years before, only 2 or 3 percent of college enrollment was female.

On the other hand, similar educational figures comparing Mexico City with other parts of the country reveal continuing and gross inequalities between the poor in urban and rural areas. In 1987, for example, the average number of years of completed education for the population over the age of fifteen in the Federal District was 8.5, the highest in the country. At the other end of the scale, in the poor southern state of Chiapas, the average was 3.7 years (Prawda 1989:43).

In the *colonias populares* of Mexico City, girls attend school, at least through junior high school, nearly as much as boys. These girls' expectations about themselves in relation to education are considerably higher than were those of their mothers and aunts; rarely do parents in Santo Domingo voice a preference that their boys, because they are boys, continue studies beyond levels reached by their daughters. It goes without saying that higher expectations on the part of girls and their families and higher educational levels achieved by girls have led to views that education—at least through junior high school—is no longer a male enclave. Having grown up in such a context, most boys and girls lack a deep sense of historical perspective and are thus unable to compare the contemporary situation with any other.

Their parents, however, both fathers and mothers, often speak with pride about daughters as well as sons who have excelled in their studies. One of the most common adornments on living-room walls throughout Santo Domingo is a child's framed diploma. "You don't want to talk to me," fifty-five-year-old Javier told me after I met him one day. I had asked if I could interview him. He explained that all he had been doing for many years was changing oil and transmission fluid in cars and buses. "I don't know anything that would interest you," he said. "You

TABLE 4

FEMALE STUDENT ENROLLMENT IN MEXICO,
AS PERCENTAGE OF ENROLLMENT

Year	Elementary School	Junior High School	University
1975	48	39	30
1980	49	47	38
1989	48	49	42

SOURCE: Data from UNESCO 1991: 3–94, 3–167, 3–260.

should talk to my daughter. She's studying computers. She knows a lot."

Residents of Santo Domingo repeatedly make a connection between higher education and lower birthrates. People talk about having fewer children, and they do have fewer children, than their parents. Many people want only two or three children so that those they do have might receive better educations than their parents had, and thereby have a better chance of getting ahead in the world. In my survey with selected people in the *colonia,* the twenty-seven men I interviewed had a average of just less than three children each; they came from families that had an average of nearly eight children.[17]

Birthrates throughout Mexico have plummeted in the past twenty years. Following tremendous population growth as a consequence of a rise in average life expectancy—from twenty-five years in 1900 to sixty-six years in 1980—birthrates have been cut nearly in half in the last two decades in Mexico (see table 5).[18] Figures reported in the Mexican census of 1990 indicate that whereas the birthrate for the country overall was 2.5 that year, for Mexico City it was a significantly lower 2.0 (INEGI 1990:265, 273). Because data for women who will go on to have other children are averaged into the totals for birthrates, one can assume that these figures are lower than the fertility rates. All in all, the drop in birthrates in the last twenty years in Mexico as a whole, and in its urban centers in particular, has been impressive.

Such demographic transitions are undoubtedly related to the meanings and practices of maternity and paternity, and to gender identities overall, in Mexican society, because female sexuality is not an essential quality, nor is it reducible to biological reproduction or demographic shifts. Yet, approaching the issue from the other side of the equation, if women and couples are having fewer and fewer children, presumably this is a result of either an increased use of birth control or decreased

TABLE 5
BIRTHRATES IN MEXICO 1900–1988, AS
AVERAGE NUMBER OF CHILDREN PER
WOMAN OVER TWELVE YEARS OLD

Year	Birthrate
1900	5.0
1940	4.6
1960	4.5
1970	4.5
1977	3.8
1981	3.4
1983	3.1
1985	2.8
1988	2.5

SOURCE: Adapted from Zavala de Cosío 1992:26, 222, 282.

sexual relations. Either way, cultural attitudes and behavior are deeply involved in the demographic statistics.

The changes involving women that are made explicit in lower birthrates imply reevaluations and changes among men as well. For if womanhood no longer is so closely tied to motherhood, for example, then manhood too may be at least partially recast, though this does not necessarily manifest itself in direct transformations regarding parenting practices on the part of women or men. Although the boys were cheerfully playing "the doll bath" at the San Bernabé Nursery School in 1992, the doll of choice among the four- and five-year-old girls there was a baby who carried in its belly a fetus that gestated for a while and was then born, I assume through a cesarean.[19]

Lower birthrates also are connected in turn to different cultural forms experienced by women and men. Valfre, thirty years old and from the sierra of Oaxaca, joked with me that birthrates were falling in the *campo* with the advent of televisions. "But don't forget, Mateo, while they love their TV programs, folks can still take advantage of the commercials!"

After he and his wife, María Elena, married in 1991, Valfre moved into María Elena's cinder-block room, next to a living-room area where her younger brother slept at night, and below the room shared by his new in-laws. Everyone shared the kitchen with its corrugated-tin roof and plastic sheeting for walls, the septic toilet in a shack, and the metal washtub used for bathing. Like several other young men I know in Colonia Santo Domingo, Valfre moved in with his wife and her parents because there was space and because they all got along well with each other.

Though patrilocality is the arrangement most commonly documented in Mexico (see Nutini, Carrasco, and Taggart 1976), kinship residence patterns do vary throughout the country. The fact that matrilocality is quite common in Santo Domingo is more indicative of intergenerational changes in gender relations within households than simply of cultural diversity. Miguel has lived for several years with Norma in a separate two-room structure, but their residence is on the property of Norma's family, and within a few feet of the bedroom of her mother and father, Angela and Juan, and of Angela's kitchen. Though Miguel and Norma have a separate toilet, they use the same shower as others in the household. In another instance, for over fifteen years Carlos, the long-haul truck driver, his wife, Leti, and their three daughters have lived in a home on the property of Leti's mother, who lives next door. Such arrangements may be generally convenient for those with limited financial resources, and at the same time they help avoid some of the often-noted problems between daughters-in-law and mothers-in-law when newlyweds move in with the husband's parents.[20]

It appears, then, that along with shifts in education and domestic divisions of labor, changes have also occurred in residence patterns as they have taken on a less gendered aspect, at least for many people, much of the time. In the past, adherence to patrilocality was often explained as a matter of "convenience" as much as cultural propriety, and today, to the extent that a transition has occurred, people in Santo Domingo, if pressed, will usually explain that when you are struggling just to get by, you should live wherever there is space and support, regardless of whose name is on the property deed. In this way they show how everyday features of their lives have become less gendered, less associated exclusively or mainly with one gender or another.

Another instance of engendering and degendering concerns the developing meanings of the word *comer* (to eat) today in the *colonia*. As well as indicating some of the diverse forms that eating takes in various households, these multiple meanings of *comer* reveal elements of what is changing and what has remained constant in gender divisions of labor.

Isabel, for instance, always prepares food for her husband and children, and she always makes sure her husband has eaten his fill before offering seconds to the children. Since the others often finish whatever meat Isabel is able to include in the meal, she frequently is left with little to eat besides beans, rice, and tortillas, and maybe some vegetables. Isabel's neighbor Juanita, on the other hand, also eats after her husband and children, but in her case there is usually meat left over. Juanita eats what they do, only later. These two situations are typical of those found in many households in the *colonia,* though more common perhaps is what occurs in the family of Inés: she prepares and serves a soup followed by the main dishes, and then sits down to eat each course, one course behind the others.

In each household *comer* has a very definite, engendered character. Even so, within this context there is marked discrepancy that leads to, among other things, Isabel complaining bitterly about eating more poorly than her husband and defensive justifications by him for this situation. As for Inés, she describes her situation in the language of mutual arrangements spouses make. In other words, it is not that eating is less linked to female work for Inés, but that the gendered division of labor is less a manifestation of subordination than of difference, where difference does not necessarily involve inequality: her husband works outside the home, and she works in it.[21]

We noted earlier with regard to identity politics that assertions of difference can be used to exclude and control, and that they can also be used by marginalized groups to assert their equal rights. Similarly, because "equality is not the elimination of difference, and difference does not preclude equality" (Scott 1990:138), divisions of labor in households in Santo Domingo cannot be analyzed merely on the basis of difference. In terms of equality between women and men, the simultaneous assertion and challenge of these and other engendered differences in the *colonia* reflect not merely rationalizations on the part of women and men with respect to housework, but the tensions of cultural contradictions and cultural norms that are espoused and defied every day in Santo Domingo.

INDEPENDENCE

The demographic shifts in employment, education, and birthrates in the past few decades in Mexico in the main represent singular, historic change. That is, unlike experiences that are often repeated from one generation to the next—in Colonia Santo Domingo, for example, most couples marry and begin having children when they are in their twen-

ties, as did their parents—these shifts (improvements in women's education, lower birthrates, and so forth) will most likely never be reversed.[22]
Even if women's remunerated employment were to decrease dramatically, the situation with regard to gender relations would hardly return
to what it had been in earlier epochs, given that so much else has
changed. Generational succession never takes place in a historical
vacuum.

The issue of women's independence from male authority and family
constraints is a common topic of discussion among men in Mexico,
especially the widely accepted perception that many young women today are demanding more of this kind of independence than their mothers had. Most of the *muchachos* feel ambivalent about these developments, which becomes apparent when they distinguish between what
they, the *muchachos,* consider the legitimate aspirations of their sisters
and the goals of their girlfriends.

Esteban told me, "For example, my sisters, they are more hung up
on this question—that women today need to be more independent, that
they should have almost the same rights as men because they live in the
same social situation. They all think, they all have arms, legs, heads. So
women are 100 percent demanding that they be given respect in society.
Demanding education, demanding a set salary, a set position in a business. In the countryside it's very different than here. They still think that
women should learn to read and write but then devote themselves to
the home."

Yet if a young man is not related to this same young woman, he may
feel and behave differently. Celso described what he seemed to view as
a justifiable cycle of male behavior toward women, with himself still
very much in the youth phase. "How are you different from your father—for instance, in how you act with women?" I asked.

"Because my father is older, he has respect for women. Because I'm
a young guy and all, well when a girl passes, I give her a *piropo.* [A
piropo can range from a flattering remark to a clever catcall to a nasty
or obscene remark.[23]] We're very different."

"So your father has more respect?" I pressed.

"Yes. I think so."

"Your father was more of a *canijo* [son of a bitch] than you," observed Pancho.

"Well, who knows? What happens is, I think that if we're talking
about young guys, I think that they all want to call out a *piropo* to

young women. Why? Because they're young and it's normal. But as far as having a lot of women, I don't think we're like our fathers." [24]

Combining a view of recent history with elements that are currently repeated to one extent or another in different generations, we may generalize that for most older men in Santo Domingo who are today grandfathers, housework has seldom been part of their lives. Most of these men never changed a diaper for their own children, though Juan told me that he has since learned how to change diapers from programs in his church and applied this knowledge when his grandchildren were infants. Among men of the older generation, assumptions of male entitlement are given more explicit voice, though even here the impact of feminism should not be underestimated, at least in public pronouncements.

Many men now in their thirties and forties still vividly recall the tumultuous events of the 1960s, and especially the 1968 massacre of hundreds of innocents at Tlatelolco prior to the Olympics in Mexico City.[25] Many of them have now been married several years and have teenage children. Among these men there is apparent if by no means uniform change both in attitudes and in behavior regarding housework and the more mundane aspects of infant care. Men and women in this age group often relate that the only way any changes came about at all was through the long back-and-forth of carefully worded requests and bitter recriminations in their marriages. Some would agree with Simón, who told me that he realizes now that he was the main person in the marriage who had to change, and that he is glad he did so. In Simón's case, as in that of countless others, the political currents of the past twenty years have mixed together with the trajectories of personal lives. The result, Simón insists, was a situation in which he and his spouse had to either resolve their earlier problems (which included violence, adultery, and excessive drinking) or separate and perhaps legally divorce.

Ordinary disputes over domestic chores, such as those that have taken place in many households in Santo Domingo in the recent past, indicate an intellectual and moral independence on the part of women in the *colonia*. The significance of this development, as Gramsci noted (1929–35:57), is that social groups dominated by others must exercise such independence and leadership if they are ever to rid themselves of their "liquidated" or subjugated status. It might seem an exaggeration to invoke Gramsci's analysis of the preliminary sites for radical change from below to describe what has occurred in Colonia Santo Domingo. After all, Gramsci was referring explicitly to the popular acquisition of governmental power and not to men scrubbing out toilet bowls. But perhaps this is not too great a stretch.

In Santo Domingo, and for Gramsci, changes of various kinds and magnitudes occur as part of the larger local and global contexts. In periods of widespread upheaval in particular regions or internationally, we may expect to find more dramatic manifestations of widespread social tumult. At other times, however, it may be that newly acquired housework responsibilities on the part of many men represent real, if limited, transformations that are carried out by more or less conscious social actors. In relation to economic and political changes occurring in Mexico and elsewhere in the late twentieth century, such activities represent contemporary rebellions against, and not mere resistance to, oppressive gender relations. In this sense, though they usually appear in muffled form, these activities are among the important creations representing popular responses to the experience of modernity. Among men and women of the '60s generation living in Santo Domingo in the 1990s, those who are today in their late thirties and forties, these developments reflect rebellion and attest to more than resistance because their aims and effect are to displace history and not merely to demean it.

CLOWNING

Younger men in the *colonia* represent more of a conundrum—still another indication of why those changes that have occurred need not follow any preordained circuit in the future. On the one hand, the youth speak sympathetically of sisters at odds with their mothers; on the other hand, their declarations often reveal personal yearnings for submissive girlfriends and wives. They wear the badge of "macho" far more often and proudly than men in the middle age group (see chapter 9). Yet once again, it may be that a fusion of history and youth is at play here, this time affecting a different generation of men.

Feminist currents in contemporary Mexico, for example, do not today exert such an obvious influence among the *muchachos,* who are at a critical period in the development of their own gender identities and sexualities. Most are not yet married. They have less experience with women sexually and romantically, and, some boast, less need to compromise. But for these same reasons, young men to varying degrees are actively seeking to define their gender and sexual identities. In the process, they frequently latch on to popular caricatures of *hombres de verdad* (real men) as the most accessible and easily assimilated models for manly emulation.

Young men in Santo Domingo have, in Gramsci's formulation of contradictory consciousness, "uncritically absorbed" truly prosaic images of *hombres de verdad*. But not only these images, for they also uncritically absorbed the influence of feminism and popular urban movements of the 1970s and 1980s when they were growing up. Because of these inherited influences, and because of their participation in the practical business of daily living, many of them speak and act in very contradictory ways with regard to women. That is, their confusion with regard to masculinity and machismo is especially apparent not simply because of their biological age, as Erikson and other psychologists might have it, but also because of their historical age as the children of the generation of the 1960s. Unless the contradictory gender identities of these youth, as cultural citizens of both society and family, are accounted for in both public and private spheres, we will be unable to understand the part played by gender in the specific, local manifestations of change in Mexico City.

Demographic factors have had a profound influence on gender identities and relations in Mexico City's *colonias populares* in the past twenty-five years. Women's employment outside the home in large numbers has not led to men assuming household chores in equal measure, but it has led to some changes in domestic divisions of labor and an even more widespread debate in homes throughout the capital regarding "women's work" and "men's work." The extent to which the teenage sons of Santo Domingo continue doing the dishes and changing diapers as they become husbands and fathers will be a key barometer of the extent to which transformations are taking place in households in the *colonia*. With birth rates in the early 1990s in Mexico as a whole roughly half what they were in the early 1970s, the identification of women with housebound motherhood is less easily realized. While there is nothing preordained about these or any other demographic changes, the spiral motion of history would argue against the possibility that domestic life for women and men in Santo Domingo will ever revert back to what it was.

In the summer of 1991, I was invited to a two-year-old's birthday party in the vast Netzahualcóyotl area, on the eastern edge of the Mexico City basin. As at many such affairs in the *clases populares,* there were some eighty people present, about equal numbers of adults and children. It was held in a neighborhood gym that had been rented for the occasion. After the guests had helped themselves to tamales, *atole* (a drink made with corn flour), cake, and giant jello molds, a clown arrived. He had games and treats for the youngsters, but he was far more than a kiddie performer. After the spectators had become sufficiently excited from watching the contests between the boys and girls, the clown shouted out, "*¿Quién manda en la casa?* [Who's the boss at home?]" On cue, all the women would shout out, "*¡Nosotras!* [We (women are)!]" Then the men would counter, "*¡Nosotros!* [We (men are)!]" The call-and-response routine went on, punctuated by periods in which individual women or men were called upon to defend the honor of their gender and explain why women or men ruled the roost in their homes.

The clown knew his audience. His purpose, of course, was not to resolve what was a silly question to begin with, but just to have some fun. A year or two later, trying to emulate the clown and finish things up on a light note, I ended my survey with the same question: "*¿Quién manda en la casa?*" The responses, serious and joking, were not especially revealing given what I already knew of Mexico City in the 1990s: nearly all the men said that both husband and wife make major decisions together; some of the women agreed with this, although several said that their husbands make most important choices. But perhaps these comments would have been more surprising had they been made twenty years ago, especially those coming from the men. That is, the very fact that gendered power and control is today a lively source of jesting and jousting, and a legitimate topic of conjecture, testifies to changes that I think have been realized and are still under way in many households in Mexico.

SEVEN

Degendering Alcohol

I regret to state, however, that today there are a great many
women quite as tipsy as the men.

Frances Calderón de la Barca, Life in Mexico
(1843)

LAS COPAS

A friend arrived at our apartment in Santo Domingo on 12 December,
the day celebrating the appearance of the Virgin of Guadalupe in 1531,
and one of the most important annual holidays in Mexico. After walking several blocks through the *colonia* from the Copilco metro stop, she
reported, "*Todos los hombres están en la calle tomados* [All the men
are in the streets drunk]."

On a basic level, this was the offhand pronouncement of someone
who had just had to weave her way over and around several congrega-
tions of male merrymakers still toasting Juan Diego's fortuitous vision.
My friend had intended not a statement of pure fact, but rather hyper-
bole with a purpose. Every day, and even more so on holidays, men are
found sipping *las copas*—alcoholic beverages—in the streets of Colonia
Santo Domingo.[1] On another level, however, the comment hints at
(mis)conceptions that are revealed in the way scholars and others sometimes refer to men and women, and in the categories we frequently employ to discuss them: "men (typically) do this"; "women (typically) are
like that."

Although anthropologically influenced concepts of multiculturalism
have served to improve the situation in the past two decades—many
now will qualify such statements by stating, for example, "Latin American men do this," "Asian women are like that," and so on—these summary statements still reveal their origins in haphazard and archaic notions of national character and personality studies. Thus they too can

blur a deeper analysis of how specific group and individual histories impinge on gender identities, as well as the significant extent to which gender relations themselves come to constitute history.

In the social science literature on Mexico, arbitrary reference to "men" and "women" is copious in discussions regarding the relation between men and alcohol. According to most anthropological studies of other locations and times in Mexico, for instance, it has been common to equate *ser hombre* (being a man) with at least periodic public inebriation.

But is this the best way to analyze the mixture of liquor and men that was occurring in Santo Domingo on 12 December 1992? What of those men who were at home and sober throughout that day? Were those men, at least implicitly, less manly than those who were drunk in the streets? In a sense, the answer must be that they were. That is, in the eyes of many commentators, the intoxicated men in the streets were the true and "typical" Mexican *hombres de verdad*.

This is not a quibble over semantics. We should subject to greater scrutiny the celebrated image of the Mexican proletarian male with a bottle of tequila in his hand and a silly, satisfied grin on his lips precisely by examining categories such as "Mexican men" and *"hombres de verdad,"* and the benefits and liabilities accruing to scholars and others who utilize such generalizations. In connection with such typologizing, too often we have landed in trouble by using the quantitative techniques of contemporary social science. For instance, one researcher, reporting on drinking in the late 1960s in a village in Morelos, states:

> Of 165 men over twenty years of age in the village, 29, or 17.6 percent, are on the list of alcoholics, while 27, or 16.3 percent, are on the heavy drinker list. The total of 56 men on both lists thus constitutes 34 percent of the men over twenty years of age. . . . Of the 22 on the violent list, 9 are found among the alcoholics and 13 among the heavy drinkers. (Romanucci-Ross 1973:137)

The construction of such categories of personality types by this investigator is based on the premise that alcoholism reflects the problems of individual psychologies. Or, more specifically, the thesis that alcoholism reveals the lack of social integration of particular individuals, and thus that alcoholics should be viewed as a problem *for* society. Such an analysis is very different from one that views alcoholism as socially created and defined, and therefore a product *of* society.[2]

On Huehuetzin Street where we lived in Colonia Santo Domingo during 1992–93, there stood what some neighbors referred to as *la casa de los borrachos* (the house of the drunks), with three generations of alcoholics living squashed together in a series of shacks. One of the younger members of the household, ten years old, told me that she had spent less than one year in school in her life; instead, she occupied her days selling candies on the curb and running to the corner store, a three-year-old sister in tow, for more *caguamas* (quarts) of beer for her elders. Although not often in so extreme a form, alcohol is part of most people's lives in one way or another in the *colonia,* from young girls who must fetch beer for their mothers and grandmothers to fathers, uncles, brothers, and cousins who miss work when they go on a *borrachera* (drinking binge) to friends who have to be taken to the emergency room when their kidneys will not tolerate another drop of rum. The fatal effects of alcoholism—direct ones like cirrhosis of the liver and alcoholic psychosis, and indirect ones like accidents and homicides—are leading causes of death among men in the so-called productive ages in Mexico (see Menéndez 1990:9).[3]

THE TEMPLE OF MEXICAN VIRILITY: *LA CANTINA*

Having already lived and conducted ethnographic research in Mexico City over a period of several years, upon arriving in Santo Domingo in 1992 I went looking for that "culturally typical" site of Mexican male bonding, the cantina. No one needed to tell me that cantinas were the characteristic meeting places of Mexican men, who after all were the subjects of my study. To my great initial disappointment, however, I was informed by neighbors that although there were a few *pulquerías* in the community, there were no cantinas whatsoever in Colonia Santo Domingo.[4]

Nor do many residents of Santo Domingo travel outside the neighborhood to go to cantinas in other *colonias.* When asked about cantinas, Héctor, who used to drink a lot, likes to lampoon the famous cantina La Guadalupana, located in the well-to-do area of Coyoacán, about a fifteen-minute *micro* ride from Santo Domingo. On any given night at La Guadalupana, says Héctor, you can spot high Mexican government officials sleeping off one too many glasses of sangría under the tables of this venerable institution. People from Santo Domingo don't go there, adds his brother-in-law Juan, because "it's a lot more pleasant to drink at home."

Not to mention less expensive. Another neighbor, a periodically em-

ployed long-haul truck driver, told me that he used to go to the cantinas
when he lived in the central-city *colonia* of Guerrero, but that was
about thirty years ago, when he was young and newly arrived in the
capital from his rancho in the state of Guanajuato. "Who's got that
kind of money today?" he asked me. He offered the following figures:
"Suppose you make a minimum salary of fifteen pesos [then about five
dollars U.S.] a day. Who can afford beer in a cantina? Say you pay one
or two pesos a beer. How long's that going to last you? Even buying a
case isn't as cheap as it used to be." Cantinas, as far as he was concerned, were for those with significantly more money than he had seen
recently.

When men do leave the *colonia* to drink, often it is to find good
pulque. Luciano the welder and his friend Ricardo, a taxi driver, stumbled toward me on their way down the street one afternoon. They told
me they had gotten away to the hills in the area known as Contreras,
in southwestern Mexico City, and that they had spent several hours
there drinking pulque. I asked why they traveled so far when there were
pulquerías in Santo Domingo, though I knew these were widely regarded as the haunts of the most pitiful drunks. It turned out there was
a reason other than the reputation of the clientele of these establishments. "That shit?" responded Luciano in giggles. He explained that in
Contreras pulque is allowed to ferment "naturally" without additives
for up to two weeks. In Santo Domingo, on the other hand, the beverage is fermented the quick way, by adding human excrement to the
brew.[5]

Three times during 1992–93 I was invited to go to cantinas, not by
friends in the neighborhood, as it turned out, but rather, each time by
one or another Mexican anthropologist. The first time, on our way to
the cantina, my companion told me that, given my interest in male identities, it was imperative that I witness firsthand *lo que hacen los hombres* (what men do) and experience this manly environment, which until
a few short years ago was by law an exclusively male refuge. ("There's
still only a men's bathroom," he pointed out to me.) The second time,
I was lectured: "You know nothing of the Mexican man if you don't
know the cantina."

The cantina *is* an important gathering place for many men in Mexico. The working class neighborhood of Colonia Obrera, in the heart
of Mexico City, for instance, is reputed to have more cantinas than taco
stands. For this and other reasons, with full justification it might be
said that Colonia Santo Domingo is not "representative" of *colonias*

populares in Mexico City. But then no neighborhood is or could be in a metropolitan area of nearly 20 million people. Undoubtedly more drinking by men occurs in cantinas in many other parts of the city and country than in Colonia Santo Domingo. Still, as we will see, according to ethnographic studies from widely scattered areas over the past twenty-five years, if there is any pattern in male drinking behavior in the country, it is one of diversity rather than homogeneity.

All of which has a number of interesting implications for gender relations in Santo Domingo, implications that may not be valid to the same degree in all other locations.[6] For many adult men in Colonia Santo Domingo in the early 1990s, drinking with your *cuates* (buddies) and *compas* (*compadres*, symbolic coparents) often similarly embodied and extended bonds of friendship, trust, and male-male intimacy. And as Lomnitz shows (1977:175 f.), *cuates* are first and foremost drinking buddies. Yet even though drinking in the home was often a markedly male activity in Santo Domingo, the very presence of women and children there, among other elements, placed constraints on the men.[7] As we will see later in this chapter, the degendering of alcohol consumption indicates that what constitutes typical male behavior does not stand still.

THE MANNERS OF DRINKING

In Colonia Santo Domingo, some men drink in the street in front of their own or friends' houses after work and on weekends. More men drink in their homes during these times, with friends or family. A few admit to occasionally drinking alone. As part of the antipollution efforts of recent years in Mexico City, each vehicle is prohibited from driving one weekday each week. For some friends whose jobs are dependent upon the use of cars or trucks, their day not to "circulate" is also considered like a weekend day, and they may drink more heavily then.

Men and women drink together at birthday parties, holiday celebrations, and when visiting friends, more often than not consuming the same beverages, sometimes in the same quantities, though most often with men drinking more than women, and with more women than men abstaining from alcohol altogether. Older teenagers are often allowed to drink during family events. Younger children are frequently offered sips of beer or *cubas* on these occasions.[8] At large and lengthy events—baptism celebrations, *quinceañera* fiestas, and weddings, for instance—

some men and less often a few women will drink to the point of intoxication. Depending on the individuals involved, this may lead to violent outbursts revealing long-simmering feuds or to tender confessional moments; in either case the parties involved are capitalizing on the belief that drunks should be held less responsible for their words and actions. My friends Juan and Tomás both seemed comfortable when they mentioned that they had reputations for being very temperate when drunk. Angela notes that whereas Juan is *impulsivo* (impulsive) in everyday life, he's the most accommodating man in the world after he's had a few *copas*.

Social drinking in moderation on a regular basis has been reported in some ethnographies of Mesoamerica (see, for example, Lewis 1951 and DeWalt 1979). Even where alcohol is more commonly consumed by men during holiday and weekend bingeing, its role in the mediation of everyday social relations is noteworthy (see Brandes 1988). In Colonia Santo Domingo, consuming one or two beers daily is common practice for many men, whereas bingeing, though not uncommon in the 1990s, was according to most accounts more common in the past. Further, nearly all women and men I have spoken with on the subject in Santo Domingo maintain that far more women today drink alcoholic beverages, and in far greater quantities, than they did in the past.[9]

On walls throughout the Pedregales one sees the painted double-"A"-within-a-circle symbol of Alcoholics Anonymous, along with meeting times, phone numbers, and other pertinent information. In this way, alcoholism in Colonia Santo Domingo has a very public presence, at least institutionally. Even the nonconformist Gabriel has attended AA sessions, and he can recite what he has learned there: "The first glass of liquor is the first step to alcoholism"; "Alcoholism is a disease." Gabi sees his drinking binges as closely connected to his attempts to escape mentally from the psychological stresses that torment him: "Sometimes I end up thinking that only drunk or asleep can I forget how fucked up everything is. Because sometimes I don't have anyone to tell about all the experiences I have, my worries, my traumas, my complexes. Because in my family I feel . . . no one understands me in my family."

Gabriel defends his sporadic participation in AA to me, saying that although he knows Alcoholics Anonymous was originally a gringo organization, he thinks that maybe alcoholism is now more resolved in the United States, whereas the streets of Mexico are still full of drunks.

From left, Marcelo, Toño, Gabriel, and Marcos clown for the camera outside Marcos's house.

The AA in Santo Domingo, through its highly visible meeting places and vocal adherents, is anything but anonymous.

Alcoholism as a daily presence in Colonia Santo Domingo takes many forms. The first time I met Claudia, she told me that her husband was an alcoholic. He had tried to quit drinking many times during their fifteen-year marriage, but without long-term success. He had lost some good jobs because of his habit. But she was no longer waiting for a miracle, she said, because she had come to the conclusion that she was the one with the problem, the problem of expecting her husband to change. Besides, she said, she really did not have all that much to complain about: he never beat her, and although on payday he always came home with a bottle in one hand, in the other he carried money for her and the children. She had to stop caring about what people said about him, because, after all, she was dependent on the money he did earn and bring home.

Claudia's husband is one kind of alcoholic. Martín and Toño explained to me one day as we sat on the curb that there are at least two other common kinds of drunks. There are drunks like the ones who live in *la casa de los borrachos,* they said—friendly and peaceful, part of the nonthreatening daily fabric of life on many blocks in Santo Domingo.

They are both women and men, though unquestionably the men are "fifty times" more prevalent and visible, according to Toño. One greets these drunks pleasantly, sometimes "lends" them a coin or two, and occasionally shares a few sips with them. Then there are the drunks in street gangs like the Nazis, overwhelmingly male, though sometimes with girlfriends in attendance. They are to be avoided if possible, and above all they are not to be antagonized, for they can turn violent rather quickly. They drink various liquors, said Martín, including the infamous "96 [percent]," and they smoke a lot of marijuana. Some sniff *cemento* (glue). Though they all may be neighbors, there are drunks and then there are *drunks,* Toño warned, crushing a just-emptied can of Modelo beer against his thigh.

GETTING DRUNK

The Mexican who does not drink and get drunk is the dead Mexican.

> *J. R. Flippin,* Sketches from the
> Mountains of Mexico *(1889)*

On another occasion in late February, Toño and I spent several hours at the corner *tienda* with Gabriel, Marcos, the Yucateco carpenter Marcial, and Marcelo, once again drinking licorice-flavored *anís.* Following a year's abstention, Toño was, two months after the New Year, still celebrating being able to drink again. Other men and a few women who stopped by to purchase something at the store were invited to share our *anís.* Some men would stay awhile, either drinking with us or buying themselves a soda instead. Although there was little pressure to drink liquor with us, only those drinking alcohol remained very long. As Marcelo commented to me at another time, it is a lot easier to enjoy the company of others if you are either all drunk or all sober.

We drank far more that day than we normally did. After we finished off the first pint of *anís,* someone went to the nearby liquor store for another, and then another, until we had consumed a half dozen of these. Finally we switched to liter bottles, ultimately polishing off two or three of the big containers. All this time, Gabriel was repairing one or another VW bus *combi,* Marcos was working on the fenders of his 1964 VW bug, and Marcelo, though enjoying his two-hour break from behind the *tienda* counter, was helping out from time to time when customers proved too much for his wife.

After several hours, Marcos's wife, Delia, brought out tacos, which she had prepared for us in their house next to the *tienda*. While she was there she scolded me in particular: "You shouldn't drink!" Though apparently resigned to my participation with the others, she was not kidding. I may have been singled out as a newcomer, and as someone who should "know better" because of being a gringo and a *profesionista* (professional). But Delia may have also felt that Marcos and the others were to a certain extent putting on a performance for me, and so I was partly responsible for her husband's growing inebriation that day.

This last idea became apparent the next week. Two days after our *borrachera* I saw Don Timoteo at his spot in the grassy median on Cerro de la Estrella. He was waiting for customers to bring him their wicker chairs for repair. "We saw you drinking the other day," he said simply, raising his eyes to stare seriously into mine. He knew that I knew that he had been an alcoholic for many years and that he spoke with authority on the subject.

The next day I bumped into Luciano. He said he had not been around the past Saturday, but that he had heard that the others and I had been *bien pedos* (literally, "well farted"; i.e., really loaded). "Pretty soon you're going to be like them," he said laughing, pointing to *la casa de los borrachos*. In Luciano's case, unlike with Don Timo, this did not seem to bother him in the least. During the rest of my fieldwork in Santo Domingo, several of my friends, and even a few men I hardly knew, would ask me, "Hey, Mateo, want some *anís?*" It became a running gag.

As much as it is true that such binges are common occurrences for some men in Colonia Santo Domingo, and therefore I chose as part of my research to suffer the indignities of later ridicule and the queasiness of hangover following our merriment, my case was also in retrospect similar to one described by Brandes in which he "tried to be more Andalusian than the Andalusians." In his paper regarding the ill-fated pursuit of anthropological preconceptions, Brandes (1987:362–63) recounts how he found himself in a bar in southern Spain in January, asking himself where all the men had gone. It turned out that although in the fall the men did spend time drinking in bars, in the winter they stayed at home in the evenings. A friend who had kindly continued drinking with Brandes into the winter despite this custom pointed out that his wife was beginning to feel neglected and suggested that they repair to his house for a change.

If I did not cause all the excess drinking at the *tienda* that afternoon in January, my presence probably did inspire some to show off. And as others demonstrated in the days following that well-oiled occasion, public tolerance for drinking is decidedly a mixture of resignation toward some and persuasive chiding and mockery toward others.

Though many in Colonia Santo Domingo speak of patterns of drinking—on the part of young men, for example—drinking is often considered more a matter of personal choice than an expression of one's inherent (for example, male) character. Juan told me of the recurring battle he had had earlier in life with alcohol:

"After work [in a factory] my friends would say to me, 'Let's go get a drink.' As they paid us on Saturdays, when we got off we went to the cantina or to the *tiendas*. I'd get home at midnight or one in the morning and Angela would be angry. We were on the verge of divorce."

"For drinking?" I asked.

"Yes, for drinking. I drank a lot, a whole lot. They thought I was going to become an alcoholic. When Noé [Juan's third child] was born, I began to cut back, to not drink so much. I continued drinking, but not like when it was every other day, or every day. My children were growing up. 'Well,' I said, 'what kind of an education am I going to give my children if I'm an alcoholic. My children are going to be ashamed of me when they become adults.' When they were small, I said, 'They are going to grow,' so I began to cut back. I didn't drink during the week or on Saturdays. Only every once in a while did I toss down my shots and get drunk. But then it was every couple of weeks."

"With the family, or with your *cuates?*"

"No, by then it was with the family. I'd left my friends. I continued drinking, getting drunk, and I'd go to sleep and wake up sick the next day. Angela has never been able to see me drinking. We used to have problems. We fought. We said things to each other, and then my children realized everything, and no, that was bad. So I began to stop drinking. I continued working in the factory, but since there were eight hundred employees, there was always someone to drag you along. Yet I always made it home with my wages. I never stopped paying the expenses."

"That was never a problem?"

"No, the problem was that I drank."

Juan's history is similar to those of other men with whom I shared experiences concerning the role alcohol had played in their lives.[10] In his case, during the year we were neighbors, on weekdays Juan sometimes settled down to watch the 8 o'clock news with a Don Pedro *cuba* or two, and at family parties he sometimes enjoyed a few more. But according to both him and Angela, the days of his problematic drinking were long past.

Thus it would be wrong to say that today Juan spends much time drinking with his friends. For Juan, as for many men in Santo Domingo, sharing a few *copas* with friends is more a periodic weekend activity than a daily occurrence. Along these same lines, some men point out that although people prefer Bacardi Añejo (dark Bacardi rum) to Bacardi Blanco (white Bacardi rum) because they like the taste better, Añejo is more expensive and they therefore drink Blanco if they want to get drunk.

In many parts of Mexico, however, ethnographers have reported far more uniform drinking patterns among men. Greenberg, for example, summarizes male leisure activities in a Chatino village in Oaxaca: "When not working, men spend a lot of time drinking with their companions" (1989:217). It is not possible to generalize about men in Santo Domingo to such an extent. There, some men will polish off a Vickys beer in the middle of a hot day as others might have a soda, more for the thirst-quenching effect or the taste than out of any desire to become intoxicated. Often while engaged in the seemingly endless task of automotive repair during evenings and weekends, men in Santo Domingo will nurse their Vickys or their Presidente *cubas* for hours, more interested in the convivial ambiance of drinking together than the chemical consequences of alcoholic intake.

Many men talk *about* drinking rather frequently, though, both while engaged in the activity and at other times, commenting on imbibing in general as well as recounting particularly memorable drinking episodes in their lives. Yet with unmistakable consistency, my friends would return to the subject of *la cruda* (the hangover). Perhaps this is a simple question of not remembering other stages of drinking experiences. Or perhaps it reflects the fact that most of my friends were well past adolescence and what were for many their first and most exciting experiences with alcohol. Nonetheless, once again, recognition of this pernicious side of alcohol use was evident as a recurring theme amid all the male camaraderie. Drinking is widely seen as a psychological problem for some men.

Gabriel was often persistent in trying to get me to stop by for a drink while he was working. He liked talking about anthropology. I would often protest that I was full, didn't feel like a drink, or had to go somewhere, but Gabi inevitably countered with his pet motto: "*Ni más ni menos de tres* [Neither more nor less than three]." Sometimes it worked and I would sit long enough for us to drink three Coronas each. (It was always easier for him to convince me on warm, dry days.) But if I did not have the time or interest, I would often reply, with a smirk, "*De regreso* [On the way back]," though we would both know that I might not be back soon. Gabi would look disappointed, but sympathetic, as if to say, "Just testing, Mateo. . . . "

ABSTINENCE, ANTIBIOTICS, AND *ESTAR JURADO*

Coercion to drink among men is a standard element of drinking habits throughout Mexico, according to most ethnographic studies to date. "*No se puede escapar a las copas* [You cannot escape liquor]" was a popular saying in one village in Oaxaca (see Kearney 1972:99).[11] Yet the extent of the obligation to drink with other men may hinge on regional patterns, possibly in conjunction with particular cultural changes in specific areas in the recent past.

When I spoke with Esteban and Felipe on the street one day, Esteban wanted me understand that "there are more drunks in the *campo*. There's nothing to do there except drink. When you go visit someone, the first thing they do *en provincia* is invite you to a pulque or a beer."

"Here I can say that I don't want one," I offered.

"There if you don't drink, it's an insult. Here you can say, 'I don't want one,' and you leave. But there you have to wait, you have to drink," Felipe insisted

"Suppose you don't drink," interjected Esteban. "It's not that they're going to force you to do it, but that the next time you come by, they're not going to invite you because you were insulting about it that time."

"It's really that different in the city?" I asked.

"Yes, it's different here," said Esteban. " 'Come on over and have a beer.' 'You know what, maybe in a while. I'll see you later.' "

The interpretations of different drinking styles in the country and city reflect more than personal experiences in both places. Among other things, in the national cinema of Mexico, the social and even physical penalties for refusing to drink when invited by a Mexican are of legendary status. Thus, again, representations of "typical" Mexican male behavior, in this case in the movies, may contribute to creating such comportment.

Of course, some men in Santo Domingo may be more persuasive than others. On the fourth night of the Posadas, the pre-Christmas nightly reenactments of Mary and Joseph's search for a place to sleep, which were followed on Huehuetzin Street by piñata breaking, I found myself watching the celebrations with Alberto. Alberto was taking large gulps of *anís* from a bottle in his hand. After each one he held the bottle out to me, offering a taste. I had no wish to drink *anís* that night, and besides, Alberto looked sickly; I most definitely did not want to share a bottle with him. But as I continued to decline his repeated offers, he grew more insistent. He began calling me *camarón* (shrimp [the shell-fish]), a nickname for gringos because when they "heat up" they turn red on the outside. Concerned about my ignorance and seeking to avoid a potential confrontation, Martín deftly intervened.

"Say," Martín asked me, "did you know that Alberto is a member of the famous Púrpuras [the Purples, a street gang whose territory extended almost to Huehuetzin Street]?" I did not. "Isn't it too bad," sympathized Martín out loud, "that Mateo is still taking antibiotics for that nasty infection of his?" I slinked away while Alberto was considering my poor health.

It turned out that I had not completely escaped my drinking obligations. In the days following, I twice bumped into Don Timoteo. Both times he said to me forcefully, "*¡Me debe!* [You owe me!]" It turned out that, from the other side of the street in front of his house, Don Timo had seen me standing with Alberto and Martín, though he could not have heard our discussion through the din. At one point Don Timoteo had gone into his house in order to get a Presidente *cuba* for me. In my flight from Alberto I had missed Don Timoteo's return and my drink. Now he expected me to collect.

Though he no longer drinks himself, there is nothing Don Timo likes better than to offer his friends some home-brewed mescal or to buy them a beer. Gabriel had talked me into a rather large glass of the mescal three days before my encounter with Alberto, and I was sent reeling. Now, at Don Timo's, Gabriel insisted I try another one—"It will help to alleviate the effects of the first . . . ," he lied to me. I demurred. Gabi kept insisting. Finally I blurted out that I was a cosponsor of that evening's Posadas, where I would be expected to help hand out candy to the children and supervise the piñata breaking. This left Gabriel unmoved, but it impressed Don Timoteo enough so that throughout the remainder of the year he praised me for my good sense that day.

It may be that because of his having grown up in a rural area, Don Timo had more of a sense of propriety when it came to community and religious responsibilities, known as *cargos* in other parts of Mexico, where excessive drinking is especially proscribed when it conflicts with fulfilling *cargo* obligations.[12] But I discovered over the course of a year several ways in which abstention from drinking in Santo Domingo was culturally sanctioned, respected, and encouraged, at least one of which has not been previously mentioned in the anthropological literature as far as I can determine.

The next time we saw each other Martín, having helped me to extricate myself from Alberto's insistent offers to drink *anís* with him, offered me some advice: "When people offer you a drink and you don't want one but they are really persistent, you can either say that you're taking antibiotics, or you can tell them, '*Estoy jurado.*'"

Estoy jurado means "I'm pledged," as in "I'm pledged not to drink" (for a period of time). Don Timoteo told me that he was drunk every day for fifteen years, but that (as of March 1993) he had been *jurado* for five years and eight months; he always knows precisely how long. He says that he had to quit for his health—"For me, I just can't help myself. It's all or nothing"—and that since then he has taken medications for the damage the alcohol previously did to his body.

When I first met him in November, Toño had been *jurado* for about eleven months, and would end his abstinence on 31 December 1992. Indeed, he spent most of the first week of 1993 making up for lost time. But he said he would never go back to the way he was. Unlike Don Timo, who had quit to save his life, Toño had pledged to stay sober for a year to prove to his family that he could stop. He said that most people are *jurado* to the Virgen de Guadalupe, but that he had made his pledge to the lesser-known Virgen de Carmen. Toño shrugged his shoulders when I asked him why he had chosen the Virgen del Carmen. A neighbor of Don Timo's told me that each of the several times during his long life that he had been *jurado,* it had always been to God. Marcos, on the other hand, said that only religious people become *jurados.* Though on other occasions Marcos described himself to me as deeply religious, while explaining this issue he simply stated that when he wants to quit drinking for a while he just does it, without invoking any saints.

The state of being *jurado* is a clearly and widely recognized cultural category among men in Colonia Santo Domingo that exempts them from drinking, and indeed often brings the respect of others. (I am unaware of the practice among women.) And although one might expect to encounter teasing with respect to a man's being *jurado*—such as what might go on among friends when one of them is trying to cut back on sweets, for instance—I never heard anyone try to tempt a man with a drink if it was known that he was *jurado*. The option of being *jurado* reflects a general concern over the perils of excessive drinking, and men's choices regarding *estar jurado* reflect the differentiated experiences and beliefs of adults in Santo Domingo with regard to alcohol.

YOUTHFUL INTEMPERANCE

I recorded the following early-morning incident in my field notes in early October:

> Street scene, 8:30 A.M., Saturday morning. Shouting in the street below, as a woman, 20-ish, walks quickly towards Las Rosas Ave. along the giant ditch carved out for the sewage pipes. Wiry fellow is shouting after her to come back. He, also around 20, has a glass of something in his hand, and is quite pickled. She looks back every few seconds, but keeps going. He gets to tortillería where another woman who's working there tries to stop him from going further. It's too dangerous with all the rocks piled up and the ditch itself. He persists, not violently, but obstinately. Another young woman, 15 or so, further up the street now tries to stop him from continuing. He's shouting all this time for the first woman, who's now out of [my] sight, to stop, to come back. Finally, five minutes after he disappears in the vicinity of the ditch, I see him being escorted by yet another woman (the fourth) back in the direction from which he first came, toward Coyamel Street.

The scene was strikingly reminiscent of one I had witnessed during Corpus Cristi celebrations in Tzintzuntzan, Michoacán, in June 1990. There, by late afternoon, many men were so inebriated they could barely stand, let alone walk unassisted, and a common sight was that of an older woman wrapping her rebozo around a man, hoisting him to his feet, and dragging him off, presumably in the direction of home.[13]

On another occasion in Santo Domingo, Michelle and I were awakened at sunrise one Sunday morning by the sound of bottles clanking, a radio blaring, people jeering, urinating, and farting, and other associated noises. Four young men, one in his thirties and the others in their early twenties, who appeared very drunk, had decided to end their night's carousing by roosting across the street from our apartment on concrete pipes not yet laid in the sewage system. Two of them argued in mock ferocious style, another dozed, and the fourth incessantly switched radio stations, always, accidentally or not, landing on ones playing English songs, from Black Sabbath heavy metal to Bee Gees disco fever. Every twenty minutes or so, one of the youths ordered another to go and buy more *caguamas* of Corona beer, no doubt at one of the tiny liquor stores operating around the clock in the *colonia,* where you receive your purchases through small holes cut out of screened cages. Other street drunks drifted by occasionally to give their regards, always politely accepting invitations to share the Coronas. Two hours after they first arrived, the young men abruptly got up and wandered off.

A half hour later, the seventy-year-old woman who lives in the house in front of which the beer party had been held came out and began trying to clean up the mess. Coincidentally or not, one of the youths happened by and, without a word being exchanged at first, began helping her set the pipes upright, sweep the urine off the sidewalk, and haul away the not inconsiderable number of bottles. Having been awakened by their loud antics myself, I was not in a charitable mood, and I looked forward to the old lady's scolding of the youth. But not a harsh word or a recriminating glance was exchanged. There were no smiles, either, to be sure, but it seemed the old woman's tolerance was far greater than my own.

On the other hand, maybe she was intimidated and chose not to say anything out of fear of later reprisals. After talking the issue over with Miguel and Noé, both in their early thirties, I came to realize that although the old woman may have been frightened, there were other, more appropriate explanations for the situation. Miguel and Noé both thought my reaction—eagerly awaiting the woman's verbal harangues—strange and excessive. The young drunks were considered members of the community, at least by some; they were familiar to neighbors and known for their positive virtues as well as their foolishness.[14] Further, the individuals involved were young men, and it is widely recognized in the *colonia* that many young men go through a stage of heavy and public drinking.

Both Miguel and Noé had spent periods in their late teens (Miguel, one and a half years; Noé, three years) in which each spent the better part of at least every weekend drunk. Noé had escaped from those years when he was sent to live and work with his uncle Héctor in Santo Domingo. In Miguel's case, *futbol* was his out. He excelled at the sport, reaching the lower levels of the professional leagues, and abusive drinking proved incompatible with the discipline required in training for and playing *futbol.* At 7:30 one morning on our way to a game of his Santo

Domingo squad, Miguel pointed to a fellow hanging out by a vat of *chicharones* (pig skins boiled in oil). He said the man was an old friend from his earlier, intemperate period, but that this man had "graduated" from drinking beer and tequila with Miguel years ago to sniffing *cemento* for the past several years. His mind had long since been permanently fried, Miguel said sadly, recalling for me what Armando Ramírez (1972:73) writes in *Chin chin el teporocho,* his tangy novel of urban Mexico: "To be a *teporocho* [wino] means you've become nobody, nothing matters to you, not even your life, or your children, or your wife. It's to lose everything, to not even have a mother anymore."

But there are others for whom heavy drinking is a period through which they pass, Miguel insisted. It seems plausible that heavy drinking, though not conceptualized by him in terms of gender categories, has been, at least until recently, largely a *male* stage through which many have passed. Teenagers often emphasized to me, however, that in the 1990s both young men and young women are drinking in a serious fashion, although young women do so less in the streets than their brothers and boyfriends.

It appears that a stage of alcohol experimentation and abuse may well be—or become—a rite of passage for many young women nearly as much as it is for young men, a complex of culturally salient experiences regarded to a degree as reasonable if not inevitable. Although some youth do not ever leave this stage, most of them do get out in one way or another, and so, Miguel and Noé emphasized to me, it is important to tolerate heavy drinking by youth. The most important thing, they said, was to keep young people from thinking that others had given up on them.

In addition to alcohol and *cemento,* marijuana has long had some currency among youth, and a few others, in Santo Domingo. Guillermo was leaning against the wall of his butcher shop taking a break one sunny June day around noon when I drove up to get another quarter kilo of ground beef for Liliana. Spotting some empty beer bottles in the back seat, Guillermo made a comment about "Mateo's *vicios* [vices]." Knowing of his fondness still, at age forty-two, for *la mota* (marijuana), and that he drinks no alcohol, I responded, "They don't sell what you like at the supermarket, do they?" He smiled contentedly, as if having already anticipated my response. "No," he pointed out, "but they do here," at which point he held up the remains of a reefer he had been smoking when I pulled up. An elderly customer glanced at Guillermo and then at me and laughed quietly to herself.

THE DEGENDERING OF ALCOHOL

Increasingly in Colonia Santo Domingo, women are engaging in adulterous liaisons and men are participating in housework. Consequently, to an extent, these activities are becoming less identified exclusively with one gender or another. In the realm of alcohol consumption, there is an even greater decentering of the perceived wisdom that associates a practice especially with men or women, a process that I refer to as *degendering*. The mere fact that values or activities are esteemed by men is not enough to call them manly or consider them unitary male attributes. Nor should we necessarily label as manly those practices that many women as well as men may respect (or despise) in men. This is because some of these same values and activities may also be similarly regarded when associated with women. What, we wonder, is the "gender" of categories like courage, meat consumption, eloquence, sexual prowess, sexual disinterest, grades in school, body hair, poise, and alcohol use? All are more or less associated with specific gender identities in particular historical and cultural contexts.

Older male residents of Santo Domingo enjoyed teaching me catch phrases that connect drinking with men in particular. Marcos, the grandfather, liked to quote a line from one of the films of the popular Mexican actor Pedro Infante to explain men's special affinity for alcohol. When he was asked, "*¿Por qué tomas vino?* [Why do you drink liquor?]," Infante answered plainly, "*¡Porque me gusta!* [Because I like it!]." When recounting this cinematic moment, Marcos leaned back and chuckled at the simplicity and truth of the punch line. (He also thought this a good explanation of why men like to have sexual relations with lots of women: "*¡Porque les gustan!* [Because they like them!]") Don Timoteo, in his early seventies, once clarified for me why men drink more than women: "*Dios y hombre, no Dios y mujer* [God and man, not God and woman]." By modifying a common expression, "*Dios y hombre*," which usually means that men deserve the same treatment accorded God, Don Timo was invoking higher orders to explain plain differences in gender proclivities.

The heavily gendered orientation of both Marcos and Timoteo when it comes to drinking patterns and much else is found as well in numerous ethnographies from other places and time periods in Mexico, not to mention throughout the world (see Heath 1987).[15] By and large, in the ethnographic literature of Mexico and Mesoamerica to date, drink-

These men are drinking pulque from the barrel. Mexico City, early
1950s. Photo courtesy José Pérez (on right).

ing is discussed as a typical male activity and drunkenness as a rather
exclusive male propensity.

In Colonia Santo Domingo in the early 1990s, male social drinking
flourished in many homes, even though the space was formally acknowledged to be shared by women and men. But even where only men
were found drinking in the home, this was occurring in a context that
was by its very nature less gender isolated than the cantina. Among
other things, confrontation between women and men, especially while
men were drinking among themselves, was a more permanent feature
of such activities by men. In addition, women often drank with men in
the home—in the early evenings, on weekends, and at fiestas—and
younger women drink nearly as much as their male age mates on many
occasions.

In Santo Domingo at this time, men on average undoubtedly were
drinking more alcoholic beverages than women were, but in many family and social situations women nearly kept pace with men. Further, the
types of alcohol consumed were generally equivalent. Such drinking on
the part of women was influenced by many things, not the least of
which were the images of feminine modernity promoted through daily
telenovelas (soap operas) and the advertising campaigns of liquor com-

panies. Bacardi ran ads on TV that featured young women and men traveling to Germany and Japan and ordering food in restaurants there that they could not stomach, but finding that, the world over, urbane sophisticates such as they enjoyed the same refreshments. These routines had little to do with the simple realities of dodging the *granaderos,* the patrol cars that irregularly cruised the streets looking for people drinking in public—a favorite game of "chicken" for many—but the slick advertising schemes showing lusty young women in slinky dresses drinking *cubas* have doubtless had an irrevocable impact upon both young men and young women. One way or another, many women in the 1990s drink more than their mothers did, and a lot of their men expect and encourage them to do so.

In the microspaces of daily living—the local sites in which changes in drinking patterns between women and men may be revealed and realized in the lives of ordinary people every day—male drinking rituals still prosper, but perhaps not so much as previously. Through greater drinking in the home on the part of women, for instance, drinking in general will increasingly be less associated with men and more with women and men—that is, with adults. To the extent that gender becomes less of a defining characteristic in alcohol consumption, drinking becomes more degendered.[16]

It is also possible that the complex of relations of *cuatismo* (close male friendship) discussed by Lomnitz (1977) is undergoing modest transformations. In many households in Santo Domingo, women, like men, do their heaviest drinking during family get-togethers. Some men in the *colonia* drink no alcohol, and many others consume no more than a Modelo beer or two at a time once or twice a week with their families. Altogether these men constitute a significant proportion of the male population of Santo Domingo, but one that is constantly shifting in its exact composition. Like Bott (1957), I find variation not simply between men and women, but among men and among women. In Bott's analysis, the previous ties people have to a community (their social networks) were of primary importance in explaining different behavior in the family. In the case of alcohol consumption in Santo Domingo, whereas gender has been a key factor in distinct drinking practices in the past, generational differences are fast becoming more significant.

"When I was about eighteen or twenty years old," Greenberg (1989:45) quotes Don Fortino from Juquila, Oaxaca, as saying, "I started to take notice of girls, but to drink? No." In the same manner,

in Santo Domingo women and alcohol are often described as among
the most important sins and pleasures of young men. Many drink and
then stop drinking, much as they follow an on-again, off-again pattern
with young women. Similarly, most men of all ages have had experience, on the street or at family gatherings, with consuming too much
beer, rum, tequila, and pulque, just as they have had experience with
refusing drinks and thus staying sober while others around them were
drinking.

My friends in the *colonia* are just as acutely aware of official images
of the Mexican male drunk as they are of widespread notions that all
Mexican men want to produce lots of boy babies. And sometimes, perhaps, my friends performed as they thought they might be expected to
by an anthropologist. That is partly what happened, I think, the day we
swallowed so much *anís*. As frustrating as it may be for many social
scientists, however, what is "typical" of men in Santo Domingo when
it comes to alcohol consumption is social drinking, abstention, drunkenness, exclusive male camaraderie, and a degendering of drinking
practices. That is to say, there is no typical Mexican male drinking pattern any more than there is a typical Mexican man.

There are nonetheless patterns of drinking in Mexico for which
women and men are paying with their lives every day.

DRINKING AND MALE VIOLENCE

On a rudimentary chemical level it is a commonplace to note that alcohol and other drugs do not affect everyone in the same manner. Thus
not all men beat other people when they become drunk. Juan and Tomás were known for mellowing after a couple of drinks, and Claudia's
husband, though a long-term alcoholic, never represented a physical
threat to her or their children.

Nonetheless, so many men do beat others when they drink that
drinking and male violence have a long association in the *colonias populares,* including the popular perception that alcohol is often the immediate and ultimately the root cause of many violent episodes on the
part of husbands, brothers, and other menfolk. To an extent, many
people utilize culturally accepted rationales to explain these violent outbursts, such as "The perpetrators were drunk and therefore were not
responsible for their actions." In this fashion, alcohol is seen as an elemental source of domestic and other violence. That is, the apparently

straightforward somatic arguments against the notion that alcohol consumption necessarily leads to violence are not believed by numerous
people, and this very disbelief itself contributes to establishing real, material links between alcohol and violence. That they are culturally and
not chemically driven does not make the explanations any less compelling.

Susana was beaten by her mother and an uncle early in childhood,
later moved out on her own, had a child with one man, and eventually
began living with another man as his wife. She recalls:

"The first few years were total sweetness, the best. He gave me everything. Then I began to have problems with him. He was very jealous
and he began to beat me a lot. Once again the beatings began. He was
drinking a lot and he'd get home and begin beating me. The truth is
that I loved him very much. I had fallen in love with him because when
I needed it most he had offered me support, his help. He made me see
life in another way and get ahead, but then his jealousies began. I began
to change a lot, as a woman I began to change. I saw myself as more
attractive, as I had settled down when my children were born. And this
made my husband very jealous. He drank a lot. He began to drink and
drink and drink."

Susana finally decided that she had to leave her husband. After much
effort, she thought she had convinced him that this was something he
too would have to accept. He told her he was reconciled and suggested
they go out for a last drink together.

"In the restaurant he cried, he kneeled in front of me and begged me
not to leave him. I told him, 'You know, I'm going.' And on our way
back in the car, it was about two in the morning, he said to me, 'So you
won't stay?' and I said no. 'Then I'm going to kill us,' and with that he
crashed the car. 'I'm going to kill us,' he told me and smashed into
another car. He was injured, and I was too. But then he drove into a
wall and that's all I remember until I woke up in the ambulance. I had
glass all over my face and body."

Susana eventually entered the United States illegally to escape her
husband, but living with her sister in Houston was difficult, and when
her husband eventually arrived and begged her to return, she relented.
For five years things were calm in their household, but then he began to
drink again. I saw Susana on Las Rosas Avenue one day with her hand
and forearm bandaged up. She told me only that she had cut herself
accidentally. A good friend of Susana's told me later that day that they
had shared a dinner two nights before, at which time the story of an-

other woman who was getting regularly beaten by her alcoholic husband was recounted. Susana had listened to the tale of the battered wife
without saying anything, but as she heard the story unfold, her grip on
a drinking glass became tighter and tighter, until the glass finally shat-
tered in Susana's hand, slicing her palm wide open.

EIGHT

Fear and Loathing in Male Violence

Tell me how you die and I will tell you who you are.

Octavio Paz, The Labyrinth of Solitude

BAGHDAD IS IN MEXICO

Because of flooding throughout the *colonia,* there was no electricity when I left the apartment one evening in early July. As I stumbled through the rain-filled potholes in the darkened street, I listened to a pocket radio carrying news that the U.S. president, Bill Clinton, had just ordered another bombardment of Iraq. It reminded me of the smoggy afternoon just before Clinton was sworn into office in January when I walked up to the *tienda* and was greeted by a noose hanging from one of the construction cranes being used to dig up volcanic rock so that sewage lines could be laid under Huehuetzin Street. Beneath the noose I saw a sign that read, "*Muera Bush y sus aliados (alias Mateo)* [Death to Bush and his allies (alias Matt)]," and another: "*Viva Sadam Huzein* [Long live Saddam Hussein]." Then I noticed an effigy with blue jeans and a stuffed plaid shirt waiting to be hung on the crane. But I still had no idea what had provoked my friends—at least I thought they were my friends—to enact this pageant.

"Haven't you heard?" Ramón asked. Then he told me about the bombing of Iraq earlier that January day by the United States, with French and British complicity. When I protested that I did not want to be lumped with George Bush and the actions of the U.S. military, Ramón and the others agreed to change the sign, erasing "alias Mateo" and putting instead "*Muera Bush Pinche Gringo* [Death to Bush, goddamned gringo]." After this was accomplished Tomás wanted me to get my camera so he could photograph me with the noose around my head

"*Muera Bush Pinche Gringo* [Death to Bush, goddamned Gringo]" and "*Viva Sadam Huzein* [Long live Saddam Hussein]." An effigy and two placards protesting the U.S. bombing of Iraq were made by some residents of Colonia Santo Domingo in January 1993.

(instead of the effigy's) and with the sign in my hands. But I declined. It was all in good fun, I suppose, but there was an angry edge to the humor motivated by real outrage against the U.S. government. If, even for an instant, I had been mistaken for a representative of U.S. military power, the situation could have become physically threatening. What's more, Tomás had been drinking a lot that afternoon.

So as I bounced along in the *combi* six months later in July, heading toward the Copilco metro stop, I was thinking about the impromptu reactions of my friends in January, the last time the United States had bombed Iraq, and wondering what this new round of aggression in July might provoke in Santo Domingo. I entered the metro station, stepping over a pool of vomit, and raced to catch the subway. Before we reached our first stop it was clear that smoke was coming from somewhere on the train. I got off, but most passengers rode on, seemingly unconcerned. I got on the next train, where two men were lying down against the opposite doors, belligerently refusing to cede space in the crowded car. The men finally got off, and my attention switched to a youngster screaming, "Maaaaaa! Maaaaaa!" The woman who had the child in her lap whispered something into his ear, but the crying persisted. She then slapped him when he tried to pick a large and painful-looking scab on his scalp. Finally the boy squirmed free and went to sit with another woman in a raggedy dress who looked as if she was well into the last trimester of her pregnancy. The boy calmed down and promptly fell asleep on the breast of another woman—a stranger, I thought—who never looked up from the television magazine she was scanning.

Finally, we arrived at my stop and I exited the metro in Colonia Juárez. I was looking for the Centro de Atención a la Violencia Intrafamiliar, where later that evening a dozen men who had beaten their wives and/or children would meet to discuss controlling their violence.

BODIES OF VIOLENCE

The Centro de Atención a la Violencia Intrafamiliar (CAVI) is formally part of the municipal police apparatus, but in its day-to-day affairs it has nothing to do with the police. In 1992, at the suggestion of women who, after being beaten, had reported their husbands to the authorities, CAVI organized groups of men who meet with psychologists once a week for three months to help them recognize and resolve their problems with domestic violence. The men who attend these sessions do so freely—none has been compelled to attend by a judge or other government authority—and are participating in what constitutes an experimental project. In this chapter I will examine violence among men by drawing on discussions in these CAVI men's groups, interviews with battered women, and incidents from the home and street life in the *colonias populares* of the Mexican capital. Yet although the immediate sources for this inquiry are quite localized, the context is global. To understand the role of violence in the lives of women and men in Santo Domingo, it is necessary to look beyond theories of alcohol abuse, faulty child-rearing patterns, urbanization, male testosterone levels, and primordially brutish cultural mores (a.k.a. machismo).

With regard to violence associated vaguely or explicitly with notions of machismo, we must also be especially careful to distinguish symbolic rationalizations from actual sources of violent conflict. Arguments by men such as "What do you expect, I'm a (macho) man?" or "She provoked me (which one shouldn't do to a macho)" cannot be accepted at face value, but must serve as starting points for discovering deeper causes and consequences of violence than some so-called cultural attribute. Because if we take violence to be the physical struggle for political power, in families as much as in nation-states, then domestic violence in Santo Domingo must be seen as part of the cultural politics of gender inequalities and not as deriving from some essential logic of Mexican men.

One night in a CAVI men's-group session a man described how for years he had been living in fear that his wife would one day take revenge on him for his having committed adultery with her best friend ten years before. It was very difficult to hear his story because, perhaps out of embarrassment, he was whispering to the floor the details of his earlier affair and the ensuing consequences for his marriage. No amount of coaxing seemed sufficient to get this man to speak louder to the others straining to catch his testimony. Yet eventually his confessional became a broader soliloquy about violent episodes in his life, and when he arrived at a specific incident involving a fight not with his wife but with another man, he suddenly became voluble. His account of the street fight with the other man as he returned from work one night had the drama of Martin Scorsese's *Raging Bull,* as he recalled in vivid detail for the rest of us how he felt and what he was thinking during each moment of the fight, exactly when and how the blows had fallen on chins, stomachs, and groins, and how the street lights looked when he regained consciousness.

The differences in tone and gesture when the man described beating

his wife versus fighting another man indicate a broader cultural distinction that most people in Santo Domingo make today. Though <u>wife beating frequently occurs, it is generally a proscribed activity in the *colonia*.
Fighting among men, on the other hand, is widely endorsed</u> if less often
<u>actually practiced.</u> Many of the fighting stories that men in the *colonia*
proudly retell involve a special style of culturally valued fighting: defending a woman from verbal abuse and physical assault. Most men
rarely have the opportunity for such heroics, and their exploits remain
in the realm of fantasies and tall tales.

Youngsters play-act such savior games, revealing their own perspective on adult social relations and public morality. Rolandito, five, and
his cousin Sara, six, used to spend many afternoons together at Rolandito's house. One of their favorite games was "Rambo." The boy,
wrapped in a headband and carrying a plastic machine gun and a toy
pistol, would tie up Sara in a chair and then proceed to save her. He
especially liked to leap around for several minutes, fending off imaginary bad guys who were trying to keep him from reaching his cousin,
while Sara sat struggling helplessly in her chair. He would make it to
the chair, get pushed away again and again by the forces of evil, fight
his way back, but always ultimately free Sara from her tormentors. At
the end of one such episode, as I stood watching the two play, Rambo-
Rolandito himself collapsed in the chair. It was hard work saving Sara
every day, and he figured he deserved something in return. With a bossy
scowl on his face, he barked, "I'm hungry now. Bring me something to
eat and drink!" Rambo had saved Sara all right. For himself!

Though not quite. In late June, I saw Rolandito with his face terribly
scratched up. He looked as if someone had dragged him over gravel,
and, I was told, Sara looked the same. Rolandito's mother said she
blamed Sara's mother, a single woman with a history of being abused
by men, who apparently was teaching Sara to fight. The girl was being
shown how to attack others when provoked, which especially irked Rolandito's mother since she and her husband had been trying to teach the
boy to turn the other cheek and not to fight.

Nearly 90 percent of those reporting domestic violence to the CAVI
center are women who have been beaten by their husbands, lovers, fathers, or, less often, brothers. Adult men, especially elderly men, are
occasionally the victims of beatings at the hands of women, but, out of
shame, they report the abuse less often. Violent attacks on male children
are inflicted with even greater regularity. In Mexico City, adult men
are overwhelmingly the perpetrators and the seeming beneficiaries of

spousal abuse, which makes the roles of men and of women in such conflicts very different. Nonetheless, many men with histories of violent mistreatment of women and children explain that they too are the products of larger forces, and some men ask how they can be blamed for what are clearly society's ills. It is largely this awkward straddling of both sides of the issue—men as victimizers and victims—that underpins arguments about male violence in Mexico being a product of a *machista* system maintained by both women and men.

As an illustration of women's role in perpetuating domestic violence, for instance, some commentators suggest that there is a common pattern in Colonia Santo Domingo and other working class areas in which men beat their wives, and mothers (more than fathers) beat their children.[1] This cannot be accounted for simply because husbands are physically larger and stronger than their wives, or because women usually spend more time with children, especially young children, than men do. Many women who are beaten by their husbands are as big and strong as the men, and many women do not beat the children with whom they spend many hours every day.

The issues of power and control are more pertinent to understanding domestic violence than are differences of sexual dimorphism and time spent with children. This analysis runs counter to the notion that violence is innate to men or simply part of urban life. It is also a critique of a view that is even more pernicious theoretically: that violence is random and inexplicable. Especially popular in the United States today, this position, if accurate at all, is so only in the narrowest, most immediate sense. In Mexico City, as in the United States, violence is understandable, foreseeable, and even predictable. Violent identities and practices associated with masculinity may be glorified or despised by men and women in Santo Domingo, but they at least "make sense."

When he was a boy, Gabriel became especially upset not when his father beat him, but when his father smashed the toys that Gabi had worked so long to purchase. For many men and women, on different sides of the beatings, violence becomes central to the social inequalities that define their lives. Susana was beaten by her mother, then by an uncle with whom she was sent to live and work, then by her mother when they lived together again, and later by the two men with whom she lived as a wife.

When adults try to gain a perspective on the violence of their childhoods and to make sense of the memories that still pain them, the scars are often very fresh.

"I remember very hard times," Rolando recounted to me. "Personally they were hard because we lived in such poverty, and because of my mother's character, which was very aggressive. My mother beat us a lot, for childish mischief; sometimes she was right, and sometimes not, but she was strong."

I asked Rolando what his mother used to beat them.

"She beat us with whatever she could—wires, sticks, belts, or rope, which was wet to hurt more. I had one experience that I've never forgotten, and I don't think I ever could forget. I was four or five. The roof of the house was cardboard. I was playing *futbol* and the ball went on the roof and didn't roll off. So I climbed up and walked along the beams and planks, but I slipped on one and broke through the roof. I got down and began to cry, knowing that my mother was going to beat me."

Despite the intervention of an uncle on his behalf, when she later caught up with him, "she dragged me off by my hair and began to beat me in the face. I was bleeding from the nose and the mouth when we got home. It was the worst beating I've ever received in my life. She washed me so you couldn't see the blood, to cover up everything so my father wouldn't ask anything. I don't understand or justify why my mother did these things, but when I think about it, maybe it was the pressure to feed fifteen of us, clothe fifteen, which was very tough for her. She beat me five times that day. When it was all over she says to me, 'If you say anything to your father, tomorrow I'll beat you again.' I managed to avoid my father seeing me the whole day, so he wouldn't notice how swollen my mouth was, and my black eyes."

Outlets for physical violence and psychological compulsion are abundant in Santo Domingo. So are the sources of fear and loathing in the everyday lives of women and men there. As to the reasons for gangs, wife beating, and street brawls, friends offer various explanations concerning the causes of the different kinds of violence that have always been part of life for even the most placid grandmother in the *colonia*.

THE VIOLENT YOUNG MEN

On leaving Angela's home after lunch one Saturday afternoon in March, I saw Jaime being dragged down the street by his girlfriend and an older man who I later learned was his father. Jaime had been drinking heavily all day at the *tienda*—I had fended off a couple of his invitations to join him in the late morning—and it appeared he had come to no good end. A big crowd was gathered in front of the *tienda,* and after

Jaime passed by me I headed in that direction. Don Timoteo's son, also named Timo, was bleeding badly from a crooked and badly discolored nose.

The details of what transpired have been spliced together from discussions beginning at this point with the participant-observers who remained. Jaime and another man began fighting. The other man was young Timo's cousin. Most people agreed that Jaime started things by his drunken, jeering, and thoroughly gratuitous insults, which ignited the cousin's short temper. Once fists started flying, Jaime extended his target and began shouting out insults to the cousin's aunt and to young Timo's mother, Catalina.

At this point the violence escalated considerably when another cousin of young Timo's pulled out a pistol and threatened Jaime. Several bystanders now jumped into the fray and tried to calm the situation, separating Jaime and the first cousin, and wresting the gun away from the second. In the course of the fracas, several people took punches, including young Timo.

Most felt that Jaime had initiated the confrontation unnecessarily. There was general consensus that "if he [Jaime] doesn't know how to drink, he shouldn't." Further, it is bad to pick fights, but unforgivable to menace an older woman, especially one in her seventies.

But as for the second cousin, named Porfirio, he had gone beyond the pale when he pulled out his pistol and began shaking it about. His actions were condemned by some with comments like "People from the *campo* are very *bravo* and think nothing of waving guns."[2] Porfirio and his brother both come from a rural area in the state of Mexico, which was all the explanation most people needed to understand their actions that Saturday in March. Beyond attributing a rural gunslinger mentality to Porfirio, several people recounted that he was still *soltero* (single) in his late twenties, the implication being that women had yet to tame him.[3] Also, he had recently lost a brother in violent and suspicious circumstances in Michoacán, and he was thus especially prone to foolish and dangerous gestures. All this despite Porfirio's being stone sober throughout the events that afternoon.

A classic Mexican male brawl? Alcohol served as a stimulant for Jaime, yet as Clausewitz's adage regarding the causes of war warns, it is very misleading to trace the origins of any violent conflict simply to whichever side fires the first shot. Brawls, like wars, begin long before the physical fighting commences. In addition to Jaime's drunkenness, other important factors, according to bystanders who witnessed the fight, had been involved: the youth of the participants, the fact that the honor of an older woman was being defended, the goading of the crowd that quickly gathered, and perhaps, on the part of the cousins, a desire to avenge the death of a sibling and a greater rural readiness to resort to gunplay.

The role of guns in violent episodes appears to be more prominent in rural areas than in the cities. One hears stories of dangerous encounters with guns in Santo Domingo, like the time a drunken teenage friend of Miguel's took a shot at him during a party, and many people may keep a shotgun in their homes "for protection." But shootings—and, still more, gun battles—are associated overwhelmingly in the minds of people in Colonia Santo Domingo with patterns of violence in the countryside (and the United States!).[4] There is even a sense that cities tend to calm men's barbarian tendencies, almost in the strict sense of *civiliz*-ing them, though all this could change in the future.

The most visible public violence in Santo Domingo is perpetrated by male youths in street gangs such as the Nazis, the Púrpuras (Purples), and the Pinoles.[5] During the year I lived continuously in Santo Domingo, one morning in early November at 7 o'clock, drugged-up gang members killed a youth with an ice pick on Las Rosas Avenue, near where we lived. Early one evening the following January, and this time a block from our apartment, another youth was jumped and repeatedly stabbed with knives by rival gang members. A month later, a *roquero* (rock fight) broke out at midnight on a Saturday at the corner of Las Rosas and Huehuetzin, a skirmish in the war over gang territories.

Most residents who live in the immediate area of a fight know about it afterward. Though gang attacks are seldom carried out at random, men and women try to avoid traveling on foot late at night. People will speak sympathetically about these young men and their girlfriends who, after all, are oppressed just like everyone else, with no jobs and nowhere to go, and who literally are their sons and daughters. It's just that the disillusionment of these youth can be dangerous to others.

The personal history of one friend describes a trajectory of gang fighting that was common for some male youth of his generation. César remembers living behind a factory in Colonia Tránsito, just southeast of downtown Mexico City. "It was a very big *vecindad* where most people, the youth anyway, dedicated themselves to robbing and getting wasted on alcohol." Later the family moved farther south in the city, to Colonia Nativitas, where "usually I got into fights two or three times a day. I was very aggressive. No one could swear at me because I'd fight them right away. Eventually my *compañeros,* friends my age, were scared of me, respected me. They gave me the nickname El Coreano."

"Why that name?"

"Because I was born during the Korean War in '51. It even got so that when someone would say, 'Here comes El Coreano,' everyone would get frightened. We had very good relations there. Then I began to drink. Not every day, because it took a lot to get the money to buy alcohol, but once a week or so. More than anything we consumed tequila. We liked it, maybe because we felt more like Mexicans, more like *lugareños* [homeboys]. You couldn't lay a finger on us in the *colonia.*"

César explained that although his father beat him once for fighting with other youngsters, his father was not by nature a violent man. His mother sometimes beat them as children when they misbehaved or refused to study and go to school, but not often. El Coreano had not learned to fight from his parents.

In the late 1960s, others arrived in Colonia Nativitas: "Let's call them Chicanos, *pochos,* Mexicans but living in the U.S." They introduced the young men to marijuana, and later to LSD and hallucinogenic mushrooms. It was the time of *rockanrol,* César remembered nostalgically. His family moved again, this time even farther south, to Colonia Santo Domingo. It was just before the invasion of the Pedregales in 1971. César said he and his brother, who also was a scrapper, tried to take advantage of their new environment and to change their "mentality."

"The mentality of being aggressive. Because . . . maybe because we were bored. We were tired of fighting all the time, of running and hiding. Because we couldn't go out alone. Because others wanted to beat us. We had to show that here [in Santo Domingo], too, others needed to respect us. And here too we had a reputation for being aggressive and good fighters. But we began to hang out at the DIF [the government family-services agency] and play *futbol, basquetbol, voli, tenis, pin pong.* We went in for billiards and running. We tried to change our lives totally. What pleases me most about this change was that more than anything it wasn't an aggressive change, but a mental one. We tried to smooth things out, to not end up in blows. We became a group of friendly friends, and everyone looked up to us because we weren't bad, we weren't aggressive."[6]

Instead of attributing violence and violent tendencies to men in general, as do some cultural feminists and sociobiologists, the example of Colonia Santo Domingo prompts us to see youth as a terribly underrated factor in the equation of many of those who are frequently the most conspicuous participants in violent episodes in the *colonia*. To be sure, most of the time this involves *male* youth, whose violence can take numerous forms—from gang fights to the daredevil antics of many young drivers in their *combis*. But whenever some of the young women next door to our apartment began punching, biting, and pulling each other's hair, I was reminded of what cramming so many bodies into such tight quarters can do to people, especially youth, male or female, and I was surprised that it did not happen more often between these sisters who were, in addition, all single mothers.

Youth was also involved, according to Tomás, in the problems of domestic violence that he and his wife had experienced early in their marriage. Tomás told me that he used to hit her a lot when they began living together. He attributed this to "a lack of experience" with marriage on both their parts. "There's violence in the best marriages, especially at first," Tomás told me. He said that this was no longer an issue in their domestic life because, now in their early thirties, they had both matured. Also, he no longer felt so impotent in the face of difficulties and differences that had earlier prompted him to beat his wife, he said.

WIFE BEATING

Men often proved reluctant to discuss their violent episodes and feelings with me. When I first interviewed him in October, César denied any domestic violence in his marriage; well, maybe his wife had beaten the girls when they were younger, he confided, but he himself had always been a "*pacifista*." It took until May, when we taped his life history, for César to trust me enough to reveal that early in his marriage he had transferred his violent propensities from the streets to the bedroom. I was further counseled by members of battered women's support groups that women would probably be even more reticent to talk with a man about domestic violence, but the opposite proved to be the case.[7] Many women seemed eager to tell their tales of physical and psychological abuse. Such was the case with three friends of Doña Fili's.

One day as she was holding chicken feet over the flame on her stove to burn off the hairs, I asked Doña Fili about domestic violence. After singeing a dozen or so of the scrawny appendages, she told me to wait in her kitchen and that she would be right back. She returned a short while later with three friends: Juanita, an elderly woman who was still suffering at the hands of her husband after decades of beatings; Elena, a woman who had been happily married for fifteen years without such problems; and Berta, a young woman who had defended her mother against her father's abuse.

Juanita and her husband were married in 1938. "Two weeks later we began to fight, over worthless things, and he beat me, he beat me. He had a plank. . . . He took his time smacking me on the hand. When he was drunk he'd fight me, smack me, beat me."

Elena related: "My mother also used to get beaten. I didn't know my father. I had a stepfather. One time he threw a pewter plate and it sliced open her nose."

I asked why the women thought these attacks occurred. Berta, in her teens, offered: "I'd say for machismo. The man says, 'I'm the man. I'm the one who's strong and you're the one who serves me. You're the one who lets me beat you.' And I'd say that Mexican women are also influenced a lot by religion: the woman should be *abnegada* [self-sacrificing] in her home. This is a popular idea, that a woman should be *abnegada* in her home, and I say this is a big influence on women letting themselves be beaten, mistreated, more than anything else."

Elena added, "I think it all has to do with how your parents raise you. How do they raise children in the pueblos and the ranchos? Well, all right, not now, but back then.[8] Back then people were more ignorant. Parents didn't know how to read because their parents and their grandparents had told them [the girls], 'No, why should you go to school? There's no need for you to go to school because you're going to marry, and then he's going to support you [financially]. So school's useless.' When I got married my [step]father told me, 'You must respect your husband and do what he tells you.' I told him, 'Well, no, I'm not going to do it.' "

She continued, relating the history of Colonia Santo Domingo to what she termed the "inculcation" of the children by their parents: "Many *compañeras* have husbands who drink too much. In addition to this problem there are those of the *colonia*. Not only the battle with husbands, but with [government] functionaries, too. Besides putting up with a *marido golpeador* [batterer husband], you have to go from office to office filling out the paperwork for land ownership. In addition to being beaten, women have had to haul water from long distances. We women were the ones who were here [in the *colonia*] during the day. There were a lot of meetings, and sometimes they came from Coyoacán to throw us out, but instead we threw them out, kicked out the mounted police and the other cops. The invasion was very violent."

Juanita remembered a particular evening when she returned home past midnight after trying to "regularize" her tenancy in the federal offices off the Zócalo in downtown Mexico City.[9]

"We got back to the house at around 12:30 A.M. He didn't let me enter. I told him I had been trying to get us this little bit of land and asked him why he wouldn't let me in. He said nothing, but just left me out there in the cold rain."

Most of my male acquaintances in Santo Domingo and elsewhere in Mexico City went mute when it came to discussions of domestic violence. Other than the occasional reference to a man having once slapped his wife, to a wife having once bitten her husband, or to the occasional belt whipping of a recalcitrant child, men frequently acted as if there were nothing to discuss about violence in the family. I was thus most appreciative when I got invited to attend the weekly sessions organized by CAVI for men with violent histories.[10] When I was introduced and requested the men's permission to participate in their meetings, they expressed appreciation for my attention to their efforts to change what for most were long-standing patterns of wife beating and fighting with other men. They told me that as long as I changed their names they were willing to have these parts of their lives publicly exposed.

Each year more complaints of domestic violence are filed with CAVI—6,289 in 1991 and 6,868 in 1992, for example.[11] Roughly one-third of both "victims" and "aggressors" are in their twenties, and another third are in their thirties. Women are victims in 88 percent of cases reported, and they are the aggressors 13 percent of the time. (Women were sometimes both victims and aggressors.) In the overwhelming number of complaints filed, both victims and aggressors are either legally married or living in *unión libre* together. CAVI divides up the types of violence that get reported to the organization into three categories: "physical violence" (81 percent); "sexual violence" (18 percent); and "psychological violence" without physical or sexual violence (1 percent). Most commonly, problems of domestic violence begin within the first five years of marriage, according to statistics compiled by CAVI.

These figures must be read with care, especially since the program is fairly new. In particular, it seems certain that there is a vast *underre-porting* of many instances of domestic violence, especially because of ignorance, fear, and inhibitions tied to social class. With regard to the latter, most of the women filing complaints with CAVI are from the lower middle or lower class, yet it is probable that this represents those who happen to seek out the center more than it does actual instances of domestic violence, which other experts report are equally numerous in the upper social strata.[12]

At a CAVI meeting one night, the first man to speak talked about an argument he had had with his wife earlier that week. He had been bathing their child, he recounted, when his wife returned home. She immediately took the child from him and began insulting his care of the boy. He became furious. This time, though, he told us, he left the house without striking her.

The central importance of children and parental care in the angry and violent episodes experienced by many men was one of a number of themes that emerged in the CAVI sessions I attended. Questions of control and power within the family often seemed to concentrate on perceived negligence by the spouse regarding the children's well-being. In contrast to the case of the man bathing his son, however, few men reported episodes in which they had become angry when their wives criticized them for inept but active participation in caring for the children. Rather, the men in these sessions complained most about their lazy wives. As one man put it, "*Me casé para que me sirviera ella* [I got married so she would serve me]." Messy homes, tortillas not ready with meals, screaming children—all were sparks that had set these men off.[13]

A plainclothes policeman was one of those attending the CAVI group one night. He voiced his problem to the others in attendance: "In my marriage, instead of one child we have two—my son and my wife. I have to teach her everything. I'm always having to do something about her ignorance. She's very *necia* [foolish]. She doesn't see the truth at first, so I always have to exert myself to get her to see the light." If this included physical reprimands, so be it. That is how children learn.

Few men I have met in Santo Domingo openly defend wife beating, but when I asked one neighbor I was interviewing, "Is violence ever justified in marriage?" he responded: "When it's justified it is. That's why a lot of times it's good to justify it, because what are you going to do when the police get there and put you in jail for beating your woman, while you can't prove anything?"

"Do women sometimes deserve the violence?" I asked.

"Yes, yes. Sometimes a man devotes himself to working, leaving early, getting home late, in order to keep his family well [supported]. And the woman sometimes begins to talk about the man fooling around, because he gets home late and is never at home. So the woman sometimes incites the man for nothing."

"Then the man's violence against the woman is justified?"

"You got it."

Most men in the CAVI sessions and in Santo Domingo generally were far less cavalier about wife beating. Perhaps this was due in part to the volunteer makeup of the men at CAVI, and no doubt some of those men in Santo Domingo who professed critical attitudes toward men who beat women were being dishonest. Yet public pronouncements count for something, and the opprobrium frequently, if not universally, heaped on men who use their fists against women and children reflects possible shifts in attitudes regarding domestic violence. Even if such shifts are occurring in what people say about wife beating, however, it is not necessarily the case that instances of domestic violence are declining. Indeed, there is good reason to believe that they may be increasing.

THE "*ESPOSAS*" OF CULTURE

The Mexican is passionate, aggressive, and warlike
out of weakness; that is to say, he lacks the will to
control his actions.

Samuel Ramos, Profile of Man and
Culture in Mexico

A man announced earnestly one evening at a CAVI session, "I have a question about history." He felt motivated to come to grips with the problem of violence in his own life, he said, but he felt overwhelmed by his ancestors. "My great-grandparents, grandparents, and my parents have all lived in a similar way, violently. The only one who has had the *criterio* [critical judgment], the choice about doing something different, is me."

Over and over the men at CAVI identified *la cultura machista* in which they had grown up as the primary culprit of their violent tendencies. The "*machista* ideas and values" were described as part of the "*machista* conditioning" process to which every boy and girl in Mexico is exposed. Ironically, in identifying elements of the matrix of male violence, the men were also, intentionally or not, explaining to themselves that they were guiltless, as if such analysis combined with remorse would atone for all prior (and future) transgressions. "We, the men in this room, we've all been taught to be machos for thirty or forty years," announced one man. "It's not fair that we get blamed for everything."

The thinking on the part of some men seemed to be that no one could expect them to change because they were also victims of an ongoing and pervasive macho ethos.

On first glance, it might be easy and tempting to dismiss such reasoning as the specious justifications of insufficiently repentant wife beaters. Yet these men are unquestionably, and in their own fashion, wrestling with issues long of concern to critical social theory. If we grant, for the sake of argument and momentary convenience, that these men in the CAVI sessions are the products of a violent society and upbringing, the question, then, would seem to be the manner in which history is made. In some of the CAVI men's rationalizations—about when it might be warranted to beat women, for instance—we can catch a glimpse of historic changes under way, transformations against which these men are often fiercely reacting. Their responses stem in part from the patrimony of violent circumstances that the men have inherited, and in part from the willful decisions that they as independent social actors have made in their lives to date. In a sense, then, there is for some of these men a distinct coincidence, and not a contradiction, between inherited and practical consciousness. Nevertheless, despite carping—"The macho culture made me hit her"—some men in the CAVI groups also have a desire to emphasize their own histories of abuse and their resolve to change themselves and their relations with those around them.

Men in the CAVI sessions frequently describe themselves as incapable of the injustices that, they are told, they have the potential of inflicting on others. Thus these men use terms like *ninguneado* (nothinged), *minimizado* (slighted), *humillado* (humiliated), and *descontrolado* (out of control) to describe how they feel as a result of how their wives, mothers, and other women treat *them*. If not for such sentiments, why else would handcuffs throughout Mexico have the popular nickname *esposas* (wives)? Many men in Santo Domingo explain the violence of men against women—and that of men against men, for that matter—as a question of men having to tolerate abuse from bosses, foremen, traffic cops, and government officials, and then seeking an outlet for their frustrations. Male violence against women, say some proponents of functionalist analysis as well, is the "displaced anger" of humiliated men, poor souls who keep their aggression pent up and finally explode in periodic paroxysms of fury against those they in turn seek to control: their wives, girlfriends, and other women. All these arguments ultimately serve to release men from responsibility for their violent actions.

The violent tempers and eruptions of the CAVI men were consistently rekindled, the men said, when they received less respect and obedience than they knew they deserved. Such challenges to their authority were personified by the women in their lives, often regardless of the immediate sources of rancor. Jealousy was cited as a particularly sensitive problem, provoked by wives wearing "extra short" skirts or more makeup than usual, or coming home late and refusing to explain where they have been. One woman filed a complaint with CAVI stating that her husband inspected her vagina whenever she got home because he was sure she had a secret lover.

Ex-boyfriends were a constant source of conflict and jealousy, according to many men. One man linked the fact that some wives want to maintain friendships with old boyfriends to a broader issue that troubles many men, which he explained as "Women want more freedom, and this quite frankly can make a lot of guys very jealous." This was one of numerous offhand remarks referring to changing demands by women and how difficult many men find it to cope with these.

A friend in Santo Domingo told me one day that he attributed violence in many marriages to men drinking, men not working, and men not fulfilling their marital obligations in general. I told him the last two reasons seemed to me reasons for *women* to beat *men*. He explained that often when men do not work wives complain, and then men beat the women. An older woman who has lived apart from her husband for several decades, though their children have regular contact with each parent, told me that he used to hit her when he was going around with other women. I asked her, "Then why did he hit *you?*" She responded, "Because he and I were no longer *coamantes* [lovers]. He was frustrated being legally stuck with me. So he beat me." Another woman informed me in an interview that violence in the marriage is always the woman's fault. This was a good friend, and I argued vigorously with her, seeking some situation in which even she would admit that the husband was to blame, but to no avail. Several minutes later I got to the last question in the interview: "Who's the boss in the house?" "I am," she quickly responded. "Always?" I asked. "Yes, always." As an example she told me, "I control the money, and he has to ask me for money." For my friend no contradiction is implied by such an allocation of responsibility and authority in her marriage and family life.

Antonio complained at a CAVI session that his family treats him like an *instrumento* (tool, instrument). "All they care about is whether I bring money home to them," he told us. Frederico added to this that he was really trying to adapt to new demands on him, demands that he said were never made on his father. But, he insisted, *"me deben de respetar* [they have to respect me]." He did not add *especially because I'm a new man,* but this is what he meant.

Thus what is new may not be so new. One of the reasons the issue of jealousy is so recurrent a theme for these men, I think, is that many men feel they are losing control over their wives in general and over their wives' sexuality in particular. They have histories of employing violence to try to regain this patriarchal authority.[14] For this reason, given what Giddens (1992:122) refers to as "the waning of female complicity," violent attacks on women may rise.

PERMISSIONS AND PARDONS

The question of historical moment is critical to an understanding of wife beating, because although such behavior may be rampant in different times and places, its causes and import are not necessarily exactly the same in each situation. Calderón, for example, writes again of her amusement at the outlook of Indians in mid-nineteenth-century Mexico regarding domestic violence:

[A]n Indian woman who complained to a padre of her husband's neglect . . . mentioned, as the crowning proof of his utter abandonment of her, that he had not given her a beating for a whole fortnight. (1843:504)[15]

While employed several years ago as a bartender in Houston, I worked with many Mexican immigrants from the state of Guerrero. I often listened to them chant a ditty about men, women, and wife beating that I later heard recited three times in Colonia Santo Domingo, each time by the same man. Coincidentally or not, it was repeated by Luis, who himself was originally from a small coastal village in Guerrero: "*No tiene perdón de Dios quien le pega a una mujer. ¡No tiene perdón de Dios si no le pega otra vez!* [God won't pardon you if you hit a woman. God won't pardon you if you don't hit her again!]"

Undoubtedly this saying is known and used by more men than just those from Guerrero.[16] Also, as I have detailed earlier in this chapter, wife beating is a widespread problem in Mexico City and throughout the Republic. Yet I was struck by the fact that such formulas were not commonly used by men in Colonia Santo Domingo. In addition, the reaction of the men who heard Luis repeat the saying surprised me. Whereas in Houston chuckling agreement inevitably followed, on each of the three occasions with Luis in Santo Domingo no one laughed appreciatively and no one picked up the spirit of the comment and added his own sayings to it; rather, the other men simply ignored Luis. That no one challenged him or the comment certainly gave an indication of contemporary beliefs, yet so did the men's silences.

According to numerous experts in the field of domestic violence, wife beating and other forms of violence in the home are on the rise. As for Santo Domingo, because I did not begin living there until 1992, I must rely rather exclusively on what my friends tell me, which is contradictory. Some report far fewer problems with wife beating in recent times, whereas others say such behavior is getting out of control. In any case, most men in the *colonia* today do not verbally approve of wife beating. On the contrary, domestic violence is discussed as a problem that, like alcoholism, needs to be overcome. Simply put, one aspect of what may be occurring is that as demands by women for greater independence rise, so do levels of wife beating and hypocrisy.

Another form of domestic abuse deserves attention. In some cases, women cannot leave their homes without the express permission of their husbands. I feel that this should also be categorized as a form male violence. I sat around the kitchen with Angela and another woman friend one evening as they ticked off the names of nearby neighbors whose husbands maintained this kind of control over their wives. Juan entered the kitchen, and I asked him to explain why some men forbade their wives to go out without permission. "*Porque las quieren* [Because they love them]," Juan responded. Angela dismissed him with a wave of her hand.

Several months later I attended a street celebration in Santo Domingo with Angela. As we passed a middle-aged woman looking out her gate, Angela urged her, "Come on, Rosa, come with us. You can come out. Did he tell you you couldn't? So, then, come on." But Rosa would not budge. Angela concluded scornfully that after so many years Rosa had no desire to end her imprisonment.

The *muchachos* explained such sanctions in the context of a generational scale. I had asked if they knew women who could not leave their homes without their husbands' approval.

"Our mothers. Well, not like in the rancho, where men ride around all macho and when they say no, well, that's it. No! Because otherwise, they'll beat you," Pancho reported.

"Is your sister going to live like that?" I asked Esteban.

"No, not anymore," he replied.

"It's going to be the reverse. *He's* going to have to ask for permission," joked Celso, poking Esteban in the ribs.

The youths told me that although they were not going to be such authoritarian husbands, and that for them marriage was going to involve greater sharing of decision making, this would be true only as long as each man's wife "*sea por la derecha* [was true]"—as long as she behaved herself, told the truth, and was always sexually faithful to her *muchacho*.

STATES OF VIOLENCE

In the surprising event that North American visitors to Mexico City were to stumble inadvertently onto Colonia Santo Domingo, few would be surprised to discover instances of male violence perpetrated against women or of young men in gangs who periodically murder and maim their opposite numbers. But to anyone who had lived in the more destitute urban sectors of the United States or who had even a passing acquaintance with those areas, the relative absence of a another form of violence would be immediately apparent: there is virtually no police presence in the *colonia*. Even for the adolescent males who spend their days hanging out in the streets, the police are mainly an occasional nuisance.

In 1992, there were thirty police officers assigned to patrol Santo Domingo, a community of around 150,000, which works out to about one police officer for every five thousand people.[17] For those officers who do drive by, there is widespread distrust, fear, and hatred among residents of Santo Domingo. The plainclothes police from La Procuraduría (La Procu, for short) are especially disliked; they are seen as hotheaded young men in their early twenties who are recruited from the *campo* and who believe they are a law unto themselves. Their Operativo Aguila (Operation Eagle), launched in spring 1993 and supposedly designed to clean up the gangs in Santo Domingo, proved ineffectual except in alienating even broader sectors of the community with its indiscriminate armed repression. The police are not a significant hourly or sometimes even a daily presence in the area, but they can be and are routinely mobilized for sweeps and crackdowns, and they have a history of brutal aggression toward opponents of the government's policies.

Given the history of Santo Domingo and some other areas in the capital, there have long been sharp antagonisms between the community and the police. Women and men in their forties and older still recount vivid tales of physical confrontations with the police in the early days of the *colonia*. "The police couldn't enter [the *colonia*]; if they did, they were attacked," one resident recalls (cited in Safa 1992:51). Vélez-Ibañez (1983:121–29) chronicles how crowds in the early 1970s in Ciudad Netzahualcóyotl used slingshots, rocks, sticks, bottles, and hardened mud clods in pitched battles with the police. The men referred to these women as "*viejas chingonas* [fucking strong women]," though the women called themselves the "*comadres* [godmothers]," no doubt utilizing some of the prestige accorded women-as-mothers to make their claim to having given birth to the community. Their violent confrontations with the police contributed to the emergence of their collective identity, but, writes Vélez-Ibañez, the "use of violence by women, as well as their participation in political action, has largely been ignored" in the social science literature.[18]

Today the police are seldom called upon to help settle disputes or problems by residents in Santo Domingo, partly because many people do not have easy access to telephones—few public phones are found in the *colonia,* and fewer still ever function—but even more because few wish to involve the police. For over twenty years people have handled many policing needs on their own or through neighborhood organizations. As in other cities in Mexico, nearly every wall surrounding private homes in Santo Domingo is topped with glass shards and, less often, barbed wire. Many households have dogs who never leave the roofs of their houses but spend their days, and nights, growling and barking at anyone who walks by or approaches the gate. Regardless of whether all this protection designed to deter would-be burglars is necessary, home robberies are uncommon in the *colonia.*

Very few of my friends in Santo Domingo have ever been arrested, much less spent time in jail, a situation that is in stark contrast to the lives of the poor, and particularly poor young men, in the United States. In fact, of those friends who have been arrested or incarcerated, most suffered those experiences at the hands of the U.S. Border Patrol, *La Migra,* while trying to make their way into Texas or California, or while living in the United States.[19] Probably the poor of Mexico City most commonly have contact with the police when they have to pay off the traffic police, also known as *mordelones* (biters), whose nickname comes from *la mordida* (the little bite, meaning a bribe).

Unless they live in a zone targeted for a specific reason—like Guerrero (drug smuggling), Chiapas (armed rebellion), or Michoacán (opposition political movements)—most people in Mexico have little contact with the federal military.[20] But when they do, the results are often deadly. The human-rights organization Americas Watch concludes: "Torture and extrajudicial killings by federal and state police and the country's security forces are disturbingly frequent in Mexico." It also reports, "Torture is endemic in Mexico" (Americas Watch Committee 1990:9).

If for most residents of Colonia Santo Domingo the police in their various guises have not to date represented a draconian presence, the state of affairs has never been that of benign neglect. And the situation in the Pedregales may soon change dramatically, because the municipal police department has been discussing plans to build a new station house in the area, probably in Colonia Ajusco, in the near future. The municipal authorities have evidently decided that the local community should no longer have as much control over itself and that the people of the Pedregales need much more intensive and consistent policing. As Weber (1919:78) ruefully remarked long ago about modernity, "Today the relation between the state and violence is an especially intimate one." Is it any wonder that men and women in Santo Domingo often appear tough, cold, and caustic to outsiders? Where the opportunities are fewer, passivity often spells failure and defeat.

VIOLENCE AND NATIONALISM

Class antagonisms may be muffled by national symbols and by claims and appeals to nationalism in both its cultural and political forms. In Mexico, violence and nationalism are not strangers. Take cockfighting or the bullfight. Beezley (1987:6) calls the latter "a metaphor of Mexico's political system, family arrangements, and even certain religious attitudes." According to television sportscasters, working class Mexican men love bullfighting. But today, at least in Santo Domingo, this metaphor of Mexican society is considered by most men as a sport of the wealthy. Few men I know have ever been to a bullring; Roberto the radiator repairman is the only friend I know of who goes often.

Although many more of my friends are interested in boxing—also associated with violence, men, and Mexican identity—their enthusiasm is often due especially to the sport's nationalist tones in an international context. The major bout in winter 1993 between Julio César Chávez and Greg Haugen was followed by many men. What they often voiced concern about, besides the bloodletting, was the fact that Mexico's political dignity was on the line in this fight. Chávez was Mexican and

Cockfighting and gambling are sometimes touted as national (male) sports in Mexico. I went with a neighbor from Santo Domingo to this 1993 cockfight, held in a village in Estado de México.

was referred to as "our *compatriota*" by most. Haugen was from the United States. The latter's defeat was quite a boon to Mexican self-esteem, yet the only person in the *colonia* I knew who actually went to Estadio Azteca to see the action live was a middle class medical student who is also an ardent boxing fan.

The cultural parallels between local-level brawls and international conflagrations are not all that tenuous for many men and women in Santo Domingo. Despite fervent attempts by residents of the *colonia* to protect themselves and their homes from violent attack, it is widely conceded that the dangers of their situation pale in comparison to the destructive and deadly world of nationalist armies and financial-market collapses. Many regard Mexico as, on the whole, more peaceful than most other parts of the globe, which is a major reason that the assassinations of two major political figures and the Chiapas uprising, all of which occurred in 1994, were so shocking to many of my friends in Santo Domingo.

My being a gringo also seemed to provoke some people. The relationship of political nationalism to violence was made apparent to me on several occasions in Mexico City, due no doubt in part to my U.S. origins. After I dropped off some of Liliana's newborn clothes with Valfre and María Elena, whose baby was due a couple of months later,

Valfre and I stepped through their gate out onto the street and were met by a thin, grizzled man holding a screwdriver in his hand and muttering something about getting himself a gringo. He may have noticed the California license plates on my car parked in the street. Valfre and I moved away quickly, trying to ignore the man and his screwdriver. I looked back and, hoping to make light of the situation, commented to this stranger, "And I thought we were friends. . . ." He looked at me in a confused way and then approached me; finally, we shook hands. He then moved on down the street, but before we knew it he had quickly picked a fight with a woman who then began beating him with her umbrella. This man was evidently violent toward many, but his was a violence set off at least on occasion by international relations and not something provoked simply by a solitary cause such as his "membership in the violent male subpopulation," alcoholism, impotence, or some other cheap "scientific" construct.

On another occasion a besotted youth hurled a piece of fruit at me, managing to hit me in the head (thus, as far as I was concerned, he had not had *enough* to drink); then he shouted "Gringo!" at me, as if this would be enough to explain his conduct. There were more than a few other times when I was the target of the invective "Gringo!"—while walking in unknown streets of the *colonia* or driving in various parts of the city. But it is important to make clear that not only did this menacing curse reflect an unmistakable anti-U.S. sentiment; it was also meant as an insult directed at the Mexican middle and upper classes. My physical appearance leaves no doubt that I am not of recent indigenous ancestry, but generally when I am observed on the street in Mexico City, I pass for Mexican. The antagonism resonating in the epithet "Gringo!" is in fact most commonly directed by youth in Santo Domingo at Mexicans who are perceived to come from better-off strata. Though people from Santo Domingo always see tourists in the Zona Rosa, the Zócalo, or Chapultepec Park, rarely do they come into direct contact with anyone from the United States, especially in their own *colonia*.[21]

Class violence is part of everyday life in the *colonias populares* of Mexico City, where the pressures to eke out a life in times of financial ruin are great. Gender violence, especially in the form of wife beating, is also ever present and probably on the rise. The consequences of this gender violence are not the same for men as for women; all are not equally injured by male violence. Thus, resolutions of the violence have required unequal responses, because men in Santo Domingo have not, as a group, relinquished their prerogative of physical domination over women unless they were forced to do so. Men have been forced to do so only when, as the saying goes, they were compelled to eat *una sopa de su propio chocolate* (a cup of their own chocolate)—that is, when they got a taste of their own medicine. As with any other aspect of daily life in Santo Domingo, whatever practical solutions to male violence against women have been found have been the result not of simply awaiting outside intervention but rather of addressing and attacking the problem from within the community and individual families.

A rise in domestic violence in Santo Domingo today provides an index not of deep-seated cultural practices by Spanish-speaking men everywhere and throughout the ages, but rather of the cultural deracination of contemporary gender relations through a sharply conflictive process.[22] Simply put, many men are finding it exceedingly difficult to cope with women's independence, and some are seeking to avoid taking responsibility for their violence by blaming "the Mexican macho system" for their outbursts.

Male violence in Mexico must be understood in its particular manifestations, but this should not lead us to an analysis that it might arise from a particular, if amorphous, culturally rooted sense of Mexican maleness, a cognitive system that some social scientists denote under the rubric *machismo*.[23] In the following chapter we direct our attention to that phenomenon known as machismo, the ethos widely held responsible for male violence in Mexico and beyond, and commonly understood as the scourge infecting all warm male bodies that speak Spanish, the culture trait that, many say, has doggedly remained unchanged through the ages, one whose resilience at least since the Conquest nearly five hundred years ago has left it impervious to history.

NINE

Machismo

Haven't you also lost something for following your father?

Rodolfo Usigli, El Gesticulador

MACHOS AND HOMBRES

"Are any of you married?" I asked the *muchachos*.

"No, *todos solteritos* [all young and single]," said Felipe.

"That bozo's got two little squirts. He's the *macho mexicano*," said Rodrigo, pointing to Celso, the father of two children who lived with their mother in another city.

"What does that mean?" I inquired.

"Macho? That you've got kids all over," said Esteban.

"That your ideology is very closed," said Pancho. "The ideology of the *macho mexicano* is very closed. He doesn't think about what might happen later, but mainly focuses on the present, on satisfaction, on pleasure, on desire. But now that's disappearing a little."

"You're not machos?" I asked.

"No, *somos hombres* [we're men]." [1]

It is common to hear women and men in Colonia Santo Domingo say that although there used to be a lot of macho men, they are not as prevalent today. Some people who make this comment are too young to know anything firsthand about bygone machos, but regardless, they are sure there was more machismo before. Some older men like to divide the world of males into machos and *mandilones* (meaning female-dominated men), where the term *macho* connotes a man who is responsible for providing financially and otherwise for his family. [2] For older men, to be macho more often means to be *un hombre de honor* (an honorable man). [3]

It is far more common for younger married men in Colonia Santo Domingo to define themselves as belonging to a third category, the "nonmacho" group. "*Ni macho, ni mandilón* [Neither macho nor *mandilón*]" is how many men describe themselves. Others may define a friend or relative as "your typical *macho mexicano*," but the same man will not infrequently reject the label, describing all the things he does to help his wife around the home, pointing out that he does not beat his wife (wife beating being one of the few generally agreed-upon attributes of machos). What is most significant is not simply how the terms *macho, machismo,* and *machista* are variously defined—there is little consensus on their meanings—but that today the terms are widely regarded by working class men in Colonia Santo Domingo, Mexico City, as pejorative and not worthy of emulation. For these younger men, then, the present period is distinguished by its liminal character with respect to male gender identities: as neither-macho-nor-*mandilón,* these men are precisely betwixt and between assigned cultural positions.

The purpose of this chapter is to describe and account for these mixed and changing sentiments regarding the terms *macho* and *machismo.* Three general points bear mentioning from the outset. First, *macho* (in its modern sense) and *machismo* (in any sense) have remarkably short word histories. Indeed, tracing the historical permutations and modulations of these words is critical to understanding the ongoing discrepancies that exist popularly and in the social sciences regarding their meanings. Carlos Monsiváis (1981, 1992) in particular has linked the emergence of the ethos of machismo especially to the golden age of Mexican cinema in the 1940s and 1950s.

Second, machismo as discussed here is not reducible to a coherent set of sexist ideas. It is not simply male chauvinism. As Roger Lancaster (1992:19) stresses in his study of Nicaragua, "machismo is resilient because it constitutes not simply a form of 'consciousness,' not 'ideology' in the classical understanding of the concept, but a field of productive relations."[4] Determining the systemic character of machismo is predicated on following the historical tracks of the term. Because these lead in various directions in different times and circumstances in Mexico and Nicaragua, for instance, the structural and material content of machismo must be kept in mind.

Finally, I would like to touch on another central, recurring theme in many if not most meanings of machismo: the physical body. This theme manifests itself in beatings, sexual episodes, alcohol consumption, daredevil antics, and the not-so-simple problem of defining the categories of "men" and "women." Regardless of how confusing gender identities may seem, they usually share relations of mutual dependence with these somatic realms.[5]

COWBOYS AND RACISM

In Mexican newspapers, academic literature, and dictionary entries, the terms *macho* and *machismo* have been used in contradictory ways. The definitions employed or implied in such official circles reveal not only a diversity of views regarding the substance of the terms, but also widely disparate conjectures as to the origins of the words and their meanings. Emphasizing sexuality, Stevens (1973:90) calls machismo "the cult of virility," adding that "[t]he chief characteristics of this cult are exaggerated aggressiveness and intransigence in male-to-male interpersonal relationships and arrogance and sexual aggression in male-to-female relationships." Greenberg (1989:227) captures some of the ambivalence of machismo when he describes an episode in which Fortino, the protagonist of his study, "was being very macho, in a nonconfrontational, almost womanly manner." *Macho* thus may be identified with nonaggressive ("womanly") behavior.[6]

Many anthropologists and psychologists writing about machismo utilize characterizations like "manly," "unmanly," and "manliness" without defining them. They seem to assume, incorrectly in my estimation, that all their readers share a common definition and understanding of such qualities. Dictionaries are in conflict over the etymological roots of *macho*, sometimes tracing them to Latin and Portuguese words for "masculine" and "mule," and at other times tracing the cultural ancestry of *macho* to Andalusian soldiers of the Conquest, or to certain indigenous peoples of the Americas, or to Yankee gringo invaders in the early part of this century.[7]

In his essay "El machismo en México," one of the first scholarly discussions on the subject, Mendoza (1962) illustrates his analysis of Mexico's "national idiosyncrasy" with the words from several dozen folk songs, *corridos*, and *cantares* sung in the late 1800s and early 1900s. Especially noteworthy in this essay is Mendoza's distinction between what he calls the two classes of machismo: the first, authentic one is characterized by courage, generosity, and stoicism; the second, which is basically false, consists of appearances—cowardice hiding behind empty boasts. Mendoza is calling attention to an essential dualism in the history of the use of the word *machismo,* similar in some respects to what friends in Colonia Santo Domingo describe as the real machos of the old days and the buffoonish machos of today.

Yet in the songs and ballads cited by Mendoza the words *macho* and *machismo* do not appear. He uses the term *machismo* to represent Mexican male rebels and cowards in the Porfiriato (1877–1911) and the ensuing revolution of the 1910s, labeling a whole genre of folklore as exemplary of machismo, but he does not explain the curious absence of the phrase in the literature of the time.

In a brilliant essay written a few years later, Américo Paredes (1967) provides several clues as to the word history of *machismo* and in the process draws clear connections between the advent of machismo and that of nationalism, racism, and international relations. Building on an earlier (1966) paper, Paredes finds that prior to the 1930s and 1940s in Mexican folklore—a good indication of popular speech at the time— the terms *macho* and *machismo* did not appear. The word *macho* existed, but almost as an obscenity, similar to later connotations of *machismo* (which Santamaría [1959:677], for instance, defines as a "crude vulgarity for manliness and virility"). Other expressions, some also semantically related to men, were far more common at the time of the Mexican Revolution: *hombrismo, hombría, muy hombre,* and *hombre de verdad* (all relating to *hombre* [man]); *valentía* and *muy valiente* (relating to valor or courage); and so forth.[8] Despite the fact that during the Mexican Revolution the phrase *muy hombre* was used to describe courageous women as well as men, the special association of such a quality with men then and now indicates certain associations of words and phrases with maleness, regardless of whether the words *macho* and *machismo* were employed.

Making a connection between courage and men during times of war in Mexico—in which men have usually been the main, though assuredly not the only, combatants—is nevertheless not the same thing as noting the full-blown "machismo syndrome," as it is sometimes called. To oversimplify, if courage was valued during the Mexican Revolution, it was valued in both men and women, though the terms used to refer to courage carried a heavy male accent. Beginning especially in the 1940s, the male accent itself came to prominence as a national(ist) symbol. For better or worse, Mexico came to mean machismo and machismo to mean Mexico.

Searching for a single national identity is a very modern project in Mexico as elsewhere. Often remembered for his blunt diagnosis of the

¿La mexicana abnegada? (The submissive Mexican woman?) Many bank guards in downtown Mexico City are women.

country's "inferiority complex," Samuel Ramos (1934) is also frequently cited as the original critic of Mexican machismo. Once again, however, Ramos never used the term *macho* or *machismo*. Yet in Ramos the connections between *lo mexicano* and manliness (however defined) were striking. He centered his account of the nation's inferiority around the "well-known Mexican type, the *pelado*," whose conduct was one of "virile protest" (Ramos 1962:9). The *pelado* is a male prole-tarian, vulgar and poorly educated, Ramos reported, who himself asso-ciates "his concept of virility with that of nationality, creating thereby the illusion that personal valor is the Mexican's particular characteris-tic" (p. 63). The particular association by Ramos of negative male qual-ities with the urban working class has been a prominent theme in writ-ings on Latin American masculinity and machismo ever since—what Mary Louise Pratt (1990:50) shows to be the "androcentrism of the modern national imaginings" in Latin America.[9] In contrast to Ramos, scholars like Paredes have linked machismo especially to Mexico's mid-dle classes, and Limón (1989, 1994) effectively critiques the class preju-dices of Ramos regarding macho *pelados*.[10]

One reason Ramos judged "the Mexican of the city" so harshly was his observation that "the *campesino* in Mexico is almost always of the indigenous race . . . [and] his role is a passive one in the present life of his country" (p. 63) whereas the "active group" of Mexicans were the mestizos and whites who lived in the city—a view that is implicitly and partially shared by some of my friends in Colonia Santo Domingo to-day. In fact, in the eyes of many working class people in Mexico in the 1990s, the (white) Mexican elites are no longer to be trusted, because they have sold out the country for their own personal financial gain. So it is ironically left to the mestizo majority in the cities to maintain the banner of Mexican national identity, including in its (male) gendered aspects. Thus *mestizaje* comes to be equated in the minds of Ramos and some of his working class subjects with masculinity, and the two are in turn made complicit in the constitution of Mexicanness itself.

In Mexico, the consolidation of nation-state and party machinery throughout the Republic and the development of the country's modern national cultural identity took place on a grand scale during the presi-dencies of Lázaro Cárdenas and Manuel Avila Camacho (1934–40 and 1940–46, respectively). After the turbulent years of the revolution and the 1920s, and following six years of national unification under the populist presidency of Cárdenas, the national election campaign of 1940 opened an era of unparalleled industrial growth and demagogic rule in Mexico. Coincidentally, one of the campaign slogans of the ulti-mately successful presidential candidate, Avila Camacho, was: "Ca . . . MACHO!" Paredes (1971:23) points out that although the president was not responsible for the use of the term *macho,* "we must remember that names lend reality to things."

As Paredes also perceptively points out, in a sense the Mexican macho is simply a joke that outsiders (foreigners) do not get. Indeed in Mexican movies, as Monsiváis (1981:107) quips, the *macho mexicano* is the Gran Macho Operático.[11] To the extent that the *macho mexicano* is a joke, both authors seem to imply, in like fashion those who grasp the humor will have their consciousness and agency restored to them, at least in part and in comparison to those who do not get the joke. Besides, although machismo in Mexico may take on quite exaggerated forms, it is hardly a phenomenon unique to that land.[12]

The word history of *machismo* is but a piece of the larger puzzle regarding the outlooks and practices codified in tautological fashion as instances of machismo. For Paredes, the peculiar history of U.S.-Mexican relations has produced a marked antipathy on the part of Mexicans toward their northern neighbors. The image of the frontier and the (Wild) West has played a special role in this tempestuous relationship, with the annexation of two-fifths of the Mexican nation to the United States in 1848 and repeated U.S. economic and military incursions into Mexico since then, putting the lie to proclamations of respect for national sovereignty. Trade between the two countries early on included the export of the Mexican *vaquero*-cowboy to the United States, Paredes reminds us. In the early nineteenth century, the frontiersmen of Texas and areas farther west were running point for the expanding Jacksonian empire, and their combination of individualism and sacrifice for the higher national good came to embody the ethos of machismo. Together with the pistol, the supreme macho symbol, such an ethos came to play a similar role in the consolidation of the Mexican nation. But today, after the fighting both in the United States and Mexico have long since ended, "*machismo* betrays a certain element of nostalgia; it is cultivated by those who feel they have been born too late" (Paredes 1971:37).

On the other side of the border, in the United States, the term *machismo* has a rather explicitly racist history; from the first appearance of the term in print in English that I can find (Griffith 1948:50–51), machismo has been associated with negative character traits not among men in general, but specifically among Mexican, Mexican American, and Latin American men.[13] Contemporary popular usage of the term *machismo* in the United States often serves to rank men according to their presumably inherent national and racial characters. Such analysis utilizes nonsexist pretensions to make denigrating generalizations about fictitious Mexican male culture traits.

JORGE NEGRETE AND *LO MEXICANO*

"You're macho, as we say. When I've needed you,
you've helped me wholeheartedly, and I'll do the same
for you."

> *Pedro, resident of Juchatengo, Oaxaca,*
> *quoted in* Blood Ties, *by James Greenberg*

The consolidation of the Mexican nation, ideologically and materially,
was fostered early on not only in the gun battles on the wild frontier,
not only in the voting rituals of presidential politics, but also in the
imagining and inventing of *lo mexicano* and *mexicanidad* in the national cinema. (Later both radio and television played starring roles in
giving people throughout the Republic a sense of themselves as sharing
a common history and destiny—in short, a national identity.) Although
there were female leads in the movies of the period, on the silver screen
it was the manly actors who most came to embody the restless and
explosive potential of the emerging Mexican nation. And of all the
movie stars of this era, one stood out as "a macho among machos."
Ever the handsome and pistol-packing *charro* (singing cowboy), with
his melodious and eminently male tenor, Jorge Negrete came to epitomize the swaggering Mexican nation, singing,

I am a Mexican, and this wild land is mine.
On the word of a macho, there's no land lovelier and wilder of its kind.
I am a Mexican, and of this I am proud.
I was born scorning life and death,
And though I have bragged, I have never been cowed.[14]

In the rural cantinas, the manly temples of the golden age of Mexican
cinema, the macho mood was forged. Mexico appeared on screen as a
single entity, however internally incongruent, while within the nation
the figures of Mexican Man and Mexican Woman loomed large—the
former

untamed, generous, cruel, womanizing, romantic, obscene, at one with family and friends, subjugated and restless . . . [the latter] obedient, seductive,
resigned, obliging, devoted to her own and slave to her husband, to her
lover, to her children, and to her essential failure. (Monsiváis 1992:18)

Other Mexican national archetypes followed Negrete, the actor Can-
tinflas playing a *pelado* more lighthearted than the one found in Ramos,

and Tin Tan, another famous actor, cast as the U.S.-experienced *pachuco*.[15] The movies of the era carried titles like *¡Vámonos con Pancho Villa!* (Let's go with Pancho Villa!), *Allá en el Rancho Grande* (Out in the Rancho Grande), *Soy puro mexicano* (I'm all-Mexican), *Flor Silvestre* (Wildflower), *Salón México,* and *Nosotros los pobres* (We the poor).

The distinctions between being a macho and being a man were starting to come into clearer focus in the Mexican cinema of the 1940s:

> To be macho is now part of the scenery. To be macho is an attitude. There are gestures, movements. It is the belief that genital potency holds the key to the universe, all that. It goes from the notion of danger to the notion of bragging; that's the difference between macho and man [*hombre*]. As the song says, "If you've got to kill me tomorrow, why don't you get it over with now?"—that is being very manly [*ser muy hombre*]. "I have four wives"—that is being very macho [*ser muy macho*]." (Carlos Monsiváis, interview by author, 20 February 1993)

Then, at the end of the 1940s, Mexican machismo underwent a most refined dissection by Octavio Paz in *El laberinto de la soledad* (1950). Despite Paz's wish to speak only to a small group "made up of those who are conscious of themselves, for one reason or another, as Mexicans" (Paz 1961:11), this work more than any other has come to represent the authoritative view of essential Mexican attributes like machismo, loneliness, and mother worship. Therefore when Paz writes, "The Mexican is always remote, from the world and from other people. And also from himself" (p. 29), he should not be taken literally but literarily. It is a beautifully written book, and part of the reason for its elegance may be that Paz was creating qualities of *mexicanidad* as much as he was reflecting on them. As he put it in his "Return to the Labyrinth of Solitude," "The book is part of the attempt of literally marginal countries to regain consciousness: to become subjects again" (Paz 1985:330).

Paz (1961:35) writes with regard to men and women in Mexico, "In a world made in man's image, woman is only a reflection of masculine will and desire." In Mexico, "woman is always vulnerable. Her social situation—as the repository of honor, in the Spanish sense—and the misfortune of her 'open' anatomy expose her to all kinds of dangers" (p. 38). Biology as destiny? But there is nothing inherently passive, or private, about vaginas in Mexico or anywhere else. Continuing with Paz, just as "the essential attribute of the *macho*"—or what the macho seeks to display, anyway—is power, so too with "the Mexican people."

The "tough hombre" image is emblematic of many popular portrayals of the *macho mexicano* and of social science stereotypes of Mexican masculinity in general. This man ran a charcoal stall in the Mexico City Centro when I took his photo in 1991.

Thus *mexicanidad,* Paz tell us, is concentrated in the macho forms of "caciques, feudal lords, hacienda owners, politicians, generals, captains of industry" (p. 82).[16]

Many Mexican men are curious about what it means to be a Mexican, and what it means to be a man. One is not born knowing these things; nor are they truly discovered. They are learned and relearned. For some, this involves a quest for one's patrimony. "Pedro Páramo is my father too," declares one of Mexico's bastard sons (Rulfo 1955 [1959]:3). Even if he is an infamous brute, a father is a father. For the Mexican macho and for the nation, it is better to have a father than to be fatherless.

In Paz and in much of the literature of cultural nationalism in Mexico in recent decades,

> [t]he problem of national identity was thus presented primarily as a problem of *male* identity, and it was male authors who debated its defects and psychoanalyzed the nation. In national allegories, women became the territory over which the quest for (male) national identity passed, or, at best, as in Juan Rulfo's *Pedro Páramo* (1955), the space of loss and of all that lies outside the male games of rivalry and revenge. (Franco 1989:131)[17]

In Santo Domingo, another authoritative source of information about machismo and national identity in addition to Paz, one that people use in the stories they tell about themselves, is Oscar Lewis. Or at least people use what they have heard about his anthropological writings; Lewis is "remembered" far more than he is read.

In the social sciences Lewis continues to be the most cited reference with regard to conclusions about modern Mexican masculinity. The affinity of anthropologists and other social scientists to stereotypes of Mexican machismo exemplifies Giddens's (1990:16) point that "the practical impact of social science and sociological theories is enormous, and sociological concepts and findings are constitutively involved in what modernity *is.*"

In fact, three particular sentences from Lewis's *The Children of Sánchez* are employed with astonishing frequency in anthropological texts to represent all Mexican males past, present, and future:

> In a fight, I would never give up or say, "Enough," even though the other was killing me. I would try to go to my death, smiling. That is what we mean by being "*macho,*" by being manly. (Lewis 1961:38)

This specific passage is cited, for example, by Marshall (1979:89) in his discussion of machismo in Micronesia, by Madsen and Madsen

(1969:712) in a paper on alcohol consumption in Mexico, and by Gilmore (1990:16) in his comparative survey of images of masculinity. A few sentences on page thirty-eight of *The Children of Sánchez* have thus come to shoulder a immense responsibility in anthropology: to provide a quotable sound bite defining Mexican masculinity/machismo.

Is this quotation really such a good and accurate description of Mexican male identity? If it were, then every male soul who finds himself south of the shallows of the Rio Grande and north of the highlands of Guatemala would have to, as if by ethnographic decree, at least try to go to his death smiling if he wished to retain his Mexican male credentials. I doubt very much if Lewis's intention was to summarize the life experiences and desires of all Mexican men in this short passage. Perhaps most revealing of all, the sentences in question are not even Lewis's own, but are actually part of a monologue by Manuel Sánchez, one of the Sánchez children. Manuel is nonetheless the man whose ideologically charged comments to Lewis on one particular day in the mid-1950s have frequently come to speak for all Mexican men since that time.[18]

MANDILONES AND DOMINATING WOMEN

In Santo Domingo there are significant differences in the uses and meanings of the terms *macho* and *machismo*. These reflect, and often concentrate, contrasting urban and rural experiences, generational differences, class stratification, stages within individuals' lives, and, in the age of television satellites, the impact on people throughout Mexico of what others around the world say about them and their national peculiarities.

Returning to the term *mandilón*, which carries a meaning that is stronger than the English "henpecked" but not nearly as vulgar as "pussy-whipped," we see by its common daily use that it is an expression produced by a *machista* system, and that it is at the same time a response to machismo.[19] As Angela, Michelle, and I were walking through the *sobre ruedas* (open-air market) one day in October, shortly after we first met, Angela remarked that perhaps Michelle should buy a *mandil* (apron) "in Mateo's size" so that I could be a proper *mandilón*. Angela added that her son Noé, whom I had not yet met, was a *mandilón*. I asked her why, and she responded by saying that Noé washed dishes, cooked, and took care of his daughter. I wanted to know how Noé had come to do these things. "*No lo creía para ser macho mexicano* [I didn't raise him to be a *macho mexicano*]" came the answer. I wondered aloud if Noé would accept this appellation. Angela insisted that he would.

In early November, after I met him, I asked Noé about his being a *mandilón*. "*No soy mandilón* [I'm not a *mandilón*]," corrected Noé. "It doesn't bother me at all to help my wife. I share everything with her." But Noé rejected the title of *mandilón,* which he defined as, "he who is dominated by women."

Noé's younger sister Norma came by our apartment in January because her husband, Miguel, had not come home and I was the last person to have seen him. After a *futbol* playoff Miguel and I had gone over to the coach's house for tacos, beans, and beer. I had left hours earlier, but by 8 P.M. Mie still had not returned, and Norma was worried. Yet she could not go looking for him herself, she said, because that might make him look like a *mandilón* in the eyes of the other young men: a wife coming to fetch her (presumably) drunk husband.

Not labeling a man a *mandilón* is not merely a matter of helping him save face, however, because for many women as well as men it carries negative connotations. That is, being a *mandilón* is seen as a positive opposite of macho to some like Angela, but to others it is but an inverse form of the macho's empty boasting. In both cases described, the definitions of *mandilón* reflect an awareness of power differences between men and women, and a contradictory consciousness with respect to male identities.

"I don't want a man who's either macho or *mandilón*," one young woman told me.

"Why not *mandilón*?" I asked.

"Because who wants someone who can't stick up for himself, who's used to getting bossed around and likes it that way?" In other words, life is hard enough as it is, and a young woman can ill afford to depend on a *mandilón* as a husband. Instead, one needs a partner who can make things happen and not just wait for orders from others, his wife included.[20]

Among men in their twenties and thirties, it was rare to hear anyone claim the title of macho for himself. "Why, I wash dishes and cook," some would protest when called macho by a friend. Machos do neither of these things, nor do they spend a lot of time with their children, many felt. However, the most common comment used to fend off being categorized as macho was "I don't beat my wife." A grandfather of sixty-seven explained to me that he was no macho, and that his own father before him had not been one, either. "Why, he never drank a beer in front of the kids," my friend told me, "and he never beat his wife."

Angela calls her brother Héctor one of the last of the dying breed of Mexican machos. But Héctor likes to joke that he is not a macho *"porque me ensillan* [because they (women) ride me]." For him, the Mexican playboy image from the cowboy movies of the 1940s typifies the golden age of machos with their *"charros, bravacones, ebrios, pe-leoneros, iresponsables, enamorados a las mujeres* [charros, braggarts, drunkards, fighters, irresponsibles, woman-lovers]." Angel García, who is active in the Christian Base Community in Colonia Ajusco, told me that for him machismo conjures up movie images of cowboys riding through the countryside, their *pistolas* firing away.

For some men today, "the macho" is also a playful role they can perform on demand. I stifled my displeasure one evening when, at her two-year-old granddaughter's birthday party, and in her capacity as pa-tron saint of my research project, Angela took me by the hand and introduced me to several men who she said were "genuine representa-tives of Mexican machismo." After I had been so presented to one young man, Angela demanded of him, "Where's your wife?" A sly smile crossed the man's face. "I sent her to the bathroom," he answered. His wife was seven months pregnant, the man added, so he, like the good macho Angela accused him of being, had to send her to the bathroom a lot. Often, as in this case, such jokes were followed by remarks that revealed an acute sensitivity to the cultural beliefs about Mexican men that many people in Mexico think are held by North Americans. "That's really what you gringos believe about us, isn't it?" people would sometimes say to me when I raised the image of Mexican men preferring to go to their death smiling rather than lose face.

Another illustration of the influence of the United States on macho self-perceptions among Mexicans was my invitation to participate, on 5 July 1993, in the Mexico City–based nationally televised talk show *María Victoria Llamas.* Along with several Mexican men, I was invited to speak on the theme "A lo macho." It was hoped that my particular presence could be used to make two points: (1) that machismo was not just a problem in Mexico, and (2) that, based on my research, it was clear that not all men in Mexico were machos. I was informed that this would sound especially convincing coming from a North American anthropologist.[21]

People in Santo Domingo and throughout Mexico City are acutely aware of gringo images of Mexico and Mexicans, including those pertaining to Mexican masculinity. Many believe that North Americans feel their men are superior to Mexican men, as men, a perception gleaned from television, cinema, and the experience of migration to the United States. What many in Mexico may fail to recognize in ideological stances expressed in statements such as "My boyfriend may not be perfect, but at least he's no Mexican macho" is the mixture of anti-Mexican racism and sexist justifications for gender relations in the United States. In this way the perpetuation in the United States of stereotypes regarding Mexican machos and self-sacrificing women helps to obscure and preserve gender inequalities in the United States.[22]

PERFORMING AS MEN

In the dramas that people in *colonias populares* offer about their own and others' marriages, the parts played by self-designated machos are not all playful by any means. But if not quite so common as the women who endure spousal abuse for decades, there are growing numbers of spirited and independent women who for one reason or another issue ultimatums to their husbands. If and when these are not met, such women file for and receive divorces from their *machos mexicanos*.

"We cheat on our wives because we're men," said one participant in a CAVI men's group that met to discuss domestic violence. Then he added, "and because we want to be macho." What does "we want to be macho" mean except that "to be macho" is an ideological stand that can be sanctified only by others—men and women—and by oneself? In my discussion with the *muchachos*, one of them said that they were not machos but rather they were *hombres* (men). Celso, however, insisted that, as men, by definition they were machos. He said that if they were going to call themselves something, *mandilón* and *marica* (queer) were obviously inappropriate. So what else did this leave except macho?

The description provided by Celso makes it appear that the youths rummage around in an identity grab bag, pulling out whatever they happen to seize upon as long as it is culturally distinct. One minute these *muchachos* identify themselves as machos who enjoy bragging about controlling women and morally and physically weaker men, clearly in tune with broader social mores. The next minute the same young men express bitterness at being the ones on the bottom. Often the two aspects of personal identities come into conflict—as, for example, when the *muchachos* enthusiastically sing along with the popular rock band Maldita Vecindad about their class hatreds:

There in the street, shining like the sun
It's his new car cruising, second to none
Flying down the street, almost taking off
Everyone watches it passing
Windshield washer boy crosses not looking
This is the car he's not missing
Hear a shout and then a thud
In this city there's too much blood.[23]

The *muchachos* do not identify with the driver in this song, and they see no contradiction in their simultaneous identification as domineering machos and as the dominated poor pitted in lifelong struggle against the rich, the ones who drive new cars.

The discussion one evening in the CAVI group also clarified an important point regarding some men's self-identification as machos. In the session on *celos* (jealousy), several men stated that they were no longer as jealous as they had once been. They spoke not only of the influence of recent sociocultural factors affecting women that had forced the men to reevaluate their own ethical standards—women working outside the home, the feminist movement, and educational levels achieved by women—but also of patterns more associated with stages in the life course. One man after another spoke of periods in his life when particular manifestations of male jealousy—and other features associated with machismo—were more pronounced and prevalent than at other times. In the cases of jealousy and violent outbursts against wives for assumed infidelity, for example, most men said that such behavior was more characteristic of the early years of their marriages.

REDEFINITIONS

[L]anguage is is at the same time a living thing and a
museum of fossils of life and civilisations.

> *Antonio Gramsci,* Selections from the Prison
> Notebooks

Machismo, then, in the minds of many younger men and women, represents a kind of option. Whether the macho is seen as good or bad, a serious threat or merely a risible fool, men have the option of letting their heads be controlled by their bodies. And quite often today in Colonia Santo Domingo, the image of the macho is linked to the male body. Women never have the option of being truly macho in the sense that men do. Above all this is because a key component of a macho's machismo is his relationship to female bodies. In Santo Domingo there are many different notions of macho, but the one element that is most commonly a part of these definitions is that of wife beating. Together with men's sexual conquest of women, abusive male physicality is for many women and men the essence of machismo.

Whether Mexican society can be characterized as macho in some overriding sense is a matter of some importance, but once again it all depends on definitions and contexts. In financial and government circles, in the arts, the universities, and the media, men predominate and dominate. In terms of who rules Mexican society and its central institutions, the issue is so straightforward that male domination there is a classic example of hegemonic, taken-for-granted control. Yet to take a more marginal example, one that reveals the interests and desires of large masses of people in Mexico City, on selected metro lines during rush hours in Mexico City, several cars are specially designated for women and children. Women can ride on the men's cars, but no men are allowed on the women's. Signs announce the segregation, and guards armed with billy clubs enforce it.

Is this separation of women from men an acknowledgment of abusive male physicality? It is. Is this an example of machismo, or an attempt—at a semiofficial level, no less—to prevent such male molestations to the extent possible? The motives are no doubt entirely mixed at the level of city government and the metro system; "protecting women," as we have seen, is part and parcel of some systems of machismo. Yet overall in this case it is more a matter of recognizing a problem and seeking a (short-term) solution to it. At rush hour women overwhelmingly avail themselves of the no-men-allowed subway cars, a means of transit that does not even exist in other societies where women are routinely fondled and harassed by men on public transport. In this way gender identities are both recognized and to a certain extent created in Mexico City.[24]

Delineating cultural identities and defining cultural categories, one's own and those of others, is not simply the pastime of ethnographers. Despite the fact that creating typologies of Mexican masculinity can result in parodies without living referents, and overlooking for the moment the not unimportant issue of how men and women in Colonia Santo Domingo understand manliness and define what *ser hombre* means, there is purpose to the quest in the social sciences for better ways to categorize men in Mexico. Although it is likely that no one in

the *colonia* would explicitly divide the population of men this way, I
think most would recognize the following four male gender groups: the
macho, the *mandilón,* the neither-macho-nor-*mandilón,* and the broad
category of men who have sex with other men. But the fact that few
men or women do or would care to divide the male population in this
manner reveals more than simply a lack of familiarity with the methods
of Weberian ideal typologizing. Masculinity, like other cultural identities, cannot be neatly confined in boxlike categories such as macho and
mandilón. Identities make sense only in relation to other identities, and
they are never firmly established for individuals or groups. Further, consensus will rarely be found as to whether a particular man deserves a
label such as neither-macho-nor-*mandilón.* He will probably think of
himself as a man in a variety of ways, none of which necessarily coincides with the views of his family and friends.

In terms of the last group of men, those who have sex with other
men, this includes among others the *putos,* who have sex for money
with other men and always play the active role, and the *homosexuales*
(*maricas, maricones,* and so on), who are marked not only by their
preference for male sex partners, but also more generally by the low
cultural esteem in which they are held by many in society. I told Gabriel
one day that in the United States a synonym for "coward" was *chicken*
and asked him what an equivalent of *cobarde* might be for him. "*Puto*
or *marica,*" he responded, adding that in the north of Mexico they
sometimes use *guajolote* (turkey) in the sense of cowardly fool. Nonetheless, men who have sex with other men are by some people's definition outside the bounds of masculinity altogether and would not even
constitute a separate male gender type.

Yet although this taxonomy may indicate some important lines of
demarcation, like all ideal typologizing it hopelessly obscures salient
differences, which are so numerous that they can hardly be considered
exceptions. And this is undoubtedly all the more true during liminal
moments historically in which by definition cultural categories lack
clearly circumscribed boundaries. No man today in Santo Domingo fits
neatly into any of the four categories, even at specific moments, much
less throughout the course of his life. Further, definitions such as these
resist other relevant but complicating factors such as class, ethnicity,
and historical epoch. "*El mexicano es muy hablador; habla mucho y
no cumple* [The Mexican man is a big talker; he talks a lot but doesn't
come through]," one young man told me. So who represents the more
archetypal *macho mexicano:* the man who wants many (male) offspring

and later abandons them, or the man who wants few, works hard to earn money for them, and calls these his manly duties? This is why attempts, even the more sophisticated ones, at quantifying Mexican masculinity on more-macho-or-less-macho scales inevitably become mired in problems of randomness, procedural errors, and, most of all, an inability to capture the existence and influence of contradictory consciousness, hegemony, and ideology among the men under investigation.

To unravel these stereotyped social roles, we must return to the point raised by Lancaster (1992): machismo, in whatever guise, is not simply a matter of ideology.[25] Machismo in Colonia Santo Domingo has been challenged ideologically, especially by grassroots feminism (see Massolo 1992a and Stephen 1996) and more indirectly by the gay and lesbian rights movements. But it has also faced real if usually ambiguous challenge through the strains of migration, falling birthrates, exposure to alternative cultures on television, and so on. These economic and sociocultural changes have not inevitably led to corresponding shifts in male domination, whether in the home, the factory, or society at large. But many men's authority has been undermined in material, if limited, ways, and this changing position for men as husbands and fathers, breadwinners and masters has in turn had real consequences for machismo in Santo Domingo.

Fidel Aguirre, a technician working in a laboratory outside the *colonia,* took pains to explain to me early one evening, "With women working outside the home it's not just a question of them having their own money now, as important as this has been. What's also involved is that women have met all sorts of different people, which has changed them forever. And this has meant that the men have changed, for if they don't, more and more they're getting left behind by women. Let me tell you, this is what's happening."[26]

To be a macho for most people in Colonia Santo Domingo involves qualities of personal belligerence, especially though not only as directed toward women, and in this sense it is very tied to appearances and style. In substance, this veneer of arrogance and hostility derives on the part of some men from feelings of superiority—and repeated and regular actions to back up these sentiments. At the same time, in the manner of Mendoza (1962) and Paredes (1967), the buffoon in Santo Domingo may seek to hide deep fears of physical inadequacy and losing male prerogative behind the guise of the macho. Women in particular talk of men who match the second description, referring to them in terms of disdain, ridicule, and even pity, and sometimes speaking of the inability of these men to sexually satisfy their wives.

Indeed, to the extent that men and women in Santo Domingo in the 1990s viewed it as a negative quality and practice, we may say that machismo had been transformed in part from a hegemonic into an ideological position that was being more openly challenged, as well as defended, in people's everyday discussions and activities in the *colonia*.

CULTURAL NATIONALISM

Authoritative discussions of machismo, or what later came to be known as machismo in some form (Ramos 1934; Paz 1950), have all made connections between the macho who "represents the masculine pole of life" (Paz 1961:81) and the broader social and political world of twentieth-century Mexico. Just as Lafaye (1976) has shown with regard to the Virgen de Guadalupe, so too with Mexican masculinity: it has not always represented the same kind of national symbol, but rather has been used for different purposes at various times to emphasize particular cultural nationalist qualities by a vast array of social forces.[27]

In Colonia Santo Domingo, as elsewhere in the Republic, the fate of machismo as an archetype of masculinity has always been closely tied to Mexican cultural nationalism. Recall César's comment to me about drinking: "More than anything we consumed tequila. We liked it, maybe because we felt more like Mexicans, more like *lugareños* [homeboys]."

For better or for worse, Ramos and Paz gave tequila-swilling machismo pride of place in the panoply of national character traits. Through their efforts and those of journalists and social scientists on both sides of the Rio Bravo/Rio Grande, the macho became "the Mexican." This is ironic, for it represents the product of a cultural nationalist invention: you note something (machismo) as existing, and in the process help foster its very existence. Mexican machismo as a national artifact was in this sense partially declared into being. Surely Paz is not the only literary figure in the world today whose authoritative descriptions about national characteristics are so continually cited that their statements become tautological arguments for the existence of these presumed traits in the first place.

And from the beginning, the portrayal of machismo (or its *pelado* forerunner) has been uniquely linked to the poor, unsophisticated, uncosmopolitan, and un–North American. From the 1920s on in Mexico, the bourgeoisie and the middle classes were, in Monsiváis's words, "obstinate in seeing nationalism as the most fruitful for their progress and internal coherence" (1976:194). The macho-*pelado,* always eminently male, represented either Mexico's homespun rural past, as did Jorge Negrete, or the essential backwardness of the nation, rural and urban, which needed to be exposed and eradicated. Regardless of the nostalgic allusion, "being *mexicano*" has been a male Mexican project. On the other side of the class ledger, nearly all union leaders and many leftist intellectuals in Mexico for much of this century have championed the cause of national progress by promoting the heroic figure of the proletarian male militant. In all versions, Mexican masculinity has been at the heart of defining a Mexican nation in terms of both its past and its future.[28]

Yet to whatever extent cultural traits like masculinity could ever have been justifiably called exclusively national in character, those days are past. Cultural processes are driven today by global ethnoscapes as never before (Appadurai 1991). In Colonia Santo Domingo in the mid-1990s, young women were watching the Miami-based, Spanish-language talk show *Cristina.* The subject of one of the first *Cristina* programs to be broadcast in Mexico concerned hospitals mixing up babies in neonatal rooms. One guest on the show was a Latino man who in the course of his story mentioned that he had been with his wife all through labor and delivery (a circumstance far more common in the United States than in Mexico, which perhaps says more about restrictions imposed by the hospitals in Mexico than it does about the desires of mothers and fathers in that country). The show's host, Cristina, interrupted the man's narrative and remarked, "That's what we'd like to see more of: real macho Latinos!" Her intention seems to have been to suggest that only real macho fathers could endure the traumas (blood and pain?) of childbirth. Where this leaves mothers in her view was not discussed, but nonetheless viewers in Mexico were treated to a Cuban-born, Miami-reared television personality defining for them the requisite components for good macho fathers.

Like religiousness, individualism, modernity, and other convenient concepts, machismo is used and understood in many ways. And history in the form of nationalism, feminism, and socioeconomic conjunctures impinges directly on gender identities in Mexico, including identities of masculinity and machismo and how they are variously regarded.[29] Either we can accept that there are multiple and shifting meanings of macho and machismo, or we can essentialize what were already reified generalizations about Mexican men in the first place. Like any identity, male identities in Mexico City do not reveal anything intrinsic about men there. The contradictory consciousness of many men in Colonia Santo Domingo about their own gender identities, their sense and experience of being *hombres* and machos, is part of the reigning chaos of their lives at least as much as is the imagined national coherence imposed from without.

TEN

Creative Contradictions

To triumph in politics is to never see, directly, life's victims.

Carlos Monsiváis, Entrada libre

IDENTITY IS DEAD, LONG LIVE IDENTITY

There is ambiguity, confusion, and contradiction in male identities throughout the putative heartland of machismo. In the case of Colonia Santo Domingo, the past two decades have witnessed a process in which numerous women and men have become aware of gender identities as impermanent and changeable, and self-reflexive about them. For some this awareness in itself has been tantamount to disputing the ideological foundations of conventional gender identities, or at least beginning such a process. Following from this, to the extent that residents of Santo Domingo have become conscious of femininity and masculinity as uncertain qualities, gender identities have consequently become less tied to inherent, natural, and immutable characteristics, a process akin to what Foucault (1980b:xiii) calls "the happy limbo of a non-identity." [1] Indeed, such indeterminacy itself is critical in the negotiation of masculinity by women and men in Mexico City today.

In the *colonia*, contradictions between consciousness inherited uncritically from the past and consciousness developed in the course of practically transforming the world—contradictory consciousness—form a crucial part of the broader political economy of systems of gender and sexuality. Contradictory consciousness is evident in the transformations I have called *degendering*, as when certain activities and beliefs become less associated with particular gender identities and more with other social groups such as adolescents, truck drivers, mestizos, or the rich. Alcohol consumption and housework are realms in which limited degendering has taken place in Santo Domingo, just as the probable rise in domestic violence of men against women there is linked to an intensified engendering of aggression as some men seek to "resolve" the contradictions and confusion in their masculinities resulting from women's increasingly declaring their independence from men. These emergent cultural practices taken as a whole describe and define gender relations and identities in Santo Domingo today.

Mexican male identities in the twentieth century have been consistently associated with the prestige and politics of the emerging Mexican nation—most of all, with the quite modern image of the Mexican macho. Changes in national identity have intimately affected Mexican masculinities, just as the shifting meanings of macho have inevitably presaged reinventions of the Mexican nation—a concentrated expression of the historical, systemic, and bodily connections between *mexicanidad* and Mexican men. In part because of this confluence of identities, a greater consciousness of gender difference and inequality within Mexican society, including an awareness of deep schisms and oppositional interests, has sometimes also led to new attitudes and behavior with respect to not only gender but also national(ist) identities.

Gender and national identities are abstractions, yet as Marx pointed out, even the most abstract categories are historically determined.[2] The male identities discussed in this book have not arisen from some timeless national approach to life found only in Mexico, but rather are products of particular, often hegemonic, historical relations, and as such cannot be understood outside the changing power contexts in which they have emerged. In Colonia Santo Domingo and in Mexico overall, men do not conform to well-behaved ideal types detached from cultural space and time. Nor are gender relations there marked by uncluttered consistency or permanent stability. The contradictory and dialectical nature of continuity and change in gender identities and relations is more substantial in Santo Domingo than is allowed by the arbitrary categories of femininity and masculinity, or even Mexican femininity and Mexican masculinity.

To belabor a point that may already seem obvious, we must guard against the tendency to regard generalizations about social categories of any kind as permanent cultural features. It is our own thinking and taxonomies that too often become ossified, and less often the beliefs and practices of those whom we would represent. This is a point on which numerous anthropologists of gender have already elaborated, and it is one that bears repeated emphasis.[3]

To note that common references to men in Colonia Santo Domingo, Mexico City, may be grouped into four rough categories—the macho, the *mandilón*, the neither-macho-nor-*mandilón*, and the homosexual—is still to flirt with (male) gender essentialism. No one man in the *colonia* is actually representative of any of these masculine identities. At the same time, it is not only social scientists who speak of *other* individuals as representatives of this or that category. The stubborn fact is that men and women in Santo Domingo themselves speak of others as typical of Mexican gender types, just as they often note the persistence or waning of Mexican archetypes such as macho men and submissive women. Thus, we may ask, if no single Mexican male identity exists in any meaningful sense, but rather there are multiple and mutable meanings of macho, why do stereotypes of male identity continue to assert themselves not only in scholarly discourse but also in everyday conversation and consciousness in Santo Domingo?

Part of the answer must lie in the fact that in this *colonia popular,* as elsewhere in the capital, many men are genuinely inspired by a "will to identity." [4] Gender distinctions were already present in society when my friends in Santo Domingo were born. Some aspects of social life were becoming more engendered while others were getting degendered, just as there was generally conflict regarding exactly how gendered different women and men considered practices as diverse as working for money, alcohol consumption, adultery, and violence. Thus, no matter how contradictory these distinctions may have seemed to my friends, they constituted culturally significant differences and therefore were key elements in the very process of how the men and women constructed themselves *as men* and *as women.*

In Santo Domingo this socialization of gender attributes begins at birth and becomes more pronounced in early childhood. Nor are men solely responsible for the definition and constitution of male identities. Women as well as men actively contribute to transforming boys into men *as men.* As social actors, men and women are presented with stages and scripts not of their own choosing. What they do creatively within these social and cultural constraints, and how originally they perform their roles, however, is not preordained. There is room to maneuver, and it is this maneuvering room that has especially occupied our attention in this study: the alcoholic fathers who rock their babies to sleep, mothers who beat their boys, boys who race their sisters to pick up the tortillas, young men drugged out on *cemento* who breed children they will never know, and mothers and fathers determined not to raise their boys to be Mexican machos.

The historical meanings of masculinity and femininity in Mexico remain diverse and contradictory as men and women throughout the country continue to engage in original discoveries and creations of future gender identities and practices.

MEXICAN MEN

Was that it? Is that where the manhood lay? In the naming done by a whiteman who was supposed to know? Who gave them the privilege not of working but of deciding how to?

Toni Morrison, Beloved

Social scientists engaged in the quest for gender and other cultural taxonomies must seek to combine numerous features in particular individuals' lives so that together they may be described as constituting male (and other) identities. Not infrequently the search for shared gender qualities leads, implicitly at least, to relegating differences of class, ethnicity, generation, and history to secondary importance. In bringing about a greater awareness of gender as a crucial complex of cultural relations, we must remember that we ourselves help make the abstract category of gender even more culturally meaningful in the very course of defining, describing, and analyzing it. Indeed, that is part of the purpose of much feminist scholarship.

Yet in the course of this ethnographically and politically important work of gender classification we must be clear that it is not simply "culture" that creates men and women; men and women create and produce culture. I did not arrive one day in Santo Domingo and announce that I was studying the impact of a macho culture on men and masculinity there; nevertheless, after a few months in the *colonia* some friends, smiling broadly, would introduce me to others as "Mateo, a gringo who's here to learn about [or from] us machos." They considered themselves my teachers in the ways of being men and women in Mexico City in the early 1990s. Though few had done much systematic thinking about machos and machismo, these were topics about which all my friends had experience and opinions. Thus it has always been a challenge for me to distinguish between my friends' more formal performances of masculinity and their more practical ones. Carrier's conclusion to his discussion of "occidentalism" proves helpful in this regard:

> The problem, then, is not essentialism itself. Instead, the problem is a failure to be conscious of essentialism, whether it springs from the assumptions with which we approach our subjects or the goals that motivate our writing. (1992:207)

The problem for me was not a matter of avoiding macho stereotypes, since this was impossible, but rather one of identifying the echo effect of official interpretations of Mexican men on these men themselves.

My own presence in Santo Domingo undoubtedly affected the way some of my friends felt and behaved regarding men's roles in parenting and housework, and I probably provoked a few new questions about masculinity in general. I, too, have been "tainted" by my research in the *colonia,* in the sense that my own understanding of gender, sexuality, fatherhood, and so on is now influenced by the perceptions, illusions, and insights of many people in Santo Domingo. This may seem an obvious point, a simple restatement of the broad aims and insights of comparative intellectual inquiry, but it is an important one for other reasons as well. From the standpoint of politically committed scholarship, for example, leaving the world "untouched" and "as we found it" is exactly not the point. In terms of scholarly methodology, on the other hand, especially when we ethnographers draw conclusions from the mass of information we tend to compile, there is often a tendency to avoid the conclusion that those we study are less interested in our research topic than we might wish. Simply put, just because gender may interest you and me does not mean that gender is necessarily significant to the people with whom we live and work.

The anthropological literature on Mexico contains a particularly abusive example of how bias and preconceptions concerning gender roles have colored how we use what we learn in the course of anthropological fieldwork. I refer to the selective utilization of the writings of Oscar Lewis, which has served to enhance and perpetuate the image and perhaps even the existence of the *macho mexicano.* The detailed descriptions of daily life in rural and urban Mexico that are available in *Life in a Mexican Village* (1951) and *The Children of Sánchez* (1961), for example, have been cited far more than analyzed. Yet one or two sensationalist passages from Lewis—or, more precisely, from one or another of his informants—have been used so often that they have come to epitomize for many an extremely homogenized view of Mexican (male) culture, a view that is at odds with the details of Lewis's studies in Mexico.

For instance, Lewis describes men in some cultural contexts—especially among the poor—as active in parenting, even when the main responsibility for child rearing has been formally female. Such ethnographic descriptions of rural Morelos in the 1940s contrast sharply with caricatures of poor Mexican men common up to the present. Instead of seeking cross-class generalizations about Mexican fathers, we would do better once again to compare detailed ethnographic studies of different populations of fathers—in this case, to compare descriptions of fathers who are *campesino* farmers with studies that examine the role that men in the urban elites in Mexico play in parenting (see Lomnitz and Pérez-Lizaur 1987). In wealthy families the *muchacha* is used as a surrogate parent, though it is not she who makes the cultural decisions about how the family's wealth is spent. In Tepoztlán of the 1940s and Colonia Santo Domingo of the 1990s, economics prevent hiring a *muchacha* and cultural mores pressure many men to actively participate in parenting. Further, as is implied in Lewis and is evident in Santo Domingo, the practice of fatherhood is central to the notions of many men and women about what it means to be a (good) man.

In light of such historical evidence regarding fathering, and in the wake of recent challenges to hegemonic gender conventions in *colonias populares* like Santo Domingo, the argument for a uniform and timeless Mexican male identity is all the more without merit. What is needed instead is a revisionist analysis that clearly calls attention to anthropological complicity in the creation of stereotypes such as that of the Mexican Macho. To posit a ubiquitous Mexican or Latin American form of masculinity basically means resorting to the archaic framework of national character traits. And ultimately any analysis that highlights the Mexican Male as a legitimate category leads us back to the perennial descriptions of *mexicanidad,* and to positing national geopolitical borders as necessarily the most significant of cultural differences in the world.

In part because of dissatisfaction with theories of national character, the native/foreign (we/they, insider/outsider, observer/observed) paradigm has been widely criticized today by anthropologists who point to the futility of clearly demarcating such arbitrary distinctions.[5] My own case again illustrates some of the issues at play here, for during my

Marcos sits with his new grandson, enjoying the afternoon sun.

fieldwork I represented a curious mixture of observer and observed. As a gringo I was a foreigner in Santo Domingo. Similarly, by social class, in the sense of education and career and income expectations, I was distinct from my neighbors. Yet as a resident of the *colonia* I was in some respects a native, at least temporarily. Despite my transient status there, I was not a daytime visitor: in material ways I shared with others certain of the joys and hardships of life in Santo Domingo that other Mexicans, for instance, did not. Life for me in Santo Domingo would also sometimes take on distinctly insider male overtones. When Michelle and Liliana left for two weeks, it was the women in the *colonia* who told me to be careful, because, they said, "we're keeping an eye on you!" Such communion, though limited, was important not only to me and my family but also to our neighbors, who often told us as much.

Further, even now that we have returned to the United States, our contact with Angela, for example, has been similar in many ways to that which we have with Liliana's other grandparents: we live far apart, we write and phone to keep in touch, and we visit at most once or twice a year. And, as we do with the other grandparents, Michelle and I often feel on the defensive when we try to justify to Angela *our* ways of doing things with *her* granddaughter.

The fact that Michelle and I were brand-new parents during the year we lived in Santo Domingo meant that, as they do with other ignorant new mothers and fathers, many of the men and women in the neighborhood gave us pointed and regular instructions on how to be good parents, from admonitions to wrap Liliana warmly to advice on the proper diet for a six-month-old to talks about the need for lactating mothers to eat lots of tortillas (and the lime in them) so that teething will be less painful for their babies. For our teachers in the arts of parenthood, this training was simply part of their moral responsibilities to us and our child, just as it was our job as new parents—and not as an anthropologist and a public-health worker—to learn these lessons from them as best we could.

Even if international geopolitical boundaries prove more porous than views of national culture will permit, however, insider/outsider frameworks can and do manifest themselves among Mexicans in several ways, doing so along lines of gender, ethnicity, and region (see Lomnitz-Adler 1994). Reflecting an understanding that modernity has precisely given rise to many, many Mexicos, recent analyses of Mexican national identity have become increasingly sophisticated. For instance, through their examinations of regional, hybrid, transnational, and postnational cultures, anthropologists have recently sought to clarify issues pertaining to the relationship between globalization and localization, including issues with regard to what have often been considered key symbols of national identity, like machismo in Mexico.[6]

If Mexican national identities, which have historically rested on par-

ticular Mexican male identities, are currently undergoing radical deconstruction and reconstruction, why shouldn't the study of gender in
Mexico similarly reject specious conclusions about ubiquitous (national) machos and *abnegadas,* and replace these stereotypes with descriptions and analyses of the diversity of changing gender identities in
Mexico at the end of the twentieth century? In this way alone we will
be able to *include* both the men who carry their babies in *canguros* and
the men who never change diapers, the women welders and truck drivers, the men who beat women who are the only wage earners, the
women who become community leaders *and* divorce their husbands,
and the homophobic talk of youth whose younger siblings are bisexual.

MAKING CHANGE IN SANTO DOMINGO

For Gramsci, contradictory consciousness refers to the fusing of transformative and inherited consciousnesses. While in the short run real
changes will emerge despite a lack of critical understanding (self-consciousness), eventually such contradictory consciousness can produce a
condition of moral and political passivity. The key process here concerns the relationship of consciousness to the emergence of cultural
change, or what Gramsci (1929–35:273) refers to as negation when he
writes, "The lower classes, historically on the defensive, can only
achieve self-awareness via a series of negations" (see also Keesing
1992:225).

In the 1970s and 1980s, the role of women in autonomous movements to obtain housing, jobs, and many social services in communities
such as Colonia Santo Domingo, together with the struggles concerning
broader issues of gender equality, gay and lesbian rights, and other factors like the widespread availability and use of contraception, have
combined to provide the seeds and soil of self-reliant opposition to
dominant gender meanings and practices in Mexico. For many in Santo
Domingo and other parts of Latin America, the emergent struggles for
social justice in recent decades represent an occasion when tens of thousands of women and men were part of a "moment in and out of time"
(Turner 1969).

In Mexico in the last twenty years, precisely the period in which
Colonia Santo Domingo has come into being, the entire society has witnessed rapid and widespread upheavals involving the economy, gender
roles, struggles over ethnic identity, regional development and stagnation, ecological catastrophes, international migration, and political in-

surgency and repression. The poor now are no longer confident that times will get better, as many in Mexico believed until the late 1970s. Today, for many, the mood is characterized by a malaise similar to that which has struck indeterminate others around the globe, what Bartra calls the cage of modern melancholy:

> There are many Mexicans who ... are unenthusiastic about an efficient modern age, and they have no desire to restore the promise of a proletarian industrial future. ... They have been hurled from the original paradise and expelled from the future. (1992:176)

For most people today in Colonia Santo Domingo there is a meanness to the contemporary epoch, when dystopian dreams have replaced the surrealism of the romantic ages. Some can trace such a nasty and miserly ethos to deep national and transnational roots that are difficult to eradicate. The more pious sometimes point skyward and speak of an unchanging human nature. All in all, the future of gender relations in Mexico City is far from clear. Nor could it be otherwise, related as gender relations are to so many other uncertainties.

Still, we need not follow the intellectual fashions of the day and refuse to even recognize change, especially when it originates from below. "We don't talk about culture change anymore," a colleague notes. "Now it's called modernity." Most members of Mexican society and of the community of Santo Domingo have better memories than such scholarly conceits would allow. Angela insisted to me one day that historically the greatest transformation in women's lives in Mexico came with the introduction and proliferation of food blenders. I laughed, but she responded by telling me that her remarks should not be dismissed as frivolous (I was actually thinking that her words represented a double form of mechanical reasoning). Yet I had forgotten that blenders made possible the early weaning of children from the breast or bottle and that they were used in place of the *molcajete* (mortar for pounding) in preparing sauces for cooking. Angela linked this time-saving device to her resulting freedom to participate in community activities and not be so tied to the home and housework.[7]

As concerns the ability of people to make change—in their lives, in the lives of people around them, and in their broader social worlds—it is evident that the constraints are formidable. But many of my friends in Colonia Santo Domingo remain adamant regarding the ethical imperative that only fools and the very rich have the freedom to leave things as they are in this world. Perhaps theirs is a sensibility similar to what Eagleton (1985:68) recounts as "the Marxist habit of extracting the progressive moment from an otherwise unpalatable or ambivalent reality."

The reverse side of the argument that culture is a primordial and resilient essence left unchanged by voluntary will is the allegation that culture remains just as unaffected by sociocultural and demographic shifts. The falling numbers of births, the higher educational levels reached by young women, and the higher rates of women's paid employment in Mexico City than elsewhere in the country do not indicate that gender roles and relations have automatically followed suit or will do so, no matter how structurally significant these changes may be. But such factors as employment, birth, and education, while not determinant, can both reflect larger cultural shifts under way and in some instances precipitate them.

Many men who have a history of wife beating invoke such "outside" social pressures when they remind us repeatedly that they grew up in a macho society. The men insist that they are products of this society and thus are merely reproducing patterns learned and relearned from prior generations. Bourdieu and others have shown that reproduction of this kind is real and is often experienced in an overwhelming fashion by social actors. Male domination in particular, Bourdieu writes, is reproduced through the imputation that cultural differences are the product of implacable biological natures; he further writes that sexism "is an essentialism" and that "among all the forms of essentialism it is undoubtedly the most difficult to uproot" (Bourdieu 1990b:12). Yet while acknowledging the perhaps more obvious realities of reproduction, we should not fail to note the development of cultural creativity, which goes against the grain and against cultural dogma. This awareness is too often missing in much contemporary social theory. As Hymes (1979:xii) points out, Bourdieu appears to think of the practical life of most peoples known to anthropology as in a state of "unquestioning acceptance of the social order as an order of nature" (see also Herzfeld 1987:212, n. 9).

Limiting analysis of cultural change to a matter of reproduction is analogous to the bottom-line ideological defense offered by some of the participants in groups for men who have histories of wife beating: "The culture made me do it!" These men often express a sense of helplessness in the face of the macho system that swaddles them—constricting and protecting them—from birth. The chain of events that leads them to the groups is most commonly one in which their wives first report being beaten and then take the initiative to help the men examine their attitudes and behaviors. Some men describe the ultimatum their wives have given them: "Either you attend the group and change, or we will get divorced and I will take the children." By the time they get to the groups, though, it is often too late to stop divorce from occurring. In any case, these women (and some of the men) are not simply "reproducing" patterns of wife beating.

Rather than seeing culture as primarily a space of distinctions, as Bourdieu does, we may view it as a space of differences and struggle, highlighting the initiative, creativity, and opposition on the part of *los de abajo,* the underdog masses of women and men, some of whom, sometimes, achieve and utilize a measure of autonomy in their everyday cultural affairs. This autonomy inevitably manifests itself in a variety of contradictory ways. Gabriel once commented to me that he used to dream of being a lawyer because he thought that in this way he might be able to help people fight the many injustices he saw around him. But halfway through seventh grade he fell in with *drogadictos,* glue-sniffing youth, and from there he began "messing up, hanging out, and not going to school." I asked Gabriel if he had robbed people during this period.

"No, never. If someone said, 'Let's go steal,' I'd go—but to rob a *bank*! What are you going to take from people? The only thing you can take is what they know. That's all they have."

The "permanently organised consent" of the oppressed in society has been repeatedly broken down among women and men in Colonia Santo Domingo in the past twenty years.[8] Through new social movements and popular urban movements in the Pedregales, for example, women especially have played the role of catalysts in changing the consciousness and practice of family and neighbors with regard to gender identities and much else. Using persuasion and coercion, women have spearheaded community activism in the *colonia* by focusing, among other things, on the needs of the family, the children, and the home. This is one reason the Mexican "popular movements, when they arise, constitute a phenomenon that is significant in itself," even though in the wake of these movements Mexico as a whole may well be "a less democratic country in the 1990s than at any time in the recent past" (Hellman 1994:137–38).

Unlike official images of Mexican men and masculinity, which have long been tied to a defense of Mexican national honor and in this way used to oppress all those who stood opposed to these images, grassroots feminism's challenge to machismo in Latin America has not developed along national lines (see Stephen 1996). The practical effect of this challenge has been felt in its distinctly nonnational character within households, workplaces, schools, and other locations throughout the region. The grassroots feminist critique of the banking official who told me that *Mexican* men don't carry babies would not concern itself with debate about commonly shared national character traits, but rather with issues of gender, class, and ethnic inequalities within the Mexican nation.

Processes involved in the degendering of alcohol consumption and in women working outside the home have led, if not inevitably, then in these particular historical circumstances, to direct challenges to popular notions of what it means to be women and men in contemporary Mexican society. More than one woman told me that her husband opposed her working outside the home because he was worried that she might avail herself of the greater opportunities she would have away from the home to take lovers. Grassroots activities and cultural creativity on the part of women who over men's objections have expressed their desire to work for money, as well as on the part of women involved in popular urban movements, certainly constitute part of women's initiative to make men change. Yet the radical implications of these women's activities and their challenge to gender conventions do not require a clear sense on the part of these women, and still less on the part of the men in their lives, as to their social role as key innovators in transcending previously existing gender relations. For many, the most radical aspect of their politics is revealed in their determination not to be forced to adapt to the system but rather to be included in it on their own terms.

FAMILY POLITICS

Contests about meaning involve the introduction of
new oppositions, the reversal of hierarchies, the
attempt to expose repressed terms, to challenge the
natural status of seemingly dichotomous pairs, and to
expose their interdependence and their internal
instability.

> *Joan Scott,* Gender and the Politics of History

At a New Year's celebration in Santo Domingo, children, grandchildren, and sons-in-law one after another offered toasts to Alicia, the

grandmother of the household. She was effusively praised for her role
as the head of the family, the person who continually brought everyone
together and the one who more than anyone else defined what they
meant to each other. Ernesto, Alicia's husband of nearly fifty years,
began to look very uncomfortable and hurt. Finally, in a belated attempt at familial propriety, someone proposed a toast to both grandfather and grandmother as together forming the core of the family.

Matrifocality in Mexico is an underreported phenomenon, and it is
by no means something unique to Colonia Santo Domingo.[9] Yet in the
working class barrios of Mexico City where popular urban movements
have in the recent past mobilized and unleashed the energies of women
as community militants and leaders, the experiences of women such as
Alicia have also become part of the historical process that begins with
a sense of being different and apart, and a feeling of independence. Feelings of independence and difference are experienced far more widely
than just in the ranks of the women activists.

Not surprisingly, the site for many skirmishes over gender identities
and relations within the *colonias populares* is often the family. Though
the family is considered by some to be among the most conservative of
social institutions, and the last refuge of male authority, it is not so easy
in the instance of Colonia Santo Domingo to dismiss what takes place
between wives and husbands, daughters and fathers, sons and mothers,
and sisters and brothers as the simple exercise of male prestige and
power.

In numerous cases on Huehuetzin Street where we lived, and
throughout the *colonia* in general, traditional patriarchal relations do
prevail with seeming imperviousness. In other households, however, the
family is the site of an ongoing struggle concerning particular gender
roles and relations. Though without broader social nurturance these
sprouts of resistance and sometimes rebellion are unable to sustain
themselves indefinitely, the expanding spheres of female authority
within many families are not merely a reflection of wider social changes.
They are simultaneously the manifestation and one of the key sources
of these transformations.[10] And, improbable as it might seem, these
changes among women are not necessarily met with a blanket of male
opposition, because though conflict is one characteristic of families in
Santo Domingo, so are the dreams, aspirations, and illusions shared by
couples, parents, and children. In the wake of important studies on divided interests and conflict within families, it is easy to lose sight of the
fact that common purposes, however irregular and fleeting, are also

important features of gender identities as they transform within families.

This duality of conflict and sharing in Santo Domingo is directly implicated in some of what makes gender unique among social categories. For although there are many analytical similarities between the classifications of gender, class, and ethnicity—for instance, each includes elements of social inequality, privilege, and organized consent—there are also particularities to each. Although aspects of gender inequality often involve physical segregation—the traditional cantina, job availability, domesticity, and so on—physical proximity, if not necessarily bodily contact between men and women, is, for most people outside the army or prison, a prominent feature of daily life. In contrast, physical isolation by class, region, and ethnic group is generally far more notable for people in Mexican society. One implication of this is that gender identities and relations have a face-to-face character that is a permanent feature of the family and the household for many women and men. Though they may talk about them frequently, few people in Santo Domingo ever have direct contact with *los ricos*.

The issue of the family as a locus of conflict has direct significance with respect to the meanings of Mexican male identities. In the lives of most men in Colonia Santo Domingo, mothers, sisters, lovers, and other women have often contributed in central ways to helping the men construct their own sense of masculinity at particular points in their lives. And for most men during most of their lives, male identities in all their various guises have in some manner been viewed in comparison to female identities. This is not to deny that the form that male gender self-identification takes is often one of contrast to other men, or that men may frequently spend much work and leisure time in the company of other men. Rather, it emphasizes the fact that, whether women are physically present or not, female identities often serve as the central point of conscious and unconscious reference for men in the development, maintenance, and transformation of their own sense of what *ser hombre* does and does not mean, and what it can and cannot mean.

Ambiguity does lie at the heart of male gender and male sexual identities in Mexico City today. But such ambiguity does not arise primarily from the overexposure of boys to their mothers, as Chodorow (1978) and certain other Freudian theorists would have it. Boys' successful identity rupture with their mothers is of less concern, I feel, than the ongoing resolution of their contradictory relations with women. Masculinity in any nonsexist sense is not achieved through the mere trans-

ference of affective bonds from mother to father. Fathers and other
adult men *are* critical in the development and transformation of gender
identities and practices among boys, but no more so than mothers and
other adult women, and for many men in Colonia Santo Domingo, for
example, their relations with their wives are far more problematic than
those they have with their mothers or fathers.

Once again, however, we must not reduce this relationship of male
and female identities to oversimplified biology and a rudimentary man-
woman binary opposition. Such a structuralist view would quickly lead
us not only to negate the existence of multiple versions of masculinity
and femininity but, even more egregiously, to overlook the reality of
other genders such as those involving androgyny or those marked by a
relative absence of gender-driven sexuality altogether.

THE IRREVERSIBLE WORLD

Colonia Santo Domingo is not a neighborhood where gender equality
flourishes or an outpost for degendered women and men. Nor is it in
any sense an isolated or closed community. But since the invasion of
September 1971, when thousands of "parachutist" families staked out
parcels of land for themselves on the south side of Mexico City, many
women and men have experienced life a little differently there than they
might have in other parts of Mexico and Latin America. The invasion
and subsequent history of Santo Domingo have made it an exceptional
and, for me, an especially appealing place in which to examine the nature, extent, and shape of noteworthy changes in gender identities and
relations in the last twenty years.

By the early 1990s, the community was more stabilized in terms of
housing and social services and the ruling government party was more
or less in control of the local political machinery, if not of all the voters
in the *colonia*. There were residents of the *colonia* who gathered food
and clothing for the Chiapas insurgents and placed "Viva EZLN [the
Zapatista army]" stickers on lampposts, for example, but they mainly
operated in semiclandestine ways, and their activities, and even more
those of the EZLN itself, were often criticized by neighbors.

In the mid-1990s, the national banking crisis of 1982 and the Mexico City earthquake of 1985 were still vivid memories for all adults in
Santo Domingo, but many at least shared the hope that stability, if not
growth, had been restored to the economy. Then, in late 1994, as Carlos Salinas de Gortari was leaving office and Ernesto Zedillo Ponce de

León was being sworn in as Mexico's new president, reports came of new market collapses and another devastating fall in the value of the peso. In early 1995, indictments were handed down against high-level government functionaries charging them with involvement in political assassinations and drug running.

By the early 1990s, cynicism was already widespread in Santo Domingo with regard to the government's and the ruling PRI party's providing any kind of democratic hope for the future. But families still had their land and their homes. With the financial crisis of 1995, and the promise of worse times still ahead, some of my friends in Santo Domingo may well be thrust even more headlong into a situation that will force many to sell their homes and move away if they are to have any hope of surviving into the twenty-first century.

The conservative pull of home ownership will lead some residents to raise self-protection as the highest social good. The bitter reality is that, except for the fact that they own their homes, most families are economically and politically far worse off than they were in the late 1970s. In the event of other land squatters' invasions in the Pedregales, for example, it is hard to imagine any scenario that would not include women fighting alongside men to defend their plots of land. Nevertheless, if the housing market continues to collapse and disaffection with state authorities goes from grumbling to organized protest, no doubt many of these same people in Santo Domingo will more actively join a political opposition.

On a basic level, what happens in Santo Domingo, including what happens with reference to gender identities, is far more dependent upon global factors than local ones. The impact of the Free Trade Agreement on industry and finance, the influence of television programming and tourism from abroad, and the further evolution of international migration as a primary component of Mexican society are among the factors that will greatly complicate the tally. Neoliberal programs designed to privatize the Mexican economy and "poverty-alleviation" campaigns like Solidaridad are sure to affect the independent organization and exercise of limited self-reliance by millions of Mexicans, for whom the 1980s in particular were a decade of growing disdain for the federal government.[11]

Though simplistic notions of social progress are easily ridiculed in academia today, we must insist on looking beneath the superficial and seemingly cyclical aspects of everyday life in the *colonias populares,* and instead accent the creativity with which men and women make and

This 1989 rally was called to protest the PRI (government-party) elections and support the opposition politician Cuauhtémoc Cárdenas. Mexico City Zocalo.

remake the world every day. Cultural creativity is a far more productive
concept than resistance in analyzing the inventiveness of the popular
classes, because it emphasizes not only the desire of ordinary people to
react to their life situations, but, more importantly, the active ways in
which men and women seek to shape their lives every day.[12]

In writing of earlier episodes in Mexico's history, Victor Turner (1974:125) reminds us that a particular sequence of events in the social drama of the insurrection of 1811 "proved to be the first phase in a process that was not cyclical but irreversible and that changed Mexican society and culture forever." Though the cultural transformations in Colonia Santo Domingo were never inevitable, they are now irreversible, and they have changed forever how men and women understand what it is to be men and women and what to do with their lives based on these beliefs. Of course, even with this understanding of the past and the present, our attempts at peering into the future of men and machismo in Santo Domingo will continue to confound us, because that future has yet to be made.

There is no absolute, cross-cultural standard of progress, but there are ethical tenets that, explicitly or not, guide us in our daily cultural practices. When the father of two daughters who had helped dig the ditch for their sidewalk told me in derisive terms of his neighbors' outrage at the sight of young women doing this kind of activity in public, and indicated to me that he sought to morally distance himself from his meddlesome neighbors, he was, in effect, seeking to create a new moral economy for gender relations.

The issue for him was not whether the world of Santo Domingo was gendered, but how it was gendered, and how and why it continued to change its gendered character. There is gender similarity and difference that is felt more deeply by some than others in the *colonia,* and gender is more important at certain moments around certain issues than at others. At the same time, though gender identities are often deeply felt, they are usually more intuited than well mapped, reflecting among other things how gender relations shift in sometimes highly unstable and unforeseen ways, and how consciousness of identity may proceed in a manner that is considerably out of sync with practical experience.

DYSTOPIAN FUTURES

In mid-July, nearing the end of my field season in Colonia Santo Domingo, I found myself on Huehuetzin Street one afternoon, once again sipping beer with several of my companions and mentors in the trials of masculinity. Gabriel was there, intermittently working on the flywheel of a neighbor's pickup. Marcos was too, so tired from work that he began falling off the bumper of his '64 VW Bug after a Vickys or two. Marcelo was home from the *campo* in Guerrero for a few days, and looking much thinner after tending the cows there. Martín looked glum. He told me that he was feeling "*mucho coraje* [really angry], something that, for no good reason, simply comes over Mexicans every now and then."[13] Toño was there, leaning against the wall, as was Gabi's new assistant, the one with the samurai haircut.

A young man drove by with paper streamers flying from either side of his rattling old station wagon. The car whipped up dust from the still-unpaved portion of the street over the new sewer pipes as it headed toward the church down the street. It was evidently going to be a newly-wed couple's getaway vehicle. "You don't know what a mistake you're making!" shouted Marcos. "Get out while you still can!" added Marcelo. Typical male sarcasm, I thought. "Why do you say that?" I tried to bait them, feigning more naïveté than was warranted. "I was much freer before I got married" (some twenty years earlier), Marcos answered. Stupidly, I pressed the issue. "What could you do then that you can't do now?" "I don't know!" he snapped back, not pleased I was spoiling their innocent jeering with a lot of inane questions. The point, of course, was to have some fun. Such taunts were not meant to reflect their deepest feelings and commitments.

As usual, things improved when I became the target of my friends' ribbing. We reminisced about our drinking bout with *anís* the past January, and several times I was offered another bottle from the corner store—for old times' sake. Gabriel recalled when I and all other gringos were symbolically hanged in effigy after the bombing of Iraq by U.S. warplanes. Closer to home, Marcelo reminded the others of driving around with me one day and having threatened to drop me off in the gang territory of the Púrpuras a few blocks from Huehuetzin. While we were all still laughing about that one, a police car appeared and everyone hustled inside a doorway, ushering me in first, since as a gringo I was the most vulnerable to harassment from the police if we were caught drinking in the street.

Sitting on milk crates in the dusty street, tossing back a few Vickys beers with the men, and baking in the high-altitude Mexico City sun, I thought of all the ways this scene seemed serenely outside of time. Gabriel came over and nudged me, breaking my reverie. We had become good friends, and I thought he might have a kind word or two for me. Instead, he said to me for the umpteenth time, "Listen, I know you have a mechanic back there in Berkeley. What's his name, Peter? Do you think you could check with him and see if he could give me a job?" Transnational unemployment, bombings in Iraq, and samurai haircuts fight for cultural space with minding the cows in Guerrero, being really pissed off because you're Mexican, and mock agony over the constraints of marriage. The outcome of this contention, when it concerns Mexican masculinities, is never final or complete.

In the *colonia popular* of Santo Domingo, Mexico City, what macho may mean and what men may do in the future are by no means apparent. What is known and what is most culturally significant today is that gender identities and relations there are characterized by inconsistency, as well as by arrogance, idealism, manipulation, discrimination, opportunism—and always, always by generous doses of humor. Not only nationalism but also class, ethnicity, generation, and other factors deeply brand Mexican male identities. Mexican machos are not dead any more than are their North American or Russian counterparts, but claims about a uniform character of Mexican masculinity, a ubiquitous *macho mexicano*, should be put to rest.

Notes

INTRODUCTION

1. At the end of the 1980s, Brandes (1988:30) provokingly concluded, "Over the years, I acquired an image of Tzintzuntzan, and the Lake Pátzcuaro region as a whole, as deviating from the usual social-science portrait of Mexican machismo." See also Brandes 1974:46. By the start of the next decade, de Barbieri (1990) would write of the "possible erosion of machismo in Mexico."

CHAPTER 1

1. For a discussion of "social constructionism," including comments about gender, see di Leonardo 1991a; see also Scott (1988:2) on defining gender and sexuality.

2. Herzfeld (1987:172–73) remarks on similar portraits by Greeks for whom the exemplars of Greekness are always the relatives of others and pointedly not the members of one's own family.

3. Unlike most topics of study in the natural sciences, the analysis of society is something undertaken by experts and lay people alike. In addition, this analysis can have a profound impact on the subject of study. That is, to a degree, we (and others) are what we think we (and others) are. Giddens (1976, 1982) has been particularly forceful in emphasizing what he notes as the "significance of reflexivity or self-awareness in human conduct," or what he sometimes refers to as the *double hermeneutic*.

4. I am not claiming that Colonia Santo Domingo is unique in this regard.

5. On the general theoretical point of intracultural variety and range, see Keesing 1987.

6. For brief discussions on Gramsci's notion of contradictory consciousness, see also Roseberry 1989:46; Comaroff and Comaroff 1991:26; and Thompson 1993:10.

7. See di Leonardo 1991a and Moore 1988 for analytical summaries of anthropological gender studies in the past two decades, part of the second wave of feminist theory actually initiated more than forty years ago with de Beauvoir 1953. Several compilations from the mid-1970s to date provide fine theoretical and ethnographic overviews of a field pioneered by Mead (1928, 1935): for instance, Rosaldo and Lamphere 1974; Reiter 1975; MacCormick and Strathern 1980; Ortner and Whitehead 1981; Collier and Yanagisako 1987; Strathern 1987; and di Leonardo 1991b. See also Sacks 1979; Scheper-Hughes 1983; Lamphere 1987; and Ortner 1989–90 on the impermanence of gender categories and anthropological theories about them.

8. As will become more apparent in subsequent chapters, the present study is grounded in previous discussion of several other prominent themes in feminist theory, such as that concerning the relations between gender and sexuality (Rubin 1975, 1982); nature and culture (Ortner 1974, 1989–90; Ortner and Whitehead 1981; MacCormack and Strathern 1980); the public and the private (Rosaldo 1974, 1980); colonialism (Sacks 1979; Etienne and Leacock 1980); and difference and inequality (Strathern 1987; Scott 1990; di Leonardo 1991a; Abu-Lughod 1993).

9. Recent anthropological works concerned with masculinity include Brandes 1980; Herdt 1981, 1987; Gregor 1985; Herzfeld 1985; Godelier 1986; Gilmore 1990; Hewlett 1991; Parker 1991; Fachel Leal 1992; Lancaster 1992; and Welzer-Lang and Filiod 1992.

The theoretical approaches and conclusions of these studies differ considerably. The best in my view ask very specific questions about very specific locales and historical situations. Those that attempt gross generalizations for entire "cultures" of supposedly homogeneous populations inevitably reinvent many of the same stale tags with which "men" as a biological group, or "the men of X" as representatives of one or another social science paradigm, have often been stamped. In addition, with important exceptions like Lancaster (1992), researchers studying men and manhood have to date made insufficient use of feminist anthropology's contributions to our knowledge of gender and sexuality and have failed to engage sufficiently in the important debates within this discourse.

One of the most difficult methodological issues raised by recent ethnographic studies with a central focus on men and masculinity is how we are to understand men's emotional (and to a lesser extent physical) relations with women. Related to this matter is the problem of "the (male) native's point of view." Simply put, some anthropologists studying masculinity have reported that women are largely irrelevant to the development of male identities and of male, *as male,* practices. As evidence of this assertion they note that their informants have told them this was the situation.

The issue is surely complicated, and one must be especially careful not to infer universal customs or beliefs that may predominate in one or even several cultural settings. Yet at least in some circumstances, I cannot help wondering how much this putative irrelevance of women to male identity is a reflection of the ethnographer's own biases. In the present study of a *colonia popular* in

Mexico City, I have tried to develop a clearer theoretical understanding of the relation of women to men-as-men, both because I think it is warranted by the case at hand and because I think such theorizing about psychological (and physical) relations between gender groupings is increasingly called for in the field of multigender studies.

I raise a final point to position this book in the field of "studies of men" (not the same field that some *Iron John*–ish "men's studies" cover; see Bly 1990). In a systematic analysis of gender and sexuality that has had broad influence among feminist scholars of masculinity in the United States and Australia, Connell (1987:xi) argues that "[m]en in general are advantaged by current social structure, heterosexual men more so than others." Connell's contention is too general and context free, but he does call our attention to something that is vital in many contexts: the position of men-as-men-as-social-group being the beneficiaries of gender inequalities. The fact that those advantages as do exist for men are constituted in more complex a manner than Connell's cross-cultural pronouncement implies does not mean that advantages do not exist.

Although I argue for a specific ethnography of men and masculinity because life is too complex to capture in facile generalizations about men-as-men or anything else, the fact that life and men are not so simple does not mean that we must abandon our ethnographies of gender to the nihilist position that truth (and oppression) are all relative and really exist only in language and text. In other words, we must guard against nuancing the politics right out of our studies.

10. For just some of the outstanding books concerned with women in Latin America, see Chiñas 1973; Arizpe 1975; Bourque and Warren 1981; de Barbieri 1984; Logan 1984; Nash and Safa 1986; Gabayet et al. 1988; Oliveira 1989; Goldsmith 1990; Jelin 1991; Stephen 1991; Massolo 1992a, 1992b; Behar 1993; and García and Oliveira 1993.

11. On the former relations, see especially Roseberry 1989; Comaroff and Comaroff 1991, 1992; Lancaster 1992; Scheper-Hughes 1992; and Rosaldo 1993. Concerning the latter, I am referring to works by those such as Turner 1969; Wolf 1969; and Stavenhagen 1975.

12. Much of the new criticism in anthropology can prove helpful if it is used to correct past imperial haughtiness and the pretense of benign impartiality. But to the extent that it represents a retreat from accepting the inherently partial character of knowledge and responsibility for the products of anthropological work, we will gain nothing in the long run. The most widely read text of ethnographic critique is Clifford and Marcus 1986; see also Marcus and Fischer 1986 and Clifford 1988.

13. This development is evidenced by the titles of two works upon which Foucault (1980b) bases his study of a French hermaphrodite, Herculine Barbin: *Question d'identité* and *Question médico-légale de l'identité*, the first of which appeared in 1860.

14. Identity, in the Marxist and dialectical sense, refers to equivalency as exemplified in the process described by Marx that is embodied in exchange value, as Jameson (1990) makes clear in his comments on Adorno (1973).

15. For a lucid analysis of the relation between identity and emergent cultures in Mexico, see Lomnitz-Adler 1992. For a critique of fixed gender categories, see Butler 1990.

16. My discussion of hegemony and ideology draws on the presentations found in the Comaroff and Comaroff 1991, 1992.

17. On hegemony and ideology, see also Bloch 1977; Williams 1977; Asad 1979; and Eagleton 1991.

18. For example, see James Scott 1985.

19. In positioning these issues as in part a dialogue between Bourdieu's and Gramsci's theories, I have benefited from García Canclini, especially 1988 and 1989, though my reading of Bourdieu in this comparison is decidedly less favorable than his. On the emerging study of popular culture, see Mukerji and Schudson 1991.

20. See especially Bourdieu 1984, though less often Bourdieu (1990:183) does implicitly acknowledge cultural creativity from below—for instance, when he lectures on movements of emancipation that "are there to prove that a certain dose of utopianism, that magic negation of the real which would elsewhere be called neurotic, may even contribute to creating the political conditions for a practical negation of the realistic view of the facts."

21. Recent edited volumes have provided insights into how cultural creativity, performance, and experience contribute to the transformation of peoples' lives (see Turner and Bruner 1986 and Lavie, Narayan, and Rosaldo 1993). For broader discussions of cultural and national(ist) imaginings and inventiveness, see Anderson 1983 [1991]; Hobsbawm and Ranger 1983; and Bartra 1992. See also Tsing (1993:290), who notes that "ethnographies . . . are a possible site for drawing attention to both local creativity and regional-to-global interconnections."

22. See Fromm and Maccoby 1970 and, to a lesser extent, Romney and Romney 1963.

23. In fact, Lewis is not even the one describing Mexican urban males here, but rather is citing one Mexican urban male, Manuel Sánchez, to this effect. See chapter 9 for further discussion of this passage.

24. See Monsiváis 1981:108.

25. Though Lewis did include machismo on his list of over sixty possible traits illustrative of the "culture of poverty" (see Rigdon 1988:114–15), he seemed ambivalent about the efficacy of using the term, inserting and deleting it in his publications (see Gutmann 1994).

26. See, for example, Simic 1969:100, 1983; Mernissi 1975:5; and Marshall 1979:90. Additional sources often cited to refer to machismo as a particularly Mexican quality include Madsen and Madsen 1969 and Maccoby 1972.

27. In yet another variant, in his study of British working class youth Willis (1979:150) speaks of "the machismo of manual work" as a masculine logic involved in the will to really work and finish a job.

28. Developing a coherent, if not always flattering, sense of national identity in twentieth-century Mexico has often involved deliberations on machismo. Certain masterpieces of Mexican literature have actually played a distinct role in popularizing notions of machismo and in the process have created popular

expectations about Mexican men. I am in substantial agreement with Lomnitz-Adler (1992:254) that *The Labyrinth of Solitude* (Paz 1950) and *Pedro Páramo* (Rulfo 1955) may be better books with which to introduce Mexican society to the uninitiated than even groundbreaking ethnographies like *Life in a Mexican Village* (Lewis 1951) or *Tzintzuntzan* (Foster 1967). But this does not mean that Paz and Rulfo are necessarily better than Lewis and Foster as guides through the ambiguous passages of Mexican cultures. And it certainly does not follow that mesmerizing writers should be spared sociological scrutiny. In the present context, whereas Paz adopts a style of "decontextualized universality," in the words of Rowe and Schelling (1991:66), I seek instead a very contextualized particularity of male identities. Further, especially with respect to the continuing influence of *Labyrinth* on gender identities in Mexico, self-fulfilling interpretation is an issue not to be overlooked. In chapter 9, I briefly comment on relevant works by Ramos, Paz, and Rulfo.

29. Herzfeld (1987:133) states more fully: "Official discourse creates a rhetoric of definitional fixity and absolute morality, and depicts the populace as falling far short of the abstract ideal. Conversely, everyday usage—the semiotic or hermeneutic common sense of people trying to make sense of an oppressive bureaucracy—constantly erodes these fixities, and critically rejects official idealizations as a poor substitute for social experience."

30. For a thoughtful recent analysis that effectively argues against generalizing about Mexican American men and traces differences among them to other sociocultural influences, see Zavella 1991.

31. Narayan (1993:671) argues in a recent paper on nativeness and the anthropologist, "Instead of the paradigm emphasizing a dichotomy between outsider/insider or observer/observed, I propose that at this historical moment we might more profitably view each anthropologist in terms of shifting identifications amid a field of interpenetrating communities and power relations."

32. Though Mannheim overestimates the detached position of intellectuals, he does (1936:168) accurately point out that "a Weltanschauung is not of necessity a source of error, but often gives access to spheres of knowledge otherwise closed." See also Giddens's (1979:171) discussion of this passage.

33. Literally, the expression means "split your mother." In a manner similar to the multiple connotations of the word *verga*, slang for "penis" (see chapter 5), which are dependent on context, the term *madre* can refer to something positive (*a toda madre*, "really great") or negative, as in the example here.

CHAPTER 2

1. See Castells 1983:188.

2. See Departamento del Distrito Federal 1988:43.

3. I am indebted to Alejandra Massolo (1992a, 1992b) both for her vivid description of the history of Santo Domingo and for help early in my research in the *colonia*. The same is true for the advice and publications of Francis Lima (1992), my field assistant for a few months, and Patricia Safa (1992) at later stages of the project. The history and description of Santo Domingo included in this chapter are also based on studies by Ward (1976, 1990) and especially

on interviews with dozens of residents, some of whom were participants in the original invasion.

4. "Estimated" because census figures are linked to tax rolls and are known for their inaccurate global counts.

5. The term *mestizo* is culturally and politically charged in Mexico. Historically *mestizo* has meant someone of mixed racial ancestry. The three official races of the Mexican nation are Indian, Spanish, and Mestizo.

6. The term *las Marías* has great resonance in Mexico today. The subtitle of Arizpe's (1975) landmark study *Indígenas en la ciudad: El caso de las "Marías"* was meant to explicitly challenge the prejudice against indigenous peoples in general and indigenous women in particular. In a characterization of more ambiguous purpose, one of the slapstick stars of Mexican television and cinema is known as La India María; her first film was called *Tonta tonta pero no tanto* (Really foolish but not so much).

7. See especially Bourque and Warren 1981; Logan 1984; Benería and Roldán 1987; Gabayet et al. 1988; Poniatowska 1988; Stephen 1991; and Massolo 1992a, 1992b.

8. For more on the subject of the PRI's methods and history of co-optation, see González Casanova 1970 and Eckstein 1977, 1990.

9. Regarding Mexico City's urbanization, among the recent important studies are Cornelius 1975; Montaño 1976; Eckstein 1977; Kemper 1977; Lomnitz 1977; Vélez-Ibáñez 1983; Navarro and Moctezuma 1989; de la Peña et al. 1990; Selby, Murphy, and Lorenzen 1990; Ward 1990; and Davis 1994.

10. Despite class polarization, however, the middle class in Mexico City and elsewhere in the country has not disappeared or even significantly withered as some predicted it would, even though many strata within this sector have had to learn to live on far less real income in the past decade (see Loaeza and Stern 1990). I was completing final revisions on this manuscript just as the financial crisis of 1995 was developing. Thus I have been unable to fully incorporate the repercussions of this latest crisis on the lives of my friends in Santo Domingo.

11. Although I emphasize the particularities of being a resident in Santo Domingo, I do not wish to imply that the differences between *colonias* in Mexico City outweigh the similarities. Eckstein (1977) and Selby et al. (1990) are correct in noting that for the poor in Mexico today, urban life is largely the same whether they are living within the capital or elsewhere in the country. Television and migration have both been prime contributors to this process. On the question of urban heterogeneity-homogeneity with regard to Mexico City, see also Cornelius 1975 and Davis 1994; for a more general discussion of the importance and particularity of space, see cultural geography studies by Soja (1989) and Watts (1992).

CHAPTER 3

1. In addition to these nicknames, Liliana was also called the more standard *muñequita* (little doll), *reina* (queen), *preciosa* (cutey), and *mamacita* (little mama).

2. On this "deceptively simple methodological approach" of Mead's, see Scheper-Hughes 1984.

3. My use of the photograph was similar to earlier ethnographers' utilization of the Thematic Apperception Test (TAT), a series of drawings of different scenes familiar worldwide that are shown to informants to elicit their cultural interpretations. I have benefited from more recent ethnographic studies by Jelin, Vila, and D'Amico (1987) and García Canclini, Safa, and Grobet (1989), and their use of photographs in Buenos Aires and Tijuana, respectively.

4. In this context my friend was using the word *mestizos* to refer to non-Indian Mexican men.

5. Following Kearney (forthcoming), I refrain from employing the ambiguous term *peasant* in this book.

6. One notable exception to these class-divided responses was by the essayist and semiofficial chronicler of Mexico City Carlos Monsiváis (interview with author, 20 February 1993), who commented on the photograph, "*Me parece normal* [It seems normal to me]."

7. I decided to define *holding* as an adult holding a child either in his or her arm(s) or by the hand. I obviously took liberties with the term *parental,* because I seldom knew for sure whether the adults involved were the parents. Based on my overall familiarity with parenting in Santo Domingo, I feel safe in assuming that in the large majority of the cases noted, the man and the woman were indeed the parents of the child(ren) being held. If more adults than one man and one woman were present, I did not count them in the sample. Similarly, when neither person in the couple held any child, the couple was not included.

For an elaboration of the deeper psychological meanings of "holding," coddling, and so on, and why these are so significant in parenting, see Erikson 1963; Winnicott 1987; Ruddick 1989; and Scheper-Hughes 1992.

8. See, for example, Taggart (1992b) on Nahua fathers in Puebla. And though men in Santo Domingo do frequently carry their children in public, they also tend to distinguish more than women between their own children and those of others. When a woman gets on the *combi* minibus with several small children in tow, other women already on board will routinely reach out and give assistance, holding the children while the first woman pays, gets settled, and so on. Generally men are far more reluctant to get involved, especially if it means touching and holding the children of strangers, though if men know the adult or the children concerned they are usually far more helpful and engaging.

9. The insight is from Leach 1958:161.

10. Nader (1990:244) writes that "a Zapotec man who abuses a woman is not thought to be abusing the honor of her family."

11. Perhaps in response to a perceived capital-city arrogance, a popular saying elsewhere in the country goes, "*Sé patriótico: ¡Mata a un chilango!* [Be patriotic: Kill a *chilango!*]" Or as an alternate wording has it, "*Haz justicia: ¡Mata a un chilango!* [Bring justice to bear: Kill a *chilango!*]"

12. This distinction people in Santo Domingo make between urban and rural areas in regard to their treatment of women is also an indication that many people in the *clases populares* in Mexico City at least make pronouncements in favor of gender equality.

13. See Redfield 1941.

14. The history of the anthropology of Mexico reveals similar analyses regarding the countryside, often in the form of discussions of indigenous cultures
as retarding influences on the country's progress and modernization. Manuel
Gamio, the father of Mexican anthropology and a student of Franz Boas, called
attention to the plight of indigenous peoples. But his emphasis on the need to
study their cultures was aimed especially at hastening their dissolution, through
"racial homogenization" and unifying the use of Spanish throughout the country. Gamio sought to facilitate the incorporation of what he regarded as stub-
bornly anachronistic forms of nationalism into the "upward march of human-
ity" (Gamio 1935:23). For more on this issue with respect to Gamio, see Hewitt
de Alcántara 1984:10 ff. Raymond Williams's (1973:289) insight that perceptions of urban-rural differences in Europe may reflect broader social convul-
sions is also germane here: "Clearly the contrast of country and city is one of
the major forms in which we become conscious of a central part of our experience and of the crises of our society."

15. Some of these differences are noted in the pages that follow, but much
work remains to be done on this question. Particularly with respect to Santo
Domingo, it is probably true that the phenomenon noted by Taylor (1979:67)
for eighteenth-century Mexico City in general has continued to exert an influence on migrants to the city's *colonias populares* more recently: "The city attracted rural traders, litigants, and supplicants with business in the capital, but
equally important, Mexico City was a place of refuge, releasing them temporarily from village rules of comportment."

16. For other studies of rural-urban migration within Mexico that illuminate but do not focus specifically on gender issues, see also Lewis 1952 and
Kemper 1977.

17. For theories that argue that bonding is more biologically driven and less
historically and culturally based, see Harlow 1971 and Bowlby 1953, 1969.

18. Nancy Scheper-Hughes (1992) has painstakingly critiqued many cultural feminist and psychological theories of maternal "instincts" and mother-
child bonding. For a recent discussion of "sharply negative attitudes about
child-bearing and child rearing" among women in a rural community of Oaxaca, see Browner 1986a. Standard histories of the changes in cultural attitudes
and behavior in Europe regarding parenting and childhood include Ariès 1962
and Shorter 1977.

19. See also Selby's (1976) discussion of how some forms of extramarital
sexual behavior were considered deviant, or morally reprehensible, and some
not in a Zapotec community in Oaxaca in the 1960s.

20. In a somewhat analogous manner, Taggart (1992a:78) reports that in
the Sierra Nahua region of Mexico, "[p]rior to adolescence, all children sleep
together on mats on the floor of the main family dwelling, with the youngest
child sleeping with the mother on one mat, the father with one or two of the
next youngest children on a second mat, and the other preadolescent children
on as many other mats as are needed." Beginning often around eighteen months
or two years, in the families Taggart has studied, children are simultaneously

weaned and they begin sleeping with the father; "they may continue to sleep with him for a number of years," and thus form close emotional ties with the father based in part on regular bodily contact with him (Taggart 1992b:444). Of further significance, both boys and girls are part of these sleeping arrangements until puberty, when they are separated. In Santo Domingo such sleeping patterns would be unusual.

21. See Nash (1970:112) on Chiapas in the 1950s and 1960s; Ingham (1986:67) on Morelos in the 1960s; and Romney and Romney (1963:672) on Oaxaca in the 1960s.

22. Significantly, in their psychoanalytic study of a village in Morelos in the 1960s, Fromm and Maccoby (1970:199) allude to broader and deeper social influences on male gender-identity development: "Our findings are not consistent with Freud's main position, which emphasized the fear of castration as the decisive factor in the boy's renouncing his primary attachment to the mother. It is our view that the breaking of the primary tie with the mother, which is necessary if a boy is to become a man, depends more on socioeconomic than on psychosexual factors."

23. Loosed from its biologically determinist moorings, this notion shares something in common with Erikson's (1963:266–68) term *generativity:* "the concern in establishing and guiding the next generation."

24. See also Taggart (1979) on inheritance and gender relations.

25. The full interview form in Spanish (with an English translation) is reproduced as an appendix in my doctoral dissertation: "Meanings of Macho: The Cultural Politics of Masculinity in Mexico City," University of California, Berkeley, 1995.

26. As Hochschild (1989) writes with regard to child care in working class families in the United States, in Colonia Santo Domingo ideals do not necessarily correlate exactly with practice.

27. In broad terms, the group was representative of tens of millions of Mexicans in the sense that it consisted of an urban population (well over 50 percent of the country's population now lives in cities of ten thousand or more) with an average household income of between one and three minimum wages (four to twelve dollars a day in 1993), living in a *colonia popular* (typical of urban housing) and including several people who had migrated from the *campo* within the past fifteen years. Of the forty-two people I interviewed, twenty-seven were men and fifteen were women. All but three people had at least one child: I interviewed a woman expecting a child, her husband, and another man who was "thinking about" having children. Most of the men and women were between twenty-five and thirty-nine years old, though a few were older than fifty-five. Most had no education beyond the junior high school (*secundaria*) level, with a low of less than a year's schooling and a high of two years of studies after high school in accounting classes. About half the women I spoke with worked outside the home for money. A few of the questions were adapted from those asked by Arizpe (1989) and her research team.

28. My generalizations on infant feeding are based on informal questioning and observations in the *colonia* rather than any systematic survey. With regard

to breast feeding, I know of no systematic network of wet nurses in Santo Domingo, nor does expressing milk that others, such as fathers, may later give to babies seem a popular alternative.

29. This minimum age may intentionally coincide with the forty-day *cuarentena* (quarantine) tradition, marking the period in some cultures in Mexico during which new mothers are traditionally not supposed to leave their homes. There are officially spaces for eighty children in the DIF center that serves tens of thousands of families in Santo Domingo.

30. See Romanucci-Ross (1973:66) and Foster (1967:62) for regional (and implicit historical) variations regarding parental divisions of labor in the beatings of children. Violence inflicted on children and many other points from my survey on parenting will be taken up in more detail and from other perspectives in subsequent chapters of this book.

31. This should not be taken to mean that extended families have ceased to play an important role in gender and kinship processes. In particular, women in various social strata in Mexico City often play a key role in keeping these ties active, making key decisions as to how to help relatives secure employment, who gets invited to family gatherings, and who is excluded from the loop. On the role of women in these family networks in Mexico, see Lomnitz and Pérez-Lizaur 1987. For comparative material on various sectors of the United States, see Stack 1974; Yanagisako 1977; and di Leonardo 1987. At the same time, neither should we assume that prior to the last twenty years everyone in Mexico lived in an extended family. Typical of many of my friends, Miguel, for example, knew only one grandmother well, met one grandfather one time, and never met his other two grandparents at all.

32. Another instance of this attitude is the use of the terms *hijo* (son) and *hija* (daughter) by spouses to refer to their partners. (Many couples also use various terms for "mother" and "father" as forms of direct address with each other.) The use of the terms *hijo* and *hija* does not infantilize the spouse so much as it emphasizes the cultural significance of the parent-child bond.

33. See, for instance, Mead and Wolfenstein 1955; Spiro 1958; and Whiting 1963.

34. "Retardation" is Gould's (1977:67) provocative phrase.

35. See Yanagisako 1979; Stacey 1990; Jelin 1991; and Thorne and Yalom 1992.

36. Tepito, a *colonia* bordering the one where Oscar Lewis's *The Children of Sánchez* (1961) was set, is akin in popular lore to New York's Lower East Side or London's East End. Today it is still the site of open-air stalls.

37. See Goldsmith (1990) on the history of domestic workers in Mexico City.

38. In this affirmation, I follow earlier studies by Bott (1957), Schneider and Smith (1973), and Stack (1974). Though their conclusions differ dramatically, these studies of Britain and the United States find, each in different ways, that certain cultural characteristics parallel class distinctions. See also Steward (1955:76) for a brief but astute comment of the relation between social class and child rearing.

39. On distinctions regarding gender issues as related to class differences, see also de Barbieri 1984.

40. In a note, Chodorow cites work from 1958, 1959, and 1961 on "cross-cultural comparisons of the relationship between family structure and men's preoccupation with masculinity" (1978:238, n. 24; see also Chodorow 1989:233, n. 26). She can hardly be blamed for the outdated comparative research she cites or faulted for the dearth of investigations. On the other hand, rather than drawing many cross-cultural conclusions from these studies, I find it more helpful to point to them as evidence that we have much work to do.

41. Thus Habermas (1987:387) is correct in noting that "epochal changes in the bourgeois family could be misunderstood; in particular, the results of the leveling out of paternal authority could be interpreted wrongly." That is, it is wrong to uncritically accept the earlier thesis of Horkheimer (1972) and others in the original Frankfurt School, because even if it were true that capitalism's impact on "the family" is everywhere and in all respects negative, still, paternal authority too would be subverted to larger systemic imperatives.

CHAPTER 4

1. On the *movimientos urbanos populares* in Mexico, see especially Montaño 1976; Alonso 1981; Ramírez Sáiz 1986; Massolo and Schteingart 1987; Monsiváis 1987; Poniatowska 1988; Mercado 1989; Navarro and Moctezuma 1989; Foweraker and Craig 1990; and Massolo 1992a, 1992b.

2. For carefully compiled histories of two women in Mexico that illustrate such changes elsewhere in Mexico, see Poniatowska's (1969) classic *Hasta no verte Jesús mío* and Behar's (1993) compelling *Translated Woman*.

3. In addition to works cited for Mexico in note 1, see Slater 1985; Nash and Safa 1986; Leacock and Safa 1986; Eckstein 1989; and Escobar and Alvarez 1992.

4. Taylor, describing eighteen-century Mexico, tells of "nasty mobs of hundreds of women brandishing spears and kitchen knives or cradling rocks in their skirts" (1979:116). (For a lovely historical parallel from England, see also Thompson 1971:116.)

5. The expression *doble jornada* (literally, "double day") is used in Latin America as the term *second shift* is used by feminists in the United States to refer to women's double duties of paid work outside the home and housework.

6. Drawing on examples from Germany in the 1970s and 1980s, Habermas (1987:393) divides popular movements into what he considers more defensive efforts (movements such as those involving squatters, the elderly, environmental activists, religious fundamentalists, and struggles for gay rights and regional autonomy) and compares these with struggles with emancipatory potential, which he considers therefore offensive. We need not subscribe to Habermas's placement of particular struggles in one category or the other—I consider many of the gay and lesbian rights struggles and autonomy movements for regional independence in the world to be emancipatory-offensive in nature—to find value in the offensive-defensive distinction itself.

7. For discussions of the theoretical importance of autonomy for women's political struggles, see Leacock 1981 and Stephen 1991, 1996.

8. See also Eckstein's (1990:224) conclusion that in some circumstances *juntas de vecinos* (committees of neighbors) have played an important role in undermining democratic currents.

9. This tenet is the flip side of an economist Marxism that many young radicals had earlier rejected: consciousness flows smoothly from people's social positions without the need for reflection and outside influence. Though some political scientists argue that in Latin America in the 1990s Marxist ideas are largely alien to the working class and that Marxist organizations are essentially revolutionary student remnants from the 1960s (see, for example, Wickham-Crowley 1992), the UCP, which is made up of homegrown radicals as well as former students, provides evidence that reform-oriented Maoism still has a small following in some poor neighborhoods in Mexico.

10. *"Hace una conducta machista en los hombres."*

11. On the CEBs and liberation theology, see Berryman 1987. In its rejection of many of the doctrines of Catholic Church orthodoxy and hierarchy, the Iglesia de la Resurrección shares something in common with the tradition of popular religion in Mexico. For an interesting ethnographic treatment of the latter in Morelos, see de la Peña 1980.

12. See also Browner's (1986b) discussion of how single motherhood in communities in Oaxaca can also bring greater freedoms to some women.

13. This view is similar to the position taken by many centers for battered women in Mexico City. In an interview in November 1992 with Ana María Cuéllar of the Centro de Investigación y Lucha Contra la Violencia Doméstica, she summarized the group's experience as showing that it is hard enough for most women to change, to realize that they can escape from a violent partner, but it is an exercise in futility to try to change the men involved.

14. *Egoismo* was the word she used.

15. Thus appeared for me in Santo Domingo anthropology's venerable incest taboo. It should be noted that older brothers and sisters in Colonia Santo Domingo frequently care for younger siblings—washing, dressing, and feeding them. (Vélez-Ibañez [1983:146] reports the same for Ciudad Netzahualcóyotl in the late 1960s, as does Nash [1970:111] for parts of Chiapas in the early 1960s.) In Miguelito's case he was too young to take much responsibility for Liliana, but throughout the year he was unfailingly sweet toward his "little sister," even taking time out from playing Rambo to attend to her needs as best he could.

16. Boys and girls dress in different uniforms beginning in elementary school. Except for days when they participate in calisthenics and everyone comes to school in sweat suits, girls wear skirts and boys wear slacks.

17. See Díaz-Guerrero 1967 and Peñalosa 1968.

18. The term *santo* refers popularly to a sacred person, and not necessarily to someone literally sanctified as a saint by the Catholic Church. Hence many people consider Jesús the most important *santo* in their lives.

CHAPTER 5

1. I draw in this chapter on Giddens's (1992) insights regarding sexuality, love, and eroticism in modern societies. The term *homosexuality* is used guardedly here to refer to sex between men and sex between women. In Santo Domingo, however, unlike the United States, people usually mean by *homosexual* only the man who is penetrated by another (not necessarily "homosexual") man in anal intercourse. For more on these meanings and practices and certain similarities with regard to sex between men in different parts of Latin America and among Chicanos, see Lancaster 1992 and Almaguer 1990.

2. Unfortunately, no demographic studies have been conducted on fertility rates for men in Mexico. In fact, discussions are just now beginning in the field of demography worldwide as to what the concept of male fertility might even mean (Eugene Hammel, personal communication).

3. As Parker (1991:92) notes in his study of sexual culture in contemporary Brazil, "It is clear that in the modern period sexuality, focused on reproduction, has become something to be managed not merely by the Catholic church or by the state, but by individuals themselves."

4. Lancaster (1992:270) continues: "It is not simply that these relations and conflicts act on some interior and preexisting sexuality 'from the outside' but that they constitute it 'from the inside' as well. Which is to say (contrary to common sense): sexual history is possible only to the extent that desire is thoroughly historicized, and sexual anthropology only to the extent that its subject is effectively relativized."

5. The National Survey was compiled from 10,142 questionnaires completed by high school students, who in Mexico come overwhelmingly from middle and upper middle class backgrounds. See Consejo Nacional de Población 1988.

6. The notion of linguistic constraints on culture is given a classic expression in the Sapir-Whorf Hypothesis: "Human beings . . . are very much at the mercy of the particular language which has become the medium of expression for their society" (Sapir 1929 [1949]:162). See Tambiah (1990:111–39) for a recent and sensible effort to analyze the question of cross-cultural translation and the commensurability of cultures.

7. For a similar approach to questions of hegemony, borrowing from Giddens's formulation of "practical consciousness," see Cowan's (1990) nuanced development of Gramscian theories in her study of gender practices in a Greek Macedonian community.

8. In March 1993, on a beach at Puerto Escondido in Oaxaca, I finally met a man who in the course of a long conversation about his life told me, "I have five kids: four daughters and a baby—*un hijo* [a son]!" He shouted those last words, clearly delighted with the maleness of the new arrival. This man and I also talked about the coincidence of both of us having lived and worked in Chicago and Houston for many years. Might his experiences in the United States have made him especially "pro-boy," or was he simply happy for the variation of a boy amid all those girls? My hunch is that the latter is closer to the truth.

9. See Secretaría de Salud 1990, especially Cuadro 6.5.8 (p. 156) and Cuadro 6.5.10 (p. 159). Other studies have arrived at dramatically different figures for condom use. Leñero (1993:9), for example, reports that 50 percent of the 250 proletarian men interviewed in his study said they used condoms, although 70 percent of respondents also said that their *wives* did not like the men to use them because they were uncomfortable (for the women!) and lessened pleasure and spontaneity.

10. Catholic Church teachings are an important influence with regard to menstruation and bodily contact. A friend told me that in Guadalajara, a city where leagues of decency have long flourished among the wealthy and conservative "señoras" (see Reguillo 1993), she once spent two hours looking for tampons before finally finding them. She attributed their scarcity to the great influence in Guadalajara of the church dogma that women must not touch their genitalia, and specifically that they must not insert anything into their vaginas—that this is a right exclusively reserved for their husbands.

11. The use of the term *verga* in Mexico differs considerably from that in Nicaragua, where Lancaster (1992:41) reports that *verga* "is necessarily a violent organ" in a world in which violence is a masculine affair. My comparison of the meanings of *verga* in Mexico and in Nicaragua argues for a highly particular reading of masculinities cross-culturally. Such has, unfortunately, not always been the practice. Instead, Herdt (1990:434) notes, "Generally . . . reductionism continues in studies of males, where there appears to be a compelling match between the cultural expectations ascribed to males, and the biological fact of their maleness."

12. In the United States this used to be called the "soul handshake" or "dapping." Some power handshakes do take place between men and women, especially younger ones attending the universities.

13. The gay and lesbian rights movement in the United States may also have indirectly played a political role in Mexico. Although there have been comparative studies of homosexuality among Mexicans in Mexico and among Mexicans in the United States (see, for example, Magaña and Carrier 1991), as far as I know there has been no research on the influence of the gay rights movement in the United States on Mexico, and of the movement in Mexico on the United States, via Mexican immigrants to the United States. For a treatment that at least raises relevant questions regarding the mutual influence of neighboring gay and Latino communities in San Francisco, see Castells 1983:99–172.

14. Such public intermingling across sexual and other cultural boundaries is also evident in Ciudad Juárez and Tijuana, both on the Mexico-U.S. border.

15. "Who [else] is going to blow forty-, fifty-, or a hundred-thousand pesos [around $15, $20, or $35] for just one screw?" (Liguori and Ortega 1990:111).

16. I am very grateful to Patricio Villalva for sharing the initial results of his unpublished research with me.

17. For certain cultural similarities, see Lancaster's (1992, Chap. 18) discussion of the role of the *hombre-hombre* and the *cochón* in the social construction of sexual practices in Nicaragua.

18. *Puto*—literally, a male whore—in this context is the equivalent to calling someone in English a sissy or a fairy.

19. In his analysis of Argentine soccer, Suárez-Orozco (1982:18) also calls attention to the previously overlooked "homosexual dimension of the macho syndrome."

20. This final observation is confirmed in recent research by Florinda Riquer (personal communication).

21. Many other ethnographers who have worked in various regions of Mexico report similar sentiments regarding male sexuality. To evoke similar popular beliefs around San Luis Potosí, Behar (1993:290) writes that "men's need for sex is insatiable." Based on fieldwork in Oaxaca, Matthews (1987:228) calls attention to "an important female view of men as being, by nature, lustful, possessing an insatiable sexual appetite. They are like animals in that they seek their own satisfaction and are not concerned with the needs of others." At the same time, such opinions should not be taken to mean that women do not share similar urges. Matthews (1987:225) also speaks of "an important male view of women as being sexually uncontrolled." We may compare these last summations with Brandes's (1980:77) research in Andalusia, Spain, where "women are seductresses, possessed of insatiable, lustful appetites."

22. In this sense, *cabrón* has a usage similar to that of the U.S. English *son of a bitch*; they can be employed as both insults and compliments. For current usage by Mexicans of the term *Sancho,* a nickname for men being cuckolded, see Conover 1987:177–78.

23. For a recent mention of the practice, though not the name, of the *casa chica,* see Bossen 1988:272 on middle class households in Guatemala City. See also Diaz 1970:60 and Fromm and Maccoby 1970:149.

24. Given my interest in fathers and fathering, I was in contact with more men who lived with their families, even if they were not necessarily active in parenting, than I was with those who had abandoned their wives and children. Single mothers were nonetheless common enough in the *colonia.*

25. In my fieldwork in Santo Domingo I was privy to very few discussions about female masturbation.

26. Within the discipline of anthropology there has been an interesting and important dialogue regarding the possibility, and appropriateness, of male ethnographers working with women (see, for example, Gregory 1984; Herzfeld 1985:48; Brandes 1987; and Gilmore 1991:29, n. 2). I believe that the anthropological study of male identities, of men *as men,* is considerably weakened when the only sources of information are men. In the same way that we have criticized as male bias an understanding of women of whatever culture that is based solely upon what men say about women (see Scheper-Hughes 1983), so too we must not depend on what only men say about themselves. Indeed, I found that on certain sensitive topics, such as domestic violence, rather than being more difficult to discuss these issues with women, it was often much easier to speak with them than it was to get men to think reflexively and report honestly about their experiences and ideas.

CHAPTER 6

1. *Vieja* literally means "old lady" and, as in some working class cultures in the United States, is employed to refer to a man's wife or one's mother. In Mexico *viejas* is also a more generic term for "females."

2. I am not proposing that getting boys to play with dolls in any manner resolves the issue of male domination. I use the example of boys playing with dolls merely as an indication of possible changes in broader sociocultural attitudes and practices.

3. Habermas's formulations on public/private share something in common with Giddens's (1990:154 ff.) discussion of "utopian realism" and his distinction between "life politics (politics of self-actualisation)" and "emancipatory politics (politics of inequality)." Both Habermas and Giddens are attempting to develop new theories to describe the ways in which men and women actually transform their lives, in smaller and larger historical contexts.

4. For recent studies that explore the relation between demography and changing gender relations in Mexico, see Selby, Murphy, and Lorenzen 1990 and García and Oliveira 1993.

5. Sánchez Gómez (1989:74 n. 6) reports that "men's help in domestic work is specific: it relates to those activities which are not close to the definition of feminine activities, those more related to the outdoors, less routine and monotonous, and the help is in most cases optional and of little significance in relation to the sum total of domestic work in the household." For a comparative study in the United States on the relation between family and paid work for women, see Lamphere, Zavella, and Gonzales 1993.

6. Lima (1992:45) cites a grandmother in Santo Domingo talking of a similar circumstance with regard to her employed daughter, her unemployed son-in-law, and the care of her grandchildren.

7. Mexican men who are migrant workers in the United States, of course, cook all the time they are there.

8. This need is also indicated in García and Oliveira's (1993:257) concluding remarks in their section on male participation in domestic work: "In our research we found a more egalitarian pattern of domestic help between sons and daughters. . . . These results are important as indications of possible intergenerational changes whose outlines might become clearer in the years to come."

9. Gudeman and Rivera (1990:98) report a somewhat different use of the term *ayudar* in rural Colombia, where "any work for the household is help. . . . All of a woman's work in the kitchen and elsewhere is help, and so is the man's work in the fields."

10. For a sociological analysis of women's household contributions through employed work, see de Barbieri 1984; Rubin-Kurtzman 1991; and García and Oliveira 1993.

11. This is also true of women in several urban areas along the border, such as Ciudad Juárez, Matamoros, and Tijuana. Early and important anthropological work on the relation between women's paid employment and cultural practices in Mexico was done by Fernández Kelly 1983.

12. Tables 2 and 3 are based on 1990 census data, which unquestionably underestimate many forms of paid employment, semiemployment, illegal employment, "informal" employment, and so forth. Nonetheless, for purposes of comparison (for example, whether more women were employed in Mexico City or in the *campo*), we may reasonably draw limited conclusions from these figures. See also figures on earlier censuses and discussion in García, Muñoz, and Oliveira 1982:34 ff.

13. To emphasize this point, Marx wrote, "Nature builds no machines, no locomotives, railways, electric telegraphs, self-acting mules, etc. These are products of human industry; natural material transformed into organs of the human will over nature, or of human participation in nature. They are *organs of the human brain, created by the human hand;* the power of knowledge, objectified" (1857–58 [1973]:706; emphasis in original).

14. The demographer Susana Lerner (personal communication) estimates that, on average, women in Mexico earn 50 percent of what men earn for the same job. The discrepancy in salaries is simultaneously a keystone of social inequality and, on a personal basis, a very considerable hurdle to economic solvency for many families.

15. This passage is alternately translated as "the first premise for the emancipation of women is the reintroduction of the entire female sex into public industry" (Engels 1884a:247).

16. As Arrom (1985:264) notes regarding certain repressive Victorian mores that were valorized in the upper classes in the late nineteenth century in Mexico City, "[t]he rationale for making the home a female domain was therefore to preserve social control [over women]."

17. Thus the people I interviewed reported on completed sibling sets but not necessarily completed sets of children. Regardless, the trend toward families having fewer children is evident in the survey responses.

18. This fall in birthrates has been the result of a number of factors, including intensive Mexican government population programs beginning in the mid-1970s. See Zavala de Cosío 1992 generally on this issue, and p. 16 for figures on life expectancy.

19. The doll was a U.S. import called Mommy's Having a Baby.

20. Larissa Lomnitz (1977:188 ff.) documents similar matrilocal residence patterns in a settlement in Mexico City in the early 1970s.

21. Compare Gudeman and Rivera 1990:101: "A man may come home at night to be served food by his spouse, or she may bring food to him in the fields, but the people see nothing servile in this."

22. For more on the relation between history and the life course, see Elder 1978, 1987 and Hareven 1978.

23. Héctor, sixty years old, taught me his favorite *piropo* so that it could be included in this book: "*Mamacita, eres más linda que la burra que cargó a la Virgen* [*Mamacita,* you are lovelier than the burro who carried the Virgin (of Guadalupe)]." Dundes and Suárez-Orozco (1987:123) write that the *piropo* tradition "is all-pervasive in contemporary Spanish and Spanish-American cultures. The piropo is . . . central to the life of males in these societies. . . . " If their description is in my view too sweeping—the *piropo* is not central to the

lives of *any* men I know in Colonia Santo Domingo—their discussion of *machismo* nonetheless adds important elements of Freudian theory to the analysis of masculinity in the region.

24. The *muchachos* wanted to know what happens when gringos call out, "Hey, *mamacita,* you're looking fine!" or, "Oh, my, my, you're so gorgeous!" "Do the young women like it, or do they get angry?" Enrique asked me. Then, answering his own question, he added, "They cut off your thing, right?"

25. Men and women who are old enough to remember the events of October 1968 and who lived in Mexico City at the time often tell where-were-you stories about them.

CHAPTER 7

1. *Las copas*—literally, "the glasses"—refers generically to alcoholic beverages of any kind.

2. Studies of alcohol consumption must pay attention not only to variation across regions and in different historical periods, but, as DeWalt (1979) points out, also to intracultural variability within regions. Further, the issues of power and control are still underdeveloped in alcohol studies in Mexico. For classic studies on alcohol in Mexico see, for example, de la Fuente 1954 and Pozas 1962.

3. For further discussion of moral and health issues related to alcohol and alcohol consumption, see Menéndez 1987, 1991, 1992; Room 1984; and Heath 1987.

4. *Pulquerías* sell pulque, an alcoholic beverage made from the sap of the maguey (agave, century plant) that has been made in Mesoamerica for centuries. It has roughly the alcoholic content of beer. Without additives it is frothy and white. A small restaurant-cantina opened in late 1992 on Papalotl Avenue, one of the main thoroughfares in Colonia Santo Domingo, but I left before it was possible to predict its success or whether other like ventures would soon follow. Men were the nearly exclusive customers in this new establishment each time I was there.

5. Vélez-Ibañez (1983:220) reports that in the early 1970s, many families from Netzahualcóyotl—a teeming settlement in Estado de México, just outside the Federal District—traveled to San Juan Chimalhuacán to drink pulque on Sunday picnics and "get away from it all."

6. On male social gatherings, see also Limón's (1989, 1994) discussion of all-male *carne asadas* (barbecues) and the "ritualistic" consumption of meat and beer in South Texas, as well as Limón 1982.

7. Not that these constraints are totally missing in the cantina. A linguist friend, Víctor Franco (personal communication), says that in many villages he is familiar with in the state of Guerrero, children are routinely sent into cantinas to retrieve their fathers. The rationale is that in these areas cantinas are still culturally if not necessarily legally off-limits to women of good repute. Then, too, the hope is that fathers will respond favorably to the sad faces of their children begging them to stop drinking and return home.

8. *Cuba* here means a drink made with Coke and either rum or brandy.

9. Yet what are we to make of the following conclusion drawn by a psychologist who studied children in a *colonia* near Santo Domingo: "[T]he men of Santa Ursula drink until they lose their memory" (Bar Din 1991:65)? All the men? All the time? Such generalizations may tell us more about researchers' preconceptions than about the ostensible subjects of study. And whereas alcohol consumption may go up in some areas in periods of increasing poverty, there are contradictory pressures in other areas that may reduce drinking. Selby (1990:175) and his colleagues found that, following the crisis of 1982, reduced incomes in the sprawling settler area of Netzahualcóyotl had meant *less* drunkenness though drunkenness had not entirely disappeared. It is difficult to draw a causal link between economic immiseration and the rise or fall of alcohol consumption, since it has been shown to go either way.

10. Compare Don Fortino's comment in Greenberg (1989:126): "Alcohol is a factor in getting people in trouble. That is why I only played with alcohol for twenty or twenty-five years."

11. See Kearney 1972 and Greenberg 1989. A more exceptional case, in the ethnographic literature if not necessarily in the cultures of Mexico, is reported in DeWalt 1979.

12. See Cancian 1965:118 and Nash 1970:192

13. I also witnessed an incident in Santo Domingo in April 1993 in which a woman in her fifties, drunk and loudly shouting "*¡Pendeja!*" was being propped up and gently coaxed down the street by a young man, and escorted by a young woman who was also drinking. But judging by my experience, situations in which a young drunk man is protected and assisted by women, family members, or simply neighbors are the most common in Santo Domingo.

14. Such community understanding of drunks of all ages has been given artistic expression in the United States by the comedian Richard Pryor. One of the popular characters in his stand-up routines is the old wino Mudbone, who loves to direct traffic around his neighborhhod housing projects while in an alcohol-induced stupor. Even though Pryor gently pokes fun at the wino, he finds much to cherish about this obstinate and loquacious fellow.

15. Ingham (1986:151), for example, writes that in Tlayacapan, Morelos, "drinking is a typically male behavior." Similarly, Kearney (1972:108) writes of an Ixtepeji man in the 1960s who was ridiculed for not drinking and thus acting "like a woman," and Vélez-Ibañez (1983:153) notes that in Netzahualcóyotl of the early 1970s, "[a]ll the men will drink brandy or tequila or sometimes beer—but not the women." See also Kennedy 1978.

16. In her "Cyborg Manifesto," Haraway (1991) discusses certain implications regarding the erosion of gender as an organizing principle in some aspects of social life.

CHAPTER 8

1. Writing about nearby Colonia Santa Ursula, Bar Din (1991:66) writes, "Husbands get home and smack their wives. Nonetheless, they don't beat the

children. Only five mothers reported 'occasional' slappings of children [by men], but not with sticks. These were reserved for the women."

2. The word *bravo* is closely associated with images of farm animals like bulls, and as such was employed to evoke a stark contrast between the wilder ("more aggressive") rural areas and a more sedate and refined way of life in the city. In addition, although women can be *bravas,* the term is especially used with reference to ("natural") male attributes. And even when it is said of women, this is generally done to point out particularly feral qualities of women from the *campo.*

3. Compare Olivia Harris's (1980:90) observation from the Bolivian Andes that "the married couple is the embodiment of society itself, and is contrasted to unmarried people who in certain respects are relegated to the wild."

4. As Greenberg (1989:152) has noted recently for the Juquila region of Oaxaca, "although the rate of fighting appears to have been fairly constant, guns have altered the outcome radically." See also Ruvalcaba 1991.

5. The Pinoles originated on the dead-end street Cerrada de Pino. Pinole is a powder made of toasted maize; it has been eaten for centuries as a sweet. There is a saying regarding pinole: "*El que tiene más saliva traga más pinole* [He who has the most saliva swallows the most pinole]," which means, roughly, "The one who talks the best game calls the shots."

6. See also Lever (1983) on *futbol* in Brazil. City clubs in Rio de Janeiro, for instance, have played a role in socially integrating into "city life" many new migrants, the young men as players and spectators and the young women as club boosters.

7. In the course of the year I met with members of the Colectivo de Lucha Contra la Violencia Hacia las Mujeres (COVAC), Centro de Investigación y Lucha Contra la Violencia Doméstica (CECOVID), Salud Integral para la Mujer (SIPAM), and other organizations.

8. Lewis, writing in 1951, observed, "Attitudes toward wife-beating and child-beating have been changing in the direction of disapproval" (1951:295). Given this commentary from over forty years ago, it is hard to know how much credence to give contemporary accounts of changes in the incidence of domestic violence. Further, while attitudes may change, there is not necessarily an organic link between these changes and changes in behavior.

9. According to residents of Colonia Santo Domingo, land and buildings can be registered in the name of only one person and thus not in the names of both wife and husband. The reader will recall that many community groups in Mexico City, operating on the assumption that many men are unreliable, have urged women to seek this exclusive title to their property. Juanita took this advice, and for this reason her land and home are legally in her name.

10. I also participated one time in the Programa de Reeducación y Compromiso Responsable para El Hombre Violento (Program for Reeducation and Responsible Commitment for Violent Men), organized by a male psychologist in a group supporting battered women, and modeled on a similar program in San Francisco, California, called ManAlive. Unlike the CAVI meetings, the Programa in Mexico City charged fifty pesos (around eighteen dollars, or better

than three days' minimum wage) per session, which probably considerably restricted its clients. For the sake of convenience, and because the content of the meetings was so similar, I have combined the comments from this session with those from the three I attended at CAVI.

11. These and the following figures from CAVI were kindly provided to me by Enrique Ortiz.

12. I base this statement on remarks by Ana María Cuéllar of CECOVID (interview by author, 5 November 1992).

13. A study group on domestic violence formed in 1993 by Irma Saucedo of the Programa Interdisciplinario de Estudios de la Mujer at the Colegio de México has gathered preliminary evidence showing that numerous men begin beating their wives during their wives' first pregnancy. Among the possible factors involved are men's feeling neglected emotionally and sometimes denied sexually.

14. Other scholars (e.g., Chodorow [1978], Stoller [1985], and Gilmore [1990]) trace additional roots of male insecurities and feelings of abandonment to more pan-historical problems in men's separation from their mothers.

15. Calderón's (1843:456) observation that the most common crime of female prisoners whom she met was "murdering their husbands" has a distinctly contemporary ring to it.

16. Foster (1967:60–61) reports similar sentiments in Tzintzuntzan in the 1960s on the part of men and women. Vogt (1970:72) notes that in wedding ceremonies in Zinacantan in the 1960s, the groom was told to work hard, provide for his wife, and not beat her.

17. This figure was cited at the 24 October 1992 meeting of the Junta de Jefes de Manzana. New York City, by contrast, has a ratio of approximately one uniformed police officer for every 350 people.

18. Taylor (1979:154–55), in his study of colonial Mexico, found that women similarly assumed an active role in violent rebellions of the period.

19. See Davis (1990, Chap. 5) for an account of recent police activities in Los Angeles, including police activities among Mexicans living there.

20. Mexico devoted just 2.2 percent of its federal budget to military expenditures in 1989 (compared with 27.5 percent in the United States), and in that same year there was an average of 1.8 soldiers per one thousand people in Mexico (compared with 9.1 in the United States). See Barry 1990:55, Table 1d.

21. On Huehuetzin Street, Michelle and I were initially greeted by acquaintances with, "Hey, gringa/gringo, how are you today?" Later, it was more common to hear, "Hey, güera/güero, how are you today?" In other words, we had been promoted from being culturally denigrated gringos to more highly regarded güeros. The term güero, meaning roughly "blondie" or "fair-skinned," is concurrently employed by many as a compliment, in the form of racist self-denigration. In the open-air markets, sellers call out to even the most dark-skinned women and men, "Hey, güera/güero, buy some melons, chiles, brushes, underwear [etc.]."

22. One study of Mexican urban households in the 1980s concludes: "Male dignity has been so assaulted by unemployment and the necessity of relying on

women for the substance that men formerly provided, that men have taken it out on their wives, and domestic violence has increased" (Selby, Murphy, and Lorenzen 1990:176).

23. One anthropologist writes that "the 'typical' situation or context of murder and violence is a probable extension of a character-type prone to intoxication and violence and of a *machismo*-centered subculture comprising the remnants of the male version of an earlier cultural horizon. That this subgroup and subculture represent a lag in the acculturative process in which the village is involved is very important" (Romanucci-Ross 1973:149).

CHAPTER 9

1. The word *hombre* may have special resonance for aficionados of Hollywood Westerns. Expressions like "He's a tough hombre" are regularly used to conjure up images of Mexican bandits for whom life means little and sexual conquest is but part of daily life. Historically there is more than a coincidental relationship between Mexican male identities and cowboys.

2. The word *mandilón* comes from *mandil* (apron) and translates literally as "apron-er."

3. Behar (1993:40) cites an incident several decades ago involving a woman who denounced her husband in front of municipal authorities in a village in San Luis Potosí using these words: "The fact is that he's no man. He's no man because he's not responsible for his family. He never treats his family well. He treats them worse than animals!"

4. However, machismo is not necessarily the same beast in every cultural context, as we will see.

5. I have greatly benefited from discussing the topic of machismo with Carlos Monsiváis and Roger Lancaster. My gratitude is due as well to Gilberto Anguiano and Luz Fernández Gordillo of the Diccionario Español Mexicano project at the Colegio de México for their help in researching the word histories of *macho, machismo, mandilón,* and other terms relevant to male identities in Mexico.

6. For a psychological-anthropological analysis of machismo, see also Gilmore and Gilmore 1979. The role of the social sciences in the United States has not been incidental in popularizing the terms *macho* and *machismo*—for instance, in national character studies and their progeny. See, for example, Peñalosa 1968. For early published references in English to *macho,* see Beals 1928a:233, 1928b:288; and Mailer 1959:19, 483–84. For *machismo,* see Griffith 1948:50–51.

7. On the etymology of *macho,* see Gómez de Silva (1988:427) and Moliner (1991:II:299–300). On diverse and contradictory aspects of the cultural history of *macho* and *machismo,* see Mendoza 1962; Santamaría 1942:210, 1959:677; and Hodges 1986:114.

8. Even though the classic novel of the Mexican Revolution, Mariano Azuela's *Los de abajo* (first published in 1915), at one point uses the expression *machito* (1915 [1958]:70; translated as simply "a man" in Azuela 1962:79),

this does not constitute a widespread use of the word *macho* or even a familiarity with the term in the sense of machismo or any of its derivatives.

9. See Bartra 1992 for more on Ramos, Paz, and *lo mexicano*. For a recent study of these "imaginings" outside Mexico, see Bolton's (1979) investigation of machismo among Peruvian truckers.

10. A review of recent literature regarding machismo and Chicanos is outside the scope of the present study, but in addition to Limón 1989 and 1994, interested readers may profitably consult Baca Zinn 1982; Mirandé 1986; and Almaguer 1991.

11. Monsiváis is conjuring up the image of the great theatrical (operatic) macho. See also Gaarder 1954.

12. Examining masculine imagery in Brazilian popular music, Oliven (1988:90) writes that "with respect to the formation of Brazilian social identity, machismo appears as a fundamental factor."

13. Representative examples in the U.S. media of popular stereotyping of Mexican and Latin American men as uniformly macho may be found in Reston 1967 and McDowell 1984.

14.

> Yo soy mexicano, mi tierra es bravía.
> Palabra de macho, que no hay otra tierra más linda
>   y más brava que la tierra mía.
> Yo soy mexicano, y orgullo lo tengo.
> Nací despreciando la vida y la muerte,
> Y si he hecho bravatas, también las sostengo.

From the song "Yo soy mexicano."

15. It will also be recalled that the *pachuco* is the character who, not coincidentally, opens Octavio Paz's examination of Mexican essence around this time, *El laberinto de la soledad* (1950). During this period, the role of the United States, and of Mexican migrants to the United States, most of whom were men, in defining Mexicanness was often emphasized by artists and other cultural critics.

16. Mellifluous, reasoned, and eminently accessible, *Laberinto* is the canonical text not only of foreigners seeking to find out about Mexico, but of many Mexicans trying to understand themselves. A friend who directs traffic in a supermarket parking lot just outside Santo Domingo commented to me one day that, like me, his brother in a village in the state of Puebla enjoyed reading books. The last time he was in the village for a visit, my friend told me, his brother was reading a book he had borrowed from the library: *El laberinto de la soledad*. For his brother it was like reading a public opinion poll in the newspaper; *this* is what Mexican men are like, it declares, and if you're not like this then you're not a real Mexican man.

17. My thanks to Jean Franco (personal communication), who first suggested that I expand the final section of an earlier paper (Gutmann 1993a), the result of which is the present chapter.

18. Another U.S.-born writer, Ernest Hemingway, is additionally responsible for popularizing ideas about Latin heroics, also known as machismo, in the

United States. See Capellán's (1985) discussion of defiance in the face of death on the part of Hemingway's characters.

19. Another way to refer to a man-as-*mandilón* is to say, "*El es muy dejado* [He's very put upon]."

20. There is a superficial resemblance between these statements and those made to Abu-Lughod (1986:89) by a Bedouin woman about "real men": "My daughter wants a man whose eyes are open—not someone nice. Girls want someone who will drive them crazy. My daughter doesn't want to be with someone she can push around, so she can come and go as she pleases. No, she wants someone who will order her around.' " To seek an independent man would seem a similar objective in both cultural contexts. Yet there is also an important distinction in that my friend in Santo Domingo did not equate, as apparently the Bedouin woman did, such male independence with the domination of women but rather with the ability to take care of oneself and one's family—that is, to dominate "outside" circumstances.

21. The ethnographic authority of anthropologists to expound on issues of supposed "national character traits" has a long history in Mexico and elsewhere, stemming back to World War II and the need at that time to place clear national labels on enemy and allied characters (see Fabian 1983:46 ff. and Yans-McLaughlin 1986). It is unclear how long it will take contemporary anthropologists to undo such simplistic "boundary maintaining" schema.

22. The imposition by the media and by social scientists of totalizing cultural histories on countries like Mexico has been effectively challenged with regard to various sites and issues by Herzfeld 1987; Anderson 1991; and Stern 1995.

23.

> *Ahí está en la calle, brilla como el sol*
> *En su auto nuevo, qué orgulloso va*
> *Vuela por la calle, gran velocidad*
> *Todas las personas lo miran pasar*
> *Limpia parabrisas, cruza sin mirar*
> *El niño no puede el auto esquivar*
> *Sólo se oye un grito, golpe y nada más*
> *Demasiada sangre en esta ciudad.*

From the song "Un poco de sangre," on the album *El circo*. The love of the stereotyped macho for automobiles and trucks is notorious; one linguistic commentator writes about the everyday usage of the term machismo, "[T]he high rate of road accidents in L/A [Latin America], particularly perhaps in Mexico, is due to notions of *machismo*; Mexicans are, admittedly, somewhat direct and impatient in their ways but the tussle to make the crossroads first . . . was activated just as much by the feeling that it would be 'sissy' to get beaten to it" (Gerrard 1952 [1972]:99).

24. Diane Davis (personal communication) also notes that the decision to segregate men and women has as much a class logic as a gender logic. Initially at least, riders on the metro were often working class men and middle class women.

25. However, it does include this aspect, as Fernández Kelly (1976) makes

clear in a paper on some of the ideological foundations of the notion of machismo.

26. For a similar analysis involving an opposite response by a different stratum of men—the New Men's Movement in the United States—see Kimmel and Kaufman 1994.

27. On Mexican national identity, nationalism, *mexicanidad,* and *lo mexicano,* see Gamio 1916; Vasconcelos 1925; Saenz 1927; Ramos 1934; Paz 1950; Ramírez 1977; Bonfil Batalla 1987; and Bartra 1992. For English surveys and analyses of this material, see Schmidt 1978 and especially Lomnitz-Adler 1992. On the Virgen de Guadalupe in particular, see also Bushnell 1958; Wolf 1958; and Alarcón 1990.

28. See Stern 1995, who argues that archetypes of masculinity and femininity were also central to Mexican national self-definitions in the late colonial period.

29. For a detailed study of nationalism in modern Europe and its relationship to male identity, homosexuality, homoeroticism, and men's domination of women, see Mosse 1985.

CHAPTER 10

1. Adorno (1973) has also spoken at length about the notion of non-identity (see also Jameson 1990).

2. See Marx 1857–58:105. What a pity so many of Marx's readers have failed to heed this historical caveat, and have thereby turned his theories into the very fossilized abstractions that Marx long rejected.

3. Strathern (1988:64), for example, paraphrases Bowden (1984) on gender and identity in the New Guinea highlands: "In seeing men's creations as likely to represent a 'man's view of the world,' the analyst assumes that what men ponder upon is themselves, so that the artifacts that visually express 'ideals relating to masculinity' represent an idealized expression 'of what it is to be a man' (as distinct from a woman) in this or that society." Other examples are provided in Herzfeld's (1985:259–74) discussion of transformations in male identity in a Cretan village; in Dundes (1976) on the ambivalent gender of male initiates; and in di Leonardo (1991a) on the embedded nature of gender.

4. The phrase is Harold Rosenberg's and appears in an essay on Jewish art and identity (1973:231).

5. See, for example, Lavie 1990; Abu-Lughod 1991; and Narayan 1993.

6. Among scholars of Mexico, see, for example, García Canclini 1989; Bartra 1992; Lomnitz-Adler 1992, 1994; and Valenzuela Arce 1992. More broadly, see also Harvey 1989; Appadurai 1991; Bhabha 1994; and Rouse 1995.

7. See Lewis's (1951:99) comments regarding technological improvements such as *nixtamals* (commercial corn mills), which freed women from long, backbreaking labor grinding corn for tortillas on a *metate:* "Not being so tied to the *metate,* women are able to leave the house more freely and undertake more extensive commercial activities."

8. The formulation belongs to Gramsci (1929–35:80 n).

9. For a notable exception, see Lomnitz and Pérez-Lizaur 1987. Matrifocality is also, oddly enough, overreported in the social sciences for other social groups such as African Americans, regarding which, see Stack's (1974) ethnographic critique. For another example of "unexpected" matrifocality, see Stacey 1991.

10. See Hartmann 1981 for an early and important discussion of the family as the locus of struggle, and not necessarily unity, regarding gender, class, and politics.

11. Partially in response to the very independence of urban social movements in the 1980s, which represented such a rupture in popular support for the regime, Salinas launched the Solidaridad-PRONASOL program early in his administration. As one government functionary put it in 1992, "The intention behind PRONASOL is to create, through public works and services, a new urban base for the Mexican state. By the end of the 1980s the social bases of the Mexican state were unraveling" (cited in Dresser 1994:148). On Solidaridad generally, see the essays in Cornelius, Craig, and Fox 1994.

12. See Rowe and Schelling (1991:2), who write of the need to reject "a lack of confidence in the inventiveness of the popular classes and in the capacity of traditional and non-Western cultures to bring about a different modernity of their own."

13. For an extended discussion of *coraje,* see Behar 1993.

Glossary

ABNEGADA Self-sacrificing, long-suffering (as applied to a woman).

ALBAÑIL Laborer in construction. Used generically to refer to those engaged in the most despised, dirtiest, lowest-paying manual labor; similar to U.S. references to "garbagemen."

ALBUR Double-entendre joke or quip, usually with sexual overtones.

ANIMADOR(A) Organizer/facilitator in a Christian Base Community.

AVENTURA "Adventure"; extramarital affair.

AYUDAR To help.

BRAVO/A Brave; for many it carries a rural flavor.

CABRÓN "Billy-goat"; often employed figuratively to mean "cuckold." The term usually carries the weight of "bastard."

CACIQUE Neighborhood (village, etc.) political boss.

CAMPO Countryside; rural area.

CANA AL AIRE "Gray hair into the air"; extramarital "fling."

CANGURO "Kangaroo"; Snugli-type pouch carrier for infants.

CASA CHICA "Small house"; refers traditionally to a mistress and the site of adulterous assignation. Contemporary usage includes a second meaning: the second wife (or subsequent wives) of a man not legally divorced from his first wife. It can also mean a woman involved in extramarital affairs.

CHAMBA Job.

CHAQUETERO Slang for "masturbator."

CHARRO Cowboy symbolic of traditional Mexican rural virtues, known for his sombrero, horsemanship, and fancy riding clothes.

CHICHIFO Male homosexual prostitute.

CHILANGO Native of Mexico City; often used disparagingly by those from outside the capital.

CLASES POPULARES The lower working class.

COLONIA Neighborhood, barrio.

COLONIAS POPULARES Poor, working class neighborhoods.

COMAL A type of grill.

COMBI Minibus (usually VW bus); one of the main forms of public transportation in Mexico City.

COMPADRE (COMPA) Symbolic coparent.

COMPAÑERO/A Carries a meaning somewhere between "friend" and "comrade."

COMUNIDADES ECLESIALES DE BASE (CEBS) Christian base communities represent a grassroots movement within the Catholic Church in Latin America aimed at securing justice through direct efforts of clergy and lay people.

COPAS Literally, "the glasses"; refers generically to alcoholic beverages of any kind.

CORONA Popular brand of beer.

CRUDA Hangover.

CUATE Used mainly by men in Mexico to refer to a close male friend. From the Nahuatl *cuatl,* meaning "twin brother."

CUBA Drink made with Coke and either rum or brandy. (Note: I never heard it called Cuba Libre in Santo Domingo.)

CUERNOS Literally, "horns"; refers to the state of being cuckolded.

DELEGACIÓN Municipal district within Mexico City.

DESARROLLO INTEGRAL DE LA FAMILIA (DIF) Government-run family-services agency.

DOBLE JORNADA Literally, "double day"; used, with reference to women, as "second shift" is in the United States, to highlight women's having to work two "jobs," one in the home and one outside.

DON PEDRO Popular brand of brandy; also called "Don Peter" (pronounced "Don Páyter").

ESCLAVO Slave.

FAENA Collective work day.

FLOJERA Laziness.

FUTBOL Soccer.

GÜERO/A The term means roughly "blondie," or "fair-skinned," and is currently employed by many as a compliment, in the form of racist self-denigration.

HOMBRE DE VERDAD Real man.

HOMBRÍA Manliness, in the sense of whatever is considered unique about being a man.

INDÍGENA Indigenous; Indian.

LO MEXICANO Phrase referring to an essential Mexicanness.

MANDILÓN Literally, "apron-er"; man who is dominated by his wife or other women. From *mandil* (apron).

MARAQUERO Slang for "masturbator."

MARIANISMO A social science term of the last twenty years used to described the cult of the so-called long-suffering Latin American woman.

MARICÓN Derogatory expression for homosexual; like *queer* or *faggot* in English.

MESTIZO Literally, "mixed"; usually refers to the "third race" mixture of Spanish (paternal) and Indian (maternal) ancestry.

METATE Stone for grinding corn for tortillas.

MEXICANIDAD Mexicanness.

MICRO Minibus.

MIJO Contraction of *mi hijo* (my son).

MODELO Popular brand of beer.

MOLCAJETE Mortar for pounding.

MOVIMIENTOS URBANOS POPULARES (MUPS) Popular urban movements.

MUJERIEGO Womanizer.

NIXTAMAL Commercial corn mill.

NORTH AMERICAN FREE TRADE AGREEMENT (NAFTA; in Spanish, TLC) Treaty between Canada, Mexico, and the United States that went into effect 1 January 1994.

NOVIO/A Boyfriend/girlfriend.

NUEVOS MOVIMIENTOS SOCIALES New social movements.

OTRO LADO Literally, "other side"; the United States. In some contexts this also refers to homosexuals.

PALETA Popsicle.

PAPELERÍA A five and ten.

PEDREGALES Area of southern Mexico City consisting of volcanic rock, of which Colonia Santo Domingo, Colonia Ajusco, and Pueblo Los Reyes are all part.

PENDEJO/A Literally, "pubic hair"; used as the word *asshole* might be in English. Both the Spanish and English terms have a scatalogical connotation that few people actually think about when they use them.

PINCHE Depending on your dialect in English, this is an adjectival curse somewhere between "goddamned" and "fucking," as in "That *pinche* gringo." (Note: in Spain, the word originally meant "chef's assistant," and one occasionally comes across this translation, though the word never has this conotation in everyday parlance in Mexico.)

PIROPO Remark, ranging from flattery to a nasty remark, directed, usually by a young man, at a (young) woman the speaker finds attractive.

POR NECESIDAD By necessity.

PRD (PARTIDO DE LA REVOLUCIÓN DEMOCRÁTICA) Party of the Democratic Revolution; left-of-center opposition party led by Cuauhtémoc Cárdenas.

PRESIDENTE Popular brand of brandy.

PRI (PARTIDO REVOLUCIONARIO INSTITUCIONAL) Institutional Revolutionary Party; party that has been in power in Mexico for more than sixty years.

PRIMARIA Elementary school.

PROSTITUTO Male prostitute; normally refers only to those prostitutes who play the "active" role in sexual relations.

PROVINCIA The provinces; the countryside.

PULQUE Alcoholic beverage made from the sap of the maguey (agave, century plant). Made in Mexico for centuries, it has roughly the alcoholic content of beer. Without additives it is frothy and white.

PULQUERÍA Bar where pulque is sold.

PUTO Male prostitute. Usually refers to those hired by other men, but is often used to mean "sissy," "fairy," etc.

QUINCEAÑERA Girl celebrating her fifteenth birthday.

REBOZO Shawl.

RICOS (LOS) The rich.

SANTO Sacred person; e.g., Catholic saints and Jesus.

SECUNDARIA Junior high school.

SEGUNDO FRENTE "Second front"; another phrase for *casa chica*.

SOBRE RUEDAS Literally, "on wheels"; open-air market, supposedly even less expensive than a tianguis.

SOLTERO/A Unmarried, single man/woman.

SUMISA Submissive (woman).

TAXISTA Taxi driver.

TERCERA EDAD Literally, "third age"; senior citizens.

TIANGUIS Open-air market. This Nahuatl word originally referred not to a place but to the activity of commercial transactions. Thus it is still said today, "Wednesday [or another day] is the day of tianguis there."

TIENDA Small sidewalk or corner store.

TRATADO DE LIBRE COMERCIO (TLC). *See* NORTH AMERICAN FREE TRADE AGREEMENT.

TRAVESTI Transvestite.

UNIÓN LIBRE Common law marriage.

VECINDAD Block of one-room apartments with communal water spigot(s) and bath(s).

VICKYS (VICTORIA) Popular brand of beer.

VINO Usually refers in Santo Domingo to rum and *not* wine, though less often to other hard liquors or wine.

Bibliography

Abu-Lughod, Lila
   1986   *Veiled Sentiments: Honor and Poetry in a Bedouin Society.*
           Berkeley: University of California Press.
   1991   "Writing against Culture." In *Recapturing Anthropology.* Rich-
           ard G. Fox, ed. Pp. 137–62. Santa Fe, NM: School of American
           Research.
   1993   *Writing Women's Worlds: Bedouin Stories.* Berkeley: University
           of California Press.
Acevedo, Marta
   1982   *El 10 de mayo.* Mexico City: SEP.
Adorno, Theodor
   1973   *Negative Dialectics.* E. B. Ashton, trans. New York: Con-
           tinuum.
Alarcón, Norma
   1990   "Traddutora, Traditora: A Paradigmatic Figure of Chicana
           Feminism." *Cultural Critique* 13:57–87.
Almaguer, Tomás
   1991   "Chicano Men: A Cartography of Homosexual Identity and Be-
           havior." *differences* 3(2):75–100.
Alonso, Jose Antonio
   1981   *Sexo, trabajo y marginalidad urbana.* Mexico City: Editorial
           Edicol.
Americas Watch Committee
   1990   *Human Rights in Mexico: A Policy of Impunity.* New York:
           Human Rights Watch.
Anderson, Benedict
   1991   *Imagined Communities: Reflections on the Origin and Spread
           of Nationalism.* Revised ed. London: Verso.
Anzaldúa, Gloria
   1987   *Borderlands/La Frontera: The New Mestiza.* San Francisco:
           Spinsters/Aunt Lute.

Appadurai, Arjun
  1991   "Global Ethnoscapes: Notes and Queries for a Transnational
              Anthropology." In *Recapturing Anthropology*. Richard G. Fox,
              ed. Pp. 191–210. Santa Fe, NM: School of American Research.
Ariès, Philippe
  1962   *Centuries of Childhood: A Social History of Family Life*. Robert
              Baldick, trans. New York: Vintage.
Arizpe, Lourdes
  1975   *Indígenas en la ciudad: El caso de las "Marías."* Mexico City:
              SEP.
  1982   "Relay Migration and the Survival of the Peasant Household."
              In *Towards a Political Economy of Urbanization in Third
              World Countries*. Helen I. Safa, ed. Pp. 19–46. Delhi: Oxford
              University Press.
  1985   *Campesinado y migración*. Mexico City: SEP.
  1989   *Cultura y desarrollo: Una etnografía de las creencias de una
              comunidad mexicana*. Mexico City: Porrúa.
  1993   "Una sociedad en movimiento." In *Antropología breve de Mé-
              xico*. Lourdes Arizpe, ed. Pp. 373–98. Mexico City: Academia
              de la Investigación Científica.
Arrom, Silvia Marina
  1985   *The Women of Mexico City, 1790–1857*. Stanford, CA: Stan-
              ford University Press.
Asad, Talal
  1979   "Anthropology and the Analysis of Ideology." *Man* (N.S.)
              14(4):607–27.
Azuela, Mariano
  1915   (1958) *Los de abajo*. Mexico City: Fondo de Cultura Eco-
              nómica.
  1962   *The Underdogs*. E. Munguía, Jr., trans. New York: Signet.
Baca Zinn, Maxine
  1982   "Chicano Men and Masculinity." *Journal of Ethnic Studies*
              10(2):29–44.
Bar Din, Anne
  1991   *Los niños de Santa Ursula: Un estudio psicosocial de la infan-
              cia*. Mexico City: Universidad Nacional Autónoma de México.
Barkin, David
  1991   *Un desarrollo distorsionado: La integración de México a la eco-
              nomía mundial*. Mexico City: Siglo Veintiuno.
Barrett, Michèle
  1988   "Comment." In *Marxism and the Interpretation of Culture*.
              Cary Nelson and Lawrence Grossberg, eds. Pp. 268–69. Ur-
              bana: University of Illinois Press.
  1992   "Words and Things: Materialism and Method in Contemporary
              Feminist Analysis." In *Destabilizing Theory: Contemporary
              Feminist Debates*. Michèle Barrett and Anne Phillips, eds. Pp.
              201–19. Stanford, CA: Stanford University Press.

Barry, Tom, ed.
1992   *Mexico: A Country Guide.* Albuquerque: Inter-Hemispheric Education Resource Center.

Bartra, Roger
1981   *Las redes imaginarias del poder político.* Mexico City: Era.
1992   *The Cage of Melancholy: Identity and Metamorphosis in the Mexican Character.* Christopher J. Hall, trans. New Brunswick, NJ: Rutgers University Press.

Beals, Carleton
1928a   "With Sandino in Nicaragua. II. On the Sandino Front." *The Nation* 126, no. 326 (29 February):232–33.
1928b   "With Sandino in Nicaragua. IV. Sandino Himself." *The Nation* 126, no. 327 (14 March):288–89.

Beezley, William
1987   *Judas at the Jockey Club and Other Episodes of Porfirian Mexico.* Lincoln: University of Nebraska Press.

Behar, Ruth
1993   *Translated Woman: Crossing the Border with Esperanza's Story.* Boston: Beacon.

Benería, Lourdes, and Martha Roldán
1987   *The Crossroads of Class and Gender: Industrial Homework, Subcontracting, and Household Dynamics in Mexico City.* Chicago: University of Chicago Press.

Bennett, Vivienne
1992   "The Evolution of Urban Popular Movements in Mexico between 1968 and 1988." In *The Making of Social Movements in Latin America: Identity, Strategy, and Democracy.* Arturo Escobar and Sonia E. Alvarez, eds. Pp. 240–59. Boulder, CO: Westview.

Berryman, Phillip
1987   *Liberation Theology: The Essential Facts about the Revolutionary Movement in Latin America and Beyond.* New York: Pantheon.

Bhabha, Homi K.
1994   *The Location of Culture.* London: Routledge.

Bloch, Maurice
1977   "The Past and the Present in the Present." *Man* (N.S.) 12(2):278–92.

Bly, Robert
1990   *Iron John: A Book about Men.* Reading, MA: Addison-Wesley.

Bolton, Ralph
1979   "Machismo in Motion: The Ethos of Peruvian Truckers." *Ethos* 7(4):312–42.

Bonfil Batalla, Guillermo
1987   *México profundo: Una civilización negada.* Mexico City: Grijalbo.

Bossen, Laurel
    1988   "Wives and Servants: Women in Middle-Class Households,
                Guatemala City." In *Urban Life: Readings in Urban Anthropol-
                ogy.* 2nd edition. George Gmelch and Walter P. Zenner, eds.
                Pp. 265–75. Prospect Heights, IL: Waveland.
Bott, Elizabeth
    1957   (1971) *Family and Social Network: Roles, Norms, and External
                Relationships in Ordinary Urban Families.* 2nd ed. New York:
                Free Press.
Bourdieu, Pierre
    1977   *Outline of a Theory of Practice.* Richard Nice, trans. Cam-
                bridge: Cambridge University Press.
    1984   *Distinction: A Social Critique of the Judgement of Taste.* Rich-
                ard Nice, trans. Cambridge: Harvard University Press.
    1990a   *In Other Words: Essays towards a Reflexive Sociology.* Mat-
                thew Adamson, trans. Stanford, CA: Stanford University Press.
    1990b   "La domination masculine." *Actes de la recherche en sciences
                sociales* 84:2–31.
Bourque, Susan C., and Kay B. Warren
    1981   *Women of the Andes: Patriarchy and Social Change in Two
                Peruvian Towns.* Ann Arbor: University of Michigan Press.
Bowden, Ross
    1984   "Art and Gender Ideology in the Sepik." *Man* (N.S.) 19(3):445–
                58.
Bowlby, John
    1953   *Child Care and the Growth of Love.* London: Pelican.
    1969   *Attachment.* 2 vols. London: Pelican.
Brandes, Stanley
    1974   "Crianza infantil y comportamiento relativo a roles familiares
                en México." *Ethnica* (Barcelona) 8:35–47.
    1980   *Metaphors of Masculinity: Sex and Status in Andalusian Folk-
                lore.* Philadelphia: University of Pennsylvania Press.
    1987   "Sex Roles and Anthropological Research in Rural Andalusia."
                Women's Studies 13:357–72.
    1988   *Power and Persuasion: Fiestas and Social Control in Rural
                Mexico.* Philadelphia: University of Pennsylvania Press.
Brecht, Bertolt
    1966   *Galileo.* Charles Laughton, trans. New York: Grove.
Browner, Carole
    1986a   "The Politics of Reproduction in a Mexican Village." *Signs*
                11(4):710–24.
    1986b   "Gender Roles and Social Change: A Mexican Case Study."
                Ethnology 25(2):89–106.
Bruner, Edward M.
    1986   "Experience and Its Expressions." In *The Anthropology of Ex-
                perience.* Victor W. Turner and Edward M. Bruner, eds. Pp. 3–
                30. Urbana: University of Illinois Press.

Bushnell, John
    1958   "La Virgen de Guadalupe as Surrogate Mother in San Juan At-
                zingo." *American Anthropologist* 60(2):261–65.
Butler, Judith
    1990   *Gender Trouble: Feminism and the Subversion of Identity.* New
                York: Routledge.
Calderón de la Barca, Frances
    1843   (1982) *Life in Mexico.* Berkeley: University of California Press.
California Chamber of Commerce
    1993   *North American Free Trade Guide: The Emerging Mexican
                Market and Opportunities in Canada under NAFTA.* Sacra-
                mento: California Chamber of Commerce.
Campbell, Howard, and Susanne Green
    1994   "A History of Representations of Isthmus Zapotec Women."
                Working paper, Department of Sociology and Anthropology,
                University of Texas at El Paso.
Cancian, Frank
    1965   *Economics and Prestige in a Maya Community: The Religious
                Cargo System in Zinacantan.* Stanford, CA: Stanford University
                Press.
Capellán, Angel
    1985   *Hemingway and the Hispanic World.* Ann Arbor, MI: UMI Re-
                search Press.
Carrier, James G.
    1992   "Occidentalism: The World Turned Upside-Down." *American
                Ethnologist* 19(2):195–212.
Castells, Manuel
    1983   *The City and the Grassroots: A Cross-Cultural Theory of Ur-
                ban Social Movements.* Berkeley: University of California Press.
Chiñas, Beverly
    1973   *The Isthmus Zapotecs: Women's Roles in Cultural Context.*
                New York: Holt, Rinehart and Winston.
Chodorow, Nancy J.
    1978   *The Reproduction of Mothering: Psychoanalysis and the Sociol-
                ogy of Gender.* Berkeley: University of California Press.
    1989   *Feminism and Psychoanalytic Theory.* New Haven, CT: Yale
                University Press.
Clifford, James
    1988   *The Predicament of Culture: Twentieth-Century Ethnography,
                Literature, and Art.* Cambridge: Harvard University Press.
Clifford, James, and George E. Marcus, eds.
    1986   *Writing Culture: The Poetics and Politics of Ethnography.*
                Berkeley: University of California Press.
Collier, Jane F., and Sylvia J. Yanagisako, eds.
    1987   *Gender and Kinship: Essays toward a Unified Analysis.* Stan-
                ford, CA: Stanford University Press.
Comaroff, Jean, and John Comaroff
    1991   *Of Revelation and Revolution: Christianity, Colonialism, and*

Consciousness in South Africa. Vol. 1. Chicago: University of Chicago Press.

1992   *Ethnography and the Historical Imagination.* Boulder, CO: Westview Press.

Connell, R. W.

1987   *Gender and Power: Society, the Person, and Sexual Politics.* Cambridge: Polity Press.

Conover, Ted

1987   *Coyotes: A Journey through the Secret World of America's Illegal Aliens.* New York: Vintage.

Consejo Nacional de Población

1988   *Encuesta nacional sobre sexualidad y familia en jóvenes de educación media superior, 1988. (Avances de investigación.)* Mexico City.

Cornelius, Wayne A.

1975   *Politics and the Migrant Poor in Mexico City.* Stanford, CA: Stanford University Press.

Cornelius, Wayne A., Ann L. Craig, and Jonanthan Fox, eds.

1994   *Transforming State-Society Relations in Mexico: The National Solidarity Strategy.* San Diego: Center for U.S.-Mexican Studies.

Cowan, Jane K.

1990   *Dance and the Body Politic in Northern Greece.* Princeton, NJ: Princeton University Press.

Davis, Diane E.

1994   *Urban Leviathan: Mexico City in the Twentieth Century.* Philadelphia: Temple University Press.

Davis, Mike

1990   *City of Quartz: Excavating the Future in Los Angeles.* New York: Vintage.

Davis, Natalie Z.

1983   *The Return of Martin Guerre.* Cambridge: Harvard University Press.

de Barbieri, Teresita

1984   *Mujeres y vida cotidiana.* Mexico City: SEP/80.

1990   "Sobre géneros, prácticas y valores: Notas acerca de posibles erosiones del machismo en México." In *Normas y prácticas: Morales y cívicas en la vida cotidiana.* Juan Manuel Ramírez Sáiz, ed. Pp. 83–105. Mexico City: Porrúa/Universidad Nacional Autónoma de México.

de Beauvoir, Simone

1953   *The Second Sex.* H. M. Parshley, trans. New York: Knopf.

de la Fuente, Julio

1954   (1991) "Alcoholismo y sociedad." In *Antropología del alcoholismo en México: Los límites culturales de la economía política, 1930–1979.* Eduardo L. Menéndez, ed. Pp.175–87. Mexico City: Centro de Investigaciones y Estudios Superiores en Antropología Social.

de la Peña, Guillermo
 1981 *A Legacy of Promises: Agriculture, Politics, and Ritual in the Morelos Highlands of Mexico.* Austin: University of Texas Press.
de la Peña, Guillermo, Juan Manuel Durán, Agustín Escobar, and Javier García de Alba, eds.
 1990 *Crisis, conflicto, y sobreviviencia: Estudios sobre la sociedad urbana en México.* Guadalajara: Universidad de Guadalajara/ Centro de Investigaciones y Estudios Superiores en Antropología.
Departamento del Distrito Federal (DDF)
 1988 *Atlas de la ciudad de México.* Mexico City: El Colegio de México.
DeWalt, Billie
 1979 "Drinking Behavior, Economic Status, and Adaptive Strategies of Modernization in a Highland Mexican Community." *American Ethnologist* 6(3):510–30.
Diaz, May N.
 1970 *Tonalá: Conservatism, Responsibility, and Authority in a Mexican Town.* Berkeley: University of California Press.
Díaz-Guerrero, Rogelio
 1967 *Psychology of the Mexican.* Austin: University of Texas Press.
di Leonardo, Micaela
 1987 "The Female World of Cards and Holidays: Women, Families, and the Work of Kinship." *Signs* 12(3):440–53.
 1991a "Gender, Culture and Historical Economy: Feminist Anthropology in Historical Perspective." In *Gender at the Crossroads of Knowledge: Feminist Anthropology in the Postmodern Era.* Micaela di Leonardo, ed. Pp.1–48. Berkeley: University of California Press.
di Leonardo, Micaela, ed.
 1991b *Gender at the Crossroads of Knowledge: Feminist Anthropology in the Postmodern Era.* Berkeley: University of California Press.
Dresser, Denise
 1994 "Bringing the Poor Back In: National Solidarity as a Strategy of Regime Legitimation." In *Transforming State-Society Relations in Mexico: The National Solidarity Strategy.* Wayne A. Cornelius, Ann L. Craig, and Jonathan Fox, eds. Pp. 143–65. San Diego: Center for U.S.-Mexican Studies.
Dundes, Alan
 1976 "A Psychoanalytic Study of the Bullroarer." *Man* (N.S.) 11(2):220–38.
 1987 "The *Piropo* and the Dual Image of Women in the Spanish-Speaking World." With Marcelo Suárez-Orozco. In *Parsing through Customs.* Pp. 118–44. Madison: University of Wisconsin Press.

Durkheim, Emile
  1895   (1964) *The Rules of Sociological Method.* Sarah A. Solovay and
                John H. Mueller, trans. Glencoe, IL: Free Press.
  1915   (1965) *The Elementary Forms of Religious Life.* Joseph W.
                Swain, trans. New York: Free Press.
Eagleton, Terry
  1985   "Capitalism, Modernism and Postmodernism." *New Left Re-
                view* 152: 60–73.
  1991   *Ideology: An Introduction.* London: Verso.
Eckstein, Susan
  1977   *The Poverty of Revolution: The State and the Urban Poor in
                Mexico.* Princeton, NJ: Princeton University Press.
  1990   "Formal versus Substantive Democracy: Poor People's Politics
                in Mexico City." *Mexican Studies/Estudios Mexicanos*
                6(2):213–39.
Eckstein, Susan, ed.
  1989   *Power and Popular Protest: Latin American Social Movements.*
                Berkeley: University of California Press.
Ehlers, Tracy
  1991   "Debunking Marianismo: Economic Vulnerability and Survival
                Strategies among Guatemalan Wives." *Ethnology* 30(1):1–16.
Elder, Glen H., Jr.
  1978   "Family History and the Life Course." In *Transitions: The Fam-
                ily and the Life Course in Historical Perspective.* Tamara K.
                Hareven, ed. Pp. 17–64. New York: Academic Press.
  1987   "Families and Lives: Some Developments in Life-Course Stud-
                ies." In *Family History at the Crossroads.* Tamara Hareven and
                Andrejs Plakans, eds. Pp. 179–99. Princeton, NJ: Princeton Uni-
                versity Press.
Engels, Frederick
  1884a   (1970) *The Origin of the Family, Private Property and the State:
                In the Light of the Researches of Lewis H. Morgan.* In *Karl
                Marx and Frederick Engels, Selected Works.* Vol. 3. Pp. 204–
                334. Moscow: Progress Publishers.
  1884b   (1972) *The Origin of the Family, Private Property and the State:
                In the Light of the Researches of Lewis H. Morgan.* Eleanor B.
                Leacock, ed. New York: International.
Erikson, Erik
  1963   *Childhood and Society.* 2nd edition. New York: W. W. Norton.
  1968   *Identity: Youth and Crisis.* New York: W. W. Norton.
  1982   *The Life Cycle Completed: A Review.* New York: W. W.
                Norton.
Escobar, Arturo, and Sonia E. Alvarez, eds.
  1992   *The Making of Social Movements in Latin America: Identity,
                Strategy, and Democracy.* Boulder, CO: Westview.
Etienne, Mona, and Eleanor B. Leacock, eds.
  1980   *Women and Colonization: Anthropological Perspectives.* New
                York: Praeger.

Fabian, Johannes
  1983   *Time and the Other: How Anthropology Makes Its Object.*
              New York: Columbia University Press.
Fachel Leal, Ondina, ed.
  1992   *Cultura e identidade masculina.* Cadernos de Antropologia,
              no.7. Porto Alegre, Brazil: Universidade Federal do Rio Grande
              do Sul.
Fernández Kelly, M. Patricia
  1976   "Ideology of Sex in Latin America: The Case of Mexican Ma-
              chismo." Working paper, Department of Anthropology, Rut-
              gers University.
  1983   *For We Are Sold: Women and Industry in Mexico's Frontier.*
              Albany: State University of New York Press.
Flippin, J. R.
  1889   *Sketches from the Mountains of Mexico.* Cincinnati: Standard.
Foster, George
  1967   *Tzintzuntzan: Mexican Peasants in a Changing World.* Boston:
              Little, Brown.
Foucault, Michel
  1980a   *The History of Sexuality: Volume 1: An Introduction.* Robert
              Hurley, trans. New York: Vintage.
  1980b   *Herculine Barbin: Being the Recently Discovered Memoirs of a
              Nineteeth-Century French Hermaphrodite.* Richard McDou-
              gall, trans. New York: Pantheon.
  1983   "The Subject and Power." Afterword in *Michel Foucault: Be-
              yond Structuralism and Hermeneutics.* 2nd edition. Hubert L.
              Dreyfus and Paul Rabinow. Pp. 208–26. Chicago: University of
              Chicago Press.
Foweraker, Joe
  1990   "Popular Movements and Political Change in Mexico." In *Pop-
              ular Movements and Political Change in Mexico.* Joe Foweraker
              and Ann L. Craig, eds. Pp. 3–20. Boulder, CO: Reinner.
Foweraker, Joe, and Ann Craig, eds.
  1990   *Popular Movements and Political Change in Mexico.* Boulder,
              CO: Rienner.
Franco, Jean
  1988   "Beyond Ethnocentrism: Gender, Power, and the Third-World
              Intelligentsia." In *Marxism and the Interpretation of Culture.*
              Cary Nelson and Lawrence Grossberg, eds. Pp. 503–15. Ur-
              bana: University of Illinois Press.
  1989   *Plotting Women: Gender and Representation in Mexico.* New
              York: Columbia University Press.
Fraser, Nancy
  1987   "What's Critical about Critical Theory? The Case of Habermas
              and Gender." In *Feminism as Critique.* Seyla Benhabib and
              Drucilla Cornell, eds. Pp. 31–56. Minneapolis: University of
              Minnesota Press.

Fromm, Erich, and Michael Maccoby
   1970   *Social Character in a Mexican Village: A Sociopsychoanalytic Study.* Englewood Cliffs, NJ: Prentice Hall.

Gaarder, Alfred Bruce
   1954   "El habla popular y la conciencia colectiva." Ph.D. dissertation, Universidad Nacional Autónoma de México, Mexico City.

Gabayet, Luisa, Patricia García, Mercedes González de la Rocha, Silvia Lailson, and Agustín Escobar, eds.
   1988   *Mujeres y sociedad: Salario, hogar y acción social en el occidente de México.* Guadalajara: El Colegio de Jalisco.

Gamio, Manuel
   1916   (1982) *Forjando patria.* Mexico City: Porrúa.
   1935   (1987) "Nacionalismo e internacionalismo." In *Hacia un México nuevo.* Pp. 21–23. Mexico City: Instituto Nacional Indigenista.

García, Brígida, and Orlandina de Oliveira
   1993   "Trabajo femenino y vida familiar en México." Book manuscript, El Colegio de México, Centros de Estudios Demográficos y Sociológicos, Mexico City.

García, Brígida, Huberto Muñoz, and Orlandina de Oliveira
   1982   *Hogares y trabajadores en la ciudad de México.* Mexico City: Universidad Nacional Autónoma de México.

García Canclini, Néstor
   1988   "La crisis teórica en la investigación sobre cultura popular." In *Teoría e investigación en la antropología social mexicana.* Pp. 67–96. Mexico City: Centro de Investigaciones y Estudios Superiores en Antropología Social.
   1989   *Culturas híbridas: Estrategias para entrar y salir de la modernidad.* Mexico City: Grijalbo.
   1991   "Conclusiones: ¿Para qué sirve el festival?" In *Públicos de arte y política cultural: Un estudio del II Festival de la ciudad de México.* Néstor García Canclini et al., eds. Pp. 159–75. Mexico City: Universidad Autonóma Metropolitana.

García Canclini, Néstor, Patricia Safa, and Lourdes Grobet
   1989   *Tijuana: La casa de toda la gente.* Mexico City: Instituto Nacional de Antropología e Historia–Escuela Nacional de Antropología e Historia/Programa Cultural de las Fronteras, Universidad Autónoma Metropolitana–Iztapalapa/Conaculta.

Geertz, Clifford
   1986   "Making Experience, Authoring Selves." In *The Anthropology of Experience.* Victor W. Turner and Edward M. Bruner, eds. Pp. 373–80. Urbana: University of Illinois Press.
   1988   *Works and Lives: The Anthropologist as Author.* Stanford, CA: Stanford University Press.

Gerrard, A. Bryson
   1952   (1972) *Beyond the Dictionary in Spanish: A Handbook of Everyday Usage.* London: Cassell.

Giddens, Anthony
  1979   (1990) *Central Problems in Social Theory: Action, Structure
              and Contradiction in Social Analysis.* Berkeley: University of
              California Press.
  1990   *The Consequences of Modernity.* Stanford, CA: Stanford Uni-
              versity Press.
  1992   *The Transformation of Intimacy: Sexuality, Love and Erot-
              icism in Modern Societies.* Stanford, CA: Stanford University
              Press.
Gilmore, David D.
  1990   *Manhood in the Making: Cultural Concepts of Masculinity.*
              New Haven, CT: Yale University Press.
  1991   "Commodity, Comity, Community: Male Exchange in Rural
              Andalusia." *Ethnology* 30(1):17–30.
Gilmore, Margaret M., and David D. Gilmore
  1979   " 'Machismo': A Psychodynamic Approach (Spain)." *Journal of
              Psychological Anthropology* 2(3):281–99.
Godelier, Maurice
  1986   *The Making of Great Men: Male Domination and Power
              among the New Guinea Baruya.* Cambridge: Cambridge Uni-
              versity Press.
Goldsmith, Mary
  1990   "Female Household Workers in the Mexico City Metropolitan
              Area." Ph.D. dissertation, University of Connecticut, Storrs.
Gómez de Silva, Guido
  1988   *Breve diccionario etimológico de la lengua española.* Mexico
              City: El Colegio de México/Fondo de Cultura Económica.
González Casanova, Pablo
  1970   *Democracy in Mexico.* Danielle Salti, trans. London: Oxford
              University Press.
Gould, Stephen J.
  1977   *Ever since Darwin: Reflections in Natural History.* New York:
              W. W. Norton.
Gramsci, Antonio
  1929–35   (1971) *Selections from the Prison Notebooks.* New York: Inter-
              national.
Greenberg, James
  1989   *Blood Ties: Life and Violence in Rural Mexico.* Tucson: Univer-
              sity of Arizona Press.
Gregor, Thomas
  1985   *Anxious Pleasures: The Sexual Lives of an Amazonian People.*
              Chicago: University of Chicago Press.
Gregory, James R.
  1984   "The Myth of the Male Ethnographer and the Woman's
              World." *American Anthropologist* 86(2):316–27.
Griffith, Beatrice
  1948   (1973) *American Me.* Westport, CT: Greenwood.

Gudeman, Stephen, and Alberto Rivera
   1990   *Conversations in Colombia: The Domestic Economy in Life and Text.* Cambridge: Cambridge University Press.

Gutmann, Matthew C.
   1993a   "Las culturas primordiales y creatividad en los orígenes de *lo mexicano.*" *La jornada semanal* (Mexico City), no. 186 (3 January):30–38.
   1993b   "Rituals of Resistance: A Critique of the Theory of Everyday Forms of Resistance." *Latin American Perspectives* 20(2):74–92.
   1994   "Los hijos de Lewis: La sensibilidad antropológica y el caso de los pobres machos." *Alteridades* (Mexico City). 4(7):9–19.
   1997   "*Mamitis* and the Traumas of Development in a *Colonia Popular* in Mexico City." In *Small Wars: The Cultural Politics of Childhood.* Nancy Scheper-Hughes and Carolyn Sargent, eds. Berkeley: University of California Press. In press.

Habermas, Jürgen
   1985   "Questions and Counterquestions." In *Habermas and Modernity.* Richard J. Bernstein, ed. Pp. 192–216. Cambridge: MIT Press.
   1987   *The Theory of Communicative Action.* Thomas McCarthy, trans. Vol. 2. Boston: Beacon.

Hall, Stuart
   1988   "The Toad in the Garden: Thatcherism among the Theorists." In *Marxism and the Interpretation of Culture.* Cary Nelson and Lawrence Grossberg, eds. Pp.35-57. Urbana: University of Illinois Press.
   1990   "Cultural Identity and Diaspora." In *Identity, Community, Culture, Difference.* Jonathan Rutherford, ed. Pp. 222–37. London: Lawrence and Wisehart.

Haraway, Donna J.
   1991   "A Cyborg Manifesto: Science, Technology, and Socialist-Feminism in the Late Twentieth Century." In *Simians, Cyborgs, and Women: The Reinvention of Nature.* Pp. 149–81.

Hareven, Tamara K., ed.
   1978   *Transitions: The Family and the Life Course in Historical Perspective.* New York: Academic Press.

Harlow, Harry
   1971   *Learning to Love.* New York: Ballantine.

Harris, Olivia
   1980   "The Power of Signs: Gender, Culture and the Wild in the Bolivian Andes." In *Nature, Culture and Gender.* Carol MacCormack and Marilyn Strathern, eds. Pp. 70–94. Cambridge: Cambridge University Press.

Hartmann, Heidi I.
   1981   "The Family as the Locus of Gender, Class, and Political Struggle: The Example of Housework." *Signs* 6(3):366–94.

Harvey, David
    1989   *The Condition of Postmodernity: An Enquiry into the Origins of Cultural Change*. Cambridge: Blackwell.

Heath, Dwight B.
    1987   "Anthropology and Alcohol Studies: Current Issues." *Annual Review of Anthropology* 16:99–120.

Herdt, Gilbert
    1981   *Guardians of the Flutes: Idioms of Masculinity*. New York: McGraw-Hill.
    1987   *The Sambia: Ritual and Gender in New Guinea*. Fort Worth, TX: Holt, Rinehart and Winston.
    1990   "Mistaken Gender: 5-Alpha Reductase Hermaphroditism and Biological Reductionism in Sexual Identity Reconsidered." *American Anthropologist* 90(2):433–46.

Herzfeld, Michael
    1985   *The Poetics of Manhood: Contest and Identity in a Cretan Mountain Village*. Princeton, NJ: Princeton University Press.
    1987   *Anthropology through the Looking-Glass: Critical Ethnography in the Margins of Europe*. Cambridge: Cambridge University Press.

Hewitt de Alcántara, Cynthia
    1984   *Anthropological Perspectives on Rural Mexico*. London: Routledge and Kegan Paul.

Hewlett, Barry S.
    1991   *Intimate Fathers: The Nature and Context of Aka Pygmy Paternal Infant Care*. Ann Arbor: University of Michigan Press.

Hobsbawm, Eric, and Terence Ranger, eds.
    1983   *The Invention of Tradition*. Cambridge: Cambridge University Press.

Hochschild, Arlie
    1989   *The Second Shift: Working Parents and the Revolution at Home*. With Anne Machung. New York: Viking.

Hodges, Donald C.
    1986   *Intellectual Foundations of the Nicaraguan Revolution*. Austin: University of Texas Press.

Horkheimer, Max
    1972   "Authority and the Family." In *Critical Theory: Selected Essays*. Matthew J. O'Connell, trans. Pp. 47–128. New York: Herder and Herder.

Hymes, Dell
    1979   Foreword to *Portraits of "The Whiteman": Linguistic Plan and Cultural Symbols among the Western Apache,* by Keith H. Basso. Pp. ix–xviii. Cambridge: Cambridge University Press.

Ingham, John M.
    1986   *Mary, Michael, and Lucifer: Folk Catholicism in Central Mexico*. Austin: University of Texas Press.

Instituto Nacional de Estadística, Geografía e Informática
   1990   *Estados Unidos Mexicanos: Resumen general, XI censo general de población y vivienda.* Mexico City: INEGI.
   1992   *La mujer en México.* Mexico City: INEGI.
Jameson, Fredric
   1990   *Late Marxism: Adorno, or, The Persistence of the Dialectic.* London: Verso.
   1991   *Postmodernism, or, The Cultural Logic of Late Capitalism.* Durham, NC: Duke University Press.
Jelin, Elizabeth, ed.
   1991   *Family, Household and Gender Relations in Latin America.* London: Kegan Paul.
Jelin, Elizabeth, Pablo Vila, and Alicia D'Amico
   1987   *Podría ser yo: Los sectores populares urbanos en imagen y palabra.* Buenos Aires: Ediciones de la Flor.
Joseph, Gilbert
   1988   *Revolution from Without: Yucatán, Mexico, and the United States.* Durham, NC: Duke University Press.
Kaplan, Temma
   1982   "Female Consciousness and Collective Action: The Case of Barcelona, 1910–1918." *Signs* 7(3):545–60.
Kearney, Michael
   1972   *The Winds of Ixtepeji: World View and Society in a Zapotec Town.* New York: Holt, Rinehart and Winston.
   1996   *Reconceptualizing the Peasantry: Anthropology in Global Perspective.* Boulder, CO: Westview Press.
Keesing, Roger M.
   1987   "Anthropology as Interpretive Quest." *Current Anthropology* 28(2):161–76.
   1992   *Custom and Confrontation: The Kwaio Struggle for Cultural Autonomy.* Chicago: University of Chicago Press.
Kemper, Robert V.
   1977   *Migration and Adaptation: Tzintzuntzan Peasants in Mexico City.* Beverly Hills, CA: SAGE.
Kennedy, John G.
   1978   *Tarahumara of the Sierra Madre: Beer, Ecology, and Social Organization.* Arlington Heights, IL: AHM Publishing.
Kimmel, Michael S., and Michael Kaufman
   1994   "Weekend Warriors: The New Men's Movement." Working paper, Department of Sociology, State University of New York at Stony Brook.
Kushner, Tony
   1992   *Angels in America, Part One: Millennium Approaches.* New York: Theatre Communications Group.
Lafaye, Jacques
   1976   *Quetzalcóatl and Guadalupe: The Formation of Mexican Na-*

tional Consciousness, 1531–1813. Benjamin Keen, trans. Chicago: University of Chicago Press.

Lamas, Marta
1992   "El feminismo mexicano y la lucha por legalizar el aborto." *Política y Cultura* (Mexico City) 1:9–22.

Lamphere, Louise
1987   "Feminism and Anthropology: The Struggle to Reshape Our Thinking about Gender." In *The Impact of Feminist Research in the Academy*. Christie Farnham, ed. Pp. 11–33. Bloomington: Indiana University Press.

Lamphere, Louise, Patricia Zavella, and Felipe Gonzales
1993   *Sunbelt Working Mothers: Reconciling Family and Factory*. Ithaca, NY: Cornell University Press.

Lancaster, Roger
1992   *Life Is Hard: Machismo, Danger, and the Intimacy of Power in Nicaragua*. Berkeley: University of California Press.

Laqueur, Thomas
1990   *Making Sex: Body and Gender from the Greeks to Freud*. Cambridge: Harvard University Press.

Lavie, Smadar
1990   *The Poetics of Military Occupation: Mzeina Allegories of Bedouin Identity under Israeli and Egyptian Rule*. Berkeley: University of California Press.

Lavie, Smadar, Kirin Narayan, and Renato Rosaldo, eds.
1993   *Creativity/Anthropology*. Ithaca, NY: Cornell University Press.

Leach, E. R.
1958   "Magical Hair." *Journal of the Royal Anthropological Institute* 88:147–64.

Leacock, Eleanor B.
1981   *Myths of Male Dominance: Collected Articles on Women Cross-Culturally*. New York: Monthly Review.

Leacock, Eleanor B., and Helen I. Safa, eds.
1986   *Women's Work: Development and the Division of Labor by Gender*. Boston: Bergin and Garvey.

Leñero Otero, Luis
1993   "Los varones mexicanos ante la planificación familiar." Working paper, Instituto Mexicano de Estudios Sociales, Cuernavaca.

Leñero, Vicente
1970   *Los albañiles*. Mexico City: Joaquín Mortiz.

Lever, Janet
1983   *Soccer Madness*. Chicago: University of Chicago Press.

Lewis, Oscar
1951   (1963) *Life in a Mexican Village: Tepoztlán Restudied*. Urbana: University of Illinois Press.
1952   "Urbanization without Breakdown." *Scientific Monthly* 75:31–41.

1959   *Five Families: Mexican Case Studies in the Culture of Poverty.*
            New York: Basic Books.
1961   *The Children of Sánchez: Autobiography of a Mexican Family.*
            New York: Vintage.

Liguori, Ana Luisa, and Gerardo Ortega
1990   "Vestidas y alborotadas." In *El nuevo arte de amar: Usos y cos-*
            tumbres sexuales en México. Hermann Bellinghausen, ed. Pp.
            107–12. Mexico City: Cal y Arena.

Lima Barrios, Francisca G.
1992   *Familia popular, sus prácticas y la conformación de una cultura.*
            Mexico City: Instituto Nacional de Antropología e Historia.

Limón, José
1982   "History, Chicano Joking, and the Varieties of Higher Educa-
            tion: Tradition and Performance as Critical Symbolic Action."
            Journal of the Folklore Institute 19:141–66.
1989   "*Carne, Carnales,* and the Carnivalesque: Bakhtinian *Batos,*
            Disorder, and Narrative Discourses." *American Ethnologist*
            16(3):471–86.
1994   *Dancing with the Devil: Society and Cultural Poetics in Mexi-*
            can-American South Texas. Madison: University of Wisconsin
            Press.

Loaeza, Soledad, and Claudio Stern, eds.
1990   *Las clases medias en la coyuntura actual.* Mexico City: El Cole-
            gio de México.

Logan, Kathleen
1984   *Haciendo Pueblo: The Development of a Guadalajaran Suburb.*
            University: University of Alabama Press.

Lomnitz, Larissa A.
1977   *Networks and Marginality: Life in a Mexican Shantytown.*
            Cinna Lomnitz, trans. New York: Academic Press.

Lomnitz, Larissa A., and Marisol Pérez-Lizaur
1987   *A Mexican Elite Family: 1820–1980.* Princeton, NJ: Princeton
            University Press.

Lomnitz-Adler, Claudio
1992   *Exits from the Labyrinth: Culture and Ideology in the Mexican*
            National Space. Berkeley: University of California Press.
1994   "Decadence in Times of Globalization." *Cultural Anthropology*
            9(2):257–67.

Maccoby, Michael
1972   "Alcoholism in a Mexican Village." In *The Drinking Man.* Da-
            vid C. McClelland et al., eds. Pp. 232–60. New York: Free
            Press.

MacCormack, Carol, and Marilyn Strathern, eds.
1980   *Nature, Culture and Gender.* Cambridge: Cambridge University
            Press.

Madsen, William, and Claudia Madsen
  1969   "The Cultural Structure of Mexican Drinking Behavior." *Quarterly Journal of Studies on Alcohol* 30(3):701–18.
Magaña, J. R., and J. M. Carrier
  1991   "Mexican and Mexican American Male Sexual Behavior and Spread of AIDS in California." *Journal of Sex Research* 28(3):425–41.
Mailer, Norman
  1959   *Advertisements for Myself.* New York: G. P. Putnam's Sons.
Malinowski, Bronislaw
  1930   (1964) "Parenthood, the Basis of Social Structure." In *The Family: Its Structure and Functions.* Rose L. Coser, ed. Pp. 3–19. New York: St. Martin's.
Mallon, Florencia E.
  1995   *Peasant and Nation: The Making of Postcolonial Mexico and Peru.* Berkeley: University of California Press.
Mannheim, Karl
  1936   *Ideology and Utopia: An Introduction to the Sociology of Knowledge.* Louis Wirth and Edward Shils, trans. New York: Harcourt, Brace.
Marcus, George E., and Michael M. J. Fischer
  1986   *Anthropology as Cultural Critique: An Experimental Moment in the Human Sciences.* Chicago: University of Chicago Press.
Marshall, Mac
  1979   *Weekend Warriors: Alcohol in a Micronesian Culture.* Palo Alto, CA: Mayfield.
Martin, JoAnn
  1990   "Motherhood and Power: The Production of a Woman's Culture of Politics in a Mexican Community." *American Ethnologist* 17(3):470–90.
Marx, Karl
  1845   (1969) "Theses on Feuerbach." In *Karl Marx and Frederick Engels, Selected Works.* Vol. 1, pp. 13–15. Moscow: Progress Publishers.
  1857–58 (1973) *Grundrisse: Foundations of the Critique of Political Economy.* Martin Nicolaus, trans. Harmonsworth, England: Penguin/New Left Review.
  1867   (1967) *Capital: A Critique of Political Economy.* 3 vols. New York: International Publishers.
Massolo, Alejandra
  1992a   *Por amor y coraje: Mujeres en movimientos urbanos de la ciudad de México.* Mexico City: El Colegio de México.
Massolo, Alejandra, ed.
  1992b   *Mujeres y ciudades: Participación social, vivienda y vida cotidiana.* Mexico City: El Colegio de México.

Massolo, Alejandra, and Martha Schteingart, eds.
1987   *Participación social, reconstrucción y mujer: El sismo de 1985.*
            Mexico City: El Colegio de México.
Matthews, Holly F.
1987   "Intracultural Variation in Beliefs about Gender in a Mexican
            Community." *American Behavioral Scientist* 31(2):219–33.
McDowell, Bart
1984   "Mexico City: An Alarming Giant." *National Geographic*
            166(2):138–78.
Mead, Margaret
1928   (1954) *Coming of Age in Samoa.* New York: Mentor.
1935   (1963) *Sex and Temperament in Three Primitive Societies.* New
            York: Laurel.
1949   *Male and Female: A Study of the Sexes in a Changing World.*
            New York: William Morrow.
Mead, Margaret, and Martha Wolfenstein, eds.
1955   *Childhood in Contemporary Cultures.* Chicago: University of
            Chicago Press.
Mendoza, Vicente T.
1962   "El machismo en México." *Cuadernos del Instituto Nacional
            de Investigaciones Folklóricas* (Buenos Aires) 3:75–86.
Menéndez, Eduardo L.
1987   *Alcoholismo II: La alcoholización, un proceso olvidado . . . pa-
            tología, integración funcional o representación cultural.* Mexico
            City: Centro de Investigaciones y Estudios Superiores en Antro-
            pología Social.
1990   *Morir de alcohol: Saber y hegemonía médica.* Mexico City: Gri-
            jalbo.
1991   "Alcoholismo y proceso de alcoholización: La construcción de
            una propuesta antropológica." In *Antropología del alcoholismo
            en México: Los límites culturales de la economía política 1930–
            1979.* Eduardo L. Menéndez, ed. Pp. 13–32. Mexico City:
            Centro de Investigaciones y Estudios Superiores en Antropo-
            logía Social.
Menéndez, Eduardo L., ed.
1992   *Práctica e ideologías "científicas" y "populares" respecto del
            "alcoholismo" en México.* Mexico City: Centro de Investiga-
            ciones y Estudios Superiores en Antropología Social.
Mercado, Angel
1989   *Arturo Loppe López: Gestor urbano.* Mexico City: Universidad
            Autónoma Metropolitana–Xochimilco.
Mernissi, Fatima
1975   (1987) *Beyond the Veil: Male-Female Dynamics in Modern
            Muslim Society.* Bloomington: University of Indiana Press.
Miano Borruso, Marinella
1993   "Mujeres zapotecas: El enigma del matriarcado." Working pa-
            per, Escuela Nacional de Antropología e Historia, Mexico City.

Mirandé, Alfredo
1986   "Qué gacho es ser macho: It's a Drag to Be a Macho Man."
        Aztlán 17(2):63–89.
Moliner, María
1991   *Diccionario de uso del español.* 2 vols. Madrid: Gredos.
Monsiváis, Carlos
1976   (1983) "La nación de unos cuantos y las esperanzas románticas
        (Notas sobre la historia del término 'Cultura Nacional' en Mé-
        xico)." In *En torno a la cultura nacional.* Héctor Aguilar
        Camín, ed. Pp. 159–221. Mexico City: Instituto Nacional Indi-
        genista/SepOchentas.
1981   *Escenas de pudor y liviandad.* Mexico City: Grijalbo.
1987   *Entrada libre: Crónicas de la sociedad que se organiza.* Mexico
        City: Era.
1990   "Paisaje de batalla entre condones." In *El nuevo arte de amar:
        Usos y costumbres sexuales en México.* Hermann Belling-
        hausen, ed. Pp. 165–79. Mexico City: Cal y Arena.
1992   "Las mitologías del cine mexicano." *Intermedios* 2:12–23.
Montaño, Jorge
1976   *Los pobres de la ciudad en los asentamientos espontáneos.*
        Mexico City: Siglo Veintiuno.
Moore, Henrietta L.
1988   *Feminism and Anthropology.* Minneapolis: University of Min-
        nesota Press.
Morrison, Toni
1987   *Beloved.* New York: New American Library.
Mosse, George L.
1985   *Nationalism and Sexuality: Respectability and Abnormal Sexu-
        ality in Modern Europe.* New York: Howard Fertig.
Mukerji, Chandra, and Michael Schudson
1991   "Rethinking Popular Culture." In *Rethinking Popular Culture:
        Contemporary Perspectives in Cultural Studies.* Chandra Muk-
        erji and Michael Schudson, eds. Pp. 1–61. Berkeley: University
        of California Press.
Nader, Laura
1986   "The Subordination of Women in Comparative Perspective."
        Urban Anthropology 15(3–4):377–97.
1990   *Harmony Ideology: Justice and Control in a Zapotec Mountain
        Village.* Stanford, CA: Stanford University Press.
Narayan, Kirin
1993   "How Native is a 'Native' Anthropologist?" *American Anthro-
        pologist* 95(3):671–86.
Nash, June
1970   (1985) *In the Eyes of the Ancestors: Belief and Behavior in a
        Mayan Community.* Prospect Heights, IL: Waveland.

Nash, June, and Helen I. Safa, eds.
  1986   *Women and Change in Latin America*. New York: Bergin and
            Garvey.
Navarro, Bernardo, and Pedro Moctezuma
  1989   *La urbanización en la ciudad de México*. Mexico City: Universi-
            dad Nacional Autónoma de México.
Nutini, Hugo, Pedro Carrasco, and James Taggart, eds.
  1976   *Essays on Mexican Kinship*. Pittsburgh: University of Pittsburgh
            Press.
Oliveira, Orlandina de, ed.
  1989   *Trabajo, poder y sexualidad*. Mexico City: El Colegio de
            México.
Oliven, Ruben George
  1988   " 'The Woman Makes (and Breaks) the Man': The Masculine
            Imagery in Brazilian Popular Music." *Latin American Music
            Review* 9(1):90–108.
Ortner, Sherry B.
  1989–90   "Gender Hegemonies." *Cultural Critique* 14:35–80.
Ortner, Sherry B., and Harriet Whitehead, eds.
  1981   *Sexual Meanings: The Cultural Construction of Gender and
            Sexuality*. Cambridge: Cambridge University Press.
Paredes, Américo
  1966   "The Anglo-American in Mexican Folklore." In *New Voices in
            American Studies*. Pp. 113–27. Lafayette, IN: Purdue University
            Press.
  1967   "Estados Unidos, México y el machismo." *Journal of Inter-
            American Studies* 9(1):65–84.
  1971   "The United States, Mexico, and Machismo." Marcy Steen,
            trans. *Journal of the Folklore Institute* 8(1):17–37.
Parker, Richard G.
  1991   *Bodies, Pleasures, and Passions: Sexual Culture in Contempo-
            rary Brazil*. Boston: Beacon.
Paz, Octavio
  1950   (1959) *El laberinto de la soledad*. Mexico City: Fondo de Cul-
            tura Económica.
  1961   *The Labyrinth of Solitude: Life and Thought in Mexico*. Ly-
            sander Kemp, trans. New York: Grove.
  1985   "Return to the Labyrinth of Solitude." In *The Labyrinth of Soli-
            tude and Other Writings*. Yara Milos, trans. Pp. 327–53. New
            York: Grove.
Peñalosa, Fernando
  1968   "Mexican Family Roles." *Journal of Marriage and the Family*
            28:680–89.
Poniatowska, Elena
  1969   *Hasta no verte Jesús mío*. Mexico City: Era.
  1975   *Massacre in Mexico*. Helen R. Lane, trans. New York: Viking.
  1988   *Nada, nadie: Las voces del temblor*. Mexico City: Era.

Pozas, Ricardo
   1962   *Juan the Chamula: An Ethnological Re-creation of the Life of a
             Mexican Indian.* Lysander Kemp, trans. Berkeley: University of
             California Press.
Pratt, Mary Louise
   1990   "Women, Literature, and National Brotherhood." In *Women,
             Culture and Politics in Latin America.* Pp. 48–73. Berkeley: Uni-
             versity of California Press.
Prawda, Juan
   1989   *Logros, inequidades y retos del futuro del sistema educativo
             mexicano.* Mexico City: Grijalbo.
Ramírez, Armando
   1972   (1985) *Chin Chin el teporocho.* Mexico City: Grijalbo.
Ramírez, Santiago
   1977   *El mexicano: Psicología de sus motivaciones.* Mexico City: Gri-
             jalbo.
Ramírez Sáiz, Juan Manuel
   1986   *El movimiento urbano popular en México.* Mexico City: Siglo
             Veintiuno.
Ramos, Samuel
   1934   (1992) *El perfil del hombre y la cultura en México.* Mexico City:
             Espasa-Calpe Mexicana.
   1962   (1975) *Profile of Man and Culture in Mexico.* Peter G. Earle,
             trans. Austin: University of Texas Press.
Redfield, Robert
   1941   *The Folk Culture of Yucatan.* Chicago: University of Chicago
             Press.
Reguillo, Rossana
   1993   "La ciudad de los milagros: Movimientos sociales y políticas
             culturales." Paper presented at International Congress of An-
             thropological and Ethnological Sciences, Mexico City.
Reiter, Rayna R., ed.
   1975   *Toward an Anthropology of Women.* New York: Monthly Re-
             view.
Reston, James
   1967   "Santiago: The Cult of Virility in Latin America." *New York
             Times,* 9 April, Sec. 4, p. 12.
Rich, Adrienne
   1976   *Of Woman Born: Motherhood as Experience and Institution.*
             New York: W. W. Norton.
Riquer, María Florinda
   1989   "Las mujeres del Movimiento Popular de Pueblos y Colonias
             del Sur (MPPCS): Un discurso sobre sí mismas." M.A. thesis,
             Universidad Iberoamericana, Mexico City.
Romanucci-Ross, Lola
   1973   *Conflict, Violence, and Morality in a Mexican Village.* Palo
             Alto, CA: National Press Books.

Romney, Kimball, and Romaine Romney
    1963   "The Mixtecans of Juxtlahuaca, Mexico." In *Six Cultures: Studies in Child Rearing*. Beatrice B. Whiting, ed. Pp. 541–691. New York: John Wiley.
Room, Robin
    1984   "Alcohol and Ethnography: A Case of Problem Deflation?" *Current Anthropology* 25(2):169–91.
Rosaldo, Michelle Z.
    1974   "Woman, Culture, and Society: A Theoretical Overview." In *Woman, Culture, and Society*. Michelle Z. Rosaldo and Louise Lamphere, eds. Pp. 17–42. Stanford, CA: Stanford University Press.
    1980   "The Use and Abuse of Anthropology: Reflections on Feminism and Cross-Cultural Understanding." *Signs* 5(3):389–417.
Rosaldo, Michelle Z., and Louise Lamphere, eds.
    1974   *Woman, Culture, and Society*. Stanford, CA: Stanford Universty Press.
Rosaldo, Renato
    1993   *Culture and Truth: The Remaking of Social Analysis*. Boston: Beacon.
Roseberry, William
    1989   *Anthropologies and Histories: Essays in Culture, History, and Political Economy*. New Brunswick, NJ: Rutgers University Press.
Rosenberg, Harold
    1973   "Pictures of Jews." In *Discovering the Present: Three Decades in Art, Culture, and Politics*. Pp. 232–35. Chicago: University of Chicago Press.
Rosenblueth, Ingrid
    1984   *Roles conyugales y redes de relaciones sociales*. Cuadernos Universitarios 15. Mexico City: Universidad Autónoma Metropolitana–Iztapalapa.
Rouse, Roger
    1991   "Mexican Migration and the Social Space of Postmodernism." *Diaspora* 1(1):8–23.
    1995   "Thinking Through Transnationalism: Notes on the Cultural Politics of Class Relations in the Contemporary United States." *Public Culture* 7(2):353–402.
Rowe, William, and Vivian Schelling
    1991   *Memory and Modernity: Popular Culture in Latin America*. London: Verso.
Rubin, Gayle
    1975   "The Traffic in Women: Notes on the 'Political Economy' of Sex." In *Toward an Anthropology of Women*. Rayna R. Reiter, ed. Pp. 157–210. New York: Monthly Review.
    1982   (1993) "Thinking Sex: Notes for a Radical Theory of the Politics of Sexuality." In *The Lesbian and Gay Studies Reader*.

Henry Abelove, Michèle Aina Barale, and David M. Halperin, eds. Pp. 3–44. New York: Routledge.

Rubin-Kurtzman, Jane Rhonda
1991   "From Prosperity to Adversity: The Labor Force Participation of Women in Mexico City, 1970–1976." Ph.D. dissertation, University of California, Los Angeles.

Ruddick, Sara
1989   *Maternal Thinking: Toward a Politics of Peace.* Boston: Beacon.

Rulfo, Juan
1955   (1986) *Pedro Páramo.* Mexico City: Fondo de Cultura Económica.

1959   *Pedro Páramo.* Lysander Kemp, trans. New York: Grove.

Ruvalcaba Mercado, Jesús
1991   *Sociedad y violencia: Extracción y concentración de excedentes en la Huasteca.* Mexico City: Centro de Investigaciones y Estudios Superiores en Antropología Social.

Sacks, Karen
1979   *Sisters and Wives: The Past and Future of Sexual Inequality.* Westport, CT: Greenwood.

1988   *Caring by the Hour: Women, Work and Organizing at Duke Medical Center.* Urbana: University of Illinois Press.

Saenz, Moises
1927   "The Two Sides of Mexican Nationalism." *Current History,* September, pp. 908–12.

Safa, Patricia
1991   *¿Por qué se envia a los hijos a la escuela?* Mexico City: Grijalbo.

Sánchez Gómez, Martha Judith
1989   "Consideraciones teórico-metodológicas en el estudio del trabajo doméstico en México." In *Trabajo, poder y sexualidad.* Orlandina de Oliveira, ed. Pp. 59–79. Mexico City: El Colegio de México.

Santamaría, Francisco J.
1942   *Diccionario general de americanismos.* 2 vols. Mexico City: Pedro Robredo.

1959   *Diccionario de mejicanismos.* Mexico City: Porrúa.

Sapir, Edward
1924   (1949) "Culture, Genuine and Spurious." In *Selected Writings of Edward Sapir.* David G. Mandelbaum, ed. Pp. 308–31. Berkeley: University of California Press.

1929   (1949) "The Status of Linguistics as a Science." In *Selected Writings of Edward Sapir,* David G. Mandelbaum, ed. Pp. 160–66. Berkeley: University of California Press.

Scheper-Hughes, Nancy
1983   "Introduction: The Problem of Bias in Androcentric and Feminist Anthropology." *Women's Studies* 10:109–16.

1984   "The Margaret Mead Controversy: Culture, Biology and Anthropological Inquiry." *Human Organization* 43(1):85–93.

1992   *Death without Weeping: The Violence of Everyday Life in Bra-*
                zil. Berkeley: University of California.
Schmidt, Henry C.
1978   *The Roots of* Lo Mexicano: *Self and Society in Mexican*
                Thought, 1900–1934. College Station: Texas A&M Press.
Schneider, David, and Raymond Smith
1973   *Class Differences and Sex Roles in American Kinship and Fam-*
                ily Structure. Englewood Cliffs, NJ: Prentice-Hall.
Scott, James C.
1985   *Weapons of the Weak: Everyday Forms of Peasant Resistance.*
                New Haven, CT: Yale University Press.
Scott, Joan W.
1988   *Gender and the Politics of History.* New York: Columbia Uni-
                versity Press.
1990   "Deconstructing Equality-versus-Difference." In *Conflicts in*
                Feminism. Marianne Hirsch and Evelyn Fox Keller, eds. Pp.
                134–48. New York: Routledge.
Secretaría de Salud, Dirección General de Planificación Familiar
1990   *Informe de la encuesta sobre conocimiento, actitud y práctica*
                en el uso de métodos anticonceptivos de la población masculina
                obrera del área metropolitana de la ciudad de México. Mexico
                City.
Sedgwick, Eve Kosofsky
1990   *Epistemology of the Closet.* Berkeley: University of California
                Press.
Selby, Henry
1976   "The Study of Social Organization in Traditional Mesoamer-
                ica." In *Essays on Mexican Kinship.* Hugo G. Nutini, Pedro
                Carrasco, and James M. Taggart, eds. Pp. 29–43. Pittsburgh:
                University of Pittsburgh Press.
Selby, Henry, Arthur Murphy, and Stephen Lorenzen
1990   *The Mexican Urban Household: Organizing for Self-Defense.*
                Austin: University of Texas Press.
Shorter, Edward
1977   *The Making of the Modern Family.* New York: Basic Books.
Simic, Andrei
1969   "Management of the Male Image in Yugoslavia." *Anthropolog-*
                ical Quarterly 42:89–101.
1983   "Machismo and Cryptomatriarchy." *Ethos* 11(1–2):66–86.
Slater, David, ed.
1985   *New Social Movements and the State in Latin America.* Cin-
                naminson, NJ: FORIS Publications.
Smith, Carol
1984   "Local History in a Global Context: Social Relations and Eco-
                nomic Transitions in Western Guatemala." *Comparative Stud-*
                ies in Society and History 26(2):193–228.

Soja, Edward W.
1989   *Postmodern Geographies: The Reassertion of Space in Critical Social Theory.* London: Verso.

Spiro, Melford E.
1958   (1975) *Children of the Kibbutz: A Study in Child Training and Personality.* Revised edition. Cambridge: Harvard University Press.

Stacey, Judith
1991   *Brave New Families: Stories of Domestic Upheaval in Late Twentieth Century America.* New York: Basic Books.

Stack, Carol
1974   *All Our Kin: Strategies for Survival in a Black Community.* New York: Harper and Row.

Stanley, Alessandra
1994   "Sexual Harassment Thrives in the New Russian Climate." *New York Times,* National Edition, 17 April, Sec. 1, pp. 1, 7.

Stavenhagen, Rodolfo
1975   *Social Classes in Agrarian Societies.* Judy Adler Hellman, trans. Garden City, NY: Anchor.

Stephen, Lynn
1991   *Zapotec Women.* Austin: University of Texas.
1997   *Women and Social Movements in Latin America: Power from Below.* Austin: University of Texas Press.

Stern, Steve
1995   *The Secret History of Gender: Women, Men, and Power in Late Colonial Mexico.* Chapel Hill: University of North Carolina Press.

Stevens, Evelyn
1973   "*Marianismo:* The Other Face of *Machismo* in Latin America." In *Male and Female in Latin America.* Ann Pescatello, ed. Pp. 89–101. Pittsburgh: University of Pittsburgh Press.

Steward, Julian
1955   (1972) *Theory of Culture Change.* Urbana: University of Illinois Press.

Stoller, Robert J.
1985   "Facts and Fancies: An Examination of Freud's Concept of Bisexuality." In *Women and Analysis: Dialogues on Psychoanalytic Views of Femininity.* Jean Strouse, ed. Pp. 343–64. Boston: G. K. Hall.

Strathern, Marilyn
1980   "No Nature, No Culture: The Hagen Case." In *Nature, Culture and Gender.* Carol MacCormack and Marilyn Strathern, eds. Pp. 174–222. Cambridge: Cambridge University Press.
1988   *Gender of the Gift: Problems with Women and Problems with Society in Melanesia.* Berkeley: University of California Press.

Strathern, Marilyn, ed.
    1987   *Dealing with Inequality: Analysing Gender Relations in Mel-
              anesia and Beyond.* Cambridge: Cambridge University Press.
Suárez-Orozco, Marcelo
    1982   "A Study of Argentine Soccer: The Dynamics of Its Fans and
              Their Folklore." *Journal of Psychoanalytic Anthropology*
              5(1):7–28.
Taggart, James M.
    1979   "Men's Changing Image of Women in Nahuat Oral Tradition."
              American Ethnologist 6(4):723–41.
    1992a   "Gender Segregation and Cultural Constructions of Sexuality in
              Two Hispanic Societies." *American Ethnologist* 19(1):75–96.
    1992b   "Fathering and the Cultural Construction of Brothers in Two
              Hispanic Societies." *Ethos* 20(4):421–52.
Tambiah, Stanley J.
    1990   *Magic, Science, Religion, and the Scope of Rationality.* Cam-
              bridge: Cambridge University Press.
Taylor, William B.
    1979   *Drinking, Homicide, and Rebellion in Colonial Mexican Vil-
              lages.* Stanford, CA: Stanford University Press.
Thompson, E. P.
    1971   "The Moral Economy of the English Crowd." *Past and Present*
              50:76–136.
    1993   "Custom and Culture." *Customs in Common: Studies in Tradi-
              tional Popular Culture.* Pp.1–15. New York: New Press.
Thorne, Barrie, and Marilyn Yalom, eds.
    1992   *Rethinking the Family: Some Feminist Questions.* Revised edi-
              tion. Boston: Northeastern University Press.
Tsing, Anna Lowenhaupt
    1993   *In the Realm of the Diamond Queen: Marginality in an Out-of-
              the-Way Place.* Princeton, NJ: Princeton University Press.
Turner, Victor W.
    1969   (1977) *The Ritual Process: Structure and Anti-Structure.* Ithaca,
              NY: Cornell University Press.
    1974   *Dramas, Fields, and Metaphors: Symbolic Action in Human So-
              ciety.* Ithaca, NY: Cornell University Press.
UNESCO
    1991   *Statistical Yearbook, 1991.* Paris: UNESCO.
Usigli, Rodolfo
    1947   (1985) *El Gesticulador.* Mexico City: Editores Mexicanos
              Unidos.
Valenzuela Arce, José Manuel, ed.
    1992   *Decadencia y auge de las identidades: Cultura nacional, identi-
              dad cultural y modernización.* Tijuana: El Colegio de la Front-
              era Norte.
Vasconcelos, José
    1925   (1992) *La raza cósmica.* Mexico City: Espasa-Calpe.

Vélez-Ibáñez, Carlos G.
  1983   *Rituals of Marginality: Politics, Process, and Culture Change in Urban Central Mexico, 1969–74.* Berkeley: University of California Press.
Vogt, Evon Z.
  1970   *The Zinacantecos of Mexico: A Modern Maya Way of Life.* New York: Holt, Rinehart and Winston.
Ward, Peter
  1976   "The Squatter Settlement as Slum or Housing Solution." *Land Economics* 52(3):330–46.
  1990   *Mexico City: The Production and Reproduction of an Urban Environment.* Boston: G. K. Hall.
Watts, Michael J.
  1992   "Capitalisms, Crises, and Cultures I: Notes toward a Totality of Fragments." In *Reworking Modernity: Capitalisms and Symbolic Discontent.* Allan Pred and Michael J. Watts, eds. Pp. 1–19. New Brunswick, NJ: Rutgers University Press.
Weber, Max
  1919   (1946) "Politics as a Vocation." In *From Max Weber: Essays in Sociology.* H. H. Gerth and C. Wright Mills, trans. and eds. Pp. 77–128. New York: Oxford University Press.
Welzer-Lang, Daniel, and Marie-France Pichevin, eds.
  1992   *Des hommes et du masculin.* Centre de Recherches et d'Etudes Anthropologiques. Lyon: Presses Universitaires.
Whiting, Beatrice B., ed.
  1963   *Six Cultures: Studies in Child Rearing.* New York: John Wiley.
Wickham-Crowley, Timothy P.
  1992   *Guerrillas and Revolution in Latin America: A Comparative Study of Insurgents and Regimes since 1956.* Princeton, NJ: Princeton University Press.
Williams, Raymond
  1973   *The Country and the City.* New York: Oxford University Press.
  1977   *Marxism and Literature.* Oxford: Oxford University Press.
Willis, Paul
  1979   *Learning to Labor: How Working Class Kids Get Working Class Jobs.* New York: Columbia University Press.
Winnicott, Donald W.
  1987   *Babies and Their Mothers.* Reading, MA: Addison-Wesley.
Wolf, Eric
  1958   "The Virgin of Guadalupe: A Mexican National Symbol." *Journal of American Folklore* 71:34–39.
  1982   *Europe and the People without History.* Berkeley: University of California Press.
Yanagisako, Sylvia J.
  1977   "Women-Centered Kin Networks in Urban Bilateral Kinship." *American Ethnologist* 3(2):207–26.

1979   "Family and Household: The Analysis of Domestic Groups."
             Annual Review of Anthropology 8:161–205.

Yanagisako, Sylvia J., and Jane F. Collier
1987   "Toward a Unified Analysis of Gender and Kinship." In *Gender
             and Kinship: Essays toward a Unified Analysis.* Jane F. Collier
             and Sylvia J. Yanagisako, eds. Pp. 14–50. Stanford, CA: Stan-
             ford University Press.

Yans-McLaughlin, Virginia
1986   "Science, Democracy, and Ethics: Mobilizing Culture and Per-
             sonality for World War II." In *Malinowski, Rivers, Benedict
             and Others.* George W. Stocking, Jr., ed. Pp. 184–217. Madi-
             son: University of Wisconsin Press.

Young, Gay
1993   "Gender Inequality and Industrial Development: The House-
             hold Connection." *Journal of Comparative Family Studies*
             24(1):1–20.

Zavala de Cosío, María Eugenia
1992   *Cambios de fecundidad en México y políticas de población.*
             Jorge Ferreiro, trans. Mexico City: El Colegio de México/Fondo
             de Cultura Económica/Economía Latinoamericana.

Zavella, Patricia
1987   *Women's Work and Chicano Families: Cannery Workers of the
             Santa Clara Valley.* Ithaca, NY: Cornell University Press.
1991   "*Mujeres* in Factories: Race and Class Perspectives on Women,
             Work, and Family." In *Gender at the Crossroads of Knowledge:
             Feminist Anthropology in the Postmodern Era.* Micaela di Leo-
             nardo, ed. Pp. 312–36. Berkeley: University of California Press.

Index

Designer: Steve Renick
Compositor: Maple-Vail Book Mfg. Group
Text: 10/13 Sabon
Display: Sabon
Printer: Maple-Vail Book Mfg. Group
Binder: Maple-Vail Book Mfg. Group